Skin *Acts*

michelle ann stephens

Skin *Acts* RACE, PSYCHOANALYSIS, AND THE BLACK MALE PERFORMER

Duke University Press   Durham and London   2014

© 2014 Duke University Press
All rights reserved
Printed in the United States of America on acid-free paper ∞
Designed by Courtney Leigh Baker and typeset in
Whitman and Helvetica Neue by Tseng Information Systems, Inc.

Library of Congress Cataloging-in-Publication Data
Stephens, Michelle Ann, 1969–
Skin acts : race, psychoanalysis, and the black male performer /
Michelle Ann Stephens.
pages cm
Includes bibliographical references and index.
ISBN 978-0-8223-5668-4 (cloth : alk. paper)
ISBN 978-0-8223-5677-6 (pbk. : alk. paper)
1. African American entertainers. 2. African American men.
3. United States—Race relations. 4. Human skin color. I. Title.
E185.86.S754 2014
305.800973—dc23
2014005682

Cover credit: Photo by Nickolas Muray; © Nickolas Muray Photo Archives.

contents

Let the trace left behind by the It-Effect be called the *afterimage*. This does not exist as an object, but rather as a sensation that persists even after the external stimulation that caused it has disappeared, like the shape of a flame that lingers in the eye after the candle has gone out.
—JOSEPH ROACH, *It*

What makes some black men icons in American society? Is it something about the men themselves, their individual talent or charisma, that makes them so appealing? Or is it a fascination not with the man himself but with some performance of difference that acts in his place? Joseph Roach describes charisma as a "sensation" created in the gazing other by a projection of the performing self. "It" or "it-ness" is not the thing in the performer himself but this sensation that "lingers in the eye[s]" of the audience long after its source has disappeared. In *Skin Acts: Race, Psychoanalysis, and the Black Male Performer*, I argue that the "It-effect," the "it-ness" of the celebrity black male performer's effect on a multiracialized audience, also exists as a haunting afterimage in the eye of the gazer, an image of the skin. What Frantz Fanon called the "fact" of blackness, race as a form of charismatic self-display, is experienced phenomenologically as a "sensation" of the "it-ness" of race, its facticity seemingly confirmed visually, prior to the black male performer's actual appearance.[1] It lingers after the performer's disappearance, ultimately contributing to his presentation of self.

This book is about men partly because we are used to thinking about masculinity as somehow able to transcend inscriptions of the skin as flesh. *Skin Acts* aims to show that when we watch and listen to charismatic black male performers, their acts perform a difference that is not just socially inscribed but also literally and materially marks their skin as no longer flesh. In *Skin Acts* I examine the vocal and cinematic performances of four black male actors and singers: Bert Williams, a turn-of-the-century blackface minstrel; Paul Robeson, a screen and stage actor and singer in the 1930s; Harry Belafonte, a matinee idol and calypso performer in the 1950s; and Bob Marley, a reggae performer and Third World superstar in the 1970s. In the different instances and genres of their performances described here — lyrical, filmic, textual, sonic, onstage and on-screen, live and technologically mediated — the epidermal text mediates between the performing black subject and his spectating other. We are intrigued by who these men were and are because of *how they appear*, how they make themselves visible to us in the skin.

These four case studies of acts of racialized masculinity display in distinctive ways the powerful relationship between the skin and the gaze in twentieth-century American popular culture. Using a range of concepts from psychoanalysis, phenomenology, performance theory and semiotics, black feminism and the study of black consciousness, *Skin Acts* explores what it means to listen and watch, retrospectively, as black men perform the inescapably intercultural meanings of blackness as a difference embodied in black skin, continually reconstructed and redefined in interaction with a white gaze. I privilege performance as the framework within which to explore deeper questions concerning race relations and the constitution of the black male subject because intercultural performances bring into view the unconscious scenes and relations of fantasy constructed between racialized performers and spectators as interactive embodied agencies.

I engage with psychoanalytic theory to foreground the ways in which the black male body, as an active, sensory, intercorporeal site, is the ground of a performative but also profoundly epidermalized psyche. Thus, the "skin act" is a performance in both a concrete and a conceptual sense. It represents first and foremost the performance itself, the performer's artistic and embodied relationship with his appreciative, watching, listening, and equally embodied audience. Second, in terms of performativity, it enacts the more subjective and subjectivizing dimensions of racialized performance, the black performer's racial, sexual, and gendered interpellation by the audience's gaze. In each of the readings that follow, the black male performer inter-acts with a subjectifying, racializing, sexualizing gaze while simultaneously reclaiming his body, re-signifying black skin, (re-)marking (upon) himself a place of unconscious speech that runs alongside but is not exclusive to his race.

In his time, the blackface minstrel comedian Bert Williams was described by the silent screen star W. C. Fields as both the "funniest man I ever saw — and the saddest man I ever knew."[2] Williams was originally born in the Caribbean and immigrated permanently to the United States in the 1880s. In 1893, he met the African American actor and comedian George Walker and the two went on to create and perform in at least three all-black minstrel musicals. After Walker's death in 1911, Williams became the first black performer in the Ziegfeld Follies, where he met W. C. Fields and earned the latter's rueful comment.

Chapter 1 focuses on Bert Williams's turn-of-the-century blackface minstrel act as represented by his very first show, *In Dahomey*, which opened in 1903. As the "first full-length musical written and played by blacks to be performed at a major Broadway house," *In Dahomey* represents an important starting point in this story of intercultural black male performances in the United States during the twentieth century.[3] The blackface minstrel's comedic act provides a narrative record of the visual fetishization of race as epidermal difference at the very moment when the New Negro movement privileged a visual politics of portraiture as a positive medium for representing the race. The visual and recording technologies of the early twentieth century facilitated the scopic act of turning a word, an element of discourse, into a thing, a material object. For American audiences of the early twentieth century, the blackface mask reinforced visual perceptions of blackness as signified by physiognomy, *faciality*, turning the colors of the flesh into a thicker, purer sign for the black subject hidden somewhere beneath. The sight of the colored, chalked, corked facial mask represented a paradigmatic instance of what Hortense Spillers describes as the skin's "concealment under the brush of discourse,"[4] and the public interaction between the white audience's gaze and the blackface minstrel's performance had an impact on the cultural representation of black, intimate, heterosexual relations that one would think lay outside of, or operated in excess of, the gaze.

Chapter 2 focuses on Paul Robeson, probably the most famous African American male actor and performer of the 1920s and 1930s. Born in 1898 as the son of an escaped slave, by the 1920s Robeson was well known in multiple venues of popular entertainment, as an accomplished athlete, a popularizer of the spirituals on the concert stage, and a stage actor playing famous lead roles in such dramas as Eugene O'Neill's *Emperor Jones* and *All God's Chillun Got Wings*, and the stage version of DuBose Heyward's novel *Porgy*. Robeson's fame was later tarnished by scandals surrounding his involvement with the Communist Party and his radical commitments to Russia and the Bolshevik revolutionary project. During his brief film career in the 1930s, however, the actor's use of his body and the language of dramatic gesture in relation to a modernist gaze turned the medium of the film screen into an intercorporeal site for the audience's haptic, as much as scopic, encounter with the subjectified black male body.

In the early decades of the twentieth century, prescriptions concerning what was visually appropriate in representing blackness evolved, offering new ways of conceptualizing the scopic interactions between a desiring white gaze and the black male body. The very surface of the black male body became an object of desire and a stage for desiring acts. The bodily interaction between an actor and his audience, his *intercorporeity*, framed Robeson's role in the paradigmatic avant-garde modernist film *Borderline*, and shaped the film's portrayal of the black heterosexual relation on-screen. Reading Robeson's filmic body engaged in the physicality of acting itself moves us away from the image of the objectified black body and fetishized black actor to a closer assessment of the power of physical gesture to evoke visually ineffable aspects of the actor's subjective reality as a *body without an image*, always in motion.

In the mid- to late 1950s, the specter of a different kind of heterosexual relation, involving physical and emotional intimacies between black men and white women, shaped the popular reception of the part-Caribbean singer and actor Harry Belafonte. Belafonte was the American-born son of a West Indian immigrant to the United States who moved her son back to Jamaica in the 1920s and 1930s for the formative years of his childhood. Upon his return to the United States, Belafonte's radical leanings placed him on the path of popular political appeal first trod by his friend and mentor Paul Robeson. When Robeson advised him to "get them to sing your song. And then they'll have to come to know who you are," Belafonte took him at his word and went on to chart a singular path in the early 1950s as both the "calypso king" and the first "Negro matinee idol."[5]

Belafonte's rise to fame as a film star, his iconic status as "negro manhood at its finest . . . the perfect hybrid of popular culture and political conscience," reflected a new phase in the visual fetishization of black masculinity at mid-century.[6] In the context of a decolonizing world, Belafonte's skin act represents the very moment when a North American cultural grid integrates the black male performer as a lead character in a twentieth-century political narrative of national self-determination and freedom. Claiming the master('s) signifier for the skin, *color*, Harry Belafonte's on-screen performances in the 1950s translate the skin act into the politics of race shaping the civil rights and decolonization eras. In Belafonte's filmic performances, the visibility of race as a color technics, an increasingly political, politicized, and politicizing field of knowledge and culture with its own rules, is mediated on-screen through the representation of miscegenation, specifically, the black male–white female sexual relation.

The commercialization and popularization of black masculinity continues to be a global site for representing new black political identities in the wake of decolonization, as evidenced in the life and career of Bob Marley, the Jamaican-born musician and songwriter who internationalized reggae music during the 1970s after the national independence movements of the Anglophone Caribbean in the 1950s and 1960s. In his rise to success, Marley introduced American audiences to the figure of the Rastafarian, a new black social identity in the Third World. As his music spread outward from Jamaica and into markets in England and the United States, his persona was adapted and incorporated to fit the mold of other American rock idols during the years he was alive.

In the decades after Marley's death of cancer in 1981, his image, music, and lyrics have become immortalized, evoking the powerful ideologies of national liberation and black power that gained momentum in the black and postcolonial world during the latter decades of the twentieth century. The uncanny, persistent representation of the black male performer's "aliveness" in death, his symbolic *life between two deaths*, avoids treating Marley as a relational, corporeal black subject whose dread performance in the 1970s was a libidinous act, representing the political, social, and cultural desires of a larger Afro-Jamaican community intent on emancipating itself from mental slavery. Marley's skin act thus allows us to think more fully about the evolution of the skin from being merely the object of the audience's desire and the performing subject's manipulation to being the very site of personal and cultural interrelation itself. Tracing in Marley's skin act his mortal relations, rather than his immortal iconicity, helps us to reconstruct the black sexual relation as it was constituted in Jamaica in the 1970s and inscribed in reggae's soundscape of black liberation and Jamaican independence.

Throughout *Skin Acts* I use a number of visual texts—album covers, book covers, song sheets, cartoons and drawings, photographs, movie and concert posters, film stills, and explanatory diagrams—to demonstrate the ways in which the field of the gaze continues to impose a difference on the black male celebrity's vocal, rhetorical, comic, and dramatic performances, turning that difference into a thing, the skin as a partial object that ultimately stands in for, covers for, the performer.[7] It is my contention here that no matter the media, the visual superimposes our desire to see difference over the physiognomy or appearance of the black male performer and his performance material so that we always see the difference in his act. The album cover, for example, as a material object, enacts mimetically the epidermal relations this book seeks to trace—it is both a cover and an afterimage of the face as a cover, blackness as a covering and the skin as the metonymic face of race.

Post-decolonization, contemporary mass and popular cultural representations of decolonial black masculinities continue to settle for a phallic investment in faciality and the symbolic power of the skin over and above the affective vulnerabilities of black skin stripped and deconstructed of its epidermalized and fetishized meanings. In relational terms, phallic skin acts of blackness offer the compensations and rewards of heterosexual and patriarchal masculinity rather than striving for full *relationality* and *consensuality* as the goal of black gendered and sexual relations, and intercultural relations between the races. *Skin Acts* asks us to consider not only the various scripts of the skin that we have inherited from this cultural history of race as epidermalization but also how they shape contemporary performances of masculinity and blackness in the age of Obama and the post-racial, post-black subject. Only those performances that take us closer to the fleshy materiality of the black body, in all its tactile color and texture, can offer pathways through and away from the skin of race as a product of colonial and biopolitical discourse.

acknowledgments

Over the course of working on this book, I have had the benefit of much support from colleagues across three institutions, specifically, the faculties of the Program of African American and African Studies and the Department of English at Mount Holyoke College, of the Africana and Latin American Studies Program and Department of English at Colgate University, and of the Departments of Africana Studies, English, and Latino and Hispanic Caribbean Studies at Rutgers University, New Brunswick. In addition, invitations to speak at or write for a number of institutions, journals, and collections have provided wonderful opportunities for feedback, developing and refining my thinking, and expanding the theoretical parameters of the work. I want to thank in particular Don Weber and Amy Martin, Amy Kaplan, Laura Wexler, and Hazel Carby, for encouraging me to take the time to write this book the way I felt it needed to be written. Erin Soros deserves a special thank-you for pointing me in the direction of Lacan; John Kucich for suggesting alternatives in psychoanalysis when Lacan was not helpful enough. For their friendship, guidance, and collaboration during the journey, thank you so much to Prudence Cumberbatch, Kathleen Clark, Ann Fabian, Sharon Kofman, David Levit, John Jackson, and Deborah Thomas, Shoshana Sokoloff, Cheryl Wall, and my co-conspirators in Critical Caribbean Studies, especially Nelson Maldonado-Torres and Yolanda Martínez-San Miguel.

This project has also benefited from the funding support of the dean of the faculty at Colgate University and at Rutgers University, especially in my securing of images. I would like to thank my contacts at the Beinecke Library, the Carl Van Vechten Trust, Douris Inc., the Schomburg Library, Twentieth Century Fox, and the artists Elia Alba, Patricia Kaersenhout, Sandra Stephens, and their representatives for granting me permission to use images of their works. I am indebted to the team at Duke University Press — the illustrator, art director, editorial associates, and proofreader, to name a few — but also to the two readers of the manuscript in its earliest stages and again in revised form. In their engagement with the work, they provided ideal critical readings, helping me to catalyze my own thinking about the stakes and goals of the project, for which I am deeply grateful. I appreciated in particular their willingness to follow and comment on the different strands of argument the book contains, their incisive suggestions for where and how those strands needed to be tightened, clarified, foregrounded, or cut. Courtney Berger, my editor, deserves a special thank-you for seeing the merits of this project early on, for understanding and sharing my vision for what I was hoping to accomplish, for sticking with it through its various stages and permutations, and for reassuring me throughout, over many phone calls and coffees and meals.

Finally, thank you Alexandria for sharing me with this book for your first years, for bearing up when writing took precedence over playtime, swimming, and just time together more generally. To my mom, my sis, Allie, Mr. and Mrs. P., Natalie, Andy and the boys, and my dad and other family members who continue to accept and love me as I am, this too has been an invaluable foundation for the work. Lou, you are amazing for being with me through every stage of this—from your first Bert Williams joke to tolerating repeated snippets of calypso and dub reggae playing throughout the house; from your first description of psychoanalytic theory's collapsing realities to actively encouraging my decision to begin psychoanalytic training. Even though you ask nothing in return, I hope you know you have my love and support, in turn, for your work.

Fleshing Out the Act

The critical notion of "epidermalization" bequeathed to our time by Frantz Fanon is valuable here. . . . It refers to a historically specific system for making bodies meaningful by endowing them with qualities of "color." It suggests a perceptual regime in which the racialized body is bounded and protected by its enclosing skin. The observer's gaze does not penetrate that membrane but rests upon it and, in doing so, receives the truths of racial difference from the other body. —PAUL GILROY, *Against Race*

Before the "body" there is the "flesh," that zero degree of social conceptualization that does not escape concealment under the brush of discourse, or the reflexes of iconography. —HORTENSE SPILLERS, "Mama's Baby, Papa's Maybe"

What is the skin? How does one experience one's skin, in itself, for others? The skin provides a boundary between self and world that serves as both an entryway to the outside world and an enclosure of interior space. It provides us with our most immediate, sensual engagement with the world and others through touch, and yet, it is often the organ we think about the least, invisible and taken for granted. The skin we see, upon which so many signs of difference can be projected and inscribed—tattoos, skin colors, ornaments, birthmarks, scars—does not feel the way it looks; no matter how different two people may look their skins feel virtually the same. The skin reminds us of ourselves in a way that differs from how we think about ourselves in the abstract; the skin brings us back in touch with ourselves, literally, as bodies.

The skin, in a black context, has also been in modern times a master sig-nifier for the specificity, the particularity, of race. It is the object produced by what Frantz Fanon and Paul Gilroy call "epidermalization." It is the sign for race understood purely as a scopic sight and the skin as the object of a specularizing gaze. This is the notion of black skin that Toni Morrison attempts to defamiliarize and deconstruct in a powerful scene in *Beloved* when the self-appointed preacher, Baby Suggs, gives an impromptu sermon in the forest to a congregation of ex-slaves.

During her speech, Baby Suggs asks everyone assembled to raise their hands and kiss them as a way of acknowledging, inhabiting, and loving their humanity. She then calls on the assembled crowd to focus on the profound nature of their status as "flesh":

> We flesh; flesh that weeps, laughs; flesh that dances on bare feet in grass. Love it. Love it hard. Yonder they do not love your flesh. They despise it. . . . No more do they love the skin on your back. Yonder they flay it. And O my people they do not love your hands. Those they only use, tie, bind, chop off and leave empty. Love your hands! Love them. Raise them up and kiss them. Touch others with them, pat them together, stroke them on your face 'cause they don't love that either. *You got to love it, you!*[1]

With these resonant words, Baby Suggs encourages the community to remember that they are alive, that they are human, but also that as free subjects they can have a different relationship to their blackness than the one they grew accustomed to seeing reflected in the eyes of their masters. If one effect of objectifying blackness historically has been the hatred of black skin, Baby Suggs suggests that re-subjectification, finding and loving oneself, begins also at the level of the skin. This is not the skin as color, however—black is beautiful—but the skin as flesh, what can be touched rather than what can be seen.

In asking her congregation to love their blackness—in their feet, on their backs, in their hands, on their faces—Baby Suggs is not asking them to *see* themselves differently. Rather, she is asking them to rediscover themselves through a different sense of their bodies, one that bypasses the gaze entirely by beginning from a different sensory location, the sense of touch. When Baby Suggs calls on her congregation to raise the part of their bodies most relevant for touching the flesh, their hands, she primes them for extending their tactile, haptic experience of themselves, of their blackness as a form of embodied subjectivity, over the entirety of their skins and bodies. In this physical act, which becomes a public, communal dance, each member of her congregation acts out and witnesses, participates in and observes, an experience of black skin as something other than just a reified object—either of the gaze or of the subject. Rather, the skin serves here as a threshold, a point of contact, a site of intersubjective encounter, between the inner and outer self and between the self and the other. Just the mere touching of skins, as William Faulkner described, can suddenly seem to shatter "shibboleths" of race and caste.[2]

Morrison's novelistic representation of the flesh in *Beloved* resonates with, expands upon, and acts out the rich notion of the flesh Hortense Spillers invokes in her canonical essay "Mama's Baby, Papa's Maybe." We are used to thinking of the skin, the surface of the body, as the baseline of what it means to be human, to be a body that matters. For Spillers, however, in the discursive order of modernity created by New World discovery, conquest, colonization, and enslavement, the "American grammar" of race fixes the black subject's skin as merely the covering of a body already trapped in the symbolic order, a body marked and named by so many multiple investments and discourses that "there is no easy way for the agents buried beneath them to come clean." This body-with-skin is an organic "resource for metaphor" but also a "defenseless target" for the aims of a racializing discursive order. This body is the victim of an original "theft" not just from the homeland but also from the African captive's body's "motive will, its active desire." Spillers's term for this body of symbolic capture throughout her essay is "the captive body," by which she means a body captive in a new symbolic order with different social conventions and gendered norms than the home ground of the African transplant.[3]

In contrast, those who are liberated have another bodily entitlement. They can imagine themselves as a body outside of the symbolic order, as the more universal body of the human covered by flesh. For those in this subject position, "before the 'body' there is the 'flesh,'" that is, another sense of the body that is a remainder of the body concealed and covered over in discourse. The skinned body that remains left behind by both physical captivity and cultural capture is what Spillers means by the "flesh." The flesh is also the organ on "the person of African females and African males [that] registered the wounding" of the traumatic transatlantic passage — it offers a "primary narrative [of] its seared, divided, ripped-apartness, riveted to the ship's hole, fallen, or 'escaped' overboard." This flesh, in other words, is not simply raw, human matter; it represents a body that also shows, that reveals, the markings of the symbolic order on its skin. It is a supplement to the black body that merely (re-)enacts its symbolic marking and naming by using the skin of race as a covering over/ of human flesh.[4]

The flesh represents the body that sits on the very edge, on the underside, of the symbolic order, pre-symbolic and pre-linguistic, just before words and meaning. It has yet to be sealed away into an image or bodily ideal. Instead, it is the underside or rough side of the bodily surface and image subsequently sealed over with racial meaning. The flesh is the side of the skin, the hide, upon which we see the scratchings of discourse. These marks of inscription are not the naturalized and normalized racial fantasies and myths of modernity. Rather, from the perspective of the flesh, they are the non-sense marks with no meaning or signification beyond their reality as traces of violence — "the anatomical specifications of rupture, of altered human tissue . . . eyes beaten out, arms, backs, skulls branded, a left jaw, a right ankle, punctured; teeth missing, as the calculated work of iron, whips, chains, knives, the canine patrol, the bullet." It is this scratched up, fleshy body, the body made subject to racially and sexually sadomasochistic acts, a body that shows the very edges and seams of its cuts and splits, which is then covered over by the skin of race: "These undecipherable markings on the captive body render a kind of hieroglyphics of the flesh whose severe disjunctures come to be hidden to the cultural seeing by skin color." In *Skin Acts: Race, Psychoanalysis, and the Black Male Performer*, this is the body the following readings of black male performances are meant to rediscover and explore. In four signature black acts, the skin is a heuristic representing the intersectional meeting point of a black body subject to symbolic and imaginary capture in racializing discourse and imagery (race as a social construction) and a bodily subject whose sensory and relational (re-) presentation of self (race as an inscription on the flesh) occurs in the experiential space of performance.[5]

I am also asking us to stay attentive to the multiple scripts of the skin that shape black subjects' interpersonal, intercultural, social, and everyday performances. Rather than forgetting about the skin, the post-racial call for us to move beneath or beyond blackness, we need a richer sense of the mind-body relation between the psyche and the skin, that is, how a historical process of seeing and understanding the skin as object and other, the site of difference, shapes the psychic formation of black subjects for whom the skin is also a bodily mode of relating to the world and others. Despite its prominence in racial thinking, black cultural studies and critical race theory have yet to develop a serious notion of the skin, a theoretically articulated account of blackness as a cutaneous medium and bodily contact zone through which modern subjects negotiate and enact a profound desire to see difference. This desire, a product of colonial modernity that leads to an alienating separation from the body, is bad enough for the black subject during slavery. The subsequent tragedy is that, even after slavery, black flesh never reclaims itself. The experience of a doubly split-off double consciousness, the epidermalized black body split off from the skinned body without an image, remains an inherent condition of modern black subjectivity.

It is no surprise that Spillers references W. E. B. Du Bois and his notion of the color line from 1903 in the opening of "Mama's Baby, Papa's Maybe." Both for Spillers and here in *Skin Acts*, this establishes the dawning of the twentieth century as a particular kind of conjuncture in which black masculinity suffered from this unacknowledged, alienating separation of the black body in its skin from the register of the black self as flesh.[6] Perhaps the primary consequence, for Spillers, of losing our concept of blackness as flesh is the subsequent inability to see black subjectivity within the frame of a relational humanity. As she puts it, in this "atomizing" of the captive body as flesh divided from itself, "we lose any hint or suggestion of a dimension of ethics, of relatedness between human personality and its anatomical features, between one human personality and another, between human personality and cultural institutions. To that extent, the procedures adopted for the captive flesh demarcate a total objectification."[7] Very specific conditions shaping black subjectivity in the United States during the twentieth century have impacted the historical evolution of a notion of the black male self as a closed, autonomous, self-sufficient subject sealed away in his skin. In each cultural moment described here, these conditions have unique, historically specific features related to the emergence of the New Negro at the start of the twentieth century and in a later iteration during the 1930s, and the emergence of a decolonized black subject in the mid-twentieth century and later in the political and cultural movements for independence of the 1960s and 1970s.

Bert Williams's and Paul Robeson's performances during the first three decades of the twentieth century are shaped by the reconstruction of the enslaved black self that two generations of New Negroes undertook in the wake of emancipation and Reconstruction. Harry Belafonte's and Bob Marley's performances occur at a slightly different conjuncture, during the era of decolonization initiated in the Third World at midcentury and continuing into the next two decades. The space between these two eras marks the shift from the black male subject's objectification to his interpellation as a subject of desire, with neither of these processes of public definition and recognition bringing him any closer to Spillers's notion of the flesh as the lost experience of a wounded, relational black body. Instead, during these four very particular cultural moments in the twentieth century, each of these black male performers became the setting or stage for certain operations of the gaze that separated the black body from the flesh and fixed it in its racial meanings. With the black male subject's entrance at midcentury into a global political order, the black male body made legible in discourses of Negritude, sovereignty, and freedom was also prescribed by interracial, intra-racial, and heterosexist cultural discourses that continue to avoid the more relational and sexually open dimensions of the black subject's experience. *Skin Acts* reads these skin acts against the grain in order to resurrect a sense of the black male performer as a body and subject in relation, interacting with his own afterimage in the space of performance between himself and his audience, and interacting with his image of the black and white female subject as "other" in the sexual relation.

Following the careers of the four performers described here, one sees specific ways in which the performer thwarts the gaze and complicates his symbolic and imaginary position by enacting a different sense of the body in the various forms of intimacy and relation made possible in the phenomenological space of performance. The voice and the ear in particular, what neuroscientists describe as the audio-vocal interface, become sites for the reappearance of the flesh as a more haptic, tactile, sensory experience of the embodied black male self beyond the limiting blind spots of the gaze. However, to understand the various dimensions in which the skin operates in black male performance on a continuum from flesh to image, one needs to retrace the varying histories of the skin in colonial discourse, Western epistemology, and modern psychoanalysis. One also needs to engage the work of the first black thinker to link these skin discourses to the psychic formation of the modern black (male) subject, the psychiatrist and theorist of decolonization Frantz Fanon in *Black Skin, White Masks*.

Histories of the Skin and Difference

For Hortense Spillers, an American grammar of race as a history of skin discourse stems all the way back to the era of conquest in the Americas. It originates, as she describes, "with a narrative self, [who] in an apparent unity of feeling . . . uncovers the means by which to subjugate the 'foreign' . . . whose most easily remarkable and irremediable difference is perceived in skin color."[8] By the mid-fifteenth century, Spillers periodizes, "a century and a half before Shakespeare's 'old black ram' of an Othello 'tups' that 'white ewe' of a Desdemona, the magic of skin color is already installed as a decisive factor in human dealings."[9] Michael Taussig also ties European attitudes toward color to "a colonially split world in which 'man in a state of nature,' as Goethe would have it, loves vivid color, while the Europeans are fearful of it."[10] In *Europe's Indians*, Vanita Seth adds historical nuance to Taussig's bold assertion that "color is a colonial subject," arguing that the attachment of color and skin to an essentialized notion of human difference is a process that evolves in Western thought as a product of European colonization, culminating in nineteenth-century biological understandings of race.[11]

Spillers's discussion of the foregrounding of skin color in colonial discourse, Taussig's contextualizing of attitudes toward color itself as deeply tied to colonialism, and Seth's linking of skin color to a deeper investment in seeing, identifying, and classifying difference, all demonstrate a paradigm shift across a number of fields, the move away from a privileging of difference in favor of discourses of relationality and even sameness. In *Flesh of My Flesh*, Kaja Silverman agrees with Seth that "the notion that we cannot be ourselves unless we are different from everyone else is relatively new. From Plato until the end of the sixteenth century, resemblance, not difference, was the organizing principle of the universe."[12] In earlier moments during the European age of discovery, explorers relied on discourses of resemblance and similitude, of relationality rather than difference, to aid in their comprehension of the other.[13] Silverman, like Morrison, explicitly links this denaturalizing of difference and return to notions of resemblance and relationality to the trope of the flesh, with the notion of resemblance functioning similarly in Silverman's account as the reminder of a premodern order based on similitude does in Seth's. The skin, in other words, becomes the primary signifier of the *meaningfulness* of difference, producing racialized difference *as* significant, as signifying. And if the skin is the site for a modern desire to see difference, Morrison and others contrast this with a very different set of meanings latent in the trope of the flesh. In all of these accounts, it is the denaturalizing of the givenness of human difference that begins to emerge as centrally at stake in contemporary discussions of the skin, and the flesh emerges as the leading trope for the shift away from difference and toward relationality.[14]

While the gaze has received much critical attention in the study of modern knowledge, power, and subjectivity, only more recently has the skin been seen as more than the object of the gaze, as having a form of knowing and interacting with the world that is all its own.[15] While some of this work can be found in an emergent discourse on the history of the senses and affect theory, my interest is in those more psychoanalytically inflected studies that understand the senses as tied to libidinous desires—to the erogenous zones, to the psychic objects and bodily organs crucial to subjective formation and psychic development—and to relational, dyadic interactions. My intention is to foreground the skin's role as a site of both libidinal conflict and intersubjective relationality—a site of drives and objects as well as transferential relations—which sets the stage for my discussion of the struggle between affinity and differentiation as a structuring force in the racialization of the human psyche. In other words, to the degree that the skin can function as both an erotogenic zone tied to the individual's conflicts and instincts, and as a site of relation and contact between the individual and others, it marks subjects' acts of differentiation and of affinity in their interpersonal dealings.

Skin-based or skin-linked knowledges have the capacity to bring the gaze back into relation with other psychic objects related to the drives but also with pre-symbolic, pre-imaginary, but still object-seeking, sensuous forms of knowing. Naomi Segal focuses on the multisensorial dimensions of the skin, using the term "consensuality" to describe the skin's capacity to take in knowledge about the world synesthetically through the utilization of more than one of the senses.[16] The skin links the various senses to each other and facilitates the subject's ability to use this linked sensorium to learn about the world and others. In a separate but related vein, Laura U. Marks identifies films made by Third World artists as harnessing a different perceptual regime, one that uses visual cues to evoke touch beyond sight, what Jennifer Barker calls also the tactile eye.[17] Much of Marks's and Barker's analyses describe how certain photographs and cinematic shots emphasize or foreground the more haptic and bodily dimensions of the image's surface, drawing texture out of the visual with the photo or film still acting as a multisensorial sight. In each instance, all three are working more or less explicitly with a distinction between more haptic, bodily forms of knowing that are prior to our imaginary idealizations of ourselves in our mirror images, and to our symbolic construction of the world of objects and others through language.[18]

While Marks's focus on epistemologies of the skin is grounded in contemporary new media, other scholars have shown that the skin as the site of an autonomous mode of knowing the self has a long and deep history in Western thought. Three works—Steven Connor's account of the "poetics of the skin" in art and intellectual thought, Claudia Benthien's sociocultural history of Western perceptions of the skin, and Nina Jablonski's natural history of the skin—take us across the humanities, social sciences, and the natural sciences, respectively, to provide a history of skin perception.[19] Despite their very different approaches, all three authors concur that a significant shift occurred over the course of modernity in the ways writers and thinkers throughout Europe and the Western hemisphere thought about the skin's interactions with an outside world.

Varying ways of thinking about the skin evolved within the context of changing understandings of the body. Gradually over the course of the Enlightenment, the skin and the body both began to harden, to be seen as less and less permeable. It is this specific history of the skin's growing impermeability, discussed in further detail below, that has the greatest significance for how we think about the skin in terms of questions of race and difference. In contrast, the notion of the skin's permeability moves it closer to the idea of the flesh as the site for a pure relationality between human subjects. Brian Massumi explicitly defines relationality as a pre-discursive, pre-symbolic mode of the body. In this mode, the body is still social but it is not the naturalized marker of difference. Rather, it is a "pure" sociality enacting social relation as "interaction-in-the-making," and "ontogenetically 'prior to' social construction."[20] This mode of the body precedes the "separating out of individuals and the identifiable groupings that they end up boxing themselves into."[21] In the context of this relational body, movement or continuity is as "elementary" as difference, "relation as primordial as individuation."[22] Given the focus of classic psychoanalysis on a libidinal body riven with the conflicts born of hereditary instincts in tension with the demands of others and culture, this turn to a pre-symbolic, relational body also suggests alternative modes of affiliation and attachment between the dyad of self and other.

Relationality has been theorized more extensively in contemporary American psychoanalytic writings that deviate from the Freudian model of drives linked to psychosexual and oedipal development, examining instead the dyadic relation between self and other as constitutive of subject formation and the workings of the unconscious. These more relational and interpersonal schools of psychoanalytic thought branch out in a number of directions, but the work of psychoanalyst and feminist theorist Jessica Benjamin offers one useful example.[23] Benjamin distinguishes between *intrapsychic* and *intersubjective* ways of knowing the other. The first operates where the subject's objects, fantasies, constitutional drives, and projections reside, turning the other into an object incorporated by the subject, producing *incorporative* forms of identification between self and other.[24] Alongside the *intrapsychic object*, however, is a separate awareness of an *intersubjective other* out there in the Real, in the world, one who cannot be fully reduced to object status. Rather than becoming the love object, a creation, a fantasy and projection of another, the *like subject* is that other who can neither be fully assimilated nor eradicated and destroyed in the subject's efforts to individuate and distinguish him or herself. This other, who is a like subject, presents a material limit to the incorporative self at the boundaries of the skin. The skin is thus the marker for a shared resistance to incorporation that runs alongside the intersubjective contact between self and other, especially in the context of sexual and psychosocial desires for intimacy and contact.

The distinction Jessica Benjamin draws between the intrapsychic objects of a desiring subject and the inescapable intersubjectivity of a Real other maps suggestively onto the tension between the skin as an object of the distancing, racializing gaze, or as the fleshy site for registering relational and reversible aspects of human touch. In *The Skin Ego*, a work of French psychoanalysis translated for an English-speaking audience in 1987, Didier Anzieu describes the skin's "echotactilism," exchanges of meaning facilitated through tactile contact, as the very model for a more reversible understanding of the relationship between self and other, self and world.[25] This reversibility—when I touch your skin I also feel your skin touching mine—is what Merleau-Ponty also described as the flesh's "reflectedness," that is, the epidermal body's particular mode of knowing.[26] As Anzieu also describes: "It is on the model of tactile reflexivity that the other sensory reflexivities (hearing oneself make sounds, smelling one's own odour, looking at oneself in the mirror), and subsequently the reflexivity of thinking, are constructed."[27] The skin, then, serves as the platform for imagining aspects of the self-other relation in more concretely epidermal terms but also reimagining the "interior intersubjectivity" of the black subject as modeled on the materiality, the material reality, of the skin as a medium of chiastic reversibility.[28]

In these various studies of the history of the skin, color ties the skin indelibly to the history of colonialism and, in consequence, to the epistemological categorization of difference; the sensorial grounds the skin in its own forms of knowing that subsume the gaze; imagining the skin's permeability moves it closer to ideas of relationality; and on the pivot point of the skin's reversible nature lies the distinction between sameness and difference that so defines the study of race. Overall, it is this focus on the relationship between samenesses and differences in human interaction that is precisely the new terrain in skin studies that would benefit from a dialogue with scholarship on the study of race.

For black subjects, the tension between skin and flesh—the skin that can be seen and represented and the flesh that can be felt and mimetically shared—emerges out of colonialism and slavery.[29] This dualistic tension between an experience of oneself as sensational flesh rather than epidermal skin has structured the lived being of black subjects throughout colonial modernity as they struggled to demonstrate their shared humanity in the face of the gaze of the white other. What is performed most acutely in the work of the four performers I discuss here is precisely this tension between these two different ways of knowing blackness and interacting with the other. In one aspect of performance, racial identity is structured as the hard exterior of a symbolic reality created by the epidermalizing gaze. In another, the performance represents an experience of the black body felt as a permeable, interior orifice, as sensational, invaginating, relatable flesh.

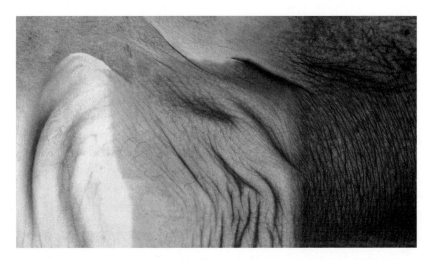

FIG I.1. *Skin*. Digital image and installation. Courtesy of Sandra Stephens.

Orifice versus Phallus (Or, the Permeable versus the Libidinous Black Body)

The converging of affect theory, psychoanalytically inflected discourses of the skin, and postcolonial and black cultural studies has the potential to sharpen our understanding of the knotty relationship between two of modernity's primary modes of difference, the racial and the sexual. This theoretical challenge, one that Kimberlé Crenshaw first named for us as the study of intersectionality, and that Hortense Spillers later challenged black cultural studies to take up as a "psychoanalytics" of blackness, is also the project I engage in here by distinguishing between epidermal skin and sensational flesh as two different but linked modes of understanding, experiencing, and performing the black body.[30] By doing this kind of cultural analysis one recognizes that there is a black subject "before race," that blackness is as much a libidinous site as one of political and cultural consciousness. Having said that, one also must note that, in a libidinal mode, the epidermal also entails an understanding of the skin as phallic versus a very different way of understanding the skinned body as erotogenic, permeable flesh.

Any dialogue between studies of racial and sexual formation benefits from engaging psychoanalysis and not eliding sexuality as somehow secondary in the black subject's psychic structure and makeup, subordinate to race rather than intimately intertwined with it. Given that intertwining, *Skin Acts'* larger theoretical stakes include demonstrating precisely how one can think race and sexuality separately but relationally—intersectionally—through the skin as the organic, material trope for both a libidinal and a racial self. This dialogue between race and sex as modes of bodily and psychic difference also detours through Western histories of the bodily surface. What emerges is the realization that our understanding of the skin as a hardened, impermeable container for difference is tied to our phallic understanding of our libidinal bodies.

It is one of *Skin Acts*' premises that, no matter the cultural period or archival text, black masculinity is a relational identity and, therefore, black male performance occurs in a radically relational and intersubjective context. Black masculinity is always engaged with the sameness and difference of the other as a like subject, whether that other is female or white. Therefore, black masculine performance always holds within it the traces of a performance of femininity, a performance of the gender relation produced by sexual difference, in much the same way racial performance has, already inscribed within it, a set of social relations based on racial difference. Throughout *Skin Acts*, each male's racial performance includes a discussion of gender relations and relevant aspects of the female performer's skin act. These readings aim to provide a model for how to think about race, sex, and gender together in black masculine performance. The relationality or intersectionality of racial and sexual difference is inscribed on the skin literally when the epidermalizing of racial difference is understood more broadly as a phallicizing of the body.

To understand what this means, how epidermalization and phallicization occur simultaneously, requires a theoretically informed history of the skin and the body, a genealogy of the construction of both racial and sexual difference, their shared trajectories in terms of how we think about the modern body and self. As powerfully suggestive as Spillers's reference to the captive black subject as flesh is in "Mama's Baby, Papa's Maybe," one finds an equally provocative insight for thinking about the *gendering* of racial and sexual difference, as both relate to the skin and the flesh, in Sylvia Wynter's equally canonical essay "Beyond Miranda's Meanings."[31] For Wynter, a substitution occurs somewhere between the early modern era of colonial encounter and the nineteenth-century development of the racial sciences that attached human difference indelibly to the epidermal surface. Racial difference essentially replaces gender difference as the structuring division understood to define man, and this substitution accompanies an even deeper epistemic shift in understanding the human body in terms of physiognomy rather than anatomy.

With the shift from anatomy to physiognomy, in the intercultural context of colonial modernity the color of the skin becomes more of a marker of an essentialized or naturalized difference between peoples than the sexual organs had been in a more homogeneous cultural and racial context. Here Wynter challenges the Freudian psychoanalytic tradition to historicize the onset of colonial modernity as precisely the moment when sexual and racial differences were linked together through different understandings of the body and its associations with the skin. While more recent histories of the skin add chronological nuance to this process, they also tend to concur with Wynter's suggestive observation that the shift from anatomy to physiognomy partly situates how Europeans thought about the *difference* of the racialized body within the deeper question of how they thought about the skin.[32]

Given the "fabulous freaks" that "roamed the pages of ancient and Renaissance texts," Vanita Seth argues, it was easy enough for the first European colonial explorers to translate the strangeness of the new peoples of the New World according to the terms of a pervasive discourse of the monstrous and the grotesque that characterized early modern Europe.[33] The world was understood as inhabited by "monstrous species" — "the dog-headed cynocephali, the horse-bodied onocentaurs, or the double-sexed androgynes of Africa" — and "monstrous individuals" — "conjoined twins, a child born with two heads."[34] "Diversity" included an imaginative array of "wild men and women, ghosts, witches, and . . . human monstrosities," and a defining feature of these monstrous creatures was their anatomical abnormality.[35] Both Seth and Benthien concur that the early modern encounter with racial difference occurred at a moment when the European colonizer saw the native other as resembling something grotesque but nonetheless *familiar* in early modern discourses, rather than signifying as something different.

In this premodern epistemological universe, the skin was seen as permeable and malleable to the point of being horrific. Europeans applied these different physical standards and meanings of difference to themselves. The differences between female and male anatomies, for example, did not mark a clear, gendered differentiation between the sexes. Rather, the female gender was seen as merely the male body's grotesque inversion.[36] Europeans believed in a "one-sex model" that informed their conceptions of the body "from the ancient Greeks to the eighteenth century."[37] In the writings of a sixth-century commentator, the female genitals were simply "inside the body and not outside it."[38] As another put it, "Turn outward the woman's, and turn inward, so to speak, and fold double the man's, and you will find the same in both in every respect."[39] While anatomy preserved a hierarchical distinction between men and women, it "nevertheless did not presume radical differences between male and female anatomy."[40] Rather, gendered anatomies and organs folded into each other to create an invaginated understanding of the body: "Medieval physicians regarded the body as a series of nested or concentric enclosures, each bounded by its own membrane or tunic." "The skin bounds the body," and enfolds the viscera of the lungs, the brain, the heart, the belly, all "thought of as enclosed in several layers of skin."[41]

If we historicize Wynter's distinction between physiognomy and anatomy, the shift from sexed anatomies to racialized physiognomies not only marks changing understandings of the meaning, or meaningfulness, of difference on the body. It also marks the shift from an anatomical understanding of the body as a site of invaginated layers to a physiognomic understanding of the body as consisting of merely the two layers of a hard, impermeable outside covering a softer organic interior. Gradually over the course of the Enlightenment, as the skin and the body both begin to harden and be seen as less and less permeable, the tying of difference to the epidermal and physiognomic also hardens the bodily surface as an impermeable container of difference. This hardening then contributes to an understanding of physiognomic difference as the marker of fundamental differences within the species. In this world of the body as a hardened container of differences, both the anatomical differences represented in the sexual organs and the physiognomic differences registered in the facial features and bodily skin color of the other become naturalized. The skin is differentiated as belonging to different genders based on the shape of the sexual organs, genital skin; the skin is differentiated as marking different races based on the body's color, epidermal skin. By the beginning of the twentieth century, with the onset of Freud's theory of psychoanalysis, it is the body with its epidermal skin and hardened physiognomy that is also understood in libidinal terms as fundamentally phallic.

The split modern body with its hardened skin contrasts in dramatic ways with the body of the medieval grotesque. The very word "complexion" that we take to refer naturally to physiognomy, the exterior surface and features of the body and the face, began as a term describing how the exterior expresses a fluid interior, the "humors" or the humorous fluids of the body.[42] For the early anatomists, "the actuality of the skin may have been invisible" in favor of "the flesh beneath the skin," the latter the site for a grotesque body that ignores the closed, regular, and smooth regions of the body surface.[43] Instead, this grotesque body is made up of its "execrescences and orifices" where what is inside can become outside: "In the grotesque body, the boundaries between body and world and those between individual bodies are much less differentiated and more open than they are in the new body canon: the very boundary of the grotesque body reveals the intermingling with the world in that protruding body parts (the nose or stomach, for example) are understood as projecting into the world, and the inside of the body comes out and mingles with the world."[44] The reverse is also true, as Benthien continues: "In this pre-Enlightenment conceptual world, there are many more body openings than we would recognize: eyes, ears, nose, mouth, breasts, navel, anus, urinary passage, and vulva."[45] Orifices were very much a feature of the grotesque body because they emphasized that body's permeability in contact with an outside world, while also leading back to the interior of the body, the visceral organs.

Contemporary affect theory and discussions of the body as sensational skin have picked up on this inner/outer/interface capacity of the skin as a way of getting back to the materiality of a more relational body. Barker organizes the body visible to a "tactile eye" into three modes, the haptic, the kinesthetic, and the visceral. For Massumi, the *quasi corporeal* or incorporeal body, "the body without an image," is one that we come to know through the linked modes of the proprioceptive (or muscular), the tactile (or haptic), and the visceral.[46] "Tactility is the sensibility of the skin as surface of contact between the perceiving subject and the perceived object. Proprioception folds tactility into the body, enveloping the skin's contact with the external world in a dimension of medium depth: between epidermis and viscera. . . . Proprioception translates [movement] into a muscular memory of relationality. . . . Proprioception effects a double translation of the subject and the object into the body, at a medium depth [that is] one of the strata proper to the corporeal; it is a dimension of the *flesh*."[47] Massumi's use of the trope of the flesh to characterize this body that escapes both the image and the signifier—the body that remains, this material remainder of the symbolic and imaginary body—points not only to the prominence of the trope in current constructions of the sensational body but also to the echoes of Merleau-Ponty's earlier constructions of the flesh as the residual trace of the grotesque body in continental philosophy and Western thought.

Prior to current accounts, the closest the contemporary body has come to resembling the grotesque medieval body with its permeable relation between the internal and the external is in Merleau-Ponty's phenomenological notion of the flesh. Since, as he describes, "every vision takes place somewhere in the tactile space," Merleau-Ponty sees the touch and the gaze as interacting in a reversible, reflecting relationship to each other.[48] Merleau-Ponty also describes a crisscrossing between the touch and the gaze, a "double and crossed situating of the visible in the tangible and of the tangible in the visible" that we can then use to envision a more interactive, intersubjective, sensorial theory of subjectivity.[49] For Merleau-Ponty, the Cartesian mind-body relation is less dualistic than circular: "The body sensed and the body sentient are as the obverse and the reverse, or again, as two segments of one sole circular course."[50] The Hegelian self-other relation is less dialectical than chiasmic: "One sole circular course which goes above from left to right and below from right to left, but which is but one sole movement in its two phases."[51] The chiasm is not just a metaphor but also a structural analog for intersubjective relations where "there is not only a me-other rivalry, but a co-functioning. We function as one unique body" in a kind of modern analog to the medieval, one-sexed, body.[52] Chiasm is the structural analog to the flesh because both function in a movement similar to that of a Möbius strip, where the lines of the Möbius strip blur and weave into and around each other in a circular movement that reaches a limit on either end around two clear and definable poles.

Invagination is the other term scholars use to describe this type of circular, reflexive, bodily relationality tied to the skin. Invagination represents the "implicative capacity of the skin—its capacity to be folded in upon itself."[53] It is part of the basic structure of Didier Anzieu's skin ego that the skin functions psychically as both "shell" and "kernel," a "matter of relations between surfaces, inserted one inside another."[54] Merleau-Ponty also characterizes these chiasmic, fleshy relations as an *intercorporeity* involving "reciprocal insertion and intertwining of one in the other. . . . There are two circles, or two vortexes, or two spheres, concentric when I live naïvely, and as soon as I question myself, the one slightly decentered with respect to the other."[55] Invagination thus takes us not only backward in time, to a grotesque conception of the body and its organs as epidermal surfaces and orifices that fold back on each other, the residue of the medieval body—but also forward to the modern twentieth-century body of phenomenology.

Invagination also takes us forward to the modern twentieth-century body of the drives. Jacques Lacan, invoking Merleau-Ponty's trope of the chiasmic "flesh of the world" to describe the subject's looping, circular, chiasmic interaction with a world felt on the boundaries of the skin, imagined the movement or "circuit" of the drives in invaginating, chiasmic terms as, "something that emerges from a rim, which redoubles its enclosed structure, following a course that returns."[56] Visualizing the movement of desire as a "turning inside-out represented by its pocket, invaginating through the erogenous zone," which he represents in a diagram of the movement of the drive between aim, rim, and goal, Lacan also describes the circuit of the drive as a circling around a rim or orifice whose erogeneity lies in the fact that it will never close (see figure 1.2).[57]

It is a crucial aspect of the Lacanian theory of the subject that the drive emerges at the very place of the signifying cut, that mark on the body that interpellates all subjects as sexually differentiated members of the social order.

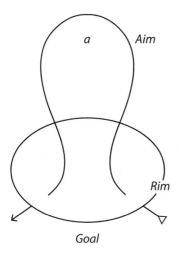

FIG 1.2. Based on Lacan's diagram of the partial drive and its circuit. Illustration.

a

Aim

Rim

Goal

"It is through sexual reality that the signifier came into the world," Lacan states, by which he means that we emerge into consciousness, social being, and language as sexually differentiated subjects.[58] Furthermore, in the symbolic order, there is nothing behind the signifying cut but lack, the sexual cut as a hard barrier between a constructed and a pre-discursive or primordial self.[59] For Lacan, sexuality is phallic precisely because it entails the subject's desire to fill up this split self, to fill up in the subject what is "not-whole."[60] The body's orifices are not seen as openings that fold unto and into each other, but rather, as holes that need to be filled, made (w)hole by the substitution of phallic objects that temporarily replace and thereby fulfill the subject's desire.

By conceiving of the libidinal body very differently, as an in(vagina)ted orifice rather than a phallic (w)hole, this turning inside out of the body and the skin has implications for how we think about modern sexuality. As Anzieu elaborates: "'Invagination,' the term used in anatomy and physiology for this relation, is a useful reminder that the vagina is not an organ of particular contexture but a fold of the skin just like the lips, the anus, the nose or the eyelids. It has no hardened layer or cornea to act as a protective shield; its mucous membrane is exposed, its sensitivity and erogeneity right on the surface."[61] The permeability of invaginating rather than phallic skin, the vagina as skin without a "hardened layer or cornea"—these associative metaphors of invagination point us neither to the hardened bodies of the Imaginary (the body as its mirror image) nor to the Symbolic body of discourse. Rather, the body as invaginated orifice(s) points us to the integration of the sensory and the consensual into the realm of the libido and the sexual drives. Erogeneity and permeability, as

Fleshing Out the Act 17

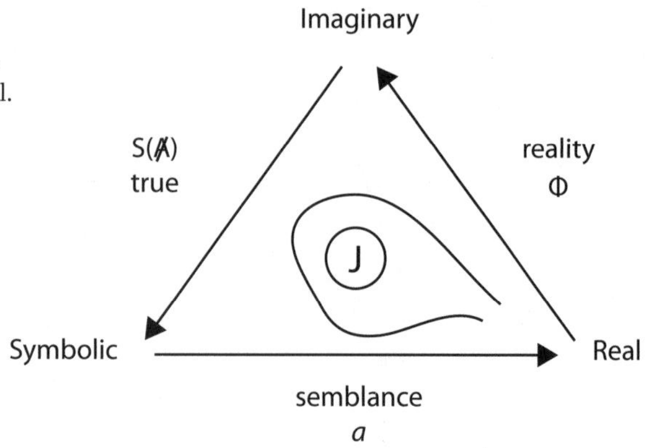

FIG 1.3. Based on Lacan's
diagram of the Imaginary,
the Symbolic, and the Real.
Illustration.

Imaginary

S(Ⱥ)
true

reality
Φ

J

Symbolic

Real

semblance
a

intensified sensation residing on the rim of the body-with-skin (on erotogenic genital skin in particular), lie alongside the instinctual conflict, deferral, and lack that characterize the phallic subject's relation to his or her drives.

Lacan literalizes this libidinous body, engaged in a constant, chiasmic search for wholeness, as itself an organ, the libido-body, with erogenous zones composed of orifices and rims, protrusions and surfaces, much like the invaginating skin.[62] "The unconscious is more like a bladder," Lacan also states, imaging the partial circuit of desire as a volume enfolding onto and into, out of and back to, the edge or rim of a bladder-like, invaginating space.[63] In one of his more famous diagrams of the Imaginary, the Symbolic, and the Real, desire presses in between them (as J for jouissance, Lacan's term for desire) in the empty space that the phallic signifier and the epidermal mirror image seek to fill in and cover up (see figure 1.3).[64] One can also think of this "libido-body" as the flesh. Elsewhere Lacan renames it the "man-let" or *lamella*, an entity he describes much like the blob or flap of skin floating between the three psychosomatic orders, on the bodily edge of the Real.

This "unreal" organ, the lamella—a physical manifestation of the libido, of the fleshiness of living being itself—is thrown off from the symbolic body, the body of symbolic capture.[65] The lamella is "an organ without body, the incorporeal and for that very reason indestructible life-substance that persists beyond the circuit of generation and corruption."[66] What is most fascinating about the lamella is the way it mimics the properties of the skin as flesh. "Extra-flat" like a "large crêpe," it "moves like the amoeba, so utterly flat that it can slip under doors."[67] Like racialized skin, it is something "that would not feel good dripping down your face" even as it "comes and envelops your face."[68] The lamella is the flap of skin, the body-skin, left behind like the "afterbirth" as the subject separates from the skin ego to become an individuated self.[69] It flies off the body rather than assimilating into word or image. It is, therefore, everything about the living being of the subject that cannot be captured by word or image and symbolized as difference.

Lacan's orifice-filled, rather than phallic, libido-body is invested with the irrepressible force of the sensational. The lamella, then, is the figure for the sensational body in Lacan's tripartite schema. Despite the fact that Lacan typically embeds the body almost fully within the symbolic order, he also conceptualized a libido-body of remainders, excesses, and surpluses that exceed the signifier, the fleshy aspects of a bodily reality that exceed the realms of discursive construction and social meaning and point to a Real outside the text.

In deference to Merleau-Ponty's notion of the flesh as a site for a different relation between the sensational self and the world of the other, in *Skin Acts* this orifice or erogenous point of contact on the skin is the site of an *intercorporeal* drive, where the skin retains a sense of the chiasmic relationship between mind and body, the gaze and the touch, the need for differentiation and attachment, encompassing both intrapsychic objects and the other as a like subject, self versus other, the field of the Other and the field of the Real. The intercorporeal drive seeks to touch (upon) the sensational body rather than the body constructed by the signifier. Linking invagination and intercorporeity, the skin becomes the reflexive site where bodies can touch each other, can be touched by the other, and can make themselves feel touched or touch themselves.[70]

Where does racial difference, the construction of both self and other as different, fit in this return to the grotesque libidinal body with its intercorporeal drives and invaginating orifices? If, as Massumi describes, the "skin is faster than the word," and if there is a body that escapes the signifier, does the sensational, fleshy black body then become androgynous, unmarked by race but also prior to the body marked by sexual difference?[71] The erogenous orifices of the libidinous body, that residual remainder of the body *as* its orifices that figured so largely in the medieval grotesque body and reappears in the Lacanian libido-body of the modern subject of the drive, are precisely the place in which one also finds a racialized body, embedded within the libidinal, pressing in rather than standing outside of the Symbolic or Imaginary orders. The libidinous black body moves chiasmically between body and flesh, the sexual and the consensual, phallic closure and invaginated openness, but also between phallic signifier and epidermal image, flowing in and around the discourse, visual codes, and languages of race.[72]

Thinking about race and sex together requires a retracing of the historical relationship between discourses of racial and sexual difference and the ways in which those intertwined discourses reveal varying modes of understanding the body. Over the course of modernity, the epistemic move from anatomy to physiognomy marks also epic shifts from medieval conceptions of the grotesque body as permeable, reversible, and invaginated to Enlightenment understandings of the body as a hardened container of both racial and sexual differences, inscribed onto epidermal and genital skin. Since the latter is the body Freud inherits at the end of the nineteenth century, the hardened epidermal body also becomes the stage for psychoanalytic understandings of the libidinal body as phallic. However, latent traces of an alternative, orifice-filled body with antecedents in the medieval grotesque find their way into the trope of the "flesh of the world" in Merleau-Ponty's phenomenology, into the idea of the body-without-an-image in Massumi's affect theory, and even into the modern libido-body of the drives theorized in Lacanian psychoanalysis. In *Skin Acts*, this body becomes the source of an intercorporeal drive that profoundly shapes the interracial and intercultural space of racialized masculine performance.

Whereas contemporary scholarship on the skin remains somewhat blind to the intertwinings of racial and sexual identities in intercultural New World modernity, in the archive of black diasporan and postcolonial writings there is one figure who undertook precisely this kind of study of the role of the skin amidst the intersectionality of colonial desire and the historical materiality of race. Frantz Fanon was a psychiatrist, anticolonial thinker, activist, and phenomenologist situated at the crossroads of multiple disciplines well before the notion of interdisciplinarity took hold. His efforts in *Black Skin, White Masks* to think blackness through the concrete metaphor of the skin provide us with a further set of conceptual tools, now originating in black studies of the psyche, for exploring how the epidermalized schema of a black racial unconscious shapes not only certain signature performances of black masculinity in interaction with a racializing white gaze but also the black male performer's intercorporeal relationship with his audience and with his own fleshy, desiring, orifice-filled, relational self. Reengaging Fanon in this context, in relation to a psychoanalytically inflected discussion of the skin and the flesh, also reveals the productivity of thinking about the phenomenology of race relations not only as it impacts contemporary performance (as one site for the working through of the self-other relation) but also as it has effects within the intraracial and the interracial sexual relation.

Epidermalization (and the Desire for Difference)

In the oft-cited, opening phrase of Fanon's fifth chapter of *Black Skin, White Masks*, the white French child's cry—"'Dirty nigger!' Or simply, 'Look, a Negro!'"—performs the gaze's other reality as unseen speech, as the "'unapprehensible' agency through which we are socially ratified or negated as spectacle."[73] With this opening, Fanon wants his readers to experience the power of this call as an interpellating speech act. The gaze takes notice of, touches upon, the skin of the black subject, and this sight is given discursive meaning by and in the child's cry.[74] While Fanon seems concerned here primarily with the appearance of blackness, how the raced subject looks and becomes visible in a racist world, I would argue that what Fanon also demonstrates powerfully in this chapter, and throughout *Black Skin, White Masks*, is the ways this epidermalizing call interpellates both the white child and the black man in a symbolic order of difference filled with racial meanings.

Fanon's observations both here and throughout the text rest on the subtlest of distinctions between seeing blackness and seeing blackness *as difference*. This latter phenomenon, the *desire for difference*, is less an inherent feature of the self than a feature of the desire of the Other, a structural aspect of the social symbolic order. It determines the psyches of modern subjects on multiple sides of the chiasmic color line, shaping the sexual relation as a site of interaction between self and other, and informing the racialized parameters of social conflict in New World political histories.

It is striking how much Fanon uses metaphors of the skin and sensation to capture the black subject's phenomenological and physiological experience of his racialization, by the Other, as different. The desire for difference is a fundamentally intersubjective formation felt on the body of the black subject as a touch. In other words, the black subject experiences symbolic capture in bodily, sensational, haptic terms. Fanon's discovery that he is seen as nothing more than a thing feels like he is being "sealed" into a "crushing objecthood," as if encased within his own skin. He apprehends the gaze as a sensation "running over" the surface of his body, first burning and then leaving him "shivering with cold, that cold that goes through your bones." He trembles, feels slapped, slashed, walled in. He wears his epidermal skin like an ugly "uniform," but is so sensitized by this skin that he becomes insect-like, "slip[ping] into corners" with his "long antennae pick[ing] up the catch-phrases strewn over the surface of things." As his antennae pick up the racial meanings written onto the skin, "catch-phrases strewn over the surface," their lexicon is physiological: "nigger underwear smells of nigger—nigger teeth are white—nigger feet are big—the nigger's barrel chest." These smells, sights, impressions of the body's volume and size are not just scopic; they are tactile and multisensorial, synesthetically fusing the racialized body and the skin on the symbolic grid.[75]

The alienating irony for Fanon is that the very gaze that objectifies him also liberates him. It acknowledges him, gives him his meaning, his location, in the signifying order. Massumi describes this order as a grid, "an oppositional framework of culturally constructed significations: male versus female, black versus white, gay versus straight, and so on. A body correspond[s] to a 'site' on the grid defined by an overlapping of one term from each pair. The body came to be defined by its pinning to the grid."[76] In the context of this grid, Fanon experiences interpellation as a physical sensation of location and belonging: "I turned beseechingly to others. Their attention was a liberation, running over my body suddenly abraded into nonbeing, endowing me once more with an agility that I had thought lost, and by taking me out of the world, restoring me to it."[77] In reality, this gaze distances him from his body. The gaze is a freeze frame, visually arresting his motion, fixing him into a socially determined position marked by his race. It then inserts this frozen body, the black body held captive on the representational grid, hardened and symbolic, as a surrogate body-image or substitute.

The gaze that places you on the grid in the first place, locating and interpellating you, is also the one that limits and constrains you, as Fanon also describes: "The movements, the attitudes, the glances of the other fixed me there, in the sense in which a chemical solution is fixed by a dye."[78] In the language of skin color, he relates his sensation of being pinned into the social frame by the epidermalizing, staining, gaze of the other. He "stumble[s]" when he realizes that in this scopic encounter between the gaze and the skin, it is the gaze that frames his movement out into the world, giving it meaning. The gaze endows as it abrades—scraping away the material flesh of the black body it puts something else in its place.

When Fanon has to "meet the white man's eyes," he feels it literally as the burden of an "unfamiliar weight." The weight (of race) is imposed so that the ideological work of privileging its removal can begin. Fanon describes researchers struggling to produce "a serum for 'denegrification'" that would allow the black subject to throw off the "corporeal malediction" of his skin. This malediction is not so much a bodily schema as a "historico-racial schema," not so much corporeal as discursive. It is a mantle, written or placed on the black body symbolically by "the white man, who had woven me out of a thousand details, anecdotes, stories." Denegrification is actually the creation of a second skin of racializing words that splits the black subject from himself.[79]

We are used to reading *Black Skin, White Masks* as a genealogy of racial dis-course, race as ideology, myth, social construction, as a form of signification and language. However, what has been written on black skin is a surface effect of an even deeper narrative of the skin as a thing woven out of "details, anec-dotes, stories" in European thought. As scholars recount how "the integument of the body has become a rigid boundary,"[80] this same history of corporeal malediction that creates the skin as a mantle or epidermal casing shapes the geo-historical space of the colony where: "identity ceases to be an ongoing process of self-making and social interaction. It becomes instead a thing to be possessed and displayed. It is a silent sign that closes down the possibility of communication. . . . Identity refers to an indelible mark or code somehow writ-ten into the bodies of its carriers [and] otherness can only be a threat."[81] This is Gilroy's description of a discursively racialized black self who is the subject most exposed to processes of epidermalization and denegrification whereby the hardened skin becomes nothing but a sign. Epidermalization repeats and reinforces the writing of a symbolic discourse of impermeability on the body.

Gilroy accurately describes racial epidermalization as an effect in the field of vision. The skin becomes a specular object, a shadowy "afterimage—a lin-gering effect of looking too casually into the damaging glare emanating from colonial conflicts at home and abroad."[82] When we extend the metaphor of the lens of the eye across the cultural field to the screen, the gaze is the in-visible social agency—ideology, discourse, cultural norms—that places us in the picture, on the image-screen, as nothing but this afterimage, as nothing beyond our symbolic status as *"photo-graphed"* subjects.[83] For Silverman, the cultural screen is a chiasmic extension of the mirror of the self into the sym-bolic realm.[84] However, the skin-as-subject is not just the visual artifact of colo-nial imaginations, powerful as that visual legacy may be in the construction of blackness. The "subject of representation" is simultaneously a spectacle and a look, an object and a subject, and neither is in the place of the gaze as the social agency with imprinting and interpellating power. The black subject racialized on the grid as a sign is not so much silent as articulating himself as he is seen, making himself seen as he is spoken (about), flesh conveying word.

The skin, in other words, is more than an afterimage; it is also a synes-thetic projection into the present that involves all of the senses. Agreeing with Gilroy's critique of race as a product of the visual regime of the sign, Ben-thien states: "Culturally, the perception of the skin was increasingly turned into a perception of distance . . . only as the observed skin of the other with whom I come face to face does skin become a sign, only through this separa-tion can the other truly become a recognizable and classifiable object. . . . The discourse about race is based on an outdated semiotic model constructed on the physiognomic ideas of the eighteenth century."[85] However, the skin as *only* the shadowy afterimage of a distancing, othering, colonial gaze from the past, as Gilroy describes it, keeps us confined to, naturalized within, the skin's symbolic and semiotic meanings. It limits our ability to see the skin as also expressive of the self's effort to subjectify itself, to speak and articulate itself, to make itself (as the) spoken (about). If on the *subjectifying* cultural screen the image is a form of speech, then also "speech about one's own skin is speech about oneself as body."[86] Benthien states further: "If the repeated, strenuous efforts at fashioning a visual semiotics of the skin are one side of the coin, the other side is the tactile experience of one's own skin and that of others, which largely escapes external categorization and attribution. The body is not only a cultural sign but also an entity with sensation and perception."[87] For the performing black subject, in other words, the *skin acts*.

Half a century after Du Bois described the black subject's double consciousness as a second sight, Fanon added in *Black Skin, White Masks* a third mode of black self-consciousness, a triple or "third-person consciousness," which he described as "a slow composition of my *self* as a body in the middle of a spatial and temporal world."[88] This is where Fanon's more radical interventions in thinking about the skin begin, as the site of a black body that is more, experiences more, signifies more, than the gaze can see. This "corporeal schema" is that of the subject-as-body, the bodily ego, the body-without-an-image that knows itself instead through "residual sensations and perceptions primarily of a tactile, vestibular, kinesthetic, and visual character."[89] Like any good phenomenologist, Fanon wanted to hold on to a sense of his own bodily experience in the world. His lament is precisely that it is this "corporeal schema" that crumbles once he discovers his black body as it is constructed from Symbolic material, from language, from the discourse of the Other.[90] The gaze hides behind difference what it cannot see of the subject, of the like subjectivity of the other, as the latter exists out there in the Real.

In reading closely Fanon's discussion of the body and the skin throughout *Black Skin, White Masks*, we need to make the crucial distinction between *epidermal* and *corporeal* blackness in parsing the multiple relationships to black skin he describes throughout the text. The bodily ego or sensational ego is tied to the skin ego, to those erogenous locations on the skin of the body around which the drive circles in search of a living being, beyond a signifying consciousness. It is this intercorporeal body, subject as it is to desire and the circuit of the drive, that sits at the intersection between the sensational body relating to the other in cultural performances and the libidinal body desiring, and being desired, and desiring to be desired, as a sexual subject-object in private relations between self and other. When the mental image of the body hardens into one's idealized mirror image, that original apprehension, an afterimage of the self as its skin, is repressed.[91]

A trace of the skin ego remains, however, in the cutaneous, sensational sense of self accessible through touch. This trace also remains in one's genitally fixed desires, and in the generalized erogeneity or sensitivity of the body as felt on the surface of the skin in contact with the world. As Freud links individual erogenous zones with the skin overall: "The erogenous zones . . . these skin regions merely show the special exaggeration of a form of sensitiveness which is, to a certain degree, found over the whole surface of the skin."[92] For Freud, the wayward desires of the consensual, multisensorial, erogenous body, if left unchecked, could fix the subject in seeking unnatural oral, anal, or genital pleasures and perverse pleasures in "touching and looking":

> At least a certain amount of touching is indispensable for a person in order to attain the normal sexual aim. . . . The same holds true in the end with looking, which is analogous to touching. . . . Covering of the body . . . continuously arouses sexual curiosity and serves to supplement the sexual object by uncovering the hidden parts. This can be turned into the artistic ("sublimation") if the interest is turned from the genitals to the form of the body. . . . On the other hand, the desire for looking becomes a perversion (a) when it is exclusively limited to the genitals.[93]

"Normal" sexuality, the transference of erogenous desires into normative heterosexual relations, depends on their sublimation from an "autoerotic" mode to an approved sexual object. The "erogenous zones subordinate themselves to the primacy of the genital zone," and the drive to seek pleasure "enters into the service of propagation"; that is, erogeneity is sublimated into, given primary social meaning as, fulfilling one's reproductive instincts.[94] Nonreproductive acts (for example, homoerotic desire but also autoerotic touching) or acts of "abnormal" desire and reproduction (for example, miscegenation but also cross-racial looking) then become perverse.

We are unaware of this apparition, the erogenous skin ego, precisely because of its twofold repression by, first, a prohibition against touch that is as powerful as the oedipal taboo is against incest, and second, a sublimation of looking "from the genitals to the form of the body," that is, from the body as its fleshy, erogenous organs to the image of the body as its idealized overall form.[95] Sealed away in prohibitions against contact with that body through touch, the skin-ego and its fleshy organs and bodily aspects are cut away; separated off they become remainders left behind in erotogenic traces on the body, and in scopic and symbolic representations of the fleshy, erogenous body as hideous.

In *Black Skin, White Masks*, Fanon theorizes a form of white psychopathology in which the (white) subject, separating from and leaving behind the skin of his own erogenous body, suddenly sees in the image of the black subject an apparition of that residual, leftover body shadowing his or her mirror image. This then becomes sublimated as a black *imago*:

> It would be interesting, on the basis of Lacan's theory of the *mirror period*, to investigate the extent to which the *imago* of his fellow built up in the young white at the usual age would undergo an imaginary aggression with the appearance of the Negro. When one has grasped the mechanism described by Lacan, one can have no further doubt that the real Other for the white man is and will continue to be the black man. And conversely. Only for the white man The Other is perceived on the level of the body image, absolutely as the not-self—that is, the unidentifiable, the unassimilable.[96]

This black imago, the "black man" that appears in the mirror of the white ego as phobic fantasy and racial stereotype, as the evil shadow of whiteness, is nothing but the afterimage of a foreclosed otherness that is "perceived on the level of the body image," that is, in the terrifying gap between the (white) subject's own felt body and his body-image. The utopian resolution of this condition, this scotoma, would be what Lacan describes as the "Jouissance of the Other," that is, an apprehension "of the body of the Other who symbolizes the Other" whereby the appreciation of the (body of the) other is linked to an appreciation of the body (the other) in the self.[97] In the dystopian colonial setting, however, the "appearance of the Negro" in the mirror has the potential to disrupt the process by which the (white) ego closes up his experience of himself as not-whole with his ideal vision of an Imaginary self.[98]

Fanon goes one step further. The black imago that appears as a shadowy apparition in the mirror of the white psyche translates onto the cultural screen as the imago of the black phallus.[99] The Negro as penis is the cultural imago that reminds us of the shadowy remainder of the body, the bodiliness of the human subject. When these "Negrophobias" get faithfully reproduced on-screen, the black phallus is not simply a hypersexualized penis. Rather, the black phallus is also, potentially, an image of the sensational body, even if now characterized negatively as biologically determined. "The Negro is fixated at the genital," "the Negro symbolizes the biological," "the Negro represents the sexual instinct (in its raw state)"—Fanon tells us this repeatedly not in order to point to the black phallic subject as a fetish arousing desire, but rather, to point to his status as a frightening, anxiety-producing figure for everything the white man uses the black phallus "to defend himself" against.[100] "The Negro . . . gives off no aura of sensuality either through his skin or through his hair. It is just that over a series of long days and long nights the image of the biological-sexual-sensual-genital-nigger has imposed itself on you and you do not know how to get free of it."[101] In Freud's oedipal narrative, sexual desire is foundationally masculine—"the libido is regularly and lawfully of a masculine nature"—and the phallus represents what one cannot have, for example, the father's sexual relationship with the mother.[102] In a Freudian world in which all genital desire is seen as fundamentally phallic, the phallus as a site of erogenous desire is transformed or sublimated into something more socially appropriate, into "normal," reproductive, heteronormative sex acts. Taboo acts, of incest, autoeroticism, with love objects of the same sex, or with those of another race, represent phallic or genital desires that are replaced with normative oedipal ones. Men are assured that they can have their sexual desires, the phallus, as it applies to other women (not the Mother). And women are assured that rather than having their own desires, they can derive their pleasure from being the phallus, that is, from being the sensual object of desire for men.[103]

The libidinal body of psychoanalysis is one in which the phallus has been symbolically separated away from the erogenous body and sublimated as a signifier for cultural authority, power, and the legitimacy that the social order can provide, including the authority of language.[104] For Fanon, the black male's dilemma is that he becomes nothing more in the symbolic order than his phallic skin, the latter seen as a meaty organ cut away from all notions of the interior intersubjectivity of the black male himself. As Silverman summarizes: "To confer a mythically large penis on the black man is not to associate him with the phallus, but to stress the distance which separates him from it," as a figure for symbolic, linguistic, and cultural authority.[105] The black male's problem is precisely that all he has, all he is, is an erogenous body whose sign is the penis rather than the phallus. However, Fanon's "phobogenic object," the Negro "penis symbol" that is also "a stimulus to anxiety," has an uncanny dimension that goes well beyond the eroticized black penis, the stereotyped, pornotroped, hypersexualized image of blackness we are used to analyzing critically in popular cultural discourse.[106] The black penis is the metonymic figure for the lost sensational and erogenous body when it reappears on the cultural screen as the phallic signifier's ugly, meaty underside.

The (black) penis is a shadow-image of the phallic signifier not because it is its opposite, but rather, because it portrays the phallus stripped down to its corporeal presence and desexualized function in a bodily Real. The desexualized Real is what Lacan calls a sexual and bodily reality that falls outside of symbolization, outside of the heteronormative, oedipal terms of phallicization. "Desexualization" is the moment when reality intrudes and the myths and fantasies governing love, sex, and other forms of social relation fall apart.[107] This desexualized Real is the hidden underbelly of the sexual relation, the moment when the like subjectivity of the other impinges upon the self's constructions and fantasies in a horrific way: "In that fall-out zone that I call desexualization and function of reality . . . the sexual object moves towards the side of reality and presents itself as a parcel of meat [and] there emerges that form of desexualization that is so obvious that it is called in the case of the hysteric a reaction of disgust."[108] Fanon's Negro fixed purely in the association of his desires with the genital is the very symbol of this meaty, desexualized Real. It is the symbolic discomfort with or negation of the Real that shapes our reactions, for example, to Robert Mapplethorpe's famous photograph *Man in Polyester Suit*, the image of a black male dressed in a three-piece polyester suit, cropped from just above the waist to just above the knee in order to emphasize and frame his exposed, uncircumcised phallus as it protrudes from the opening in his pants.[109] What disturbs the gaze in Mapplethorpe's photograph is precisely the visibility of the fleshy skin of the phallic signifier — or the phallic signifier *as a fleshy black foreskin* covering over what is frightening about the erogenous body. In the exposure of the black phallus, this erogenous body, despite being clothed, presses into the picture from the Real. The "hyperbolic black penis" is the phallus shorn of "the clothing of the self-image that envelops the object cause of desire" and on the basis of which "the object relationship is most often sustained."[110] One could go so far as to say that this is the phallus shorn of whiteness, where it is whiteness that stands as the racial dressing, the clothing of the signifier, draped over (black and other) flesh. The black-and-white photograph's high definition reproduces the leathery skin of the penis, drawing our attention as much to the phallus as to its tactile covering foreskin, and the black veiny hand posed nearby serves as a reminder of all the dangerous possibilities of touch. The overdressing of the black male body in his synthetic polyester suit only further highlights the photograph's obscene unclothing of the phallic signifier as mere meat, the bared black phallus as the disgusting, hysteria-producing reality of the sexual organ as mere flesh.

Mapplethorpe's image manages to capture and expose black genital skin as much more than just a fetish. The blatantly exposed phallus poking through the crack or orifice of the Real is stripped of its symbolic skin, providing instead a glimmer of its other form as the separated, shed, foreclosed and disavowed erogenous body, the stripped or skinned body, the fleshy underside of the modern, photo-graphed, black subject. However, Mapplethorpe's spotlight on the black phallus still carries with it some remaining investments in clothing the posed or performing black male body in a phallic suit or foreskin. Both here and throughout his oeuvre, his images fluctuate between desexualizing the black phallus as meat and re-symbolizing or re-eroticizing phallic meat as signifiers for the desired, black male object. In *Skin Acts*, through the analysis of performances of black masculinity that never fully escape the grid of a variety of visual texts, that is, embodied performance represented here not simply as lived experience, but rather, as the body without an image simultaneously, or in the process of being, captured and reified by the cultural screen, I seek to offer a different option. In the chapters that follow, I propose an understanding of black male performance as an invaginated phallic experience layered over by and situated within dyadic and relational, performance and performative contexts. The goal is to offer a more complex image of the phallic black body that reveals its symbolic inscription in the very moment of enacting its "motive desire and active will" as flesh.

If the captive body, the black-body-with-skin, is the object of an exterior gaze, the fleshy body, the body-without-an-image, keeps in tension the psychoanalytic truth that the black subject experiences his or her own skin and re-creates it as a partial object in play with the gaze of the other. In the creative imagination, experience, and performance of one's own blackness, the skin is a fleshy site of relation between self and other, a liminal space of inter-action in which the body left behind, the body as flesh without an image, can appear briefly in various specters, shapes, and forms—as the throaty, glottal, vocal lining of the word in Bert Williams's minstrel act; as the shadowy, blurred, gestural outline of a body in motion in Paul Robeson's physical acting on-screen; as the cracked underside of a smooth, symbolic mask of color in the Technicolor optics of Harry Belafonte's films; as the meaty phallus desexualized, that is, made real and stripped of its symbolic skin, in the sexual politics of Bob Marley's performances of liveness. Each of these specters of the flesh appears in the cultural scripts of the skin left behind, and read anew, in the four performers' stage and screen acts.

In *Skin Acts* I introduce another set of meanings to blackness by understanding its most material signifier, the skin, as the site of sensory, interpersonal contact and racial, intersubjective knowing. Blackness is lived and performed in the flesh, this flesh serving as a threshold or meeting point of human contact, a contact zone in which black subjects negotiate the relations of sameness and difference they share with each other, and with those against whom they have been defined as Other. As in Morrison's scene in *Beloved*, so too in the history of blacks in the New World, racialized skin has signified as both a despised object and as an object of love and desire. The skin act, the circularity of the act of objectifying and subjectifying one's skin, is a process of simultaneously witnessing and performing, seeing and being seen. By fleshing out the performance of black subjectivity as a skin act I am asking us to think about black skin not just in terms of the gaze—skin color, epidermalization, racialization—but also in terms of the flesh, as flesh circulating and performing in a multisensory and interpersonal world.

one

Seeing Faces, Hearing Signs

I ain't never done nothin' to nobody,
I ain't never got nothin' from nobody, no time!
And until I get somethin' from somebody, sometime,
I don't intend to do nothin' for nobody, no time!
—BERT WILLIAMS, lyrics, "Nobody"

The obverse of the voice that gives body to what we can never see, to what
eludes our gaze, is an image that renders present the failure of the voice [as]
a sound that doesn't yet resonate but remains stuck in the throat.
—SLAVOJ ŽIŽEK, "I Hear You with My Eyes; or, The Invisible Master"

In 1906 Bert Williams's partner, George Walker, wrote an essay for the *Theatre Magazine* entitled "The Real 'Coon' on the American Stage." In this piece he expressed his hope that "the black man on the American stage [could] rise above being a mere minstrel man," and yet, he knew that the black entertainer in turn-of-the-century America still had to focus on the expectations of a white audience "always interested in what they call 'darky' singing and dancing."[1] Walker was confident that he "could entertain in that way as no white boy could," especially after he observed white performers acting in blackface: "Bert and I watched the white 'coons,' and were often much amused at seeing white men with black cork on their faces trying to imitate black folks. Nothing about these white men's actions was natural, and therefore nothing was as interesting as if black performers had been dancing and singing their own songs in their own way." The very real distinction between caricatures of black performance and the actual movements and songs of black subjects of this period may have influenced Walker's idea of what constituted an authentic black performance.

FIG 1.1. Postcard, "Mr. B. A. Williams as 'Shylock Homestead' in *In Dahomey*." Image provided by Yale Collection of American Literature, Beinecke Rare Book and Manuscript Library.

However, by billing themselves as "Two Real Coons," Williams and Walker's "darky act" made literal the idea that black actors *are* coons rather than actors *playing* coons, inviting audiences to observe them doing what seemingly came naturally.[2]

The play on authenticity that the notion of the "real coon" captures—where is the distinction between the self and what the self performs—mirrors the ways in which the blackface mask functioned as an epidermal sign at the turn of the twentieth century. In Williams and Walker's performances, the blackface mask literally extended its racialized meanings over their skin. The body of the minstrel became "facialized," that is, ruled by that aspect of the symbolic grid in which the most obvious sign of the intersection between signification and subjectification is the human face, a *"white wall/black hole* system."[3] Unlike Deleuze and Guattari's face on the symbolic grid, however, which is that of the "White Man himself, with his broad white cheeks and the black hole of his eyes," the hole is now the black facial surface and the white wall the unseen gaze of the cultural grid or screen.⁴ In the interaction between the two, "the mask is now the face itself," that is, blackness becomes, signifies as, a reified image or thing.⁵ Physiognomy and skin color were not only parodied in the blackface mask; they became the primary frame through which white audiences understood the black minstrel's body, speech, and song.

Blackface minstrelsy, then, as both the emblematization and the embodiment of *faciality*—the process by which the self becomes a subject in the signifying order through surface signifiers such as the face—reflects the popularization of blackness according to a deeper physiognomic logic undergirding colonial modernity. As an aesthetic strategy for black artists seeking recognition at the beginning of the twentieth century, the visual logic of faciality *was* the primary playing field they had to operate within to assert a sense of self recognizable to American audiences at that time. The first stirrings of the New Negro movement in the Harlem Renaissance of the 1920s could be seen in the earlier visual politics of African Americans from the 1890s onward.⁶ The turn of the century saw an African American preoccupation with presenting a newly emancipated race to the nation by literally presenting a new face of the race, that is, reconstructing the black image. For all of their ideological differences, two of the leading black male figures of the period, Booker T. Washington and W. E. B. Du Bois, took advantage of the new medium of photography and the genre of the portrait to engage in a very similar visual project. In 1900 Booker T. Washington edited the book *A New Negro for A New Century*, which included sixty portraits of idealized black subjects representing members of the race's "progressive class." For the International Exposition in Paris in 1900, Du Bois prepared an exhibit on the lives of African Americans that included hundreds of photographs and individual and family portraits depicting the industry and intelligence of African Americans following slavery and Reconstruction.⁷

The portrait photograph, far from an authentic representation of the black ex-slave at the dawn of the new century, is the very medium through which the modern black subject was turned into a sign that could be recognized, seen: "The head, even the human head, is not necessarily a face. The face is produced only when the head ceases to be a part of the body, when it ceases to be coded by the body, when it ceases to have a multidimensional, polyvocal corporeal code—when the body, head included, has been decoded and has to be *overcoded* by something we shall call The Face. This amounts to saying that the head, all the volume-cavity elements of the head, have to be facialized."⁸ In the portrait photograph, the body of the black subject was as facialized as the body of the blackface minstrel, but here the makeup and props were also gendered codes, producing respectable New Negro men and women as powerful visual signifiers of the race's potential for a fuller form of American citizenship. As Deleuze and Guattari also describe: "The difference between our uniforms and clothes and primitive paintings and garb is that the former effect a facialization of the body, with buttons for black holes against the white wall of the material."[9] In the portrait photographs of the New Negro neither the head nor the body was present; rather, the face and the respectably dressed body of the New Negro were the phallic signifiers and gendered signs through which a newly interpellated black subject addressed a broader American culture.

Black performers like Walker and Williams, working and creating together in the entertainment industries during the early decades of the twentieth century, saw themselves as part of this new effort to present a new face of the Negro to the world. In his fictional biography of Williams in the years surrounding his first show with Walker, *In Dahomey*, the British Caribbean author Caryl Phillips reconstructs turn-of-the-century Harlem as "a respectable colored world peopled by those who had yet to learn how to grin and bend over for the white man."[10] In this space, Bert Williams the celebrity entertainer "was king, and his subjects were happy to bask in his long, ambling shadow."[11] A "tall, light-skinned man," Williams the elegant performer with his upright public bearing epitomized the idealized New Negro male: "Back then he dressed well, he walked tall, and the bright glare from his shoes could pick a man's eyes clean out of his knobby head. Women watched him pass by, his hardback carriage upright, and they whispered half sentences about him from behind perfumed handkerchiefs. . . . Men watched him too, with their collars turned high, pulling on ash-heavy cigarettes, their broad feet helplessly anchored to the earth. . . . Children followed him at a respectable distance . . . but the neighborhood *man* continued on his way, stepping purposefully."[12] In this depiction, repeated in a photograph of the dashing Williams in his three-piece suit with phallic cigarette dangling, Williams wears the joint persona of the New Negro and the West Indian gentleman, Anglophone and Victorian in his sensibilities and carriage (see figure 1.2).[13] In Phillips's reconstruction, Harlem was the perfect setting for Williams and Walker's early ambitions on the American stage because both Williams and the black metropolis shared a turn-of-the-century ideal image of blackness, one based on "that old-fashioned dignity and civic pride," which allowed black "men [to] appear where previously only shades lived."[14] Offstage as New Negroes, the gentleman and the dandy arm in arm, Williams and Walker suited up in an attempt to remove the mantle of the Negro as phobogenic object that they donned onstage as the "Two Real Coons" (see figures 1.3 and 1.4).[15]

FIG 1.2. Three-quarter length portrait of Bert Williams, entertainer. Photographer Samuel Lumiere, ca. 1911. Photographs and Prints Division, Schomburg Center for Research in Black Culture, the New York Public Library, Astor, Lenox and Tilden Foundations.

FIG 1.3. Photograph of Bert Williams and George Walker. Image provided by Yale Collection of American Literature, Beinecke Rare Book and Manuscript Library.

FIG 1.4. Bert Williams and George Walker as "Two Real Coons," Lottie Album #56. Image provided by Yale Collection of American Literature, Beinecke Rare Book and Manuscript Library.

The visual politics of the New Negro make sense when one remembers what they were up against, prolific racist caricatures of black people distributed at the turn of the century on postcards that anyone could purchase.[16] While Washington and Du Bois hoped to use portraiture to move the black subject beyond caricature, for the blackface minstrel the two worked as synonyms for each other rather than opposing visual mediums. Although the photograph and the illustration are two distinct mediums with different visual vocabularies, in representing the blackface minstrel they worked together to reinforce blackness in the social field as a speck of difference, evident to the sight.[17]

Song sheets from the period illustrate well the chiasmic relationship between portraiture and caricature in representing the blackface minstrel as the phobogenic object, that is, as the signifier for a form of racial difference substituted for, standing in the place of, white audiences' experiences of the like subjectivity of black performers. At the turn of the century, since a performer's celebrity depended on the popularity of his songs, sheet music provided a way for the performer to advertise himself with his songs. In so doing, they also tended to bind the voice, as an alternative register for experiencing the performer, to certain images. On one song sheet advertising Williams and Walker's song "Good Morning, Carrie!," the performers' portraits are bound to the field of racist cartoons that surround them, the latter effectively undercutting the photographs' efforts to differentiate them from those caricatures.[18] Just as their voices are the absent register behind the words advertising their song, their embodied selves, already represented at one remove in their portraits, are further enfolded and subsumed within the cartoon images and words, and the comedic effect they produce on the page. On song sheets more generally, often the placement of black performers' portraits alongside derogatory images of blackness reinforced the drawings' ability to modify the picture of reality the photographs tried to present. Sitting squarely between image and text, the illustration becomes the key form of visual inscription on the song sheets, "drawing" blackness farther from the framed body and fixing it, like a dye, in the realm of the signifier.

In another popular song sheet, caricature ultimately works to assign the portrait a subordinate signifying status. The insert photo of minstrel performer Lew Dockstader in blackface literalizes blackness as a face that can be drawn onto the head of the performer himself (see figure 1.5). A clever visual pun, the animated word-image of the COON, dominates and overshadows the portrait of the performer on the top right corner of the page. The stereotypical image of ears, eyes, and lips cohere into the three repeated faces of a black person. When the word "COON" is literally animated into a visual caricature of a black

FIG 1.5. Sheet music cover "Coon Coon Coon" from 1901; with insert photo of minstrel performer Lew Dockstader in blackface. Courtesy of the Library of Congress, http://hdl.loc.gov /loc.award/rpbaasm.0489.

face, with the white letters and words standing in for the eyes and ears of a human, the facial caricature naturalizes in the words "COON COON COON" the idea that the signifier of the coon stands in for something real in the world, blackness as the site of difference. "COON COON COON" provides both a literal instance of and a perfect metaphor for the process by which a word becomes a thing. The COON, a discursive construction, becomes Real, material and visible, in a chain of metonymic associations that lead us from a sound-image (the written letters of the word) to a physiognomic illustration (the drawing of a face) to the visual logic that links blackness and whiteness to skin color — "the *white wall/black hole* system" of racialization through facialization.[19]

As the image of the word "COON" bores through the black subject from one ear to another he becomes nothing more than that word and image, a violent, univocal instance of racist interpellation. He is what he hears, that interpellating call, and what he hears is imposed upon the skin as seen. The cartoon image of the black face as a "real coon" represents the ways in which blackness as a sign exceeds even the boundaries of the photograph in early twentieth-century American culture. The photograph is not creating stereotypical images of blackness; rather, it is recording symbolic understandings and codings of blackness as, primarily, a visual sign of the difference of the racial other. Exceeding the frame of the portrait, blackness is already an ideogram, an image that is always already a word—race, difference, coon—before the emerging technology of photography offers a new medium for reinforcing racial codes inherited from colonial discourse. A comparison of the "COON COON COON" image with the photograph of Williams in blackface as Shylock Homestead at the beginning of this chapter (see figure 1.1) offers a graphic representation of the blackface mask as merely a drawing or caricature of blackness pasted on to the face itself. Bert Williams's photo-graphed, blackfaced depiction blurs the lines between portrait photography and caricature, revealing the ways in which both functioned as visual interpellations of the black subject into the symbolic order as his stereotypical image, the black imago, the facialized form of the anxiety-producing body of the black performer.

At the time of Bert Williams's first blackface performance, the early twentieth-century photograph recorded the activity of a gaze, an act of sight, which was already shaped by the racial discourses of modernity, its social languages and its political unconscious. By the turn of the century, white American audiences were already trained to see black corporeality reductively, as meaningful only in terms of its epidermal surface. As a synecdoche for the body, the skin was both an index of and a container for biological racial difference. The term "physiognomy" refers both to the features of the face and to the surface features of the body. By first facializing the head and then racializing the face of the black subject, "a concerted effort is made to do away with the body and corporeal coordinates through which the multidimensional or polyvocal semiotics operated. Bodies are disciplined, corporeality dismantled."[20] The blackface mask doubled the effect of "the thickening into visibility of the skin" of the raced subject.[21] The blackface mask extracted the face and its meanings one step further away from the corporeality, the bodiliness, of the (black) body.

What the mask also thickens is the idea that one's likeness, one's face, is a perfect index to subjectivity, to the truth of the person. The reliance on the visual is tied up in the ideal that one's likeness represents the "selfsame body," that is, it is like the self.[22] While this idea of the face as a sign of the person shapes Bert Williams's portrayal in the two visual mediums, portraiture and caricature, popular at the turn of the century, Williams the performer did find ways to play with his own facialization on the early twentieth-century grid. An elaborate photo spread in *Vanity Fair*, which depicted the performers engaged in "a series of specially posed facial stunts," provides a powerful example of a main argument of *Skin Acts*. Reading the bodily performance retrospectively back into an image can break up some of the equivalences between the performer's likeness and the racist imago that portraits and caricatures of blackness work to link and underscore in different periods.

As much as the *Vanity Fair* series placed the two black performers on the social grid much like "a chemical solution is fixed by a dye," the title caption of the series also points to the performative gap between the natural man—Williams and Walker as *Nature's Black-Face Comedians*—and the man performing nature, with his series of *Specially Posed Facial Stunts* (see figures 1.6 and 1.7).[23]

The sixteen photographs are arranged as a grid with six poses on the top row of George Walker, six on the bottom row of Bert Williams, and four in the middle, two of each performer, sharing space with two boxes of text. In George Walker's images, the actor is not in blackface and in five shots in the top row he performs an exaggerated array of facial poses, clearly indicating that he is acting.[24] The performer's posed aspect carries over into the two more "natural" shots of Walker, one in which he is sitting before the camera in his street clothes as if posing for a studio portrait. The other, an idiosyncratic portrayal of the actor shirtless, with his bare back to the camera as he throws us a grin from over his shoulder, fits within the field of images precisely because the photograph literally presents the skin (of the back) as the face of the actor's bodiliness, black flesh bared as skin dressed up for the gaze.[25]

The first line of accompanying text commends Williams and Walker for being unlike other "colored actors" who "frequently failed because they aimed higher than the white theatre-going public wanted to look." Since "every image embodies a way of seeing" and the photograph is "a sight which has been recreated or reproduced," in the *Vanity Fair* pictures, reproduced as posters and publicity sheets for *In Dahomey*, the gaze of Williams's blackface coon situates his audience historically.[26] Walker's unwillingness to meet the "eyes" of the camera places less pressure on the viewer to change the terms of his or her relationship to the image by acknowledging the black subject as a like subjectivity. Bert Williams's gaze in his headshots communicates with the viewer differently, producing the effect of an irrepressible force pushing in from the space of real racial interaction and social conflict. Bert Williams's facial stunts represent subtle attempts to draw the aim of the gaze to the gap between the performer and his skin.

On the bottom row, Williams's series of facial expressions are all subtle shadings and variations of one distinct expression. From the wide and squinty-eyed grin to the rueful balanced pose, it is as if Williams, very much in the persona of the blackface minstrel, is addressing the viewer as an audience directly, as an "interaction-in-the-making"; it is as if he is trying on a series of linked faces for our approval and viewing pleasure until we pick or authorize the right shot.[27] This solicits a level of interactivity, recognition, awareness, and acknowledgment on the part of the audience, or at the minimum, expresses visually a direct appeal from the performer. Williams's bottom-row series of shots animate the closed cartoon sign of the blackface mask. They are the closest approximation to a moving image that the still, photo-graphed, blackface mask (graphed onto the face, graphed into the photo) can provide, the serial images of a moving face functioning as metonyms of bodily movement and ephemeral presence. Williams's linked shots work as a kind of stop-motion animation in which the blackface performer and the camera together mimic the incorporeal motion of his invisible body sliding between the frames.[28]

Even more successful are Williams's middle shots that surround the frame of text. Williams faces the mirror first as the blackfaced minstrel putting on or taking off his makeup. In the second image, the mask-less performer is distinguished from his former image not only by the absence of blackface but also by his change of clothes and his turn away from the mirror. This is facialization in action; in the act of putting on his face the performer presents to his viewers an image of his moving head, a face rounded out to reveal its "corporeal coordinates" as the performer engages in the "multidimensional or polyvocal semiotics" of dressing and undressing the self.[29] This doubling of images has a very different effect than Walker's middle-row shots. Rather than collapsing Williams's performances both on and off the stage, they each put the other into question.

Unlike the image of Walker's bare back, in the picture of the black male performer putting on and taking off his mask, the skin of the facial signifier is denaturalized as something the performer is painting onto the surface of his body. The black face is no longer naturalized as a likeness, but rather, made visible as a canvas, a separate surface with its own materiality. In the image on the left, the face of the actor in the mirror is also detached from and doubled by the head and back of the performer. The face in the hardened, cork-brushed, epidermal mask is then separated further from the body of the mask-less performer, turned away from the mirror of the gaze, by the text in between the two shots.[30] Finally, in both, the black face in the mirror stares back at a performer positioned on this side, the viewer's side, of the mirror.[31] Taken together, Williams's two middle-row shots offer a picture of the body in its polyvalent, multiple, signifying forms—both in front of the cultural mirror and reflected in it, dressed and undressing, being and being performed, a head in the aftermath of motion as much as a face posed and graphed onto the grid.

FIG 1.6. "Williams and Walker, Nature's Black-Face Comedians in a Series of Specially Posed Facial Stunts." *Vanity Fair* ca. 1910, page 1. Anonymous. Photomechanical print. Billy Rose Theatre Division, the New York Public Library for the Performing Arts, Astor, Lenox and Tilden Foundations.

element. These prototypes in color of the white Rogers Brothers drew crowded houses to the New York theatres, won plaudits in England, and came back to renew their American success at the Grand Opera House. New York critics generally agreed that not only Williams and Walker but the entire "In Dahomey" company set a pace for white comedians and comediennes to follow in an entire absence of slap-stick comedy and in a strict regard for only niceties in fun-making. "In Dahomey" is under the direction of Hurtig & Seamon.

y Fair, is believed to be the only series of the two colored artists to be posed for and peculiar style of dramatic humor make this page of exceptional value, and of what—to say the least—is a most novel and valuable set of faces.

PICTURES OF THE SEASON AND WORTH THREE TIMES THE REGULAR ADMISSION PRICE!!

FIG 1.7. "Williams and Walker, Nature's Black-Face Comedians in a Series of Specially Posed Facial Stunts." *Vanity Fair*, ca. 1910, page 2. Anonymous. Photomechanical print. Billy Rose Theatre Division, the New York Public Library for the Performing Arts, Astor, Lenox and Tilden Foundations.

Throughout Caryl Phillips's novel *Dancing in the Dark*, scenes of Williams in his dressing room, at his makeup table, staring at his mirror and putting on his mask, provide self-reflexive moments for the author to imagine the performer talking to and hearing himself. A similar self-reflexivity is evident in the novel's opening scene of Williams onstage in the role of Shylock Homestead, his character from *In Dahomey*. As Phillips describes: "He stares at the contented white faces in the orchestra stalls knowing that he can hold an audience like nobody else in the city. He knows when to go gently with them, and he carefully observes their mood; he knows not to strain the color line for he respects their violence. At other times, when he can sense something close to warmth, he might push and cajole a little, and try to show them something that they had not thought of before."[32] Speaking in the voice of Bert Williams the performer, Phillips describes a scene of mutual gazing and encounter between the black performer and his turn-of-the-century white American audience, an audience as visible to the performer as the faces we imagine him looking out at in the *Vanity Fair* photographic series. Williams's ability to read the intercultural, racial politics of the American scene he found himself in during the early decades of the century are evident in his essay "The Comic Side of Trouble," originally published in January 1918 in the *American Magazine*, where we find Williams on record explaining the self-reflexivity and self-consciousness required for him to perfect his craft.[33]

Over the course of his career, Bert Williams's minstrel act effectively captured the performative tensions involved in acting black at the turn of a new century. He left behind a permanent photographic record of himself as the denigrated "jolly colored coon." However, even from within his minstrel performances Bert Williams speaks back to us from behind the mask, his vocal performance reversing the terms upon which he was placed on the social grid. As the site on the face for the polyvocality that facialization seeks to displace, the hole that phallic symbolicization seeks to fill, the mouth and the object-voice offer a different kind of corporeal coordinate, an orifice or rim, on the black performing body. Directed at the open ear rather than the eyes wide shut, the voice addresses the audience from the gap between the performer and his act. The voice, as the object of an invocatory drive, evokes and invokes the lost body of the black performer, the aspects of his corporeal subjectivity silenced by the facial signifier.

Bert Williams speaks in those moments when something he does in his performance reverses the relationship between image and sound, between the signifier and the object-voice, and places meaning back in the body of the performer. In its written form, the blackface minstrel show actually offers a textual and visual alternative to the portrait photograph during this period, a way of *seeing the voice* held in abeyance just on the edge or rim of the sign. The sound-images and eye-dialects used to represent black speech on the page also serve as an image of blackness, even if a less obvious one, than the photograph or the drawing reproduced on a song sheet. Bert Williams was part of a cohort of black entertainers and performers on the vaudeville and minstrel stages who attempted to speak back to popular representations of blackness from within the parameters of the "coon song," using the rhythms and signifyin' potential of black speech.[34] A written record of these black sounds can be found in the librettos, musical scores, and dramatic scripts of the shows from Bert Williams's era. On these pages we find modes of speaking back to the era's racist portraits of a fixed black self. These modes engaged the signifier both on visual and acoustic terms, foregrounding the raw material of symbolic speech, the black letter, as an "instance of the [black] unconscious" captured in both word and sound.[35]

The challenge for a performer such as Bert Williams, a comedian skilled in the arts of mime and black folk mannerisms and gestures from across the diaspora, was how to navigate the terms of a distinctly visual American popular culture that muted the voice of the black performer and defined the meaning of blackness in favor of the face of the body. The voices of the "tan maidens," "muscular men fresh off the ships from the Caribbean," and "excited southerners" Caryl Phillips describes as migrating to the New World city of Harlem, found expression in the black musical sounds and speech patterns performed onstage and recorded in the burgeoning race-records industry emerging in the North.[36] While dialect was an important medium for portraying the sentiments of those blacks inhabiting modernity from a different class position than that of the educated black elites, black popular music and entertainment also became the staging ground for a cultural battle waged by educated and well-trained black musicians and performers. As the eye-dialects of black speech were captured and written into the librettos and scripts of the blackface minstrel show, a signifyin' and syncopated black vocality reappeared in the field of the visual to reclaim the body of blackness from the sign.[37]

In the years between the publication of Paul Laurence Dunbar's first African American dialect poem, "A Banjo Song," in 1893 and Claude McKay's two published collections of Jamaican dialect verse, *Constab Ballads* and *Songs of Jamaica*, in 1912, an entire recording industry emerged in the United States in which black music and syncopation played a key role.[38] Dunbar's choice to title his poem a song was fitting in the 1890s when, more so than artists, the popularity of individual songs sold records and the "coon song" was one of the staples of late nineteenth-century American musical culture. In New York Dunbar joined songwriters such as Will Marion Cook, Bob Cole, and the two brothers J. Rosamond and James Weldon Johnson (the latter himself a leading literary figure and intellectual of the Harlem Renaissance), and with Bert Williams and George Walker they came together to develop black musical comedy as a genre during this period.[39] Together they attempted to find a small space for their own artistic talents within the constraints of an American popular music industry disinterested in moving beyond racial stereotypes. All of these lyricists and musicians contributed to William and Walker's show, *In Dahomey*, the first black musical production of its kind to appear on the mainstream American stage.[40]

Both dialect speech and some African-derived rhythms have a quality that shares the same descriptive term, syncopation, which can refer both to the act of placing accents on the weak beat of a musical bar, a common feature of ragtime music at the turn of the century, and to the act of shortening a word by losing one or more sounds or letters in the middle, a common feature of black dialects as they are spoken and then recorded in writing. The coon song included both of these forms of syncopation, one describing rhythmic accents and the other the special features of the black letter. While the coon song initially developed in the context of white blackface minstrel shows, it took on both a life of its own and a higher level of musical complexity as it gained independence from the framework of the minstrel routine.

The Caribbean poet Edward Kamau Brathwaite describes the capacities of the voice for communicating meaning as "get[ting] the sound of it, rather than the sight of it," and Gates coins the term "signifyin(g)," which I have rewritten here as signifyin', as a way of making us attentive to the rhetorical differences of black speech, its excesses in sound and pronunciation, its puns on meaning.[41] If the spoken and the written have long been in tension in black diasporic cultures, they come together in the creation and transcription of complex black musical sounds, rhetorical figures, and speech rhythms.[42]

In Dahomey's script works with rhetorical wordplay and the sounds of the black letter to recapture the black subject lost to racist stereotypes and imagery. Whereas signifyin' represents the pleasure of black speech, the play with the sounds and meanings of words, syncopation calls our attention to the silences at the back of the throat, the visceral breaks in the rhythm of speech felt in the beat of the body. This is why Lacan describes the opening and closing of the subject—aphanisis and interpellation—as having a rhythm "that is, of its nature, syncopated," and located "in the gullet of the signifier," at the bodily juncture between silence and symbolic speech.[43] Underneath the signifier we find the echoes of a silent scream, the voice ultimately failing, as Žižek also describes, to become a "sound that doesn't yet resonate but remains stuck in the throat."[44]

The specter of a syncopated black silence that remains on the rim of the symbolic can appear as a punctuation mark on the page. Jennifer DeVere Brody, in her work on punctuation "as (a) matter of life and death as well as embodiment," describes punctuation marks as "shadow figures that both compose and haunt writing's substance," like the apparition who disappears at the first sign of the subject's emergence in the symbolic order, and yet, his disappearance is the very ground upon which the subject emerges.[45] The syncopated silences of the black letter, and therefore of the black subject, are written into the text as brackets or apostrophes marking, and thereby replacing, missing sounds. The apostrophe's very name invokes its homonym, a form of poetic speech that addresses someone who is absent or imaginary, lost or dead—the lost black speaker addressing a (white) listener who remains unaware.

The rise of the coon song was coincident with the popular reproduction of such derogatory images as the "jolly colored coon" in early twentieth-century American entertainment culture. Negative depictions of black subjects traveled into the lyrics of these songs: "By the 1890s, coon songs had acquired a degree of syncopation that distinguished them from other dialect and comic songs; meanwhile, coon-song texts had begun to exhibit a level of malice, violence, and viciousness rarely stressed in the minstrel songs from the previous half-century. Whereas dialect minstrel show tunes had worked to be funny via exaggerated images showing behaviors of a benighted but generally unthreatening group, the new coon songs consistently portrayed blacks as quarrelsome thieves, obsessive gamblers, violent drunks, and sexual predators."[46] Despite and alongside the racist images of black people in the coon songs, syncopation also opened up a space for representing blackness in a different medium. Written into the lyrics as eye-dialects of black speech, men such as Will Cook self-consciously attempted to rework dialect and find its "poetic possibilities" within the constraints of musical comedy.[47] As a small intellectual and cultural formation running alongside and in tension with the New Negro arts and literature movement, black entertainers such as Williams and Walker, the Johnson Brothers, and Will Cook fit awkwardly in the space between the popular and the cultured, musical form and literary speech. However, black vaudeville and minstrel acts brought together multiple media for conveying racial narratives—song, music, dialect, and the body of the black performer.

In a lecture presented at Harvard in 1979 entitled "History of the Voice," the Caribbean poet Edward Kamau Brathwaite described the "*total expression*" of Caribbean vocal forms where meaning resides on a continuum between "the noise and sounds that the poet makes."[48] Brathwaite argued that it was precisely in the "riddmic" aspects of Caribbean speech, "not only semantic but sound elements," the sound "rather than the sight of it," that one could hear alternative, resistant black consciousnesses inhabiting modernity from a different historical location than that of the colonizers.[49] In contrast, important black artists and intellectuals in the United States have found it difficult to accept minstrel forms such as the coon song as part of a liberatory narrative of black music and orality.[50] However, if we throw out the coon song and minstrelsy as simply the by-products of white racist imaginations, we miss the story told in the signifyin' and syncopated features of these cultural art forms.

Caribbean scholars also argue that prior to literacy, the performed black speech act captured some of the violence of the "irruption into modernity" lived viscerally by the New World slave.[51] As Glissant elaborates: "The alienated body of the slave, in the time of slavery, is in fact deprived, in an attempt at complete dispossession, of speech. Self-expression is not only forbidden, but impossible to envisage. Even in his reproductive function, the slave is not in control of himself. He reproduces, but it is for the master. All pleasure is silent: that is, thwarted, deformed, denied. In such a situation, expression is cautious, reticent, whispered, spun thread by thread in the dark."[52] The black body of pleasure and sensation is reproduced as a silenced body, a no-body, under the conditions of slavery. This history of silence and speech adds another dimension to understanding both the noise and the silence of the black-on-black minstrel's speech acts, its resistant elements. The skin of the voice reinvokes not just the body but also the negated, embodied history of the black slave left behind on the black letter as a material trace. Here the black letter is a figure for the evocation of the black performing subject in the G clefs, the quavers and semi-quavers, the half notes and quarter notes, beamed notes and breath marks of the musical sign, with blackness signifying as a missing sound or vocality swallowed and left behind on the rim of the coon song's racist imagery and words.

In 1901 when the Victor Talking Machine Company introduced the Victrola phonograph, the instrument that would predate film to become the first mass sound medium of the twentieth century, Bert Williams and George Walker made their first of fifteen recordings.[53] By 1911, the artist had become more of the draw in selling records, and it was Bert Williams, the celebrity and star, who was the object of value rather than his individual songs. Žižek argues that upon our entrance into the symbolic order, the voice acquires a "spectral autonomy," an "unbridgeable gap" emerging that forever separates "a human body from 'its' voice": "it never quite belongs to the body we see, so that even when we see a living person talking, there is always some degree of ventriloquism at work."[54] That sense of a ventriloquism that sounds in the gap between the performer and his speech is the visual metaphor evident in the following photograph, a picture of the performer and his shadow, with Williams dressed as the character "Nobody" from one of his signature songs (see figure 1.8).

As Williams's shadow looms behind him in his costumed blackfaced persona, one is reminded of Trinculo's comment about Ariel's singing in Shakespeare's *The Tempest*: "This is the tune of our catch, played by the picture of Nobody."[55] While the sight of Bert Williams in blackface is mortifying, the mask eerily demonstrating a human being in the process of becoming a thing, listening to a Williams recording produces the opposite effect, an enlivening sensation, as Williams comes alive once again in the animated resonances of his voice. Thomas Riis describes further: "On sound recordings nearly every word that Williams speaks takes on a life of its own and has the potential to overturn a cliché—to make us think twice about what has just been said— because the tempo is being radically shifted by Williams' unfailing ability to hold our attention. . . . This is not to suggest that Williams did away with minstrel images, only that he shifted them in ways that have not been accounted for."[56] As Brathwaite also described the impact of Claude McKay's oral recitation of his poetry: "In the tradition of the spoken word. . . . the noise that it makes is part of the meaning, and if you ignore the noise (or what you would think of as noise . . .), then you lose part of the meaning."[57] Through very intentional performance effects, the performer can attempt to bridge the gap between his social reality, his performativity, and his actual or bodily voice.

Bert Williams's vocal talent created the space for some sense of his subjectivity to exceed the confines of the blackface mask, his voice reaching out to us from the body lost in the shadows of the epidermal image.[58] Of the cast of *In Dahomey*, including Williams's and Walker's wives Lottie Williams and the prominent dancer Ada Overton Walker, only Bert Williams left behind a vast recording legacy. Riis provides some insight into Williams's impressive oeuvre by explaining in musical terms the performance effects he was able to achieve through vocal modulations. By controlling his pitch and tone, Williams shaped a song's emotional registers: "Although Williams was not a trained singer, he made the most of a resonant, somewhat hooty baritone. . . . He tended to intone as much as sing his songs [contributing] to the general estimate of Williams as a singer of emotion and pathos."[59] Riis also describes how Williams manipulated his "deadpan speaking tone and sure sense of timing," cutting a

FIG 1.8. Bert Williams in top hat, holding cigarette, singing "Nobody." Photographer Samuel Lumiere. Photographs and Prints Division, Schomburg Center for Research in Black Culture, the New York Public Library, Astor, Lenox and Tilden Foundations.

word or phrase here and there and using these "surprising shifts of accent [to] produce a comic effect."[60] Williams also created humorous effects by matching his voice to the music's sound. The most famous example of this occurs in "Nobody" where Williams mimics the sound of the trombone: "Trombone slides and stutters in 'Nobody,' his most celebrated song after *In Dahomey*, are precisely imitated by Williams immediately after they are played, and comic noises from bassoons, clarinets, and percussion are also in evidence."[61]

An additional rhetorical feature also creates a powerful effect in "Nobody," a lyrical confusion concerning first-person intentionality in the song. Certain lyrics use comedy to pose the question of whether the performer's persona is doing or not doing something in the song, is acting or not acting for someone else. These flashes of a subject fading in and out of speech are registered in a punning on double negatives most evident in the song's chorus:

> I ain't never done nothin' to nobody,
> I ain't never got nothin' from nobody, no time!
> And until I get somethin' from somebody, sometime,
> I don't intend to do nothin' for nobody, no time![62]

Williams's nonsense lyrics depend for their comic effect on the clear distinction between the actor and the act, the black speaking self and the black self spoken. The black actor as the speaker (the subject of the enunciation) voices the statement, "I ain't never done nothin' to nobody," but he speaks from a different location than the self indicated as the subject of his speech act—namely, the enunciated, the "coon" who is complaining about receiving nothing. Mirroring a Lacanian formulation, as a speech act Williams's lyrics can be better understood as, "I am the one saying, 'I ain't never done nothin' to nobody,'" with the first "I" functioning here as that silent and invisible voice of the performing subject stuck at the point of enunciation in the throat of "no-body," the performative shadow silhouetted behind the enunciated coon.[63]

If the joke in "Nobody" rests on whether there is a *somebody* in the song, the doleful humor lies in the idea of a *nobody* or *not-body* performing, an incorporeal black subject appearing and disappearing in flashes of presence and absence, as literalized in the profusion of double negatives throughout the song. The nonsense lyrics implicate both the doer and the receiver—the "I" doing nothing and the somebody from whom the doer gets nothing—and thereby underscores the reality that a speaker does not exist, does not signify, without an interlocutor and without the recognition that interlocutor provides and returns in language. At the moment in "Nobody" when Williams uses his voice to mimic the trombone slide, the performer slides from the intentional accents and clear pronunciation of verses against a light melodic background, to a chorus in which his voice slides out of "view" as it sounds more and more like the trombone. The humor of the trombone/voice slide rests precisely in our enjoyment of this as a performance by no/body, that is, by a human body whose speech is now silenced behind a non-signifying, even nonhuman sound. This performance effect is only heightened when the performer himself is a social nobody in the years the song was produced, a fetishized object-body bought and consumed in the form of his recorded signature song.

On the surface, the joke of "Nobody" is the enunciated subject's lack of knowledge about his own absence or presence in the song. At its deepest levels, however, the song reflects, in the belligerence and purposeful willfulness of its tone, the black male performer's awareness that the minstrel song is the only place his audience is willing to look for him.[64] In the midst of his vocal performances, Bert Williams often stepped out of his coon role to make interjections "as if connecting with the audience by stepping outside of the formality of the song."[65] Addressing the audience directly, he attempted to draw their attention to his presence as the performer rather than the performed in his speech act. As Riis also describes, many of Williams's and Walker's contemporaries believed that "more radical text departures were possible within the new upbeat, frequently syncopated, musical idiom . . . which [they] recognized as a genuine product of black culture."[66] The African American writers and musicians who helped to create In Dahomey had to find their own ways to use their words, even when sung in another's voice, to mark their presence.

In the song "On Broadway in Dahomey Bye and Bye," the musician Will Cook uses forms of black signifyin' speech, which "mandates the use of the tongue in a certain way, the use of sound in a certain way," to capture "the actual rhythm and the syllables, the very body work, in a way, of the language."[67] Made up of signifyin' strategies that enhanced "the effect that words have on the ear, their sound as well as their meaning, and the delight we take from their merely sounding," neither the speech nor the lyrics of In Dahomey fully transcend or subvert the coon song's racist meanings.[68] Rather, they elaborate upon the coon song's surface, syncopating on the rim of meaning, demonstrating in a type of negative comparison both the conditions of the show's production and the commitment of the black entertainers who sought to push beyond those limits.[69]

"On Broadway in Dahomey Bye and Bye," begins with the conditional, "If we went to Da-ho-mey sup-pose the king would say," and imagines what the aftermath and repercussions of the idyllic back to Africa migration narrative might be.[70] Chude-Sokei describes this song as "a broad satire of political positions within a black transatlantic community," the song encapsulating in a more compact form one version of *In Dahomey*'s closing scene in which power shifts back and forth between colonizing African American swindlers and the leaders of the Dahomey and Ashanti nations.[71] While "On Broadway in Dahomey Bye and Bye" does provide a humorous take on African Americans' renewed servitude to a modern, updated vision of the old colonialist's civilizing mission, it also gestures beyond the back-to-Africa migration story to the very act the performers are engaged in—the minstrel show itself and its place on the American stage.

The song links an older discourse of colonial imperialism to the new global spread of American consumer culture and values. The king of Dahomey demands all the trappings of the modern American entertainment and consumer industries, including a "Broadway built for us" and "a big department store." In his wishes he rearticulates American commercial values in African forms. Similarly, the new African American colonists act as the old European masters: "We'd build a nice roof gar-den some-where a-long the line, / Serve Gi-raffe High Balls and real Coke-nut wine. / We'd use Mon-tan-a Di-a-monds to make E-lec-tric light / And then have Wag-ner sung by par-rots ev-'ry night." Alex Roger's ironic lyrics parody and demystify an America of false promises while also pointing to the impossibility of return to any romanticized African past. As the black emigrationists emulate commercial values that are against the political interests of their people, it becomes clear that the dream they have sold themselves for is a farce — "You'll see on the sides of rocks and hills, — 'Use Carter's Lit-tle Liv-er pills' / On Broadway in Dahomey bye and bye." The American dream is not exportable because it is a symbolic fiction, a mirage requiring the constant support of a barrage of advertising and commercial information.[72]

Our contemporary view of minstrelsy is shaped to some degree by Ralph Ellison's very harsh critique in *Shadow and Act*, where he described the minstrel act as reducing "The Negro" to a "negative sign . . . in a comedy of the grotesque and unacceptable" and entailing nothing more entertaining or skilled than "Negro-deprived choreography . . . ringing of banjos and rattling of bones . . . voices cackling jokes in pseudo-Negro dialect . . . nonsense songs [and] bright costumes and sweating performers."[73] What Ellison discounted, however, was the presence of an ironic performing consciousness in the songs and lyrics created by the musicians and composers who produced black minstrel acts such as *In Dahomey*. *In Dahomey* has the semblance of a minstrel show's structure, with three acts, interlocutors and delineators, stump speeches, stock characters, malapropisms, nonsense speeches and songs, and a core of four to six staple songs that remained relatively stable throughout its many performances. The show's organization along the lines of the minstrel show also determines its deep structure, composed of various rhetorical and symbolic acts that drive the show's performance effects as much as any narrative elements of plot.

Signifyin' speech acts are a deep structural element of the show. They revolve around a group of characters led by the two protagonists, Shylock Homestead and Rareback Pinkerton played by Williams and Walker, and an entourage of trickster figures called "the syndicate," who are linked to meaningful objects or props. Jesse Shipp, the scriptwriter, worked with Williams and Walker to produce a script that includes all the classic rhetorical devices of Shakespearean comedy, "repetition, doubling, preposterous reversal, amplification and multiplication of words and errors."[74] Overall, the text of *In Dahomey* exemplifies both African American and Caribbean uses and histories of the black voice. As a performative utterance, *In Dahomey* makes visible the intercultural context these black entertainers worked in, the cultural scene of the "darky act" itself, with the black entertainers working as *delineators* of the very forces that subvert the black liberatory narrative, addressing the white audience as *interlocutors* equally structured by New World histories of conquest, slavery, colonialism, and racism.[75]

The Itinerary of the Letter: *In Dahomey*'s Signifying Acts

By "letter" I designate the material medium [support] that concrete discourse borrows from language. — JACQUES LACAN, *Écrits*

In Dahomey opens with a stump speech that has all the elements of a classic minstrel routine. Dr. Straight, a local hustler, attempts to sell a crowd of onlookers two products—"Straightaline," the "greatest hair tonic on earth" that promises to straighten "knappy or knotty hair"; and "Oblicutis," a "wonderful face bleach [that] removes the outer skin."[76] Dr. Straight then offers a tongue-in-cheek, academic explanation of each product's name: "*obli*—in this case being an abbreviation of the word obliterate, *cuti*—taken from the word *cuticle*, the outer skin, and *cuss* is what everybody does when the desired results are not obtained." Dr. Straight's description foregrounds the role of the visual and of language in defining blackness. Straightening black hair and stripping black skin are precisely effects produced when race is seen as a "faciality machine," entailing "the social production of face, because it performs the facialization of the entire body and all its surroundings and objects. . . . The decoding of the body . . . the collapse of corporeal coordinates or milieus."[77] Dr. Straight's opening stump speech names and parodies the alienating discourse of blackness understood in terms of appearance, physiognomy, and the skin.

The terms "straightaline" and "oblicutis" also pun on the signifyin', sound-based, meaning-deprived, properties of language. They hint at the fact that the minstrel show will not run in a straight line but will have oblique meanings, nonsense elements that ultimately parody the darky act's tendency to strip the skin from the face and build it up into a master signifier of black identity. In another interesting wordplay, Dr. Straight professes not to be selling the commodities he is displaying. As he proclaims: "I'm not here to sell but to advertise. I'm not here to make money but to give it away."[78] When Dr. Straight claims to be merely advertising rather than selling his products, he demonstrates the slippery nature of language in concealing truth and intention. To give something away does not preclude one's desire to sell a version of it later, as is obviously true of Dr. Straight, who in advertising his product publicizes its qualities precisely in the hopes that he can capitalize later on the value of that product.[79] Dr. Straight's malapropisms and puns reference what cannot be captured in the photo-graphed image of the black, the density of language as a site that records the performative intentionality of the playwright, Jesse Shipp, and his collaborators Williams and Walker.

Dr. Straight announces his commercial intentions in almost exactly the same words at least three times in his speech. His phrasing signals his rhetorical intentions in a method of speech Bertolt Brecht linked directly to a self-reflexive style of acting: "When [the actor] appears on the stage, besides what he actually is doing he will at all essential points discover, specify, imply what he is not doing; that is to say he will act in such a way that the alternative emerges as clearly as possible, that his acting allows the other possibilities to be inferred and only represents one out of the possible variants."[80] This acting out of hidden, disavowed, or unanticipated alternatives to the actor's actions has its corollary in a type of speech that the skilled actor uses to gesture actively toward the alternatives to his speech as he or she is speaking. Brecht identifies this acting strategy, of using a grammatical formulation as a tool to distance the audience so they look beyond the surface meanings of a word or text, as "fixing the 'not . . . but.'"[81] Many of Dr. Straight's phrases, such as his statement, "I'm *not* here to sell *but* to advertise. I'm *not* here to make money *but* to give it away" (emphasis mine), follow this syntactic logic of "fixing the 'not . . . but.'" Brecht argues that the merit of the "not . . . but" strategy is that it compels the audience to question the actor's absence or presence in his performance: "Where is the man himself, the living, unmistakable man, who is not quite identical with those identified with him?"[82] Similarly, the motives and meanings of the black performer become unstable once one recognizes in his language a signifyin', trickster consciousness.[83]

In the first scene that follows Dr. Straight's stump speech, George Reeder opens and reads a letter that introduces the lost object around which one of the plots of *In Dahomey* revolves, a box owned by Cicero Lightfoot. The ostensible purpose of the letter is to request that Mr. Reeder, as the man who could "furnish anything," hire two detectives to locate his missing box. This innocuous box is described often and in multiple ways throughout the script and each mention modifies the object's original meaning. Variously, it is called a "silver casket," a "lost article," a "coffin," "a little silver box beautifully ornamented," "a perfectly smooth and highly polished surface," and an object "engraved with a cat." The box soon takes on a fetish-like quality reminiscent of the commodities Dr. Straight professed not to be selling in the opening scene.[84]

In contrast to Dr. Straight's circumlocutions, however, the opening sentence of Cicero Lightfoot's letter is straightforward: "I lost last Friday, which was the 13th of the month, a silver casket with a cat drawed on the outside and a cat's eye on the inside."[85] Something definitive has happened at a certain time to an identifiable object. Here the text of *In Dahomey* finds a different way to signal the "not . . . but" as a grammatical performance strategy. When Mr. Reeder hires Williams's and Walker's characters as detectives to hunt down this box, he also modifies the letter's meaning. Describing the box as "an insignificant article to which [Lightfoot] sets great store," an insignificant object "of inestimate value," Reeder sums up: "Now I've come to the conclusion that the old man in question has *not* lost the article, *but*, being over-careful, has hid the aforementioned article from himself, as it were."[86] With this latter statement, Reeder invites speculation not on the mystery of the box itself, but rather, on the loss of the box as precisely the act that gives the box meaning. In other words, the box becomes meaningful as something lost or as loss itself, and the letter that details this loss becomes what remains, of the box.

The "letter"—both the individual unit of the word-sign and the epistolary form in which those units combine to take on syntactic and narrative meaning—is an eerily apt choice for representing this gap between meaning and loss in a text as deceptively simple as *In Dahomey*. Lacan describes the orthographical letter as the "material medium" or support that discourse "borrows from language."[87] However, in a famous lecture on the narrative meaningfulness of the "purloined letter" in Edgar Allan Poe's detective story of the same title, Lacan goes further, arguing that letters are props signifying the absent presence of their authors.[88] They are surrogates that act in the subject's place and represent more figuratively the subject's futile struggle to be in the same place as his letter, that is, to represent himself fully in written language. As Reeder translates and puts his own spin on Cicero Lightfoot's letter, he places in question the reliability of the first-person author of the letter to determine the real value of the lost object. Instead, he ridicules Lightfoot for being a man seeking something that is merely hidden in its place.

In Dahomey begins with a profusion of letters written either by or to the Lightfoot brothers, and these letters change hands as quickly and confusedly as the itinerary traveled by the lost box. The letters ultimately lead to the fundamental question of In Dahomey as a blackface performance text. Can the author, the performer, ever really control the meaning of his letter when the recipient, the audience, can always make the letter mean something other than what the author intends? As the letter and the box travel through the minstrel show, serving as the catalyst for plot movements and characters' dialogue, their itineraries force the question of where we should look for the black minstrel as a performing subject — is he in the place of the performer as author of his text or is he more present as a sound(-effect) of his words?

The letters and the lost box also play a linguistic role as metonymic and metaphoric props for forms of language that produce certain ironic and burlesque effects, aimed at the expectations of the audience (or reader).[89] Always part of a signifyin' joke or a figure of speech, they distance the spectator to provide the possibility for their questioning of the social values shaping the text's production. George Reeder's description of Cicero Lightfoot's box introduces the idea of an object that is not so much lost as misplaced, in another place than where everyone has chosen to look. At first it is Cicero the character who is doing the overlooking. Over the course of the script, however, the lost box becomes a mysterious object that always escapes being caught and increases in value with each shift to a new potential owner.

When Shylock Homestead and Rareback Pinkerton are hired to find the lost box, they realize that it was already recently in their possession. The box traveled north with the two phony detectives before they heard of it from George Reeder, as Shylock relates its route:

SHYLOCK. Yes, fust that man with the rusty yellow coat offered to sell it for a dollar and six bits. Then I come purty near having it. (Pause). Say don't you know every time I think of how near I come to havin' that box it gives me the shivers. . . . He finally sold the box for six bits, and that bowlegged cook that bought it had that box for just thirteen minutes when he got broke, and the man he sold it to had thirteen dollars, and after speculatin' with a cross-eyed barber about four minutes the thirteen dollars and the box changed hands agin.[90]

Like Cicero, the two detectives also had the box in their grasp and "lost sight of it."[91] From then on, Shylock Homestead, the no/body in blackface, can never seem to keep his hands on the box or gain any profit from it. As he describes further: "Jist about that time I begun speculatin' myself and I lost sight of it until I saw you with it jist before the boat landed." As the banter between Rareback and Shylock continues, it becomes clear that, in addition to where the box is, there is another question concerning the box's seemingly indeterminate nature.

What is the box exactly—a thing in itself or an object that contains, represents, another thing? Is it the valued missing object itself or merely its covering? On the surface of the box there is a drawing of a cat's eye, leading Rareback and Shylock to speculate on whether there is a live cat's eye inside the box itself:

RAREBACK. Shy, did you see inside that box?
SHYLOCK. No sah, the outside was enough for me.
RAREBACK. There was a cat's eye in that box, and it looked as if the eye
    was alive.[92]

When Shylock says, "No sah, the outside was enough for me," he literally describes his own condition as the blackfaced minstrel for whom surface alone is enough to understand his role and meaning as a figure for the black subject. Elsewhere the box is also referred to as a casket, raising the question of whether what has been lost is really the agalma, another name for the precious, animate corporeal flesh inside the box of the inanimate, symbolic self.[93]

The script of *In Dahomey* never resolves this mystery, and it would have had a marginal significance in audiences' appreciation of the show itself at the time of its production. Nevertheless, in the hands and words of the show's skillful black producers and performers, it marks the truth hidden behind the blackface mask that the performer Bert Williams hoped the audience would uncover, namely, that the mystery of the black performing male subject, as a like subjectivity, can never be found fully on the surface of his performance. As characters continue to speculate about the location and the nature of the box, the slippage between the drawing of a cat on the cover and an actual, live cat's eye within the box leads to a discussion of speculation itself as one of *In Dahomey*'s key tropes. Each time the word appears it references the indeterminacy of speech and the speculative aspects of black signifyin' that provide *In Dahomey*'s underlying frame of reference.

Reprimanded by Walker's character, Rareback Pinkerton, for gambling, Shylock puns on the meaning of the word "speculation" to draw our attention not just to what the word means but how it means, or signifies, as a series of stuttering sounds:

RAREBACK. Now I told you not to speculate with your money.
SHYLOCK. Spec-a-late, spec-a-late, den I didn't lose my money shootin' craps? I lost it speculatin'?[94]

Shylock's comic confusion about the meaning of the word "speculate" is answered in a nonsymbolic register when he breaks down the word into its syllabic units. The sound is the meaning, that is, the meaning of the word lies solely in its performance effect as a humorous chain of staccato, broken-up sounds.

Linguists and semioticians argue that the meaning of the word "c-a-t," for example, is determined less by something inherent to the sign itself than by "its differences from other combinations of sound in English. The sound (*ket*) is . . . distinguishable from *bat, cot, Kate, cats, etc.*"[95] Similarly, in an almost literal application of this linguistic observation, the meaning of the cat's eye box in *In Dahomey* is only significant as it constitutes a certain kind of vocal performance of blackness, a certain form of intercultural address from black male performer to audience, and a certain play on language as we follow the shifting journey of the chain of signifiers that each character associates with the box. When George Reeder describes Cicero's box with enough detail for Shylock and Rareback to realize that the box they had been traveling with is one and the same, the following dialogue ensues:

REEDER. The lost article is a silver casket.
SHYLOCK. What's he talkin' about, a coffin?
RAREBACK. Who ever heard of a coffin made of silver?
REEDER. The casket in this instance happens to be a little silver box beautifully ornamented. On the center of a perfectly smooth and highly polished surface is engraved a cat. (SHYLOCK. *funny fall*) What's the matter with your friend?
RAREBACK. He has cat-aleptic fits.[96]

Shylock's "cat-a-leptic" fit provides a fitting point of closure to this repeating nonsense metaphor of the cat's eye box which, like the blackface mask, may or may not be a surface reflection of a live thing, but is never the thing itself, the cat.

Shylock's "cat-alepsy" combines three complex figures of speech, catachresis, metalepsis, and malapropism. Phonetically it begins like the figure it has the least in common with, *cat-a*-chresis, which means using a real word in a false or incorrect manner much like Dr. Straight's wordplay in the opening scene. "Cat-a-leptic" works more basically here as a malapropism, the incorrect use of a word by substituting a similar-sounding word with different meaning for comic effect (the joke lies in Rareback incorrectly describing Shylock's "epileptic" fit as "cat-aleptic").[97] The phonetic ending of the word "cat-*a-leptic*," however, appropriately evokes a more complex figure of speech that aptly describes the way wordplay works throughout *In Dahomey*. The word "cat-a-leptic" functions as a form of *metalepsis* in that Shylock's "cat-a-leptic fit" becomes the reader's, the listener's, passage back to the joke of the cat's eye box in all of its significations.[98]

The idea of the "cat-a-leptic fit" tropes on the already very complex figure of the metaphoric cat's drawing and the metonymic cat's eye, working through a complex signifying and rhetorical chain to link us back to the actual cat's box itself. Harold Bloom describes metalepsis as "a metonymy of a metonymy," that is: "the trope of a trope, the metonymic substitution of a word for a word already figurative . . . frequently allusive, that refers the reader back to any previous figurative scheme."[99] Linguistically, Rareback's nonsense word *does* more than it *means*, or more to the point, its meaning lies in its sound as a joke derived purely from its link back to the broader metaphor of the cat's eye box itself. *In Dahomey*'s play with words and their sounds reveals the fundamental problem with using an object—blackface, the skin—to represent something else. When Shylock states, "Jist as soon as I seen dat a cat was scratched on the back I turned round three times, walked backward four steps, throwed a hand full of salt over my left shoulder, and I give him back that box so quick. If I was superstitious I'd a swore I seen that cat's whiskers move," he evokes the uncanniness of the gap between the literal and the figurative, between the symbolic grid of language, the imaginary order of the image, and the real world of the material thing, as all converge, but never fully come together, in the material sound-sign-word, "cat."[100]

Fixing the not . . . but, the traveling letters, and the prop of the lost cat's eye box, all form the basis of important rhetorical, signifying acts that structure *In Dahomey*. All play with language in order to problematize what lies both on the surface of meaning, the skin of words, and on the edge of meaning, the fleshy sound of the voice. A final rhetorical act involves more broadly the question of what is missed in this encounter between voice and word, body and face. It occurs in relation to a scene toward the end of *In Dahomey* when Shylock Homestead inexplicably goes missing, right after he mistakenly wanders into the dressing room of the emigrationist Mrs. Stringer, a widow also described as a "dealer in forsaken patterns."[101]

The stage instruction, referring to Mrs. Stringer's occupation as a dress-maker, also references her meta-textual role as a trickster figure representing the signifier's capacity to dress the flesh with meaning. As the allegorical figure in the show for gendered masquerade, Mrs. Stringer links the minstrel's racial costume to the symbolic costumes and stylized performances of gender that the actors engage in, for example, in the show's famous cakewalk scene. The cakewalk dance was a key component of *In Dahomey*'s crossover appeal. Williams and Walker came to be known as masters of the dance routine, so much so that they were asked to add it to their performance of *In Dahomey* in England and to teach it to the members of the British royal family. Like forms of gender masquerade and cross-dressing, when Shylock Homestead walks into Mrs. Stringer's dressing room he accidentally places his masculinity in question, an act he is teased for when he reappears later in the show. Audre Lorde described the inability to see the black body in relational terms as a gendered body as "an American disease in blackface," but in this instance, the blackface act includes a dressing of the flesh of the New Negro in gendered layers.[102] If signification "is what comes to seal, to close, to gather up the multiplicity of the physical, physiological, linguistic means of elocution, to contract them into one sole act," gender masquerade offered one significant form of sealing up the blackface act represented by the New Negro both on and off the stage.[103] What are the costs of gaining a voice through the gendered colorations of the signifier, as Lorde also put it elegantly when she noted that sound always "comes into a word, coloured / By who pays what for speaking?"[104] Rather than subverting the fixing of racial difference onto the black body, gender performance exacerbated the epidermal condition of the early twentieth-century New Negro. Affixing blackness to a fixed set of gendered codes and meanings, gender performance closed back down the polyvocality of meanings expressed in black sounds, tying the object-voice or the voice of the body once again to its facialized image.

In his essay "The Instance of the Letter in the Unconscious," Lacan uses two instructive examples to demonstrate how semiological meaning works through differentiation and deferral. One recalls the dressing rooms and restrooms Bert Williams traveled through as he constructed his identity as a blackface performer. Lacan tells the following anecdote: "A train arrives at a station. A little boy and a little girl, brother and sister, are seated across from each other in a compartment next to the outside window that provides a view of the station platform buildings going by as the train comes to a stop. 'Look,' says the brother, 'we're at Ladies!' 'Imbecile!' replies his sister, 'Don't you see we're at Gentlemen.'"[105] Lacan's story demonstrates allegorically how movement across the symbolic grid of language is blocked by the impermeability of difference as it structures meaning. Fanon's account of his epidermalization by the child's speech act—"Look, a Negro!"—is doubled here in the gendered interpellation of the body onto the symbolic grid by these children's cries—"Look," says the brother, "we're at Ladies!" "Imbecile!" replies his sister, "Don't you see we're at Gentlemen."[106] Lacan's anecdote essentially reveals how much meaning moves across the grid by noting increments of difference. As he describes this form of misrecognition further: "For the signifier will raise Dissension. . . . To these children, Gentlemen and Ladies will henceforth be two homelands towards which each of their souls will take flight on divergent wings, and regarding which it will be all the more impossible for them to reach an agreement since, being in fact the same homeland, neither can give ground."[107] The symbolic grid's linkage of linguistic difference and semantic meaning ties the meaning of the other's body to its irrevocable difference from our own.

In Lacan's second example, he describes the way in which the signifier "always anticipates meaning by deploying [it] in some sense before it."[108] He illustrates this with the phrase, "I am black, but comely" from the "Song of Songs," stating further: "The phenomenon is no different, which—making her appear, with the sole postponement of a 'but,' as comely as the Shulamite . . . adorns and readies the Negress for the wedding."[109] Everything that follows the "but" represents the sentence to which the Negress will be consigned once her meaning as gendered difference has been established in the symbolic order.[110] Here the wedding becomes the figure for how gender, like race, can close up the subject of the black voice whose sentence was originally left open to the play of signification and syncopation.[111]

Both Lacan's train story and his story of the Negress emphasize the fatal structural flaw of symbolization, that is, the naturalization of prescribed forms of difference as the only options for experiencing others. When the children look out at reality from the window provided by the symbolic grid's frame of reference, what they learn is to locate themselves as subjects of (sexual and racial) difference—"Look, a Negro!" "Look, we're at ladies!" The story of the Negress dressed for her wedding stresses further how difference itself becomes a form of symbolic masquerade.[112] In mimicry one blends in by becoming "mottled" in order to join an already mottled terrain. An unexpected cost of epidermalization, then, for the black entertainers and minstrels of the turn of the twentieth century was the impact of their public, "mottled" gender performances on their private sexual identities and relations.

The Final Act: Blackface Minstrelsy and Gender Masquerade

The song sheet for "Good Enough!," the first cakewalk song published in 1871, shows a caricature of a black man and woman dressed in the exaggerated, dandyish, and frilly costumes of the minstrel performer. The couple is depicted as high-steppin' and hip-swayin(g) to the minstrel song, with arms akimbo, legs kicking, and the stereotypical blackface minstrel grin on the man's face. The drawing contrasts sharply with another image from the same period, of two black couples on the cover page of the sheet music for the "Maple Leaf Rag" (1899). Here the couples present a more stately and dignified posture, promenading as if in a procession rather than a dance. Mirroring each other, the men appear in profile with both feet firmly placed on the ground; the women stand behind them, swaying and leaning over gently to look at the viewer over the men's shoulders. Both of these song sheets from the period represent the extension of the blackface mask over the body, the coming together of portraiture and caricature to depict the "darky act" as a full-bodied, gendered performance.

Both song sheets float between illustration and photography as was typical of the genre. The illustration of the more stately couple on the "Maple Leaf Rag," however, also merges the photograph and the drawing literally, for it is a tracing of the final image (*Cake Walk [Negro Dance] NO.4*) in a series of photographs taken of two black couples performing the cakewalk during a photo shoot for a tobacco company ad (see figures 1.9, 1.10, 1.11, 1.12).

As Caryl Phillips describes in *Dancing in the Dark*, the male models for the cakewalking ad were Bert Williams and George Walker, while one of the female models was the woman who would become George Walker's wife, the African American dancer Ada Walker. Phillips chooses to focus on this photo shoot, and the striking images it produced, as they impacted both the Williamses and the Walkers as couples. In so doing, Phillips privileges the scene as a performative, photo-graphed enactment of aspects of the black heterosexual relation. The private space of the black couple becomes a site for enacting the traumas of epidermal racialization, and reifying gender performance, shaping New Negro social worlds in the early decades of the twentieth century.[113]

The commercially successful cakewalk dance prescribed a certain picture of black heterosexuality. The tobacco ad photographs and Phillips's novelis-

Franz Huld, Publisher, N.Y.   Cake Walk (Negro Dance) Nº1.

Franz Huld, Publisher, N.Y.   Cake Walk (Negro Dance) Nº2.

FIGS 1.9–1.10. *Cake Walk (Negro Dance) NO.1.* (top) and *NO.2.* (above); 8 × 10 photo prints provided by Yale Collection of American Literature, Beinecke Rare Book and Manuscript Library.

Franz Huld, Publisher, N.Y.   Cake Walk (Negro Dance) N°3.

Franz Huld, Publisher, N.Y.   Cake Walk (Negro Dance) N°4.

FIGS 1.11–1.12. *Cake Walk (Negro Dance) NO.3.* (top) and *NO.4.* (above); 8 × 10 photo prints provided by Yale Collection of American Literature, Beinecke Rare Book and Manuscript Library.

tic depiction of the photo shoot are artifacts of what Lacan described as the reifying gaze's "arrest of movement": "The gaze in itself not only terminates the movement, it freezes it [like] those dances I mentioned—they are always punctuated by a series of times of arrest in which the actors pause in a frozen attitude."[114] Like "actors pause[d] in a frozen attitude," the subdued bodies of the cakewalking dancers wearing the dignified dress of New Negro gentlemen and their ladies represented an idealizing, reconstructed image of the black couple in the attempt to wrest the photograph from the realm of racist stereotype. The photo-graphic effect is an image of bodily restraint that captures perfectly the ways the models were compelled to place themselves, as subjects, as black couples, in the social picture in a prescribed way. What we are left with are mannequins.

In *Dancing in the Dark*, it is this dimension of the New Negro couple's performance that Caryl Phillips captures as the blackface minstrel's final act. His inspired choice to organize the story of these two couples around the tobacco ad and cakewalking scene allows him to explore the tensions produced by the extension of the New Negro's performance into the intimate space of the sexual relation. All four performers are left dancing in the dark by the novel's end, as the husbands' crises of masculinity impact both wives' senses of their femininity and sexuality. In Phillips's reconstruction, Bert and Lottie Williams and George and Ada Walker first meet as couples in the photography studio and, years later, George, Ada, and Lottie all reflect on the photographs produced by the tobacco ad shoot as a record of their intimate relations.

The couples' reflections begin with George Walker's character looking around the living space he shares with Ada and noticing one of the photographs:

> The framed photograph on the mantelpiece of the living room seizes his attention, and he recalls the anxious white man who corralled together the four finely dressed colored entertainers for this promotional picture. The man barked instructions and tried to position the Negro dancers without actually touching any of them. . . . The man was used to people who were keen to strike poses that might satisfy him—snap quickly, one, two, then a third, head held high, hold it, a pose, recline the neck, drape the arm, that's it, that's it, good—but these colored dancers moved nervously around one another in his studio.[115]

Walker's version of the photo session portrays vividly the difference between spontaneous and posed movement. The restrictions and taboos against interracial touch within the scene shape the stiffness of the photo-graphed black body that results. As he snaps his pictures, the white photographer barks instructions—Look! Pose! Act!—demanding that the "finely dressed colored" actors place themselves in the picture in a socially determined way. In the studio, the black performers move "nervously around one another," their choreographed bodies captured in ornate color photographs. George Walker's description undermines the slick, commercial, reified visual effect of the two couples' dancing poses by emphasizing the far-from-natural demeanors of the performers as they struggled to give the white photographer the sight he desired.

The awkwardness of this initial masquerade has long-lasting effects on both couples' intimate relations. During the session, Phillips continues, "the more he worked with the chocolate dandies the clearer it became that all four of them were a trifle unsure of themselves."[116] This lack of surety continues into George and Ada's relationship as a history of tension and infidelity erases any sense of closeness and familiarity between them as a couple. Their living space is barren: "Beyond this one photograph there are no images of him in their apartment. She does not keep any of him alone, nor does she treasure any of them together. This one photograph only. A beginning, but no story going forward."[117] As a story of black heterosexuality the photographic session is nongenerative, infertile, closed off, and sealed up with no spillover meaning. Its finished product, the photograph, becomes a hardened reflection of the lack of relation, physical intimacy, and affection in their marriage.

In a follow-up scene, Ada's character reacts to George Walker's "evening adventures," especially his long-term relationship with a white woman. Ada's comments move beyond the frame of the picture into the messier terrain of black heterosexual desire and interracial fantasies: "When Ada returns home she discovers that George has already set forth on his evening adventures, and the framed photograph has been removed from the mantelpiece and is lying abandoned on the sofa. . . . Although he may betray her with a chorus line of impressionable girls, she has managed to convince herself that in every other way he remains faithful to her. . . . Having hurriedly removed the photograph from its ornate brass frame, she carefully slices the offending image into neat strips."[118] As one of the more proactive characters in Phillips's novel, Ada attacks the photograph in recognition of the fact that, far from the idealized image of her beloved, it represents the sense of lack, the mysterious loss, which perpetually structures her and George's dysfunction as a couple.

Lottie Williams's character, in contrast, describes the scene much more romantically than her friend. As she observes George, Ada, Bert, and the fourth female model during the photo shoot:

On that momentous day she accompanied her friend Ada, and sat quietly in the corner of the photographer's studio. The tobacco advertisement was to feature [the two women] all dressed up in their finery, sophisticated ladies ready to step out on the arms of two gentlemen. Quality colored ladies, quality product, and then the two dandies entered the studio, one tall and tan, one dark and short, and her eyes were drawn to the tall man [who] turned to her and smiles with a sweetness that caused her body to tremble. . . . His image was burned deeply into her soul. . . . And yet again the photographer moved this tall man . . . into another position that suggested both courtliness and intimacy, and the tall man turned his head so that his eyes once more met those of Lottie, who remained seated quietly in the corner.[119]

Lottie's description provides in words a picture of everything the reconstructed New Negro hoped his and her portraits could represent: "Quality colored ladies, quality product . . . dandies" who are "all dressed up in their finery" like the metaphoric Negress adorning herself for the wedding. Lottie Williams's character is a more passive, melancholic figure than Ada's. Her depression later in the novel reflects her nostalgic unwillingness to let go of the mental image of her husband as the love object who was, at the time of the tobacco ad, "handsome, well dressed, and still in his mid-twenties, he possessed courtesies that belonged to an earlier era."[120] In reality, as Lottie laments in her reflections on her and Ada's marriages: "Between us two husbands straying, one in mind, one in body, although it is unclear to me which is the greater betrayal. A long time since the photograph, the four of us, each in our own way excited, each in our own way consumed by nerves."[121]

Much like Lottie's character in Phillips's novel, if our memories of Bert Williams as a performer rest solely on the image of the actor in his blackface mask, we continue to see him very much in terms of a dominant narrative that privileges sight. Hence the significance of those songs of *In Dahomey* in which black songwriters and performers strove to make audible, if not visible, the way black heterosexual love looks, in a space beyond the epidermalizing gaze. "Society," for example, brought together the songwriting talents of Paul Laurence Dunbar and the musical expertise of Will Marion Cook, and the song's punch line comes in the form of a black female response that focuses not on the value of black people as objects one looks at, but rather, on the nature and signifying intent of the look itself:

Love looks not at es-tate Oh No!
'Twere fol-ly one should think it so.

The beg-gar maid be-comes a queen
Who through her lov-er's eyes is seen.[122]

In the context of her black lover's gaze, the "black, but comely" Negress from the "Song of Songs" takes on different corporeal coordinates, and rather than meaning moving toward an inevitable ending sentence, the "queen" doubles back on herself to become a reflexive, chiastic mirror image reflected in her lover's eye. In "Brown-Skin Baby Mine," Will Cook signifies on classic figures of speech to exalt the black woman's skin in the face of her desexualization and negation:

She is no vi-o-let, She is no red, red rose;
An' though de lil-y of de val-ley's sweet,
She's sweet-er yet, I knows.
She is no tu-lip rare Nor morn-in' glo-ry fine;
But 'mongst de flow-ers fair can't none com-pare
Wid Brown-skin Ba-by mine.[123]

"Brown-Skin Baby Mine" finds beauty in female blackness by putting the tropes, language, and figures of the sonnet to the syncopated rhythms of dialect music and speech.

At the turn of the twentieth century, the epidermalizing visual politics of blackface performance shaped the terrain Bert Williams negotiated as a mainstream entertainer crossing over in American popular culture. It also shaped the strategies he utilized, as a performer, to reclaim the black male body. The song sheet, as a material object and cultural artifact of this history, records the power of the image in facializing and mortifying the black performer as a sign of difference. However, in the traces of the black letter left behind on the song sheet's pages, it also recalls his voice as an echo of the lost body of the blackface minstrel, revivifying his sounds and silences. Merleau-Ponty describes "the finger of the glove that is turned inside out" as the perfect figure for a relationality in which, "there is no need of a spectator who would be *on each side*. . . . In reality there is neither me nor the other as positive, positive subjectivities. There are two caverns, two opennesses, two stages where something will take place."[124] Performance helps us to flip the script of facialization, providing us with a retrospective echo of Bert Williams's unconscious dialogue with his audience as it reverberates in the sounds of his act.[125]

In Dahomey's script is like a letter from Bert Williams that has taken almost a century to arrive. As a minstrel act, more than Ralph Ellison's dismissal, it deserves at the very least a more attentive form of listening. In another iconic

FIG 1.13. Bert Williams in white gloves. Image provided by Yale Collection of American Literature, Beinecke Rare Book and Manuscript Library.

photograph, Bert Williams the blackface minstrel is caught mid-gesture in the silent speech of the mime. The comedian's white-gloved black hand signals not just the prescribed speech of a fetishized object but also the black male performer as a "ready-to-speak," a muted subjectivity just about to reach out and touch his audience with a different kind of intercorporeal address and appeal (see figure 1.13).[126]

two

Bodylines, Borderlines, Color Lines

All actors are limited by their physique. A slender five-footer can't play a giant;
a buxom, heavyweight lady can't play an ingénue. Well, I've got limitations, too—
size and color. Same limitations as other actors have, plus.
—PAUL ROBESON

The outline of the skin is not felt as a smooth and straight surface. . . . This outline is
blurred. There are no sharp borderlines between the outside world and the body.
—PAUL SCHILDER

Paul Robeson, the African American actor and singer, fascinated a number
of white modernists during the early decades of the twentieth century. For
Gertrude Stein he personified the outsider who "knew American values and
American life as only one in it but not of it could know them."[1] "And yet," she
continued, "as soon as any other person came into the room he became definitely a negro." To be "definitely a negro" meant to be static, immobile, with
no claim to even the forms and cultural products tied to African American history: "Negroes were not suffering from persecution, they were suffering from
nothingness. . . . The African is not primitive, he has a very ancient but a very
narrow culture and there it remains. Consequently nothing does or can happen."[2] Stein's observations fit within a particular form of colonialist discourse
in which nonwhite or non-Western cultures with their own ancient histories
are seen as bound in the static form of "tradition," as opposed to modern Western nations' ongoing, progressive temporality and "history."[3]

Perhaps it was this sense of Robeson's monumental immobility that made
him such an ideal model for various modernist artists throughout the 1920s

FIG 2.1. *Borderline* production: Paul Robeson. Image provided by Yale Collection of American Literature, Beinecke Rare Book and Manuscript Library. Permission for still from *Borderline* provided by Douris UK Ltd.

and 1930s. Many individuals working in a variety of media—from sculpture to photography, poetry, and film—approached the actor through an aesthetic appreciation of his physique. As the first epigraph to this chapter reveals, Robeson himself was aware of his physique as an element or tool in his performances, something to work with or work against, a "limitation" as he put it, specifically in relation to his acting. The question is whether Paul Robeson posed a different kind of sight for a modernist gaze than Bert Williams had for white American audiences a mere one to two decades earlier. Robeson's various encounters with white artists during the 1920s and the 1930s mark an important shift in the visual culture of modernism. While American audiences in the 1900s wanted to look at the "thickening into visibility of the skin" of blackness facilitated by the blackface mask, in the era of the new modernism, blackness became a surface to get close to and take pleasure in, a tactility extending from the face across the entire body.[4] Unlike the portrait photography of an earlier era, white modernists' efforts to capture Robeson in the nude point to the centrality of his physique in the actor's charismatic appeal.

FIG 2.2. Tony Salemme's studio: Paul Robeson. Photographer Carl Van Vechten, September 20, 1937. Van Vechten Trust / Yale Collection of American Literature, Beinecke Rare Book and Manuscript Library.

In one of his first encounters, Robeson crossed paths with the Italian American sculptor Antonio Salemme. As Paul Robeson Jr. describes: "Salemme created two magnificent bronzes of my father in 1925–1926. . . . The first sculpture, one of Salemme's greatest works, bore the title *Negro Spiritual* [see figure 2.2]. It was a life-size nude with arms and face upraised to the heavens. Philadelphia banned the work in 1930 because it depicted a nude black man, but it was exhibited to great acclaim in the Brooklyn Museum and in Paris's Salon des Tuileries in 1930–1931."[5] Robeson began sitting for Salemme's sculptures between 1924 and 1926. Based on the sculptor's and Robeson Jr.'s accounts, these sessions were quite an event. As one of the first African American male entertainers to sit for nude studies, Robeson's act of self-exhibition drew both fascinated and scornful gazes.[6] His collaboration and friendship with Salemme, a "particularly satisfying diversion," became the occasion for a cross-cultural exchange between more conservative New Negro values and the liberalism of the avant-garde set: "Salemme introduced Paul to the best of Greenwich Village's bohemian artists who congregated at his studio loft. Their unfettered lifestyle had made Paul uncomfortable when he had first arrived in New York, but during the years with Salemme, Paul grew to enjoy them. In return, he often took the sculptor up to Harlem."[7] By the time Philadelphia officials refused to exhibit Salemme's life-size statue of Robeson, both had agreed not to allow them to use a fig leaf or any other aesthetic covering to hide the figure's genitals from public view.[8]

Robeson's relationship with Salemme placed him right at the heart of a New York circle of white modernist artists and intellectuals whom he engaged with at various degrees of closeness. In turn, Salemme's life-size sculpture also reflects the sculptor's desire to capture Robeson with a certain degree of intimacy—that is, to imagine that the artist can re-create, in Robeson's bodily likeness, as close an approximation to the real-life actor that one can get in an artistic form. The statue becomes a kind of surrogate for the immediacy of the actor's presence in the world. What moves the sculpture beyond facialization, however, is the way, like the body and the head, it inhabits three-dimensional space. Rather than serving as a mere metaphoric substitute for the body, in the medium of sculpture something of the body always remains.

The sculpture is more than a visual likeness. It sits in space with a solidity that is mimetically and tactilely similar to the body's corporeal presence. The artist "circling round the sculpture," is driven by something that moves between the scopic and the haptic, "part of a sense experience midway between touching and seeing."[9] It mimics, as Schilder describes in this chapter's epigraph, the sense that there are "no sharp borderlines" between the body and the world—the "outline is blurred."[10] The "limitations" of Robeson's body as he experienced them, his size and color, leave a trace on the viewer in his or her interaction with the sculptural representation itself. Both the sculptor and the viewers of a life-size nude inadvertently retain a sense of the actual lines, contours, shape, size, even texture, of the body sculpted, closing the space between model and sculptor, audience and sculpture.

This type of tactile, intercorporeal engagement with Robeson's body carried over from sculpture into the more visual and discursive mediums of photography and poetry. In Carl Van Vechten's photograph of Salemme's *Negro Spiritual*, the photographic image retains some of the haptic dimensions of the sculpted body, moving the distancing gaze closer to the gleaming, tactile surface of the skin. Modernist photographer Nickolas Muray's series of nudes of Robeson from 1926 continued a neoclassical visual aesthetic evident in Salemme's statue (see figure 2.3). His photographs also reveal an absorption with the texture of the corporeal surface, the definition of muscles, dimples of cheeks, lines of tendons in Robeson's forearms, and the attempt to reproduce a photographic surface that captures the body in such fine, close-up detail. His photographs record the incorporative aspects of a "miscegenated gaze" on blackness, that is, one focused on grasping all there is to see of epidermal difference on the corporeal surface.[11] They also record Robeson's desire, as the subject of a body-to-be-sculpted, to present his body to the gaze and pose for the grid in a certain way.[12]

In her discussion of the sculptural arts and the "neoclassical nude" specifically as a mode of representing the body-with-skin, Segal argues that the spectator's appreciation involves "a heterosexualizing of viewing" that positions him or her as masculine: "Whatever the sex of the viewing body, the stance of this desire is penetrative."[13] The neoclassical nude draws in a spectatorial gaze that is already gendered, what John Berger describes also as the gaze of a male spectator-owner in his discussion of Renaissance paintings of the European female nude.[14] There is an even more subtle way, however, in which the neoclassical nude manages and directs the sexuated, scopic desires of its audience. The heterosexualizing of viewing can be seen as the erotics of desiring to see sexual difference in aestheticized terms. To look at Robeson's sculpture with a masculine, penetrative gaze and a heterosexualizing erotic logic is to look for the phallus as the aesthetic signifier rather than as desexualized, grotesque flesh, the male nude as an aesthetically closed, sealed, even phallic, volume. This is not the phallus understood literally as the genitals, but rather, a phallicizing of male anatomy as muscular and hard that has a long history in European representations of the impermeable, sealed off, whole and closed, white male ecorche.[15] This aesthetic was well in place by the 1920s as a way of representing an idealized, that is phallic, masculinity.

Paul Robeson's nude figured and idealized the New Negro's newborn autonomy in the suggestion of the lines and contours of a masculine muscularity that lies just beneath the skin. A different aspect of the materiality of the New Negro's actual body remains, however, a fleshy, uncanny kernel of the Real. One might say that the lost sensational body hovers on the lining or rim of sculptural form, a bodily depth hidden within the surface of the neoclassical nude like a "firm, fruitful kernel," in a mass whose "final, lightest contour is swinging air."[16] The modernists were intensely fascinated with this sculptural borderline between mass and air, the tangible object and the incorporeal body it evokes, sculpture as a sensory object beyond the visual.[17] For the modern-

FIG 2.3. Nude photograph of Paul Robeson. Photographer Nickolas Muray. Image provided by Yale Collection of American Literature, Beinecke Rare Book and Manuscript Library.

ist gaze, neoclassical photography offered a way of bringing the viewer closer to the actual surface and lining of Robeson's body, and the black male body offered itself up to the gaze as an object that could be touched.[18] These sculptural portrayals of Robeson exhibit qualities that go beyond those of Fanon's phobogenic "hyperbolic penis" that causes anxiety in the white subject.[19] If anything, the controversial exposure of Robeson's genitals without the aesthetic cover-up of a fig leaf reflects not just the sexual but also the multisensorial desire to access, to have a relationship with, the black actor in all of his phallic flesh, and concomitant fears such a desire also produces.

In the title poem of her collection, *Red Roses for Bronze* (1931), the modernist poet H. D. describes an artistic process reminiscent of the one that created Salemme's bronze and plaster statue of Robeson. This process creates a relationship between the artist and the model that goes beyond sight to a sense of touch.[20] In the poem, H. D.'s poetic persona expresses a desire, like Salemme's and Muray's, to sculpt a Robeson-like figure as a "weight of bronze." As the poet describes, she wishes to "sate my wretched fingers in ecstatic work . . . fashion eyes and mouth and chin . . . take dark bronze and hammer in," like a sculptor molding skin.[21] Of all three modernist engagements with Robeson's body and image, H. D.'s is the most self-revealing. She literally wants to rip into the skin of the black phallic signifier, tear off its symbolic covering, and grasp the meat of the subject it can never fully portray—the "ripple and flash and gleam / of indrawn muscle / . . . from the moulded thigh and hip." In her desire for connection she seeks to expose the body, but it is an act intended to force a more direct recognition of herself: to "force you to grasp my soul's sincerity, / and single out / me, / me, / something to challenge, / handle differently." Establishing a relationship with the bronzed body-object in its materiality, she imagines herself stroking repeatedly "at—something (stone, marble)," but this hardness is not that of the blackface mask, distanced and confined to where the audience wants to look. Instead, the poetic persona's tactile engagement with the bronzed body and skin entails a more intimate form of recognition. She sees a like subject in the stone, a like subject she in turn wants recognition from.[22]

What distinguishes H. D.'s poem is the intersubjectivity of the interaction between the poetic persona and the subject who has become the object of her interest and desire. It points to a desired boundary-lessness between bodies, and between the body and the outside world, which Paul Schilder describes when he suggests that "the outline of the skin is not felt as a smooth and straight surface. . . . This outline is blurred. There are no sharp borderlines between the outside world and the body."[23] As a "weight of bronze," the Robeson-like figure offers himself up to H. D.'s gaze as a lure, holding out the promise of a deeper, relational consciousness she can access, and who will allow her to open herself up further to him. While his inaccessibility as a like subject is evident in "the slightly mocking, slightly cynical smile you choose to wear," as the poem progresses the poetic persona continues to seek something beneath the surface of the subject-object's face, something hidden behind that slightly mocking smile. She makes demands of the entertainer, refusing to be the silly recipient of "the casual sort of homage that you care to flick toward this or that odd passing whim."[24] Appreciating his look, his physical demeanor, his outward appearance — "neither too tall for some taste, none too slight" — she wants the kind of intimacy that comes with a more intense interaction with the actual surface of his body.

"Red Roses for Bronze" goes beyond the mere objectification or eroticization of the black male actor. It also performs, in writing, a deeper level of intersubjective interaction, across racial lines, at work in the relationship between the white modernist artist and the black male performing body. H. D.'s poem expresses the relational desire, the dream, to cross the barrier of Robeson's skin with a touch. In the poem, H. D. falls short of her goal precisely because the intensity of her engagement with the black male body overwhelms her — as she laments, "Such is my jealousy . . . that no mere woman's love could long endure." For Massumi, "intensity" is the autonomic reaction of the body to powerful emotion, to experiencing something, experiencing others, as an "effect" on the skin of the body itself.[25] The eye, in contrast, "seeks relaxation from the gaze," from this intensity, modulating and distancing it when the gaze gets too close to the body.[26] In "Red Roses for Bronze," as much as the poet desires to "strip" or flay Robeson's clothed body in order to lay him bare for her gaze, she ultimately closes back up and reifies that body, sets it back in stone, when she turns black skin into a "weight of bronze." Like Muray, she ends up cloaking the embodied black subject in aesthetic form, the poetic metaphor creating, like the sculptural line or the camera's gleaming shot or sight, a second skin over the body, a calcified shell mediating and constraining our desire to touch. Hence she tells us at the poem's end, "I would set your bronzed head in its place," sealing up the love object and firmly placing it outside the boundaries of the white, female, poetic self. To read H. D.'s poem in this way is not to discount her own racialized construction of Robeson, but rather, to acknowledge race as a relation of intimacy between different subjects and to recognize the equally fraught permeability of black and white relations running alongside their reification by laws of racial hierarchy.

It was a particular goal of the modernist writer to use language to capture the materiality of the body, often by attending to the materiality of language.[27]

Asking, "How, then, are we to touch upon the body, rather than signify it or make it signify," Jean-Luc Nancy describes this mode of writing as an engagement with the body as a tactile border: "Writing touches upon bodies *along the absolute limit* separating the sense of the one from the skin and nerves of the other. Nothing *gets through*, which is why it touches."[28] This form of writing aims to touch upon, brush up against, the cutaneous surface of the body, "along the border, at the limit, the tip, the furthest edge."[29] This form of haptic writing takes place not just on the borderline but *on the bodyline* of the self. The bodyline marks the tension of a form of representation—writing, photography, sculpture—that, while distancing itself from the body to create its mirror image in language, simultaneously comes as close as it can to the edge of the body, as close as it can to the body's *intercorporeity*, on the borderline or lining between the self and the world.

The multimedia array of modernist nudes of Robeson in the 1930s reveals a complex interplay between his body and the tension of different kinds of looks: the scopic (invoking a black male body hardened by a phallicizing, aestheticizing gaze) and the haptic (the same body attracting a type of looking that imitates touch). Even more so than sculpture, photography, and poetry, film offered a particularly effective medium for capturing the incorporeal dimensions of Robeson's body—the body without an image, the body on the lining of the image. This is because the movies attempt to represent movement itself: "The mobility of the moving image situates it symbolically on the side of vitality and movement, and those values make the film and video cameras less appropriate signifiers for the gaze."[30] Film can offer the kind of look that is "perspectival ('from behind, from the side')."[31] For Jennifer Barker, the sight lines in cinematic space also create a common, relational skin, a space where neither meaning nor emotion resides solely in films or viewers but rather emerges "in the intimate, tactile encounter between them," and "meaning and affect emerge in [a] fleshy, visceral encounter" through tactile, kinesthetic, and visceral actor-effects.[32] The film screen itself becomes a metaphoric body lining or skin, with one side facing the gaze and the symbolic screen, while the other side faces the body as an interface and interactive site.

While the film's body can be said to evoke the incorporeal human body in its very form, Barker does not factor in enough the figure at the heart of that convergence between the body of the film and the body on film. This is the actor himself, whose own corporeality helps to flesh out further the effects created by the film's body. The bodyline therefore offers a useful metaphor both for the intercorporeity of cinematic projections of Robeson's body as a mobile, tactile, and interactive surface, and for the liminal or borderline space created by the actor himself, whose gestures, expressing affect, physical action, and motion, lure the spectator into a self-reflexive experience of corporeality as more than inanimate physique.

The Black Male Bodyline as Tactile Gesture and Lure

In her discussion of the race men of the 1920s and 1930s, Hazel Carby uses the notion of the bodyline to describe Caribbean critic C. L. R. James's appreciation of the black cricket player's physique and presence.[33] In a specific batting move in cricket known as the bodyline maneuver, the bowler deliberately aims the cricket ball at the body of the opposing batsman like a lure, hoping to create leg-side deflections that could be caught by one of several fielders.[34] Considered an instance of bad sportsmanship and banned from the game after its first appearance, the bodyline maneuver can be thought of as the appearance of a spontaneous gesture, an unexpected move, in an otherwise uniformly coded field of play. This type of gesture occurs when an unprecedented element of individual style emerges in a game or performance. The gesture individualizes the player, requiring the imposition of new rules to incorporate his or her bodily maneuver as a new element of play, or as an element to be banned.[35] In cricket the bodyline maneuver was just such a spontaneous gesture. As a broader metaphor for the significance of the performer's individual gestures and style, the bodyline points to what lies just beyond sight, the actor's incorporeal motion that exceeds the camera and the grid, reaching out to the spectator from the very lining or edge of the image.

In his photographs Muray posed Robeson in classical poses, turning the performer in different directions simultaneously, at the knees, the hips, the shoulders, and the head, in order to emphasize the beautiful line of the body (see figure 2.3).[36] In contrast, in *Beyond a Boundary*, C. L. R. James argued that, in the context of the game of cricket's significance for a postcolonial world, the broader *artistic* significance of the black athlete's physicality rested in the body's emphasis on tactile values and motion rather than on the aesthetic value of the line. In a chapter entitled "What Is Art?," James discusses the emphasis on the line in Renaissance art and aesthetics and argues instead that the more important aesthetic elements of a work captured viewers' attentions with "tactile values" emphasizing movement and spatial composition.[37] For James, these were the important values evoked by the sculptural nude: "The idea of tactile values could be most clearly grasped by observing the manner in which truly great artists rendered the nude human body. They so posed their figures, they manipulated, arranged, shortened, lengthened, foreshortened, they so articulated the movements of the joints that they stimulated the tactile consciousness of the viewer, his special artistic sense."[38]

The point of such an artistic vision was "not that such a painting looked more real, made the object more lifelike [but rather] significant form makes the painting life-giving, life-enhancing, *to the viewer*. Significant form, or 'decoration' . . . sets off physical processes in the spectator."[39] The goal of the artist's manipulation was not to achieve a more accurate representation of the body, but rather, to stimulate a tactile sensibility in the audience as their primary experience of the work.

In "What Is Art?," James describes the black athlete as embodying a poetics in motion that facilitates, relationally and interpersonally, what Massumi calls the "movement-vision" of the spectator: "a kind of vision that grasps exactly and exclusively what mirror-vision misses: the movement, only the movement ('walking, standing, moving normally through a room')."[40] Movement-vision reflects "a way of appearing that goes beyond text and visualization, script and picture."[41] What elevated sports as an art beyond painting and sculpture was its ability to press tactility into the service of proprioception: "Cricket, in fact any ball game, to the visual image adds the sense of physical coordination, of harmonious action, of timing. The visual image of a diving fieldsman is a frame for his rhythmic contact with the flying ball. Here two art forms meet."[42] The incorporeal body emerges consensually through the interaction of the various senses, as Massumi also describes further: "Proprioception translates the exertions and ease of the body's encounters with objects into a muscular memory of relationality. This is the cumulative memory of skill, habit, posture. At the same time as proprioception folds tactility in, it draws out the subject's reactions to the qualities of the objects it perceives through all five senses, bringing them into the motor realm of externalizable response."[43] Only this kind of return to the body through muscular memory and multisensorial perception moves us away from a purely visual appreciation of art. The tactile values of the black athlete-artist's bodywork focus our attention away from the line of the body as a more abstract visual form, and toward the more haptic visuality of a bodyline engaged in "the perfect flow of motion," where the gaze is supported by the other senses and by sensory memory.[44]

James also believed that one's enjoyment of the spectacle of the black body in motion derived from the athlete's ability to engage not only the eyes but also the body of the spectator in a visceral way. He linked spectators' visual appreciation of the athlete to the spectators' own muscle memory, their proprioceptive sensibility, the memory of their own movement. The athlete's physicality forged an intercorporeal, proprioceptive connection between player and spectator. His motion triggered in the spectator a self-reflexive appreciation of his or her own body through the memory of repeated action: "These motions are not caught and permanently fixed for us to make repeated visits to them. They are repeated often enough to become a permanent possession of the spectator which he can renew at will."[45] This quality also linked the physicality of athletes to the charismatic style of entertainers: "In our world human beings are on view for artistic enjoyment only on the field of sport or on the entertainment stage [but] what is not visible is received in the tactile consciousness of thousands who have themselves for years practiced the same motion."[46] Both the celebrity actor and the star athlete played to their audiences by using distinctive gestures and physical features of their bodies to capture their attention.

The athlete's or entertainer's physical performance expressed his or her own unique, incorporeal style. For James, while the artwork's proprioceptive significance mattered "*to the viewer,*" it also incorporated the actions and intentions of the athlete *as* artist, actor, player, and performer, in a distinctive way. The lesson James took from the "truly great artists" was that they used physical action, gesture, and motion to transform the body's nakedness into their own distinctive style. Style, the idiosyncratic movements and gestures of a particular body, is an important force in animating an objectified body-image, opening up the rules of a game, adding the potential for spontaneity to a performance's formal codes, subjectifying the body-object. As James also describes: "Sometimes it is a total performance branching out in many directions by a single player who stamps all he does with the hallmark of an individual style. . . . It can be and often is a particular image. . . . The image can be a single stroke, made on a certain day, which has been seen and never forgotten."[47] The unique and original athlete-star particularizes his movements to create unprecedented bodily gestures that then become anticipated, repeat actions, linked to his idiosyncratic style.

James's linkage of the athlete and the film star through the bodily features of action, motion, gesture, and style opens up ways of thinking about Robeson's on-screen acting and presence. The black actor's spontaneous gestures, his bodywork, become sites for locating his body-without-an-image as it appears and disappears, leaving its traces behind on the cultural screen. James's observations are quickly becoming standard in contemporary affect, movement, and sensation studies. For example, Massumi describes style in terms strikingly similar to James's: "Style is what makes the player. What makes a player a star is more than perfection of technique. . . . To technical perfection the star adds something extra. Perhaps a way of catching the eye of players on the opposite team to make them self-conscious and throw them off their own game. Perhaps a feint added to every kick. Or an imperceptible spin. Little extras. Small but effective ways of skewing the potential movements composing the field."[48] For James, this notion of style was both an act unique to the performer and expected by the audience, as he describes the movie star further: "World-famous and rightly so [they] mumble words and go through motions which neither they nor their audience care very much about. [Their] appeal is themselves, how they walk, how they move, how they do anything or nothing, so long as they are themselves and their particular quality shines through."[49]

In a project similar to Massumi's, James strove to put the body of the audience back in its place as participating actively in the process of drawing meaning from their observation of the actor's or the athlete's gesture and physical action. The line of the body extends outward in three dimensions to the body and gaze of the viewer, an incorporeal touching that extends from the screen and the body on-screen back to the viewer and vice versa, arriving at an image of the body viewed as more than simply an image in the eye of the beholder but also as a felt sensation in the body of the spectator.

Not surprisingly, then, it was also C. L. R. James who noted the significance of Robeson's athletic physique for his star appeal. At the height of his stage and film career in the 1930s, Robeson and James worked together when the actor played the lead role of Toussaint L'Ouverture in the British stage production of James's play on the Haitian Revolution in 1937. Later, James expressed a deep appreciation for the actor's athletic talents: "He was some six feet six inches in height and built in proportion, but he always had the silhouette and litheness of a great athlete."[50] This impressive physique shaped the actor's powerful presence and charisma, which seemed to spill beyond his roles: "He was here, as elsewhere, always the centre of attention, a not easy role to fill" and "all who were connected with the stages where we rehearsed had their eyes fastened on him and were all ears when he spoke."[51] For James, Robeson's impressive voice was tied to its deeper, kinesthetic unity with his body. Robeson's physique evoked what the actor could *do* with his body as much as how he looked in it, his muscular figure enacting the dynamic union between motion and gesture that could not be captured in the image of an arrested pose.

Originally trained as a stage actor, Robeson came to film in the 1930s with a conscious awareness of his physique, especially after working actively to make any kinesthetic awkwardness on his part due to his size a productive aspect of his stage performances. He was familiar with the work of Russian director Constantin Stanislavski, whose pioneering Method of Physical Action focused on the idea that good acting depended on the use of the body.[52] Since the only thing an actor had full control of was his body, the actor and the director were to use the body's performance of physical action as a type of raw material. While for many contemporary critics Robeson's physicality was so forceful that they debated whether he had any real talent as an actor beyond it, rather than detracting from his performances, his physicality should be seen as one of their distinguishing features.[53] This was especially true when the actor chose not to smooth out a performance's rougher physical edges. His physical acting, his mobilization of his kinesics, his size, his awkwardness, his powerful voice, even the texture and color of his skin, all of these shaped the translation of his bodily presence onto the image on the film screen.[54]

Robeson's allure as a film star rested in part on how he presented himself to the audience, how he made himself present, through the gestures of his body. In the essay "What Is Painting?," similar to James's discussion of the actor's and athlete-artist's intentionality in "What Is Art?," Lacan asks rhetorically: "When a human subject is engaged in making a picture of himself, in putting into operation that something that has as its centre the gaze, what is taking place?"[55] He responds: "It might be thought that, like the actor, the painter wishes to be looked at. I do not think so. I think there is a relation with the gaze of the spectator, but that it is more complex. The painter gives something to the person who must stand in front of his painting which, in part, at least, of the painting, might be summed up thus—*You want to see? Well, take a look at this!*"[56] The actor does not simply act; instead, like the painter, he makes "a picture of himself," and like the athlete, this requires him moving his body in particular ways. Lacan suggests that in the act, in the image of the embodied self the actor presents and projects, there is a lure designed to draw the audience's attention. The lure is what the subject chooses to give back to an audience, partly to satisfy their symbolic expectations, but also, partly to entice them away from the interpellations of the gaze.[57]

How does one capture the ephemerality of the moving body, the body without an image, in visual form? The subject, like the artist, like the athlete, and like the celebrity actor, tames the gaze by providing something more than an object for the other's consumption. The subject-as-artist, the artist-as-actor, offers up a glimmer of his or her missing, invisible, absent, bodily subjectivity that the gazing subject both desires and is fearful of seeing. This glimmer of a lost body and a like subjectivity rests on the bodyline of the film screen, as a trace on the cinematic image of the incorporeal body in motion, a body of gestures caught just barely out of the sight of the arresting gaze.[58]

In one sense this offering, this skin act, is a feint, a "*trompe-l'œil,*" an object painted with the intention of fooling the viewer as to its three-dimensionality, a painting that veils the Real by imitating it.[59] In another sense, the black celebrity actor's and athletic performer's offering up of himself as a lure presents a new kind of opportunity. Just as the painter wants his art object to be more than the merely looked at, the actor wants to be engaged in more than the creation of a mere image of the self. The black actor, faced with an epidermalized image of himself on the cultural and symbolic screen, attempts, like a painter, to deflect or deceive the gaze while simultaneously appealing to something in the look of the other that goes beyond the gaze: "The being gives of himself, or receives from the other, something that is like a mask, a double, an envelope, a thrown-off skin, thrown off in order to cover the frame of a shield. It is through this separated form of himself that the being comes into play in his effects."[60]

The acting subject is both "a thrown-off skin," a projected and "separated form of himself," and a "cover [on] the frame of a shield," an epidermal surface irrevocably attached to his embodied subjectivity. The skin functions here as both metonym and synecdoche for the doubled, always reversible, subject-object the performer creates, a chiasmic site where both the painter and the actor in the self meet, the creator of images and the maker of corporeal gestures of the self.

In his discussion of the relationship between the gesture and the gaze, Lacan slides between the different artistic mediums of the photograph, the painting, and the film reel, to find an example of the type of spontaneous, individualized gesture and motion that the painter uses to draw from his audience a more haptic and tactile sight. Ultimately, "as if to insist upon the hand [as] the corporeal locus of the eye," he finds it in the brushstroke whereby, the painter's gesture, "*those little blues, those little browns, those little whites,* those touches that fall like rain from the painter's brush," emphasize the haptic qualities of both painting and performing the self.[61] This is the incorporeal self as physical action-in-process, as an "interaction-in-the-making" rather than an action with a terminated end.[62]

The final image painted onto a canvas can only register the fall of the artist's brushstroke as an "end," a "terminal moment," and as "haste," that is, motion subordinated to its outcome, the produced image. The total artistic act, however, includes the incorporeal gesture of the brushstroke itself as an action less available for capture and freezing. The corporeal movements of the painter only appear, retroactively, in their incorporeal traces, in the impression of brushstrokes left behind on the canvas, recorded on the painting's surface. In this way, in the screen surface's inescapable representation of invisible presence through gestural motion—the director's, the actor's, even that of the reflected audience behind the fourth wall—what is restless and cannot be fixed leaves its trace on the physiognomy of the pictured black male subject.

There is something theatrical and performative in the battle waged between the gesture and the terminal act.[63] Whether in sculpture, the photograph, the poem, or painting, one could say that all seek to represent the artist *as an actor*, as an active force pressing into and onto the surface of the image. All of these mediums struggle to make visible the ephemeral motion of the body embedded within the act, the gesture contained within the picture, the bodily within the body-image. However, the act can only reveal the gesture in retrospect, as an image of the action already performed rather than of the gesture in the act of being performed. This relationship between the actor and the painter as different modes of performative self-representation is crucial for thinking in more complicated ways about Paul Robeson's film performances of the 1930s.

Robeson's performance in the film *Borderline* (1930) demonstrates how the medium of the moving image can function less as a frame than as a threshold, the "I—my body-chiasm" of the theatre acting as an intercorporeal space.[64] Attentiveness to the role of the body in both modernist and New Negro experiences of blackness in the 1920s and 1930s remaps the ground of the interracial interactions of the period, redefining new dimensions of consensuality shaping the relations between New Negro and modernist artists and audiences. In Paul and Essie Robeson's performances in *Borderline*, the bodyline of the actor crossed the borderline of the film screen to complicate and reverse the racializing operations of the color line shaping the modernist gaze of the 1930s. Despite Essie Robeson's concerns that her husband's interactions with white modernists included his many flirtations and affairs with white women, the film created an intercultural container for forms of interracial desire and intercorporeal bodily engagement that went beyond the tropes of miscegenation, even as they depended upon them for their more obvious significations and meanings.

"The Borderline, Or Rather the Line of the Border, Whose Is It?"

The film still from *Borderline* that opens this chapter provides an example of physical acting, the broad range of exaggerated, even melodramatic, body movements required of the actor onstage that were an integral aspect of Robeson's (self-)training (see figure 2.1). The actor holds his hand to his forehead in a standardized gesture for the swoon, evincing here strong emotion, a wistful happiness, in relation to what he is looking at below. The headshots on the cover of the brochure advertising the film *Borderline* offer examples of a different kind of cinematic shot, the classic close-up (see figure 2.4). In the early twentieth-century transition from theatre to film, cinematic devices such as

FIG 2.4. *Borderline*, A *Pool* film with Paul Robeson (program). Image provided by Yale Collection of American Literature, Beinecke Rare Book and Manuscript Library.

the close-up shot were thought to diminish the need for the kind of exaggerated gesture required in physical acting. As D. W. Griffith observed: "When you saw only the small full-length figures [on the stage] it was necessary to have exaggerated acting, what might be called 'physical' acting, the waving of the hand, and so on. The close-up enabled us to reach real acting, restraint, acting that is a duplicate of real life."[65] Robeson's early interest in film reflected a similar enthusiasm for the camera's ability, through such devices as the close-up, to bring the actor's performance, if not the actor himself, closer to his audience than was possible on stage.

Of a piece, however, with his general skepticism concerning the ontological differences between live performance and mediated forms, Philip Auslander argues that the development of the close-up was shaped as much by theatrical imperatives as cinematic ones.[66] Auslander shifts us away from thinking of the cinema and the theatre as competing modes of performance. Rather, both position the audience in an attitude of embodied viewing. The bodily interaction between the audience of a film and the audience of a play share striking similarities: "Early film modeled itself directly on theatrical practice," and "cinematic staging and editing in the 1910s" attempted to meet the same theatrical and narrative goals with new means.[67] Auslander continues: "The narrative structures and visual devices of cinema, including the close-up and the fade-in/fade-out, and parallel editing, had all been fully developed on stage before becoming the foundations of the new medium's language, at least in its narrative forms." The close-up freezes the frame to produce a similar effect as a melodramatic actor's gestures onstage. One might even say the close-up shot is the camera's distinctive, theatrical gesture. The actor physically "acts" for the close-up shot, playing to the camera, producing his or her own "facial stunts," even if these are more muted and less melodramatic than those produced on stage.[68]

Borderline's director, Kenneth Macpherson, used the close-up shot very consciously to enhance the tactile and expressive dimensions of Robeson's recognizable face and form. H. D. described one close-up of Robeson as the cinematic version of a "weight of bronze": "We have here an exquisite pen and ink sketch of a negro head almost filling the space of the little frame allotted."[69] H. D. played a large role in Borderline's production not just as Robeson's costar but also as an editor of the final product. Essie Robeson, Borderline's other lead actress, was "surprised to see how well we both filmed" and described her husband's face on-screen as "marvelous," his face in close-up "so big and mobile and expressive."[70] Scholars and critics have argued that in Borderline the cinematic screen becomes the perfect lens for effacing a story of race, sacrificing narrative scenario in favor of the individual close-up shot. Carby's concern is that ultimately "the effect was to freeze Robeson into a modernist ideal of the Negro male, outside of history."[71] Martin Duberman adds that Macpherson, with his "meticulously planned camera angles and movement," created a film that was mainly "a series of . . . snapshots [so that] the camera is in the end the real actor."[72] The loving but immobilizing gaze of the camera creates a beautiful still image of the black actor's face, his dramatic expression enhanced by the play of light and shadow that produces dramatic angles, dips, and planes.

As a cinematic effect, however, the close-up shot can be shaped by other imperatives such as the viewer's desire for a more haptic, intimate engagement with Robeson's body. In the film, close-ups of Robeson's face are often followed by shots emphasizing the actor's veined hands, pointing the spectator to the muscular memory of touch. In her notion of the body of the film, rather than film as a mere series of images, Barker also describes the ways in which the viewer's seated body can mimic the motion of the camera. Close-ups encourage the audience to lean in and physically mimic the camera's motion: "It is those muscular movements that inspire the close-up, the zoom, and the crane shot. . . . Film and viewer share certain deep-seated muscular habits."[73] This is how the film screen moves theatrically, gesturing like the brushstroke toward the acting and moving body. Rather than distancing the viewer from the actor as a pure, reified image-object, the close-up can bring the bodylines of the actor and the viewer in closer relationship to each other.

As a cultural document, *Borderline* sits at the intersection of the black modernists of the Harlem Renaissance and the avant-garde modernism of the white *Pool* magazine group, with racialized sexuality as the meeting point between these two worlds. The phantasm of miscegenation underlies the film's strong prohibitions against both interracial and homosexual attachment and touch. At the same time, the camera work plays out the intercorporeal significance of different types of touches and skin relations as these are embodied in the interactions and gazes between the film's characters. The film points in its very title, *Borderline*, to the skin's role as interface, as meeting point, between self, other, and world.

Borderline's promotional material contained this dialectical tension between the miscegenation narrative and a more consensual experience of black and white skins moving and touching in close proximity to each other. Using key words lifted directly from white colonial fantasies of the Negro, as Fanon would describe them years later in *Black Skin, White Masks*, the film's accompanying brochure described it's fragmented plot: "The border, or rather the line of the border, whose is it? . . . In this biological ground . . . we have 'BORDER-LINE': a negro couple in a white country, a couple that were separated, for she lived with a white man. . . . The drama between the white couple and the negro couple. The whites are neuroses; the negroes, nature. Nature turns to nature: . . . and Pete, negro among whites, is expelled as undesirable."[74] The borderline exists in a "biological ground" composed of white "neuroses" and black "nature," with the Negro positioned at the preconscious, non-neurotic, genital level as the black hyperbolic penis which, like Robeson's character Pete, must be "expelled as undesirable." However, the brochure's cover image, which this section opens with, also used close-ups of the actors' faces and shots of the actors' bodies to suggest cleverly the intimate relations between the two interracial couples placed in erotic proximity with each other (see figure 2.4). As examples of both facialization and racialization, together the brochure's cover and text simultaneously code the bodies of both the white and black actors onto the symbolic grid in the racialist language of older colonialist narratives. They mimetically picture the intimacies and border violations produced when the skins of different racial subjects brush up against each other and touch.

Despite the film's narrative focus on two couples, the brochure's cover is filled with a disproportionate number of images of Robeson's face. Seven Robeson cutouts are arrayed against the dark, blotchy background and present the black male actor from multiple camera angles, including one shot of the back of his body. All of Robeson's face shots are nuanced variations of a common expression, slightly belligerent with flat affect. The seven images of Robeson's character, Pete, surround in a kind of circular, clocklike motion, the images of the other characters, converging at the center of the poster on the doubled image of Pete facing himself. The other close-ups include two of Thorne, the male partner in the white couple, played by Gavin Arthur; one of H. D.'s character, Astrid; and one of Essie Robeson, who appears as a reduced outline standing behind Robeson in the medium shot on the lower left corner of the poster. Both women also appear on the poster as body parts—Adah's eyes look toward Astrid, and Astrid's lips float behind and between the doubled image of Pete looking at himself at the center of the poster. The outline of H. D.'s lips touches the outlines of Robeson's faces, and lips, in a kind of intercorporeal caress.[75]

The master signifier of the black male face ties together all of the other characters' faces and bodies. As such, the black male face mimics, more so than it consciously represents, epidermalization itself as a process of ideological interpellation tying together all of the subjects represented in the image. Robeson's image(s) on the poster reflects the fact that his character, Pete, who is not the sole or even primary focus of the film's plot, will nevertheless become by the film's end the ultimate signifier for the white characters' traumatic, neurotic contact with the borderline of their own desires for the other's difference.

In asking, "the border, or rather the line of the border, whose is it?" the film also asks, where is the actual line or point of differentiation between one skin and another when two skins touch? *Borderline* speculates on the new sexual borderlines and renegotiations of old ones in the social system of sexual relations that were emerging in the modern interracial encounters of the early twentieth century.[76] Sexual relations are the field upon which *Borderline* negotiates what are, in effect, social skin relations, the psychopathologies of epidermalization and denegrification, of being raced and of shedding one's race, in a modern, early twentieth-century world. *Borderline* has long attracted the attention of modernist scholars due to H. D.'s performance as the wife in the film's white couple. The film also has a special status in film studies as the only feature film produced by Macpherson, who started his film magazine, *Pool*, with

H. D. and a circle of British and American avant-garde filmmakers in the early 1900s. Jean Walton argues that any "critical analysis of the film's racialized sexual politics must be preceded by a biographical account of the interrelationships of the POOL group," scholars such as herself pointing to the lesbian love relationship between H. D. and Macpherson's wife Bryher, who plays a tavern keeper in the film.[77] The film's lingering camera shots on Robeson also gesture toward white male homosexual desire, the film reflecting Macpherson's homoerotic fascination with black men.

However, another set of biographical facts and sexual dynamics are elided from scholars' accounts of the film, namely, the fact that the two black protagonists are played by a very prominent, married New Negro couple. Given its assumed status as a film about white desire, perhaps it is not surprising that we never hear of the domestic tensions in the Robesons' life as a couple at that time, tensions exacerbated by Paul Robeson's general desirability and intermittent affairs with his white leading ladies.[78] As much as the film explores the complexities of white love and desire across the color line, black sexual politics also play a role in shaping the black actors' portrayals and bodily interpretations of the film's thematics. Current analyses miss the ways in which the film tells us as much about the *black* love relation, as it intersects with questions of race and sexuality, as it does about the white love relations portrayed both directly and indirectly in the film.[79]

In a film such as *Borderline*, the less explored context of the black sexual relation reveals more about the film's intercorporeity, and the consensuality between the New Negro and the modernist, than the film's more blatant miscegenation narrative. Whether the directors fully intended so or not, and whether white audiences fully appreciated this or not, the film itself presents a field of bodily relations that exceeds the film's narrative frame.[80] By reading *Borderline* against the grain of its miscegenation tropes and thematics, one rediscovers the powerful ways in which the black actor and actress in the film convey, through their performances, other kinds of bodily and libidinal relations. In *Borderline*, the black love relation provides a milieu for the bodily portrayal of dimensions of the black actors' experience that escape or are hidden from the film's symbolic narrative. Alongside those close-up shots that immobilize Robeson and make him fully available to the camera are others that animate Pete as a character actively moving through the story line in response to both his own and other characters' memories and feelings.

In *Borderline* Robeson the actor uses physical action and gesture to signal the shift in mode between word and image, character and flesh. In an early scene, which includes the still shot that opens this chapter, Pete flashes back to a memory of Adah in happier times, waving to him from outside as he stands in front of the window of their boarding house bedroom (see figure 2.1). First Pete moves from the bed, dislodging his body from those still shots that initially lure our gaze. Then, in long shots of Pete framed against the sky, laughing, beckoning, and then returning once again to the bed despondent, we get a sense of the depth of the character's feelings for Adah. This is all cued visually through shots in which Robeson the actor is much less still and composed than in the preceding close-ups. "The activity of the actor is less to imitate a character in a script," Massumi reminds us, "than to mimic in the flesh the incorporeality of the event."[81] It is the actor's job, in other words, to turn the character into flesh: "The actor makes words into images, visualizes text, then renders that visualization public by embodying it before the camera."[82] Through his motion and gestures, Robeson animates Pete, fleshing out a character whose memories spur him into action as he dons his hat and coat and sets out in search of Adah. The camera then follows him on a brisk walk through the village seeking Adah in order to recapture her love and attention (see figures 2.5, 2.6, 2.7).

In these scenes of Pete following Adah, *Borderline* offers an extended visual metaphor of the black, heterosexual love relation as we follow him tracking her through the streets of a small Swiss town. In these active, enfolding, and enwrapping scenes of movement and action, the camera shadows Pete and Adah as they move around buildings, walk through archways, hide behind walls, and stride down and along brick walkways, all in long and medium range shots at a greater distance from the camera than the close-up. These shots portray the black characters not so much in nature as in space, what Barker also describes as the kinesthetic dimensions of the film's body.[83] These scenes and shots conjure up for the spectating viewer a sense of spatiality—the muscular impression of the outside as space, a feeling for the monumental shape, architectural form, and the tactility of concrete objects.

These long scenes of the characters' proprioceptive amble also capture, metaphorically and mimetically, the circuit of never-ending desire that constitutes the black sexual relation. In a classic example of the film's technique of clatter montage, an image of a cat playing with fish is interspersed with the scenes of Pete following Adah. Both scenes combine to create the visual metaphor of heterosexual desire as a cat and mouse game. As the actors reenact the incorporeal, mobile, and bodily dimensions of this game, the line between play and menace, pleasure and death, blurs. Despite the framing attempted by the film's brochure—"Nature turns to nature"—Pete and Adah's walk outside is not a mere expression of the simple and timeless nature of black heterosexual love. As Pete follows Adah through the town's cobbled streets, the couple mimics a certain gendered itinerary, the well-worn heteronormative conventions of his aggression and determination set against her coy flirtatiousness and fear.

In another evocative close-up, Adah's face peeks out from behind a wall whose ragged and grainy texture gives it the membrane-like appearance of a veil (see figure 2.8). Evoking a strip of skin or a swath of her hair, the wall partially shrouds Adah, sealing her up behind the veil while also promising us access, luring us to ask who she is, this mysterious female catalyst for the love affair that sparks the various interactions between the couples that drive the plot. As Adah, half playfully and half seriously, runs and hides from Pete, their cat and mouse (or in this case, cat and fish) game with the viewer underscores the elusive nature of black desire. When the film asks, "The borderline, whose is it?" it points to the confusion of roles within the love relation; here we are unclear who the cat is and who is the fish, who is doing the leading and who is being led, Pete or Adah? As Pete looms behind Adah in dark alleyways and tunnels, the sense of menace, of suspense and tension, grows, and when Pete finally catches (up to) Adah we see a question in her eyes whether, in response to Pete's desiring gaze, she really wants to be found (see figure 2.9).

Black heterosexuality figures prominently on *Borderline*'s tactile, visual screen even as it is being marginalized by the film's miscegenation story line. While most critics focus on homosexuality as the film's most potent, sexual counternarrative, black heterosexuality also comments on white heteronormativity in the film, signifying on the latter as a racialized formation with the fear of miscegenation at its center. The black couple's interactions are framed within a web of intra- and interracial relations that, far from being natural, are all chiasmic and neurotic.[84] The film's multiple, potentially transgressive relationships, typically figured by shots of gazes between characters and hands, occur within a relational sexual field where a variety of lines of gender, race, and sexuality are crossed. In some of the film's strongest scenes, the black characters' actions thwart our expectations, suggesting in their physical acting and gestures that the film includes more complex subjective and social formations than simply "the whites are neuroses; the negroes, nature."

Adah's Gaze and Pete's Laugh: Breaking the Fourth Wall

In an early scene of confrontation between Adah (played by Essie Robeson) and Astrid (played by H. D.), a profile shot of the two actresses facing each other includes a picture of a stylish, modern woman mounted on the wall between them. Throughout this opening scene, many images of fashionable women are scattered on the walls of Thorne and Astrid's sitting room. They represent H. D.

FIGS 2.5–2.6. *Borderline*, Pete outside following Adah—brick wall (top) and Pete outside following Adah—archway (above). Permission for stills from *Borderline* provided by Douris UK Ltd.

FIG 2.7. *Borderline*, Pete outside following Adah—around building. Permission for still from *Borderline* provided by Douris UK Ltd.

FIGS 2.8–2.9. *Borderline*, Adah behind the wall (top). Paul and Essie Robeson (above). Image provided by Yale Collection of American Literature, Beinecke Rare Book and Manuscript Library. Permission for stills from *Borderline* provided by Douris UK Ltd.

the modernist poet as the "New Woman" of the era, liberated in her sexuality and artistically independent.[85] However, they also represent Essie Robeson as her New Negro female counterpart. Dressed in the style we have come to associate with a modern, stylish, black femininity, in her smart cloches, heels, fur-lined coats, and "tut-cut," Adah is the classic female figure of a contemporaneous black modernism, the New Negro sensibility of the 1930s.[86]

Perhaps it is the New Negro Woman's brash self-confidence (performed at its utmost by Zora Neale Hurston) that Essie Robeson was thinking of when, throughout the film, she portrays Adah as neither the long-suffering and wronged wife of black male infidelity nor the rejected and tragic mulatta mistress.[87] When Astrid demands of Adah, "You must go back to Pete and leave Thorne," she mockingly responds, ". . . and leave Thorne—for you?" assuming a surprisingly brash and proprietary attitude toward Thorne in complete defiance of Astrid's actual status as his wife.[88] This caption accompanies a close-up of Adah, looking mockingly over her shoulder with a seductive and knowing smile.

Essie Robeson performs Adah as a modern black woman who was herself the wife of a prominent New Negro performer, well versed in the politics and style of the entertainment industry even if not a practicing professional herself. In other words, even if unrecognized and invisible to a white audience and the *Pool* group of modernist filmmakers, Adah's racialized femininity is a palpable presence on-screen, part of the film's signifying, bodily language. Rather than harkening back to older tropes of the tragic mulatto, hers is a presence befitting its cultural moment, the emergence of the liberated, modern, new black woman freed from Victorian prescriptions. Adah not only instigates the drama of the film around which all the couples, and the crisis in the town, revolve, but also she does so as a character whose cool attitude of critical detachment produces an almost Brechtian-like alienation effect in relation to the film's drama of white neurosis. Essie Robeson's Adah thus provides us with another way in which the unanticipated actions, gestures, and style of the black actor produce meanings in the film that disrupt its phantasm of miscegenation and primary story line of white neurosis.[89]

Throughout *Borderline*, Essie Robeson's portrayal of Adah is noticeably deadpan, her emotionless stares and stillness in direct contrast with Pete's expressive lightheartedness and Thorne's and Astrid's angst. This is nowhere more evident than in a climactic scene of confrontation between Thorne and Pete close to the end of the film. While certainly a sign of her lack of professional training as an actress, Adah/Essie Robeson's affective and physical acts of separation from the diegetic action of the film in this scene also work to produce the kind of reflexive, alienating effect a modernist such as Brecht hoped to create onstage. During the confrontation between Thorne and Pete, Adah's flattened affect, reflected in her corporeal stance and facial demeanor, heightens the ironies of masculine bravado that are shaping the confrontation.

Ada's most significant opening gesture in the scene involves a prop, a small rectangular mirror she is holding up when Thorne first bursts into the bedroom. Staring toward Thorne at the entryway of the room, Adah's look indicates her lack of emotional involvement in the melodrama about to take place between the two male characters. The actress also breaks a rule any accomplished director would have coached her against. Accidentally or intentionally, Adah breaks the fourth wall, that is, she stares directly into the camera and shatters the illusion of the viewer's absence from the scene/screen. Her stare raises the potentially alienating awareness of our specular presence, as

FIG 2.11. *Borderline*, Adah and the mirror. Permission for still from *Borderline* provided by Douris UK Ltd.

she seems to be staring directly at the camera, and at us, rather than at Thorne (see figure 2.11).

As Adah, both literally and figuratively, holds up a mirror to the audience, an even more dramatic error occurs, once again, drawing our attention away from the diegetic action of the film and instead toward the surface of the screen as an interface between the actor, the camera/director, and the audience. Throughout most of this scene the camera follows Adah from the right of the screen, mimicking the sight lines of Pete and the other characters as they look into the bedroom from the door. As Pete stands up to engage Thorne, however, the camera places Essie Robeson in a position that should be physically impossible given the geographic configuration of the room, and the orientations of the various sight lines and eye lines that have dominated the scene thus far. Suddenly we are presented with a profile shot of her from the left, from a corner where no one is standing but a wall. Here the camera commits another cinematographic taboo by "crossing the line" to produce a shot otherwise known as a cheat shot, a sight line impossible in the layout of the room pictured in the scene. If in the shot before, Adah's gaze crosses the line and reminds us of the world outside the film, now the camera shot of her profile

FIG 2.12. *Borderline*, Adah in the angled mirror. Permission for still from *Borderline* provided by Douris UK Ltd.

breaks the fourth wall by literally placing itself in a position only available to the viewer outside of the scene. The camera allows the audience to have a sight line on Adah that, diegetically, could only represent the perspective of an eye in the wall of the room, or alternatively, an eye in the mirror Adah has been holding up.

These two shots created by the technical play of McPherson's camera then set up a third, even more self-reflexive shot that captures a part of Adah's reflection on the angled face of the small mirror. Clearly a virtuoso shot meant to draw our attention to the artificial aesthetic reality the camera constructs and imposes, mirror shots in general often suggest diegetically that a character is engaging in an act of self-reflection. Thus, Essie Robeson's detached demeanor is underscored by a shot which, now composed intentionally by the editors and director, offers the viewer access to psychological elements in Adah's character that go beyond mere appearance. However, in Adah's mirror shot we do not see her looking at herself. The mirror is oddly angled such that instead, we see a reflection of her eye alone as she looks toward Pete and Thorne (see figure 2.12).

In the mirror Adah inhabits the scene metonymically, as an eye observing and responding to the male drama ensuing at the doorway, while her hand is detached and engaged in the very separate activity of angling the mirror for the camera to get this particular, inventive shot. Even more so than the previous two shots of Adah, the mirror shot is purely performative and artistic for it has no purpose within the sight lines composing the scene. One of the effects of Adah's mirror shot is to point us to the very artificiality of the performance of masculinity Thorne and Pete are engaged in. The shot graphically matches the shot that follows, of Pete and Thorne squaring off at the door. As their staring contest becomes a symbol of masculine confrontation, Pete and Thorne are also represented formally as eyes and parts of faces, chopped off, partitioned, the body in bits and pieces cut off by the rim of the film screen.

Adah's shot thus anticipates and comments on Pete's and Thorne's. To some degree she mimics the director in framing the scene to come, literally angling her arm to catch, in a reflection of her female sight line, an angle on this confrontation between men. Her physical acting in this scene—used here to convey the broader sense of the specific way she uses her body to convey meaning—is crucial, for none of this visual virtuosity would be as effective without her performance of a certain skepticism and emotional detachment, as if she does not fully inhabit the scene or believe in any of the respective characters' gender performances.[90] In the beginning of the scene, her lack of passion makes Thorne's melodrama appear ridiculous; by the end, in the aftermath of this masculine encounter, her lack of affection makes Pete appear sheepish. Throughout the scene she never appears as weak or cringing, the affect conveyed by Astrid. Instead, as she peers out from behind Robeson's large, blocking shoulders in the moment of Pete's stare down with Thorne, her body movement conveys the slow and detached demeanor of someone observing an accident in which he or she plays no part (see figures 2.13, 2.14, 2.15).[91] Essie's body swaying slowly behind Pete is a gesture that also demonstrates an attitude of the body of the film itself. As Barker describes:

> Often a film encourages a muscular gesture in the viewer and then expresses its empathy with us by performing the same gesture itself. . . . The mimetic, empathetic relationship between film and viewer goes both ways [and] film's structures are based on human structures of perception, attention, memory, and imagination. The close-up, for example, evolved as a result of viewers' need for a closer view [but also] our mental structures are embodied, borne out and at the same time inflected by our bodily behaviors (which are themselves embedded in culture and history). We want to see more closely, so we lean in, step forward, or crane our necks.[92]

FIGS 2.13–2.15.
Borderline, Adah
swaying behind
Pete. Permission
for stills from *Bor-
derline* provided
by Douris UK Ltd.

The intercorporeal relationship between the actor and the audience, the black body and the camera/screen, is performed in and by the film itself. In this scene the actor's movement, Essie's/Adah's swaying, becomes the medium by which the film communicates her detachment to the audience but also encourages a similar attitude of critical detachment in their bodies as they observe the diegetic action of male confrontation that is the scene's central plot.

In the character Thorne's desperate stance at the threshold of the doorway, he also weaves back and forth but his actions work to support the plot, expressing bodily his struggle to achieve some form of vindication for his affair with Adah. Thorne is filmed very much as Pete's foil, and in this sense he also stands in as a surrogate for the homoerotic gaze of the white male director behind the camera.[93] However, in his response to Thorne, Robeson also speaks back to the camera and to the audience in his signature gestures throughout the scene. Pete and Adah are in their private room upstairs when Thorne storms into the tavern. Arriving at the doorway of their room, Thorne stands at the borderline or threshold of a black interior space, the private terrain of Pete and Adah's relationship. Five characters — Pete and Adah in the room, the pianist and the bar owner just outside in the hall, and Thorne at the threshold — exchange a series of glances culminating in the primary stare down and face off between Adah's black and white male lovers. The graininess of the film, the black-and-white backdrops of a wall and a curtain behind Thorne and Pete, the director's enhancement of black-and-white film, all mimic and reinforce the epidermal contours of this racialized and sexualized confrontation. Pete's response, however, is to laugh boisterously in Thorne's face and then to wryly chuckle and shake his head after Thorne leaves. In most of Pete's shots throughout this scene he is laughing or smiling (see figure 2.16). When the camera zooms in for a close-up of Pete's look, Robeson the actor also intentionally breaks the fourth wall, the smile on his face and in his eyes suggesting his sardonic feelings about the entire event. In this manner, this shot goes beyond the scene of white male hysteria to include the off-screen, behind the scenes, racial production of *Borderline* itself as a film that mirrors the attitudes, beliefs, and symbolic structures of the white modernist viewers beyond the camera.[94]

The Robesons were certainly conscious of the racial dynamics on *Borderline*'s film set. In her diary Essie commented amusedly on the racial naïveté of their costars by stating: "Kenneth and H. D. used to make us so shriek with laughter with their naïve ideas of Negroes that Paul and I often completely ruined our make-up."[95] This laugh that leaves the body as a "shriek" disrupts the director's posing and setting-up of the black actors for their scene. It is one of those unscripted, corporeal acts in which the black actor communicates

FIG 2.16. *Borderline*, close-up of Pete smiling. Permission for still from *Borderline* provided by Douris UK Ltd.

through his or her style and mannerisms what cannot be conveyed in words, in a film's formal dialogue, diegetic action, or explicit camera work: "Little extras. Small but effective ways of skewing the potential movements composing the field."[96] At the threshold to Pete and Adah's room, as these intercorporeal dynamics play out between characters, between actors, and between the camera and the audience, these are the dynamics that the film's narrative logic attempts to erase. The miscegenation morality tale—who gets punished for committing inappropriate acts of desire—becomes the narrative device policing all of the other forms of sexuality and manifestations of desire that clutter the film, the latter all neatly subsumed by the movie's ending, the scapegoating and eviction of "poor Pete."

In their gestures, the black actor and actress signal the relational context of their performance, two bodies interacting with each other against the backdrop of dynamics that extend beyond the screen into their real life as a black couple, and into their relationship with the film's white filmmakers and costars. These embodied acts move this cinematic portrayal of black heterosexuality beyond the masqueraded stiffness, for example, of the tobacco ad and photographic series featuring the Williamses and the Walkers. Instead, Paul and Essie Robeson are engaged in a conversation with the camera about what escapes, even contradicts, the film's primary story line of the distraught, tragic black female torn between two men, and the irate, jealous black male in self-righteous defense of his beloved. Instead, we get Paul Robeson's humor, and Essie Robeson's direct gaze and metadiegetic address, all reminding viewers of their existence outside of the terms of the film's plot, in a cultural space shared by the film's director, the camera, and the audience's gaze.

Escaping the Frame-Up: Blurring the Black Body in *Borderline* and *Song of Freedom*

Movement-vision is sight turned proprioceptive, the eyes reabsorbed into the flesh through a black hole in the geometry of empirical space and a gash in bodily form.
—BRIAN MASSUMI, *Parables for the Virtual*

In *Heavenly Bodies*, his study of Paul Robeson's screen roles, Richard Dyer argues that the actor was unable to translate his strident political activism on-screen and failed to bring a sense of agency to his roles that transcended his being fixed in stereotypical ways by the camera. For Dyer, "even as a leader" in his films Robeson "seldom had a role that involved actions that had an effect on the plot, unless it was in white interests. . . . He is effectively ineffective."[97] Focusing on Robeson's use of his body Dyer continues: "All performers use their bodies and have their bodies used, but in the case of Robeson in the twenties and thirties he was often little more than a body and a voice. . . . Hence, finally, a figure like Robeson, whose body can be, in sport, in feats of strength, in sculpturable muscularity, in sheer presence, in a voice [—] the correlative of manly power, but whose body finally does nothing, contained by frames, montage, narrative, direction, vocal restraint."[98] Dyer's assessment of Robeson is ultimately that he was "put into a position of female 'subordination' within the dynamics of looking that are built into any portrait-image of a human being in this culture."[99] Like the female object of the gaze, he could not "act," either politically or dramatically, since his personality was subordinated to the compelling power of the image and his own appearance.

Richard Dyer's assessment that, on-screen, Paul Robeson was primarily contained within the borders of the cinematic frame, his black masculinity projected as appearance rather than in terms of psychological cognition and action, positions Robeson as merely the *object* of white desire and fantasy. His critique is a familiar one, the idea that black celebrity performers' images and acts only allow them to function as the objects of the gaze of the spectator. Their only form of resistance to the gaze is to act in a manner that demonstrates their own agency and thereby thwarts the reifying effects of the audience's looks. Hence the more positive and racially uplifting images of Robeson as the black ruler or emperor throughout the 1920s and 1930s, a role he made famous in three incarnations as Othello, the ultimate representation of the black male performer as sovereign subject rather than fetish object (see figure 2.17).[100] In such roles as the black ruler in *Othello*, or the black emperor in *The Emperor Jones* and *Song of Freedom*, Robeson was the inscribed subject-object of, as H. D. eloquently proclaimed, "the touch the world proclaims / perfection . . . / the tall god standing / where the race is run."[101]

In his critique, however, Dyer misses the ways in which Robeson embodied not just the idealized fantasy but also the uncanny specter of a black like subject. The performance that escapes the traps of the epidermal and symbolic grid most effectively is not one that tries to picture the sovereignty of the black male subject, but rather, his bodily relationality at the very moment in which it appears to exceed or escape from the symbolic frame. Massumi describes this as the true definition of "*suspense*": that charged moment when, on the borders of the cultural screen — on "the edge of the hole in empirical space into which the eyes of movement-vision disappear" — the incorporeal body appears outlined on "the rim of the virtual at the crossroads of the actual."[102] This evocation of a haptic, tactile embodied black subject exceeds both the black male's incorporation as pure object-image and his idealization as the embodiment of sovereignty.

There are glimpses of this Robeson in his films from the 1930s, in those shots that image the black male body as a shadowy apparition on the surface or screen of the intercorporeal gaze. This is the cinematic image of the black male "body stripped of its skin," appearing as a pure epidermal outline in "the black hole" and "crack in the texture of [symbolic] reality," where we encounter him in the materiality of the flesh itself: "movement-vision is sight turned proprioceptive, the eyes reabsorbed into the flesh through a black hole in the geometry of empirical space and a gash in bodily form."[103] In *Borderline*, this is the haunting body we see in the blurry silhouette of a black male shadow captured on a poster that frames the raised fist of one of the white men from the village, as the latter confronts Pete in another scene in the tavern (see figure 2.18).

The shadowy and blurred aspects of the image, which remain so even as the camera moves in for a sharper close-up, epitomize Laura U. Marks's definition of the haptic image, one that is figural, more texture than substance, and hard to resolve into a narrative. The feathery texture of light and shadow falls on the surface of the shot like the brushstrokes on a painting. The image also represents mimetically the physical touch of white skin against black skin as the fist in the foreground appears to squeeze and crush the silhouetted black

FIG 2.17. Paul Robeson as "Othello," No. 16. Photographer Carl Van Vechten. Van Vechten Trust / Yale Collection of American Literature, Beinecke Rare Book and Manuscript Library.

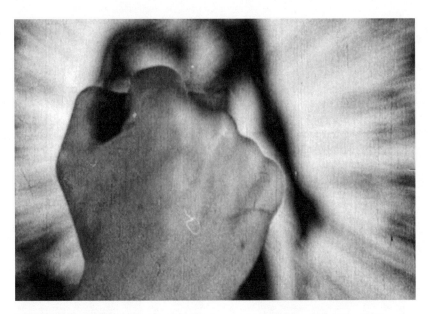

FIG 2.18. *Borderline*, the fist and the silhouette. Permission for still from *Borderline* provided by Douris UK Ltd.

male body at its midpoint. The white halo of light behind the silhouette registers that touch in a kind of animation of the fist's point of impact on the mid-areas of the black male body. The action of the fist also mimics a different kind of homoerotic touch, the white hand thrust upward in the imitation of a firm clasp on the black phallus, either violently or erotically.

This shadowy figure of the black male actor as a relational body but also as an inaccessible subject just out of the reach of the embodied audience beyond the camera also appears at the end of Robeson's paradigmatic film of black male sovereignty in this period, *Song of Freedom*. Robeson plays John Zinga, a concert singer who abandons his stage career in the United States to pursue his family connections to African royalty.[104] The main trope of the film is a sacred song that Zinga uses as proof of his lineage; in one scene, his performance of this song saves himself and his wife, played by Elisabeth Welch, from certain death by distrustful African tribesmen. Zinga sings from a place of power, the voice as a kind of phallic signifier representing the power and authority of the speech of a sovereign black masculinity. The emperor's song is replayed a number of times in the film as a symbol of Zinga's triumphant reclaiming of his African heritage.[105]

FIGS 2.19–2.20. *Song of Freedom*, the king onstage. Permission for stills from *Song of Freedom* provided by Douris UK Ltd.

In Zinga's final performance of the emperor's song, however, a relaxed and shirtless Robeson is shot as he is seated on a concert stage, singing at a fund-raising benefit for the character's rediscovered African land. In a series of shots, the figure of the performer shrinks to that of a dark speck within a blurry white oval with jagged edges (see figures 2.19 and 2.20).

The white blur, evoking the blurry, moist, filmy lining of the eye, turns the gaze of the film screen into a white hole, the frightening crack of the REAL. If the face is a white wall/black hole system at the intersection of signification and subjectification, *Song of Freedom* ends with the black hole of subjectivity now imaged as the stripped and vulnerable body of the black male performer appearing in the fissure of the gaze. As Robeson's image shrinks in the blurry gash of the film lens, we get a glimpse of our own "movement-vision," that is, "sight turned proprioceptive, the eyes reabsorbed into the flesh through a black hole in the geometry of empirical space and a gash in bodily form."[106] As we watch the African king diminish from the grandness of the sovereign ego-subject to the subject fading away in the gaze's dazzling spotlight, he leaves behind Robeson's bare-chested silhouette less as an image of agency than as the bodily canvas, the bodyline, across which the intertwined agencies of the actor and the viewer communicate on the skin of the film screen.

three

The Problem of Color

In the history of whiteness as a performance practice, organizing the world on the basis of skin, miscegenation constitutes the primal scene, especially when the liaison is between a black man and white woman.
—JOSEPH ROACH, *It*

As long as we're alive the world's still alive. We're monuments you and me.
— HARRY BELAFONTE, *The World, the Flesh and the Devil*

In an essay published in 1966 for the *Ebony* collection, *The White Problem in America*, James Baldwin recalls marching in the streets of Montgomery, Alabama, "the Confederate flag . . . flying from the Capitol dome [and] the Federalized National Guard, assigned to protect the marchers, [wearing] Confederate flags on their jackets."[1] As he watched, white businessmen stood on the balconies of buildings "jeering" at the marchers with "eyes—which could not face ours." Baldwin also noted the more "schizophrenic" gaze of the white female spectators when they saw his friend and fellow marcher, Harry Belafonte, the movie star, singer, and one of the most popular black male celebrities of this period:

> From upstairs office windows, white American secretaries were leaning out of windows, jeering and mocking, and using the ancient Roman sentence of death: thumbs down. Then they saw Harry, who is my very dear friend and a beautiful cat, and who is also, in this most desperately schizophrenic of republics, a major, reigning matinee idol. . . . When the girls saw Harry Belafonte, a collision occurred in them so visible as to be at once hilarious and unutterably sad. At one moment the thumbs

FIG 3.1. Harry Belafonte. NO. 1165. Photographer Carl Van Vechten. Van Vechten Trust / Yale Collection of American Literature, Beinecke Rare Book and Manuscript Library.

were down, they were barricaded within their skins, at the next moment, those down turned thumbs flew to their mouths, their fingers pointed, their faces changed, and . . . they oohed, and aahed and moaned.[2]

In his description of this dramatic encounter, Baldwin references what Joseph Roach has described as a "primal scene" of colonial modernity, that is, the emblematic scenario of miscegenation as a primary taboo governing interracial sexual relations in the eras of New World discovery and colonization. Roach also suggests, however, that what is "primal" about this scene is not just its racial but also its specific gendered components—that the fear of miscegenation rests most fundamentally on the archetypal dyad of the white female/black male. Baldwin was drawn to the difference between the white women's two gazes, from one second to another. One was "barricaded" within white skin and unable to meet black Americans' eyes; the other was a look of unconscious desire, lured to the black male celebrity and expressed in incoherent gasps.[3] Together, the two gazes represented a bodily and sensory "collision" connecting the women libidinously to the black man marching below.

In his prose during the period, Baldwin often explored the topic of what drew white viewers to, and repelled them from, the black actors appearing more frequently on North American movie and television screens in the 1950s. A different kind of public encounter between black celebrities and their civil rights contemporaries was captured in a famous pair of press photographs with Baldwin and Belafonte but also including other celebrities such as Sidney Poitier, Charlton Heston, and Marlon Brando. In one photo, the well-known activist-entertainers of the period pose together amidst the press of an eager crowd. Marlon Brando's and James Baldwin's hands are positioned at the center of the image almost as if they are touching, while other luminaries such as Charlton Heston, Harry Belafonte, and Sidney Poitier look on. In another photo of the same event, Poitier and Belafonte talk against the backdrop of the stony statue of Abraham Lincoln, an apt posing since both of the photographs work to transmit official state messages about racial and social equality as the nation's civic ideals. In one photograph, social equality between the races at midcentury is portrayed as a matter of black and white men touching hands; in the other, the stony statue of Abraham Lincoln reminds viewers that the investment in such ideals is a crucial aspect of the nation's identity and racial history.

In the picture that includes him, James Baldwin looks a bit like the trickster figure he was in American public life during this period. In his exploration of the space between the bodily and the political in American race relations, he revealed a much more fraught and messy terrain than the two official photographs captured. As civil rights became more and more the state's official language of racial political equality, it contradicted the deeply embedded fear among whites that social equality was merely code for sexual equality between the races.[4] Ironically, it was film that captured both the messiness of American race relations during the 1950s and those cinematic strategies that served to contain the emerging new dynamics in race relations during this era of civil rights and decolonization. During the 1950s, film technologies of color reproduced on-screen fantasies of miscegenation that resurrected what the official black-and-white photographs attempted to whitewash: the messy intercultural, sexualized space between bodies racialized as different.

If the street scene in Montgomery, Alabama, describes one public space for reenactments of mid-twentieth-century race relations in the United States, the theatre and the cinema were also public spaces involved in the staging of race, settings for public encounters between the bodies of white audiences and those of actors of color. Baldwin argued, however, that in the space of the cinema, Belafonte and other black actors and actresses became ciphers for white America to work through sexual anxieties concerning their relationship to black bodiliness. As he commented: "Life does not produce ciphers like these: when people have become this empty they are not ciphers any longer, but monsters. The creation of such ciphers proves, however, that Americans are far from empty; they are, on the contrary, very deeply disturbed."[5]

The cipher represented the thickness, rather than the emptiness, of black-white proximal relations in the 1950s, a thickness American society tried to gloss over with new racial narratives and new color technologies on-screen. Baldwin spent much of his career anatomizing the problem of color in the United States at midcentury precisely because it was his sense that, by the 1950s, Americans had become comfortable interacting with each other through epidermal ciphers or masks of color. Race functioned socially as a protective covering, and black skin and the white gaze were the two opposing sides of this difference mask.

Skin color, as a stain on both the black face and the lining of the gaze, represented the hardening of epidermal skin into new ways of marking difference. Both the gaze and the skin operated as ciphers or surrogates on behalf of the subjects in whose place they stood. For Baldwin, the primary loss in the American cultural transition from stage to screen was the deadening of the audience's ability to see itself. Now it was "the camera [that] sees what you want it to see," further limiting and circumscribing where the audience wanted to look in relation to the other.[6] The camera facilitated the covering over of the audience's look by the gaze, by the camera's sight line, like a veneer. In the movie theatre, cinematic technical effects effaced and replaced the embodied agency of the audience. This would have a profound effect on the relations between the skin and the gaze, between the black actor and the white spectator.[7]

The black actor also lost something in the transition from the stage to the Technicolor screen. As in Robeson's screen performances, race films in the 1950s continued the myth that audiences could have intimate access to the real self of the black performer: "No one . . . will ever really know whether [movie stars] can, or could, really act, or not, nor does anyone care: acting is not what they are required to do. Their acting ability, so far from being what attracts their audience, can often be what drives their audience away. One does not go to see them act: one goes to watch them be."[8] Here Baldwin's comments sound similar, at first, to James's discussion of the celebrity entertainer's idiosyncratic bodily style. For James, however, this dynamic still pointed to some of the relational elements of the player's interaction with his audience. In the 1950s, the black actor on-screen created a more synthetic experience of intimacy with the audience.

A false intimacy masqueraded as relationality in the movie star's performance: "The distance between oneself—the audience—and a screen performer is an absolute: a paradoxical absolute, masquerading as intimacy."[9] The theatre remained an idealized space for Baldwin precisely because "one is not in the presence of shadows, but responding to one's flesh and blood; in the theater, we are recreating each other."[10] Baldwin pointed specifically to the distracting consequences of heightened cinematic color and sound for representing blackness on the cultural screen. In contrast to the audience and actor "recreating each other" as "flesh and blood," the camera lens falsely lessens the distance between actor and audience with a veil or lure. Color closes the gap; cinematic color offered a trompe l'oeil projection of the fact that "we are all each other's flesh and blood" rather than a representation of the fleshy relation itself.[11] In the 1950s, the sense of intimacy created in the interaction with the black movie star's charisma, his or her "It-ness," became more a function of the camera's color technics than the actor's bodily gestures, a performance of intimacy hiding deeper and more fraught relations of distance on the one hand, alikeness on the other, shaping interracial interactions.

If we remember 1960 more as "the year that constituted the climax of the Technicolor, CinemaScope 1950s, rather than the onset of the 60s per se," then that also reminds us of the staying power of Technicolor as a visual metaphor for the look of the decade, shaping and pervading the visual field.[12] In posters advertising the films of the era, the phrases "in CinemaScope" and "Color by Deluxe" signaled the use of a wide-screen technique and a coloring technology that would come to characterize the look of fifties films more broadly.

In 1952, Twentieth Century Fox bought the rights to the CinemaScope, a wide-screen format that promised even greater visual realism in comparison to 3-D. CinemaScope technology was based on the anamorphic lens made by Henri Chrétien during World War I, which employed an optical trick to produce an image twice as wide as that produced with conventional lenses. Technicolor was the trademark name for a color film process pioneered by Technicolor Motion Picture Corporation and celebrated for bringing hyperrealistic, saturated levels of color to film. In 1953, the movie industry adopted the stereoscopic camera and wide-screen systems such as CinemaScope, and retrofitted movie theatres for stereophonic sound, a third technique designed to give movie spectators the impression that they were hearing sounds in a film from various directions, much like natural hearing.

CinemaScope, Technicolor, and stereophonic sound were three key developments in the film industry's efforts to use heightened sensory modes to draw an audience back to movie theatres and away from the increasingly popular television screen. Chrétien's wide-scope lens took its name from the process of anamorphosis, which describes a distorted projection or perspective that requires the viewer to use special devices or to occupy a specific vantage point to reconstitute an image. CinemaScope, Panavision, Technirama, and other wide-screen formats introduced this new technique of projecting a wider image from a narrower film frame. The fundamental technique of anamorphosis, however, had been used as early as the sixteenth century in Renaissance paintings such as Hans Holbein's *The Ambassadors* (1533), the painting Lacan uses to demonstrate how anamorphosis situates a gaze that is detached from the world and striving for a distanced realism, as opposed to a look that becomes aware of itself as a form of situated, distorted viewing constituted by its own subjective sight lines.

Was the visual regime we associate with the Technicolor 1950s in the United States harnessed in any way to the racial dynamics of the period? In the showcasing of color, 3-D, and wide-screen, the lures drawing audiences to watch black actors on film were now more a function of the symbolic grid than the charismatic corporeality of the performer.[13] CinemaScope and other anamorphic technologies were constructed, cinematic sight lines masquerading as specialized, objective re-creations of reality on-screen. They were the product of what Jean-Paul Sartre called the "privileges of our race, of our color, of our technics," that is, the symbolic gaze manipulating social reality with the benefit of color technology.[14]

As the use of color on-screen manipulated the social politics of color in visual forms, the fear of black sexuality and desire was harnessed to these new scopic innovations. Wide screens promised to bring actors and scenes even closer to the viewer, while bright splashes of color assured audiences of a synthetic experience of blackness that would not touch white bodies. Both the skin and the screen became canvases on which racial color could be given commercial meaning. On these saturated surfaces, color became a central trope through which audiences could think about race in terms of surfaces that could not meet, rather than in terms of bodies interacting and in contact with each other in intercultural space.

In a scene toward the end of his novel, *Tell Me How Long the Train's Been Gone*, Baldwin's Belafonte-like character, the actor Leo Proudhammer, sees his face projected on a large set of movie screens: "On the wall were four screens, and, on those screens, ectoplasmic figures and faces endlessly writhed, moving in and out of each other, in a tremendous sexual rhythm which made me think of nameless creatures blindly coupling in all the slime of the world. . . . From time to time, on this screen, one recognized a face. . . . I thought I saw my own."[15] Here the "ectoplasmic" figures "blindly coupling" lie on a border between the synthetic and the fleshy. Alongside the gaze's ability to facialize and mortify, the actors' "ectoplasmic" bodies also throw off, like amoeba-shaped lamellas or ghostly skins, a sense of the corporeality of living being. The libidinous body exceeds the screen's neat frame, slipping and sliding over into "the slime of the world." Technicolor, as an evolving visual technology in a scopic regime of race and intercultural relations, used the formal properties of cinematic color to clean up such scenes, divesting them of their worldly, desexualized reality.

The spot of racial difference on the surface of the gaze also signifies as a disturbing, slimy remainder, and reminder, of the Real. In Technicolor films with black actors of the 1950s, everything disturbing about this spot or stain was cleaned away in the dazzling glare of color and light. As Baldwin described further: "[On-screen] the color itself then becomes a kind of vacuum which each spectator will fill with his own fantasies. . . . The word that springs immediately to mind to describe the appallingly technicolored sets—an army camp, a room, and a street on Chicago's South Side, presumably, which Bigger Thomas would certainly fail to recognize—is 'spotless.'"[16]

A pair of Carl Van Vechten's studio photographs of Belafonte capture some of these dynamics, the coloring over of race relations and the masking of the black performer as a cipher in a cinematic pretense of public intimacy with the black star (see figures 3.2 and 3.3).

The two images come from Carl Van Vechten's collection of photographs of famous black artists, writers, and performers, which he began taking in the early years of the Harlem Renaissance. As a whole, the collection provides a powerful visual archive of black celebrity figures from the first half of the twentieth century. Often Van Vechten was able to capture something distinctive about the style and body of a particular figure, especially as it related to that figure's broader cultural role or significance. In his photograph of Robeson as Othello, for example, he caught the actor in a signature pose—frozen in the middle of a dramatic song or oration, his straight back, wide-legged stance and outreaching hand similar to his poses as the black emperor in Song of Freedom (see figure 2.17). His photograph of Paul and Essie Robeson together captures simultaneously the clever boldness of her gaze but also a certain proprietary

FIG 3.2. Harry Belafonte. NO. 1168. Photographer Carl Van Vechten. Van Vechten Trust / Yale Collection of American Literature, Beinecke Rare Book and Manuscript Library.

gleam as she looks at Robeson, whose matching eye-line gaze acknowledges their intimacy while his face in profile retains that "slightly mocking, slightly cynical smile" that so intrigued H. D. (see figure 2.10).[17]

Van Vechten's photographs of Belafonte capture the actor in the act of masking and revealing his face. In representing this paradigmatic performance gesture, there are subtle variations in meaning, affect, and effect between the two photographs. On the one hand, in the photograph of Belafonte removing the mask, he offers his face and body to his viewers as a lure. The subject opens himself to signification, to his interpellation as a subject by the gaze. His eyes look away; they do not press the image or pressure the gazer into an interaction with his look back. In not meeting our eyes, he lowers the mask to reveal the

FIG 3.3. Harry Belafonte. NO. 1167. Photographer Carl Van Vechten. Van Vechten Trust / Yale Collection of American Literature, Beinecke Rare Book and Manuscript Library.

face of someone to be looked at, someone whose body is available for the camera and the photographer. In the second, colorful image, however, Belafonte holds the silver mask up to partially hide his face. Together the mask and the face create two pairs of eyes, the black hole/white wall system of facialization revealed as a covering that now floats above, and veils, Belafonte's narrowing gaze. The latter, while still turned away from the viewer, seems less available and more indeterminate in its meaning, the face of the black male performer now hidden beneath the coverings of both his symbolic white mask and black skin. Even Belafonte's bodily pose shifts slightly between the two photographs. In the brighter image, his face, the deep V of his chest, his hands, are all open and shining with light, the silver mask shunted more to the side and in the shadows. In the second, darker image, the shadows bleed out more across the photograph's surface and Belafonte's hunched shoulders and clenched fist obstruct the viewer's access to his chest and hand exposed in the previous photograph.

This latter photograph is the image of the performer this chapter seeks to recapture, the actor holding something back from his audience, signaling with his very performance that he is also somewhere else and someone else behind the mask. The prop of the mask itself links Belafonte to the "player," the ritualized theatrical performer, and the performance tradition of black-on-black minstrelsy that first placed the black male actor before white American popular audiences in the first place. As in the case of Bert Williams's blackface mask, the silver mask here is a metonym for the performative visuality of skin color as a body covering that signifies race to the gaze. Here the gaze is not a personal look but the symbolic order's most powerful mechanism for assigning epidermal difference with meaning.

Unlike earlier in Bert Williams's moment, in the 1950s it is not black skin itself that hardens—if anything the epidermal surface, like the colorful film screen, becomes even more manipulable, even more the physiognomic ground for new performative identities and new processes of self-display for the black performer. In on-screen representations of skin color in the 1950s, it is the gaze itself that hardens, reifying and phallicizing blackness as "color" in a new social and political ideal. Through technologies of color, the gaze takes on its own kind of new, epidermalizing gestures, closing down and sealing up the liminal space of the film screen as a permeable borderline. In the twenty years or so since Paul Robeson's experiments with film, the cinematic screen of the Technicolor 1950s was less a membrane of intercorporeity than a hard canvas for the gaze's projection of a racializing stain that would define some of the political forms of blackness developing in what would also come to be known as the Bandung era.

Harry Belafonte's film career in the United States during the 1950s was shaped by the reality James Baldwin characterized in the opening statement of *Nobody Knows My Name*: "The question of color, especially in this country, operates to hide the graver questions of the self."[18] In his Technicolor films, skin color becomes the flip side of the gaze's reification of racial relations, covering over the complexities of the interracial sexual relation as a space of intercultural interaction in a decolonizing world. Both the tropes and the technics of color created a cinematic medium for freezing race relations visually as a thing rather than as a process, as a social problem of othering rather than the psychic encounter of like subjectivities. Cinematic technologies of light and color became the means of refiguring both black and white actors and actresses as ciphers moving in a choreographed fantasy landscape of miscegenation.

Like Van Vechten's paired images of the masked and unmasked actor, however, two signature Belafonte films from this decade, *Island in the Sun* and *The World, the Flesh and the Devil*, both revealed the ways in which the actor and his audiences were invested in the new political meanings of skin color emerging in this decade and found ways to crack the shell of color to reveal the deeper problem of epidermalization as a way of representing male blackness as an idealized, eroticized image on-screen. Once again, the black male actor's relationship with his predominantly white American audience in the 1950s, and the dynamics of interracial cultural proximity and social intimacy such a relationship entailed, played out in public portrayals of black-white love and sexual relations that aimed to tame and regulate the potentials for consensuality between multiracial bodies.

"Will Hollywood Let Negroes Make Love?"

What makes any man so appealing to the nation's women (or youngsters) that they swoon over him, sigh and squeal over him, rave and pant over him, is partly an enigma. But, as the saying goes, you have it or you don't. Harry Belafonte does. —ARNOLD SHAW, *Belafonte*

A common explanation for Harry Belafonte's appeal during the 1950s was his "color," a term encompassing both the color of his skin and the white standards of male beauty the actor was seen to possess. As the black novelist Bill Attaway described in an unauthorized biography written by Arnold Shaw: "At the present stage of the struggle for human freedom, the need is for a bridge Negro—one who serves to connect white and Negro. Harry fills that need remarkably. Although he is brown-skinned and unmistakably Negro, his handsomeness is acceptable in terms of white standards of beauty. Brown up Tab Hunter, and you could hardly tell him from Harry Belafonte."[19] By 1960, the year Shaw published his biography, Belafonte had so become the standard of male beauty that he in turn became the model for white matinee idols like Tab Hunter, as one of Belafonte's white female costars exclaimed: "That man has no bad angles! . . . Why, he's a white Belafonte!" Attaway felt that Belafonte's status as an "interim Negro" partly accounted for his "phenomenal rise and his widespread acceptance as a matinee idol."[20]

Color, complexion, and physiognomy alone, however, do not offer a thick enough explanation for Belafonte's star appeal, especially since just a few years later, a man with a similar West Indian background but very different features would emerge as the new, iconic African American male movie star—Sidney

Poitier. Attaway understood the white public's acceptance of both Belafonte and Poitier, in different decades, as evidence for the progress of the movement for racial integration:

> But the fact is that we are at an interim stage in humanity's fight for racial equality. First, we had movies like Pinky . . . acceptance only of the Negro who did not seem to be Negro. . . . The present level of public taste—a higher one—is one of accepting the Negro as a Negro, provided his physical appeal is that of a white person. That's Harry. . . . The third stage is Sidney Poitier, who is less handsome in Caucasian terms but beautiful on a Negro level. It is a testimonial to the work of the good people who have been conducting the fight for freedom that Sidney's acceptance is so rapid. We are moving.[21]

In the passage of time between the two black male actors' rise to prominence, however, color served as both a trope and a template for reconfiguring and projecting American race relations in epidermal terms. To sharpen, then, what it means to say that color was a source of Belafonte's success and acceptance in white American society during the 1950s and 1960s, we need to specify how the treatment of color can be linked to the hardening of black-white relations during the period.

Harry Belafonte, or what he represented in the white popular cultural imagination of the 1950s, became the trope for containing the sociocultural permeability between the races within the boundaries of a new set of politico-cultural laws. James Baldwin argued that in *Carmen Jones*, the actor's second film with Dorothy Dandridge, one of the most prominent black actresses at the time, "the Negro male is still too loaded a quantity for [the moviemakers] to know quite how to handle. The result is that Mr. Belafonte is really not allowed to do anything more than walk around looking like a spaniel."[22] It feels almost trite to say that Harry Belafonte's sex appeal was another key component of his star appeal. As Joseph Roach also observes about "It," his term for an entertainer's indefinable charisma: "Most of us immediately assume that It has to do with sex, and we're right, but mainly because everything has to do with sex."[23] However, the sexuality Shaw describes as being at the heart of the black film star's "it-ness" or charisma—"you have it or you don't"—refers directly back to the primal scene that Roach also argues was a defining force in performance cultures of the circum-atlantic Americas. Repeated here as an epigraph to this chapter, it is this same primal scene, relations between black men and white women, that extended across the cultural screen to shape the psychosocial dimensions of Belafonte's celebrity, his "it-ness," as the 1950s' first "Negro matinee idol." The focus on Belafonte's sexuality during his popular reign in the United States in the 1950s opens up a set of questions about the place of the miscegenation narrative, with its primal scene of black male–white female intimacy, at that midcentury moment, in the heart of an American racial unconscious and a distinctly New World history of sexual formation.

In white audiences' responses and reactions to Harry Belafonte in the 1950s, histories of colonial desire were sublimated through the presentation of cross-racial desire on the colorful film screen. In the 1950s, the world of "Gaze Esthetics," as Charles Eidsvik describes, was one "in which film-makers left time for the viewer to contemplate the mise-en-scène," and the contemplation of color itself became a cinematic medium for renegotiating race relations made more tense in the context of the emergent civil rights and decolonization movements.[24] Technicolor films created "a vacuum in which the spectacle of color," in its racial dimensions, could be "divested of its danger."[25] The reemergence of miscegenation as a racy topic, paired with the cinematographic use of color for an anamorphic white gaze, exposed once again the not-so-secret secret shaping intercultural interaction. This was the historical reality that the races do mix, and have mixed, despite all prescriptions and regulations to the contrary. New World discourses of miscegenation have always legislated against the forbidden sexual act of crossing racial lines, while simultaneously attesting to the very prevalence of such acts and colonial desires in the creole Atlantic world.

The fifties saw a surge in films of interracial romance in the United States, a surge partially inspired by Belafonte and Dandridge's later film together, *Island in the Sun*.[26] However, this surge takes place within the context of an increased and more generalized interest in representing blackness itself on-screen. Later miscegenation films would crystallize the intimate dynamic between white audiences and black actors by substituting the white female love interest as a surrogate for the audience's gaze. As early as *Carmen Jones*, however, a film with an all-black cast still engaged the miscegenated gaze of an audience preoccupied with the representation of blackness. As an issue of *Tan* magazine revealed, with its cover image of Belafonte and his costar, Dorothy Dandridge, framed by the screaming headline "Will Hollywood Let Negroes Make Love?," regardless of a film's intra-racial rather than interracial setting the issue of black people making love still shaped the film's fraught cultural terrain.[27]

In his review of *Carmen Jones*, James Baldwin pointed to a more layered reading of those Technicolor films from the 1950s in which color signifies as both medium and message, form and content, technological vehicle and framing plot, for containing America's messy, contradictory, desegregating, sociocultural reality. Engaging in the type of in-depth analysis of cinematic representations of the black body that figures such as Dyer, Silverman, and Roach have performed more recently, Baldwin focused on the representation of those bodies as they revealed something about American conceptions of race and the sexual relation. Baldwin argued that "the only reason, finally, that the eroticism of *Carmen Jones* is more potent than, say, the eroticism of a Lana Turner vehicle is that *Carmen Jones* has Negro bodies before the camera and Negroes are associated in the public mind with sex."[28] He then clarified: "Since darker races always seem to have for lighter races an aura of sexuality, this fact is not distressing in itself. What is distressing is the conjecture this movie leaves one with as to what Americans take sex to be." For Baldwin, such films highlighted the haunting of official narratives of social equality by deeper cultural fears of the sexual mixing of the races. To contain such a fear, Technicolor films projected "in color, on a screen a block wide, and in stereophonic sound," a black "irreality" without the messy colors of either blacks' or whites' historicity, transforming black bodies and their fleshy relations instead into synthetic objects with colorful skins (see figure 3.4).[29]

Over the course of three films together, *Bright Road* in 1953, *Carmen Jones* in 1954, and *Island in the Sun* in 1957, Belafonte and Dandridge became star vehicles for transferring the Negro problem of the 1930s into the problem of color for the 1950s. *Carmen Jones* was director Otto Preminger's first Technicolor film, and the movie's publicity and advertising emphasized his use of the new visual technologies, "in CinemaScope" and "Color by Deluxe," to create the "lifeless unreality" of the colored world the film projected.[30] Baldwin critiqued the oft-hailed Technicolor-CinemaScope-Stereo triad for covering over and erasing the anamorphic (white) gaze in colorful, noisy spectacles of blackness, which "assuages their guilt about Negroes and it attacks none of their fantasies."[31] Instead, the mortifying of the black body in color was something "dreamed up by someone determined to prove that Negroes are as 'clean' and as 'modern' as white people."[32]

In the title of his review of *Carmen Jones*, "The Dark Is Light Enough," Baldwin played with the multiple cultural meanings of color, using the notion of "lightening" blackness to convey the sanitizing ways in which Hollywood used color to represent blackness to an American audience fearful of new forms of social and political integration between the races. In regards to the sexuality of the black actor or actress, in a film like *Carmen Jones*, "the technicolored bodies of Dandridge and Belafonte . . . are used for the maximum erotic effect [which] is a sterile and distressing eroticism, however, because it is occurring in a vacuum between two mannequins who clearly are not involved in anything more

serious than giving the customers a run for their money."[33] In the reception of such films as *Carmen Jones*, black love was as much an aspect of the miscegenated gaze as the filming of the black-white sexual relation. Crossing one cultural prohibition, the filming of black actors' erotic interactions on-screen, was merely a precursor to crossing another.

Creole Relations and the Color Complex in *Island in the Sun*

We have to justify our mores, our technics, our undercooked paleness and our verdigris vegetation. We are eaten away to the bones by these quiet and corrosive looks. . . . we can no longer rely on the privileges of our race, of our color, of our technics.
—JEAN-PAUL SARTRE, "Black Orpheus"

Between 1952 and 1953, as Harry Belafonte was receiving his first RCA Victor contract to record folk music, both James Baldwin and the Anglophone Caribbean writer George Lamming published their first novels, *Go Tell It On the*

FIG 3.5. *Island in the Sun*, David and Mavis. *Island in the Sun* © 1957 Twentieth Century Fox. All rights reserved.

Mountain and *In the Castle of My Skin*. As Belafonte was starring in his first feature film with Dandridge, *Bright Road*, Fanon was publishing *Black Skin, White Masks*, and Richard Wright was publishing his existential novel, *The Outsider*. One year later in 1954, Amiri Baraka moved to Greenwich Village to begin the first phase of his career as a Beat poet while Belafonte and Dandridge were teaming up again to film their much better known star vehicle, *Carmen Jones*. Among this group of writers, James Baldwin was the one who most effectively bridged the popular and literary worlds by explicitly connecting media images of blackness to older colonial discourses but also by observing the black and colonial male writer's investments in crafting a new sense of the freed black self.

Belafonte's early crossover success with white American audiences had partly to do with the romantic place of the West Indies in the United States imagination during the 1950s.[34] Hailed as the "calypso king," Belafonte's celebrity rivaled that of the other king of North American popular culture, Elvis Presley.[35] Together with his second public persona, that of the first "Negro matinee idol," Belafonte embodied both on and off the screen a new way for American audiences to manage the tensions and forces spilling out from the colonial worlds outside of the nation and the black worlds within it.

One film in particular captured Belafonte's unique place at the intersection of decolonization and civil rights politics, the Twentieth Century Fox production, *Island in the Sun* (1957). A Hollywood film with an American director, based on a novel by a British writer, set on an island in the West Indies on the brink of ending British colonial rule, and starring a transatlantic cast of actors, *Island in the Sun* was "a Caribbean metaphor for American racial tensions . . . as much a crusade as a moneymaker."[36] Rather than substituting one narrative for the other, *Island in the Sun* portrays hybrid discussions of race converging in the space between the early civil rights movement in the United States and the first signs of global decolonization evident in the organizing around the Bandung conference in 1955.

Just two years before the film's production, the world was abuzz with news of a planned meeting of African and Asian leaders in Bandung, Indonesia. This meeting put geopolitical questions of African and Asian sovereignty, economics, and ideology on the table, marking also the historical emergence of a transnational consciousness defined by coloniality.[37] The 1950s turned out to be a watershed decade in the black world's organized efforts to update the Pan-African framework of social transformation for a decolonizing world. A new name for black and colonial peoples emerged from the discussions in and around Bandung, the idea of a "Third World" of nonaligned states, which some imagined as the late twentieth-century version of the Third Estate, creating a third space beyond the tensions of the Cold War.[38]

For some, Bandung was also a catalyst for the further consolidating of a black anticolonial politics, what Sartre, describing the Negritude authors in 1948–1951, referred to as the rise of a "Black Orpheus": "Here are black men standing, looking at us, and I hope that you—like me—will feel the shock of being seen."[39] In the mirror of the black gaze, Sartre saw the "undercooked paleness and . . . verdigris vegetation" of a dying colonialism and its white racial imaginary. One year after Bandung, in 1956, a group of prominent black male writers held their own international meeting, the first Conference of Negro-African Writers and Artists in Paris at the Sorbonne. Together they focused on the cultural implications of the political moment for a poetics of blackness. Two distinct positions emerged on the question of the cultural legacies blacks shared across New and Old Worlds.

The Negritude poet Aimé Césaire called for the decolonization of the black mind, the eradication of the "inferiority complex . . . inculcated by the colonizer," while Richard Wright argued for the benefits of the intercultural encounter between colonizer and colonized, such as the inheritances of the Enlightenment.[40] For Baldwin, what both speeches left out was the black interior, the realm of the black cultural unconscious. Between political notions and cultural expressions of blackness, Baldwin wondered about a third and neglected space that held the unconscious strategies black and colonial peoples had constructed in their struggle to endure the vicissitudes of colonial modernity.[41] Baldwin felt that only George Lamming, a "genuine writer," redirected the discussion toward the internal and unconscious black life.[42] In a phrase insightfully pitting epidermal politics against a more affective notion of black identity freed from colonial rule, Baldwin quoted with admiration Lamming's dismay that "a great many Negroes . . . were in what he called 'the skin trade' [whereas] Lamming was insisting on the respect which is due the private life."[43] Lamming's words resonated with Baldwin's interrogations of the "private life" and sexual fantasies of blackness Americans linked to each other in the politics and discourses of the skin.[44]

Two years after Bandung and one year after the black writers' conference, Belafonte and Dandridge teamed up for *Island in the Sun*. While their earlier films, *Bright Road* and *Carmen Jones*, explored dimensions of black heterosexual love, *Island in the Sun* was an intercultural compendium of black-white heterosexual romances, playing out in a space that spread between the Caribbean and the United States.[45] In this same year, "Harry became big news to the big circulation magazines—[it was] the year in which he became a celebrity as distinguished from a celebrated artist."[46] *Island in the Sun* played an important role in the actor's crossover celebrity. Much of the hubbub surrounding him involved accounts of a reputed kiss between the black actor and his white female costar in the film, Joan Fontaine. As reported in the pages of *Ebony* in July of that year, the prospect of an interracial kiss in the film caused quite a stir. This would have been the first time such an event was captured on American film.[47] The public discourse surrounding this kiss set certain parameters and limits that governed the representation of interracial sexual relations onscreen more broadly.

"'To Kiss Or Not to Kiss?,'" an inset within the broader *Ebony* article on the film's interracial politics, focuses on the prohibition against interracial kissing that shaped the film's reception—"the Hollywood censors had made their [concerns] felt on the interracial love scenes. . . . Even though Dandridge and Rennie and Belafonte and Fontaine are supposed to be in love, they are not allowed to kiss for the cameras."[48] The producer Darryl F. Zanuck responded that "there is no scene that calls for kissing. . . . There was no conscious effort to avoid it." He was right, but only in the sense that the prohibition against kissing reflects a deeper interdiction against miscegenation—social equality as sexual equality—that the film is not explicitly aware it is avoiding crossing, especially given the moviemakers' overt goal to use the film to take American racial discourse in a more liberally progressive direction.

The significance of this virtual kiss, as one lens through which an audience experienced Belafonte as a figure for integration, can be seen in the simultaneous coverage of Belafonte's marriage to the white and Native American dancer Julie Robinson that same year. To an *Ebony* readership, Belafonte's personal adventures in crossing the color line were as fascinating as the interracial politics of the film. To nail home the point that the two were related, the *Ebony* issue published in July 1957 included a picture of Belafonte and Robinson on the cover, appearing less than a year after *Jet*'s cover image of the actor with his first wife, Marguerite.[49] The *Ebony* issue also included a "first person piece" by Belafonte entitled, "Why I Married Julie," which ran with the following introductory caption: "Harry Belafonte, acknowledged king of the folk singers and the reluctant king of calypso, shocked many of his female fans when he divorced his wife Marguerite and married dancer Julie Robinson. 'Why,' they asked, 'Why did he do it?' To give Harry a chance to answer, EBONY has opened its pages to the singer."[50] Placing Belafonte's essay under the section "Race," and the piece on *Island in the Sun* under the section "Entertainment," *Ebony* contributed to a national conversation concerning integration and, by implication, miscegenation, in a decolonizing civil rights world.

The controversies concerning whether both Belafonte and Dandridge could kiss, touch, or marry white partners and costars in the 1950s also represented white America's much deeper wrestling with their greater access to blackness during this period. Articles in the American press debated not just whether a black man could kiss a white woman on-screen—blacks' sexual freedom and agency—but also whether the white audience was ready to look publicly at such a scene given its powerful, private meanings. *Island in the Sun* tested, in a sense, the parameters of the gaze concerning its specular claims on blackness and the fascination with Belafonte's indefinable charisma.[51]

Island in the Sun displaces civil rights tensions between black and white Americans onto the colonial desires of creole subjects in a postindependence, self-governing Caribbean. The "creole" is the figure for both the colonial of New World origin (of any and all races) and the New World subject of mixed race (a later evolution of the term). It is also, as Robert Young argues about the hybrid, "a resolutely heterosexual category."[52] Interracial heterosexuality becomes the space where sexual difference converges with racial difference, and both revolve around the question of color. For Sean Goudie, "creole" also refers to the state of political independence and economic dependence that the United States found itself in after the Revolutionary War. Goudie coins the phrase "creole complex" to describe the chiasmic mixture of economic and cultural relations still tying the new republic to the rest of the New World colonies.[53] Here the notion of a creole complex becomes useful for naming the matrix of interracial, heterosexual relations that we find in an American film, set in the Caribbean, with American, African American, Caribbean, and British actors, and using the trope of miscegenation to hybridize American race relations with intersecting issues of Caribbean self-governance and separation from colonial rule.[54]

Island in the Sun uses the political question of black self-government as a cover story for what are really fears of social and cultural intermixture once the era of independence on the island has come and gone. In a scene late in the film, an American journalist asks the island's police commissioner if he thinks that West Indians can govern themselves. The real question of the film, however, is whether black and white subjects can learn to govern their own unruly sexual desires in an emerging, intercultural, decolonizing world. The fact that the American reporter asks this question of a British policeman is also relevant since the latter is the figure responsible for determining whether the prohibitions of colonial law will prevail, whether creole people as a whole will discipline themselves and obey racial laws as an internal compulsion once the political barriers upholding the old colonial color lines fall.

The film begins with a shot of Harry Belafonte guiding us into the world of the island of Santa Marta. Here the camera's gaze is very much that of the American tourist. In the issue of *Ebony* dated November 1948, Langston Hughes had introduced Jamaica to African Americans as a "prejudice-free" tourist destination with "an English-African charm all its own."[55] This "English-African charm" is much less evident in one of the film's main protagonists, the English creole Maxwell Fleury (played by the British actor James Mason). In the film's opening, Fleury is irrationally concerned that his wife is having an affair. He suffers from an inferiority complex concerning his status as a second son, the less appropriate inheritor of his father's colonial legacy.[56] Maxwell Fleury's insecurities are juxtaposed against the manly confidence of the governor's son, Ewan Templeton, recently returned to Santa Marta from the Middle East. Associated with British colonial power and the romantic image of the European colonialist as a foreign adventurer, Templeton is more worldly than Fleury, the latter representing the European son still bound to the colonial past.

An early scene at the Government House, an architectural symbol of empire's colonial governmentality, sets in motion all the different romantic subplots of the film. These include Ewan Templeton's attraction to Jocelyn Fleury, Maxwell's sister, played by Joan Collins, and a second romance between a young shopgirl from the island, played by Dorothy Dandridge, and the governor's aide, a kind of adopted son of the governor. Jocelyn Fleury, the creole woman, and Margot Seaton, the local woman of color, act as foils for each other, representing the two different faces of a creolized, colonial femininity. They both fall somewhere on the color spectrum between the blackness of the local island women and the racial and sexual purity of Maxwell Fleury's white wife, Sylvia. While Jocelyn Fleury is clearly in her element at the Government House, Dorothy Dandridge's character does not belong. She attends the party as an uninvited guest, the date of the local trade unionist David Boyeur, played by Harry Belafonte. Throughout the film, Margot Seaton finds her proper place in outdoor scenes that also introduce the black people and culture of the island. Her racial position is marked symbolically in one important scene indoors when the governor's aide, Dennis Archer, proclaims his love.

Posed purposefully beside an ethnic black mask, a still shot captures Margot's association with epidermal blackness on the island (see figure 3.6). Throughout the film, versions of this stylized black mask will figure as an important marker of racial identity, both overdetermining and demonstrating the incapacity of physiognomy alone to register the deeper symbolic meanings of blackness in the decolonizing realities of the film. In the world outside the film, Dorothy Dandridge's own "color" placed her in a complicated relation to blackness, part of the social context the film indirectly refers to (what it "skin trades" on, one might say, using Lamming's phrase). Dandridge was the era's quintessential "brown girl," the female figure of racial mixture invoked by those who feared social equality. The discourse of sexual equality and the fear of the brown girl always shadowed discourses of social equality in the 1950s.[57] For both blacks and whites of the era, the brown girl was the figure for blackness in a creolizing relation with whiteness, and while she was idealized by some she was vilified by others in the much more ambivalent national discussions of integration and miscegenation.

In Margot Seaton and Dennis Archer's idealized romance, *Island in the Sun* attempts to offer a multiracial audience a way of transforming the old psychological effects of miscegenation between master and slave into a new romance of interracial love. After asking Margot to marry him, Archer abandons his post with the governor to fulfill his dream of becoming a writer. Symbolically, he gains the power to rewrite the colonial narrative of miscegenation as a modern romance with a woman of color from the islands. In *Black Skin, White Masks*, Fanon had nothing but scorn for the kind of option Margot's choice represents, describing the woman of color's desire for a white man as "an attempt to acquire — by internalizing them — assets that were originally prohibited," namely, the benefits accruing from the privileged status of whiteness.[58] In *Island in the Sun*, however, this reading of the black woman's desire as subjugated to whiteness breaks up in the actress's performance on-screen.

Dorothy Dandridge brings a coquettish wryness to her portrayals of Margot's interactions with her white male lover during his courtship. In the still shot of Dandridge beside the mask, one sees the glimmers of this attitude as the camera captures the wry smile on her face, the slight upturn to the corner of her lips suggesting both resignation and amusement. Together, these facial expressions capture the complex power dynamics of her position in relation to Archer and his proposal. Baldwin argued that even within the constraints of the film industry's "misuse" of the black actor and actress, both still manage to give "moments—indelible moments, created, miraculously, beyond the confines of the script: hints of reality, smuggled like contraband into a maudlin tale, and with enough force, if unleashed, to shatter the tale to fragments."[59] In this instance the camera catches one such moment as Dandridge comments, in her facial gestures, on some of the contradictions that slip outside of the film's frame.[60] The ironies of this scene lie precisely in the lacunae of the kiss that never happens, which marks on the screen the absent presence of the world outside of the film.

This absent kiss, in limiting the degree of interracial physical intimacy the film can portray, also undermines the guiding premise of this perfect interracial romance. The romance between Margot and Dennis feels unreal not because of unconvincing acting but because of the "irreality" of the diegetic world the film seeks to convey. Dandridge's look and smile at the camera take the place of the kiss that should have been and put to the test the reality being constructed in the scene itself, the romance of crossing the taboo of the color line. Even with Dandridge's graceful gesture, however, there is nothing radical in the structure of Margot and Dennis's romance. Together they simply repeat older colonial sexual relations between white masters and the women of color, their slaves and servants, to whom they had free sexual access during colonialism and slavery. In the social system of sexual relations prescribed for a soon-to-be ex-colonial society, Margot and Dennis's romance merely rewrites the old narrative of miscegenation as regulated rather than forbidden. Their open secret is legitimized by the law of marriage, as evident on Margot's hand in the engagement ring she wears in her new position as the secretary for the governor.

No such legitimation attends Jocelyn Fleury's romance, whose sexual aggression as the creole daughter in pursuit of Ewan Templeton is in direct contrast to Margot Seaton's demure flirtatiousness. During a romantic interlude, Jocelyn and Ewan Templeton are stranded together at the old plantation, Belle Fontaine. A local islander's prank of disabling their car leads to their decision to spend the night at the plantation, their illicit act taking on by association an atmosphere of black mischief. This association is made literal in the sinister shot of a black man in a white mask watching them, his gaze literally represent-

FIG 3.7. *Island in the Sun*, the man in the mask. *Island in the Sun* © 1957 Twentieth Century Fox. All rights reserved.

ing the messy, loosening social boundaries between the races, the dangerous stain of black flesh lying beneath the mask's white skin (see figure 3.7). While this trickster figure connotes black sedition, he also signifies Jocelyn's sexual "corruption," the white mask signaling the possibility of a stain of blackness hidden underneath white feminine virtue. The stain attaches to both Jocelyn's and Fleury's skin literally when, later in the film, the scandal emerges that their grandmother may have been black. Jocelyn's willingness to have sex with Templeton outside of marriage already introduces the stain of miscegenation by the time this scandal emerges in the plot.

Harry Belafonte enters the film as the brash trade unionist David Boyeur in the early scene at the Government House party. Flinging his cigarette at the car of a local member of the European elite, he personifies the ideal of the home-grown island revolutionary, the aggressive display of his racialized masculinity contrasting with an earlier scene in which a cigarette butt becomes the catalyst for Maxwell Fleury's fears of his wife's infidelity. Boyeur is the second male figure whose confidence places him in direct contrast with Fleury, the insecure white creole. Belafonte's anatomical perfection, imaged often in the camera's many full-body shots of the actor, places him at the center of this complex of creolized sexual relations and hierarchies on the island. The goal of the film is to show how Belafonte's character must, for political reasons, transform the story of black male subjugation and romantic denial Fanon described as that of the black male abandonment-neurotic—"I do not wish to be loved and I will flee from love-objects"—into a narrative of his heroic self-separation from the complex of creole relations that characterize the film.[61] In the development of Belafonte's character, the mask of color, the mask of the skin, is politicized as his difference is idealized for the noblest of reasons, black self-determination.

In another scene Boyeur takes his white female love interest, Mavis Norman, on a tour of those areas on the island she has not been exposed to as a daughter of the colonial elite. As Sylvia Fleury's sister, her romance with Boyeur acts as a foil for Maxwell and Sylvia Fleury's marriage. Both couplings are linked by the sexuality of the white women, and the actress Joan Fontaine becomes the real-life "belle Fontaine" whose name puns on that of the Fleurys' plantation. The beautiful Fontaine is the primary stand-in for the audience whose sight line she shares as Belafonte introduces her to black Santa Marta.

When the couple stops to listen to a group of singing fishermen, Boyeur tells Mavis that she is hearing a song no tourist has ever heard, a kind of privileged hearing of the island's folk world.[62] A beautiful Technicolor shot captures this idealized, romantic moment as the couple shares a coconut while watching the fishermen singing (see figure 3.5). This very coconut, it turns out, is the replacement object for the missing kiss, as Joan Fontaine describes in "'To Kiss Or Not to Kiss?'": "At least I made them agree that Harry and I can drink out of the same cocoanut together in a scene. But they insist no kissing."[63] Belafonte holds up the coconut between them as the only tactile reminder of a kiss that was (never) to have been, marking the extra-diegetic reality of the film's racialized cultural context as the blind spot or vanishing point in the film.

Falling victim to his own fantasies of the interracial sexual relation, Fanon described black male–white female pairings as having "automatically a romantic aspect" because "when a white woman accepts a black man [it] is a giving, not a seizing."[64] In Mavis and David's relationship, due to his developing self-sufficiency and autonomy, the white female has nothing to give him but her loyalty. At a certain point on their island tour, Mavis makes the gauche mistake of putting on a black mask hanging in a vendor's stall. With Dandridge's shot with the ebony mask as an earlier reference point, the scene's not-so-subtle symbolism is that, in desiring to wear the black mask, Mavis gives herself over to blackness and her desire for Boyeur, the local black male. Boyeur responds aggressively to her act, however, slapping the mask away with a blur of his hand against the brilliant Technicolor backdrop of the scene. The violence of his action reestablishes the necessary boundaries between blackness and whiteness in this newly politicized creole environment. She is prohibited from displaying any of the qualities of the "seizing" colonial elites. Boyeur also polices himself, delineating where the colonial past ends and where the new future of a black nation begins. His act foreshadows the role he will play later as a political leader on the island.

Island in the Sun's real strength lies in the way it manages to speak in two filmic voices, reminding us that despite the plot, the real answer to the film's questions concerning self-governance exists at the level of sexual desire. The "color problem" in Santa Marta takes on a specific meaning when the scandal erupts that Maxwell and Jocelyn's father had a black slave mother. Fleury's hysterical repetition of the words "tar brush" as he commits a murder of passion makes it clear how race becomes the cover story for his own inadequate sense of manhood. Soon after, he turns his discovery of a black ancestor to his advantage by deciding to run against David Boyeur in an upcoming local election. In the scene of the political rally that follows, Fleury and Boyeur are pitted against each other as antagonists, figures for the colonizer and the colonized, Boyeur's hostile skepticism evident as he and a crowd of black islanders watch Maxwell's opening speech (see figure 3.8). Following Fleury's speech, the confrontation between Fleury and Boyeur escalates in shots that emphasize visually the many kinds of lines that separate them. When Fleury tries to cross a bridge between himself and his black audience, unbridgeable political lines and impermeable color lines are reinforced in the imagery of the roped-off ramp that leads from the podium to the assembled crowd (see figure 3.9). The vertical poles and lines of ropes serve as barriers separating the men from each other and defining each of their relationships to the crowd. Boyeur asserts in his speech that color — as a social and historical relation of power, sexual exploitation, and oppression — is the only truth the black audience should take away from Fleury's discourse of the master. Color is a truth that keeps the creolized worlds of colonizer and native apart, and it cannot be covered over by new fantasies of miscegenation. Boyeur steps forward to speak, blocking Fleury's exit and forcing his retreat back to the stage. He returns to the platform and stands underneath a banner that, partially cut off in the shot, proclaims where his true racial loyalties lie, as "Eury" rather than "Fleury for the People." Boyeur stares forward into the camera but points at Fleury, accusing the gaze beyond the camera of its complicity with "Eury," the European colonial's descendant (see figure 3.10). David Boyeur (Boy-Eur), Europe's boy who once maintained the grounds of plantations such as Belle Fontaine, replaces Maxwell Fleury as politics steps in to place the fate of the island in his hands.

When filmmakers first started working with Technicolor, they worried that color would be too prominent an aspect of a film and would take away from the

FIG 3.8. *Island in the Sun*, Boyeur at the political rally. *Island in the Sun* © 1957 Twentieth Century Fox. All rights reserved.

FIG 3.9. *Island in the Sun*, Harry Belafonte and James Mason #1. *Island in the Sun* © 1957 Twentieth Century Fox. All rights reserved.

FIG 3.10. *Island in the Sun*, Harry Belafonte and James Mason #2. *Island in the Sun*
© 1957 Twentieth Century Fox. All rights reserved.

film's narrative in the audience's viewing experience. In *Island in the Sun* color
is itself the narrative; it provides both the content and the form of the cover
story in the film's nervous exploration of interracial proximity and desire. New
visual technologies aestheticize and romanticize older colonial relations in a
new miscegenation fantasy, while the color technics of the film offer powerful
visual support to a new symbolic fiction of race emerging in the era of decolonization. This fiction frames both black and colonial masculinity, and the black
male–white female love relation, in a new narrative of renunciation and political radicalism held together by the trope of the skin.

In the denouement of Mavis and Boyeur's romance, the couple stands on a
beach watching a plane fly overhead as it leaves for England with the film's two
other couples, Margot and Dennis, and Jocelyn and Ewan. Noting their happy
endings, Mavis wistfully asks whether the white female and the black male can
have their own miscegenation fantasy. In the dialogue that follows, the film
works to assert a Caribbean, black nationalist politics over and above its sexual
subplots. Boyeur's immediate, abrupt response establishes that the freedoms
afforded by independence and self-governance stop firmly at the sexual color
line, even in these soon-to-be ex-colonies. However, the ironies of the intercultural sexual relation also play out in their conversation as they each tell a

pair of "lies" that unconsciously reveals their control over the fiction of their romance's inevitable end, and the deeper tensions undergirding their black male–white female sexual relation:

MAVIS. In the girl's case, does it work the other way around? . . .
   When it's the other way around, does it make any difference?
DAVID. Out here, yes.
MAVIS. How big is Santa Marta? It's 50 miles long. There are . . .
   other countries.
DAVID. My skin is my country. . . .
MAVIS. Do you care what stupid and prejudiced people think?
DAVID. . . . It would be inevitable.
MAVIS. What would be?
DAVID. That night that you'd forget yourself and call me a nigger.
MAVIS. You can't mean that. You can't possibly mean that!
DAVID. No, I don't.
MAVIS. Then why did you say it?
DAVID. Because here is my world. These are my people and this is
   where I belong. If I went to England who would I be? What would
   I be? . . . My people have their freedom. They've got a vote, they've
   got power now and I've got to show them how to use it. . . . Here
   in Santa Marta, or go to St. Kitts, and Barbados, and Grenada, the
   whole archipelago.
MAVIS. . . . You don't want that power for your people, you want it for
   yourself! . . . People don't count with you. Nothing counts with you
   but power!
DAVID. You can't mean that.
MAVIS. No I don't. You're right and I'm wrong, I'm wrong and you're
   right.
DAVID. And that's the end is it?
MAVIS. Yes, that's the end.⁶⁵

David and Mavis's dialogue draws our attention to the discursive nature of romance itself, with its sexualized projections about the other that are more symbolic and imaginary than real. David's renunciation of Mavis serves a nationalist politics that extends across the Caribbean archipelago, the film thereby providing, in his voice, a new ideological rationale against miscegenation more suited to decolonizing times. However, as each confesses to a lie about what they said but did not mean, or did not mean to say, the film reopens the gap it has tried to close when the character's reasons—her racism, his will to power—are revealed as flimsy excuses hiding the most secret knowledge of the film. This is the reality that what thwarts their romance is less their individual choices than a social taboo against miscegenation that still stands as the overarching logic of the film. That taboo must be constantly re-created and reasserted in different historical moments because the deeper truth of the interracial sexual relation is that a politics of skin color alone is a very thin veil covering over the problems and fraught dynamics of intercultural intimacy and interracial desire.[66]

"Does Belafonte Get Girl in 'End of World?'": Escaping the Miscegenation Fantasy in *The World, the Flesh and the Devil*

The postindependence miscegenation fantasy of *Island in the Sun* relies less on an authoritative, social injunction against mixing than on the internal injunction that one must police oneself by choosing freely not to mix; self-regulating not what you do but what you *want* to do.[67] At the film's end, Boyeur rejects "la belle Fontaine," renouncing everything Joan Fontaine's character represents as an object of his desire. For those watching the film and carried along by their unfolding romance, this resolution is satisfactory since we have already enjoyed the synthetic experience of stymied black male–white female desire, as it has been performed alongside the film's ending of poetic self-denial and heroic restraint. Belafonte's character in *Island in the Sun* offers one phallic fiction of blackness, the renunciation of whiteness as love-object for the sake of a higher racial cause.

In 1959 Belafonte used financing from his own production company, Harbel Productions, to make *The World, the Flesh and the Devil*, another film that explicitly addressed the complications of interracial desire. Once again the black male hero rejects the white female character as an embodiment of the temptations of the "flesh," and the film seems to arrive at the same narrative impasse as *Island in the Sun*. The cover of the issue of *Jet* dated December 1958 ran with the headline "Does Belafonte Get Girl in 'End of World?'" as if wondering whether this time, white audiences would get to consummate their relationship with Belafonte through another miscegenation romance and another white female cipher.

The World, the Flesh and the Devil goes much further than *Island in the Sun*, however, choosing not to idealize the black male act of rejection as if it is in the service of some higher ideal or greater political narrative. Rather than falling back on easy notions of black political autonomy and masculine self-sufficiency, Belafonte's character Ralph Burton must instead take responsibility for his own internalization of the "world's" symbolic fictions, including the white female eroticization of black masculinity, and crack the shell of an idealized and calcified blackness to make possible alternative aspects of identity in an apocalyptic, insecure, uncharted, relational, and interpersonal world. *The World, the Flesh and the Devil* leaves us at the very point that Fanon described as the epitome of the black male's critical self-reflection in a post-colonial world: "Mak[e] people ashamed of their existence. . . . to become aware of the potentials they have forbidden themselves, of the passivity they have paraded . . . to upset, if necessary, the chain of command, but in any case, and most assuredly, *to stand up to the world*."[68] The film's protagonists, the last three people left on earth after a devastating atomic explosion, are very much in a confrontation with the world, a seemingly inanimate world deprived of other people, and yet, still shaped by the laws of human society.[69]

In *The World, the Flesh and the Devil*, the interracial couple Ralph Burton and Sarah Crandall, played by Belafonte and Inger Stevens, cannot leave their doomsday scenario and escape either to England or to another island. Since there is no other social or political reality to escape into, the primary social forces Ralph Burton and Sarah Crandall face are those that they have internalized and are fighting within themselves. By the time the white male character, Ben Hacker, joins them in the last third of the film, his role as the oppressive white male rival is almost incidental. Hacker simply presents an outlet for the unbearable tension Sarah and Ralph have been carrying between them throughout the film as they negotiate the terms of their interracial attraction and relation.[70] Ben Hacker relieves the couple and the audience of the incredible burden of their own unacted-upon fantasies and unsymbolizable desires. He becomes the externalization and rationalization of the big Other's prohibition against black male–white female desire that both the characters and the audience have been wrestling with throughout the film. Moreover, he *is* the other, embodied most obviously by the audience, whose gaze is the necessary precondition for the sexual tension exhibited by the interracial couple.

For most critics, the power of *The World, the Flesh and the Devil* lies in its black-and-white, CinemaScope enhanced imagery of an evacuated, empty New York City as seen from Ralph Burton's perspective soon after he arrives there from Pennsylvania. Belafonte is filmed against the backdrop of towering bridges, immense skyscrapers, and mammoth monuments as they loom over and around him. The viewer gets a powerful visual impression of the city as testimony to a human civilization now facing extinction. This monumental, architecturally dominant New York City landscape is inhuman in affect. As Ralph arrives in New York and develops a relationship with Sarah amidst the emptiness of this urban landscape, the film conveys timeless questions concerning human loneliness and the forces that draw very different kinds of people together and keep them apart.

What is less obvious in the film's surface narrative is the ways in which Ralph Burton's isolation in this surreal landscape is not that dissimilar from his earlier position at the very start of the film before the world's end. As a black miner working in Pennsylvania, Ralph Burton is already isolated before he ever arrives in New York City, and the film spends quite a bit of time with him in these early scenes as he is buried alive underground in a mine. When Ralph emerges from the mine and realizes that he may be the last man left on earth, the world he faces merely reflects the isolation he has already lived with among his coworkers. In the opening scenes of the film, Burton sits in the dark mine with only a flickering candle for company. As he calls out to his fellow miners, Belafonte laces his voice and tone with a mix of brashness, sarcasm, and desperation, all of which work together to convey the character's consternation that no one on the outside will care enough to rescue him. As he digs himself out of the mine, he exits through a boxlike shaped tunnel that we see from the perspective of a long shot, as we look down the ladder he will climb up. Almost as if he is ascending from the underworld, this shot matches the viewer's sensation of Ralph's physical and social distance, buried deep and far away as he is from an audience who may or may not be listening to his cries for help.

Ralph's solitude in the film's opening scenes draws us into sympathy with his aloneness as we put ourselves in his place in an act of identification. An attraction of the "end of the world" survivor narrative is precisely the protagonist's journey to find his real self when distanced from the clamor and demands of the symbolic order, the system of social rules and values by which he has heretofore lived his life. As Ralph Burton climbs out of the Pennsylvania mine, the audience prepares to undergo this journey with him, both out into the world and further into the self. In shots of empty buildings and streets the camera conveys how frightening it is to be left alone without the shelter and protection of that social world.

At a deeper interpretive level, however, the camera's angles and visual perspectives in *The World, the Flesh and the Devil* also work to reassure the viewer that Ralph Burton is really *never* alone. In actuality, he is *always* in the viewer's sight lines. Burton's exit from the mine is filmed from the viewer's perspective. He remains a full-length figure in the frame as the camera moves backward and pans around him to capture the abandoned area of the mine site. Rather than looking at the scene through his eyes, we are looking at him dwarfed by the scene's surrounding landscape. At no point are we afforded a sight line from

Ralph's point of view. Thus, the audience never experiences for itself the desolation of looking out and seeing no one; that experience is Burton's alone, on the grid, and instead we watch him from the security of our populated world.

This gap between Ralph Burton's subjective perspective on his dilemma and the anamorphic perspective of the camera and the audience watching him is part of what makes his arrival in New York City so eerie. As he runs through the streets identifying himself, yelling, "It's me, Ralph Burton, I'm alive," the camera's high-angle shots leave the impression that the city is a silent but sentient entity looking back at him. As his shouts bounce and echo from sky-high buildings, extremely high-angled camera shots place the audience in the omniscient position of looking down at the character. Anamorphic camera angles point sharply down on Ralph Burton, positioning and locating him in their sight line from city buildings so high that the shots create an intense boxed-in feeling, filled with vertiginous lines and an overall claustrophobic effect. These sight lines do not evoke a godly figure so much as a visual point of view stemming from the actual buildings themselves looming over him. This is the mortal city, a monument to civilization that, even when abandoned by human society, retains its anamorphic perspectives and angles of vision. When Burton's voice echoes throughout the streets, the Other, Man in the abstract, answers back, New York's built environment serving as an echoing testament to human civilization itself.

In shots that emphasize the angles and corners of buildings, the perpendicular lines of objects in the environment, the camera creates a visual echo of our perception that Ralph Burton is not completely alone, or rather, that he is still the specular subject being watched and photo-graphed. Even the last man on earth, experiencing such intense feelings of isolation and dislocation, is still a located subject situated in the tangible remnants of the social world left standing around him. What is eerie is less the loss of the symbolic order than the fear that reality may now start pressing in too keenly. The camera goes to great lengths to create the visual impression of Ralph Burton being boxed in, as if reality is much too close, the Real pressing in much too insistently, frightening and sinister in its uncanny immediacy, without the mediating narratives and symbolic systems we use to live and navigate in the world.

If freedom results from liberating oneself from one's inner conflicts and voices, in Ralph Burton's end-of-the-world scenario such a freedom is terrifying. In this film, "world" stands as much for material reality as for the social order that constructs and defines that reality. "World" also stands for Ralph Burton's symbiotic, intercorporeal relation to the world, not as a man now separated from it, but rather, as one revealed ever more starkly to be watched by the world as much as he is the one watching it. When Ralph accepts his dilemma, he essentially takes responsibility for preserving the symbolic order whose remnants are left behind in the buildings of New York. Burton becomes the custodian of the world civilization he once knew; he is the man left behind to preserve its most precious artifacts, for whomever or whatever comes afterward.

Like the spools of newsreel Ralph finds in the WKYL — NEWS BUREAU recording the last minutes of the end of the world, Burton's mission in the first third of the film becomes the recovery of a record of humanity's lost time at world's end. Burton needs to believe that the world of the past can be preserved for the future in his present. As he shops for groceries and engages in the routines of everyday life, *The World, the Flesh and the Devil* finds an ingenious way of figuring Ralph's efforts to memorialize the social relations of the world that has just ended. Ralph adopts two life-size department store mannequins as his companions, Betsy and Mr. Snodgrass, and his interactions with these two mannequins rehearse the dramatic conflict to come in the interracial triangle between Ralph, Sarah, and Ben Hacker.

Betsy and Snodgrass are effigies of white heteronormativity. Ideal types in dress, manner, and posture, down to the placement of their hands, they represent the reified best of everything world civilization had to offer, humanity at its most perfect and idealized. However, as mannequins they are also the ultimate ciphers, the ultimate representatives of the unreal — the irrealities — in human social relations. The male mannequin, Snodgrass, foreshadows and explains why the white male character, Ben Hacker, will need to appear in the last third of the film. Ralph's desire for Snodgrass's company reflects the average citizen's need for a figure — the ubiquitous "They," the subjectivized big Other — to whom one can attribute societal standards and expectations of behavior, even as one distances oneself from those standards as a rebellious, self-defined individual. Žižek terms this "interpassivity," our need to believe that someone else is out there believing what we know we should believe, doing the believing for us — of religious credos, liberal ideologies, multicultural discourses — thereby freeing us up to distance ourselves as individuals from the main tenets that regulate society.[71] An interpassive subjectivity is the underside of our symbolic fictions of individuality, allowing us to preserve the appearance of a gap between our individual subjectivity and the big Other's gaze.

The mannequin Snodgrass represents Burton's need for a social figure of regulation against whom he can rebel. Ralph looks at Snodgrass and complains, "Always smiling. Nobody can be that happy." Snodgrass is the big Other, the internalized gaze, the set of social codes that interpellate us as normal and happy. In the dynamic interplay between Betsy's aloof but potentially de-siring white female gaze and Snodgrass's friendly but ultimately regulatory look back, Ralph performs his sense of normalcy with an eye toward the gaze of the Other. He takes it as a given that he is excluded from Betsy and Snodgrass's imaginary world, even as he flirtatiously tells the mannequin Betsy that she is "too good for" Snodgrass.

In another scene, a distinctive, V-shaped tracking shot swivels to follow Belafonte as he walks between the mannequins singing them a song. Bela-fonte moves from the right corner of the room, where he pauses to turn Snod-grass's head so that the mannequin is watching him, to the left side of the room where he continues his song to Betsy. In this zigzag trajectory across the room, traversing the space, Burton reveals both his dependence on Snodgrass's gaze and his need to exert some form of agency, to take control by determining what he presents of himself on the grid for the big Other, Snodgrass, to look at. The social roles available to him, however, are limited to handy man, janitor, and — in this scene — entertainer. Ralph is only recognizable to the gaze in the image of Harry Belafonte the performer, the black entertainer, whose song actually removes him, briefly, from the diegetic action of the film.

In another set of photographs from his collection, Van Vechten captured again Harry Belafonte's distinctive social identity as the beloved black enter-tainer of American culture for the synthetic 1950s. Posed in the striped pants of a Harlequin-type figure, Belafonte is photo-graphed dancing, in an arrested twisting motion that creates for the gaze a beautiful, graceful line of the body (see figures 3.11 and 3.12). Ralph's act of traversing the room and manipulating the mannequins' gazes calls on them to recognize him in similar ways, as the "calypso singer" and "matinee idol" stepping like a puppet across the curtained space of the screen framed by the camera. Both in Van Vechten's photographs and in the shots from the scene, Harry himself becomes a kind of mannequin as gracefully posed as Betsy and Snodgrass.

In the film, however, this scene also marks the beginning of Ralph's "stand-ing up to the world," his act of rebellion against his own position on the grid and the social codes and laws embedded in Snodgrass as a projection of the black male's own inherited interdictions. Moments later, fed up with Snod-grass's ever-smiling presence, Burton throws the mannequin off the balcony of a penthouse apartment in a fit of rage. In Miklós Rózsa's musical score for the film, this scene is aptly titled "Snodgrass's Suicide," for it intentionally suggests the thin line, the symbiosis, between Snodgrass's passive, symbolic agency as a mannequin and Belafonte's act of aggression in throwing him away. When Ralph exclaims, "No sense, no feeling . . . You look at me but you don't see me,"

he expresses his frustration that he is also treated like a mannequin-object rather than a like subject in his relationship with the Other. It is less that Snodgrass does something than that his silent, social happiness does nothing to address the deep loneliness of the black male subject figured here by Ralph. Ralph accuses Snodgrass, "What's so funny? I'm lonely and you're laughing." The prohibitions and interpellations Snodgrass represents, his role as a lifeless cipher for social reality, can do nothing to address what Burton needs in this end-of-the-world scenario, affective and relational resources that go well beyond the purview of the everyday codes of the big Other.

Explaining the metaphor of the Devil he used to organize *The Devil Finds Work*, his essay collection on Hollywood films, Baldwin argued that where the devil finds his work is as the symbolic support for the fantasy selves we wish to see projected onto the film screen, those beguiling mirror images of our selves we project onto the social world.[72] "The Devil was that mirror which could

never be smashed," Baldwin describes, that hard shell or skin of an ego-image
and self-fiction invulnerable to the impulses and desires buried with the sensational, affective body.[73] However, Baldwin continued, "To look into the mirror
every day . . . was to engage Satan in a battle which we knew could never end."
In the act of facing off against that mirror image, seeking the crack or fracture
of reality embedded within it, the egoic subject's potential disintegration could
afford a different kind of vantage point on the black male as a relational self.

In a scene that follows Ben Hacker's arrival in the last third of the film,
Ralph Burton stares into a mirror while holding another relic he has saved and
mutters, "Poor slob. All alone in the world." The relic is a painting by Winslow
Homer, *The Gulf Stream* (1899), depicting a lone black male lost at sea. The
bare-chested man in the painting mirrors Belafonte's status as the isolated and
vulnerable black male, stripped from his culture, both an object of the gaze's
hyper-attention and a figure of profound human loneliness.[74] Simultaneously,

however, as he looks in the mirror Ralph also dis-identifies with the "poor slob" who remains perpetually isolated from the flesh of the world. Looking the devil squarely in the face, Ralph smashes the mirror with the painting asserting that his relations, with Ben, with Sarah, extend beyond the power of the symbolic gaze. When Ralph smashes the mirror with the painting, he acts as the man who, turned with his head and back to us and whose face we cannot fully see, is the man outside of the mirror, positioned on our side of the screen.

In this shot we are then given four images of Belafonte. First, the actor with his back to us is the subject who cannot be fully seen, whose (back of the) head cannot be fully facialized, who represents a bodily ego the camera can never fully capture. Second, Belafonte is also the cracked mirror image, that underside of the smooth symbolic surface that reveals its cuts and cracks, its scars and ruptures. Third, there is the painting, which represents the black male subject produced from a colonialist, historico-racial schema, his symbolic and discursive history on the grid defined by the discourse of and desire for difference. Finally, the shadow on the painting represents that fading apparition of the subject that can never be fully seen in the symbolic and imaginary frame, a hint of something of the embodied subject that lies elsewhere, in the body without an image.

In the second third of the film, once Sarah Crandall reveals herself as sharing the space of the lonely city with Ralph, for many viewers the narrative tension of the film lies in his unwillingness to tolerate her growing affection and to reciprocate her desire.[75] As the lonely black male, possibly the last man of the human species, refuses to accept Sarah's sexual companionship, he seems deluded at best, suicidal at worst. However, the film is less interested in what would save the two main characters from themselves than in exploring more fully what it is that Sarah and Ralph are trying to save. Ralph and Sarah's unconsummated relationship is merely a logical reflection of the world civilization Burton is so intent on preserving. Therefore, the very actions that make him a heroic savior figure go hand in hand with the old color lines, racial hierarchies, and taboos against miscegenation that constituted his lost world.

Burton's unbending pride and resistance to Sarah's attraction represent more than another heroic act of renunciation, another instance when Burton/Belafonte goes against his own desires as a black male. Rather, as Ralph denies Sarah, counterintuitively going against his own reproductive interests and placing humanity's survival in jeopardy, he is literally saving the world, that is, the world and customs of the culture he has charged himself with preserving.

The narrative of racial and civilizational decline that structures *The World, the Flesh and the Devil* was based on a novel, *The Purple Cloud*, written by M. P.

Shiel and published in 1901.[76] In this "last man" novel, when the protagonist discovers the destruction of the world by a noxious purple cloud, he laments that the universe is a place of strife between vague "powers" struggling for dominance, "The White" and "The Black," situating the end of the world firmly within the context of race war.[77] It is this world ruled by race that the protagonist sees no sense in preserving. The inevitability of race war leads to his vow to do his part to destroy any remainder of the human race, a vow which then shapes his unwillingness to consummate a relationship with the one other human he finds on his journeys, a young woman.

Shiel's narrative makes the explicit connection between race war and the end-of-the-world scenario, but not simply because one might lead to the other. M. P. Shiel was a prolific British writer of the late nineteenth and early twentieth century. Of West Indian descent, he was born on the island of Montserrat, the product of a mixed-race encounter between Priscilla Ann Blake, most likely the daughter of freed slaves, and Matthew Dowdy Shiell, most likely the illegitimate child of an Irish customs officer and a slave woman. Born only nine years before Bert Williams, Shiel was educated in a British context, thus his sense of world history would have been shaped by the kind of apocalyptic, end-of-the-world sensibilities forged in the contradictory founding moments of colonial modernity, when New World societies reflected both the decline of one set of Native American and African worlds and the rise of new capitalist economies and republics.[78]

Not surprisingly, Shiel's story draws deeper genealogical connections between *Island in the Sun*'s troubled discourse of race, creole love, and desire set in the founding of a newly national Caribbean society of the twentieth century, and *The World, the Flesh and the Devil*'s apocalyptic discourse of race warfare shaped by the end-of-the-world sensibilities of a nineteenth- century author of creole, West Indian descent. In the second, more dystopian film, it becomes clear that the end of racial classification and epidermalization would also be a wrenching process that would signal the end of the world as we know it, a form of symbolic death.

It is this premonition of the destruction of the symbolic order, the uncanny return to the world of the flesh, that structures the fatalism of the end-of-the-world scenario, especially one that revolves so centrally around the question of race. While *Island in the Sun* resorts to the romantic fantasy of miscegenation to resolve racially determined, intersubjective, and intercultural conflict, *The World, the Flesh and the Devil* turns instead to portraying that which cannot be symbolized, the phantasmatic specter of the world's fictions, the contradictions those fictions cannot resolve. Belafonte does not "get the girl" at the end of the world precisely because the film succeeds in symbolizing the fact that the interracial sexual relation never simply works out, and never works out simply. Sexuality is not the ground for resolving difference, but rather, the stage for recognizing that it is the other's fundamental likeness to the self that makes them inaccessible and immune to full incorporation.

Unlike *Island in the Sun*, *The World, the Flesh and the Devil* works to de-eroticize black male–white female relations, traversing the very fantasy of miscegenation with a depiction of the mutual condition of fleshly mortality a black man and a white woman share as desiring human beings. The scene that marks the end of Sarah's, and the movie's, fantasy of miscegenation occurs as Ralph helps Sarah celebrate a fictional birthday to cheer her up after one of their quarrels. A dreamy, romantic tone is established by a fade-in, montage shot of a dashing, suited Belafonte preparing the setting for a lovely meal at a restaurant. As Ralph escorts Sarah in and seats her when she arrives, the sound of his own voice also serenades her in music piped in over a recording, and he jokes about the multiple roles he is playing in the scene. He is both the waiter and the performer, both the romantic suitor and the transgressive, erotic lover in Sarah's fantasy world.

When Sarah crosses the line and expresses her desire, however, she is brutally put in check by Ralph. He does this by reminding everyone—the audience, the female protagonist, and himself—that the symbolic grid is still in place even at the world's end. Belafonte's voice croons romantically in the background in sharp contrast to Ralph's tone and demeanor when he tells Sarah firmly, "Mr. Burton isn't permitted to sit with the customers ma'am." In a setting that is both three-dimensional like a stage, and two-dimensional with its grid-like, geometrical backdrop, Ralph refuses to play the Imaginary role that Sarah would like to assign him and bows, leaving her sitting alone at the end of the scene.

In an earlier scene, Sarah justified her desire for Ralph by asserting, "I'm free, white and I'm 21 and I'm gonna do what I please!" When Ralph states wryly in this scene, "You and I are not alone in the world anymore. Civilization's back," he reminds Sarah of the symbolic realities they live within that thwart her narcissistic desires: "The narcissist seeks to include everything (good) within himself. . . . The opposite is true: the world contains us."[79] Announcing that he has finally achieved radio contact with other people, he reminds her that the symbolic world did not simply get erased because she now wills it. Rather, unlike Margot and Archer, but also unlike David and Mavis from *Island in the Sun*, the black male, the white female, and later, the white male are all still bound together in time, bound together by history. As Ralph also tells Sarah: "As long as we're alive the world's still alive. We're monuments you and me." Throughout the film, Ralph's actions and feelings are based on his resigned acceptance of these internalized social codes and his resistance to Sarah's naïve desire to pretend that they do not exist. As he responds ironically to her suggestion that they live in the same building: "No. People might talk." The ingenuity of *The World, the Flesh and the Devil* is precisely the film's, and the main protagonist's, seemingly illogical resistance to a utopian, narcissistic ending to the romantic narrative of black male–white female love.

In their very first meeting, Sarah exclaims with terror, "Don't touch me!" The strength of her internal prohibition explains her hesitation in approaching him earlier in the film. Ralph responds ruefully: "That's good. That's very funny. We're probably the only two people left in the world and all you can say is 'Don't touch me!'" Prior to their meeting, Sarah remains distant like the audience and the camera's gaze, spying on Ralph as he engages in everyday routines and silly moments of play to keep himself sane in his new world. In one such scene, Sarah watches from a corner, a Snodgrass-like puppet lit up in the shop window behind her, while Ralph walks down an abandoned street. Belafonte walks onto the screen from the left corner of the shot and as he notices his magnified shadow on the facade of an opera house, he steps back out of the shot to dance. The camera captures his enlarged silhouette shadow dancing on the wall.

The shadow of the black male performer conveys the underlying pathos of this scene in a manner very different from the sight of the black male performer as a mannequin or photo-graphed image. At the very limits of an epidermalized symbolic order, the incorporeal aspect of the black male performer acts as a body without an image, a sensory, bodily impression, the shadowy brushstroke of the dancing self projected on a wall, a self that has no audience. The erasure of the gaze denies the black performer his specular existence. Without the gaze, Burton has no one to watch him in this shadowy performance but himself. The shadow is therefore the very negation of his narcissistic, performing ego, reminding us of the more spectral and incorporeal aspects of the black entertainer dancing in the shadows of the symbolic world.[80]

four

In the Flesh, Living Sound

[The] phallus is a kind of organ without a body which I put on, which gets attached to my body, but never becomes an organic part, forever sticking out as its incoherent, excessive prosthesis.
—SLAVOJ ŽIŽEK, *How to Read Lacan*

"Rasta no abide amputation . . . I and I . . . don't allow a mon ta be dismantled . . . no scalpel shall crease me flesh! . . . Rastamon live out."
—BOB MARLEY, *Songs of Freedom*

In 1976, five years before the singer's death, *Rolling Stone* featured an article on Robert Nesta Marley, the world's first "Third World superstar." The magazine used for its cover a photo taken from a shoot that year with Annie Leibovitz. The accompanying article referenced Marley's single "I Shot the Sheriff" (1973), which climbed to the number one spot on Billboard's Hot 100 chart when Eric Clapton covered it in 1974. This same shoot furnished two additional photographs for *Rolling Stone* covers in the decades after Marley's death. The first appeared on the cover of the issue dated February 24, 1994, and coincided with Marley's admission into the Rock and Roll Hall of Fame. The second, reproduced here, appeared on the cover of the issue of March 10, 2005 (see figure 4.1).

The banner-like headline across the cover image from 1994 proclaimed: "Sex, Drugs and Rock and Roll: Bob Marley's Reggae Legacy: Hall of Fame '94." Not surprisingly, the accompanying article claimed him definitively as a rock-and-roll artist. The second posthumous cover image accompanied an article entitled "The Life and Times of Bob Marley: How He Changed Our World Forever." This headline also advertised the by-now iconic "Portraits by Annie Lei-

FIG 4.1. Cover of *Rolling Stone* magazine, March 2005, featuring Bob Marley.

On cover: MARS VOLTA ★ ARCADE FIRE ★ 50 CENT — Issue 969 ≫ March 10, 2005 ≫ $3.95 — rollingstone.com — *Rolling Stone* — THE LIFE AND TIMES OF Bob Marley — *How He Changed Our World Forever* — PORTRAITS BY ANNIE LEIBOVITZ — FASHION — Kings *of* Leon — *The Preacher's Kids Party Down With Models and Music* — Surviving Fallujah — *Hangin' With the Boys Who Fought the Big One* — New CD Preview *Sneak Peeks From* BRUCE SPRINGSTEEN — DAVE MATTHEWS BAND — ROBERT PLANT — BECK — MOBY — NINE INCH NAILS — MARIAH CAREY — STEVIE WONDER — BLACK EYED PEAS — JENNIFER LOPEZ

bovitz," marking the importance of her cultural representations of Marley as much as the singer's representation of himself. Taken together, this series of *Rolling Stone* covers demonstrates the various ways in which the Jamaican performer has been integrated into First World, North American popular musical culture. Each cover, or one might say, each face, reproduces meanings assigned to Marley's performance at different moments in his career, beginning with the cover from 1976 that focused on Marley alive and onstage.

With dreadlocks flying, his eyes tightly closed, and his mouth smiling but also expressive, as if in the midst of singing, on the *Rolling Stone* cover from 1976, Marley raises his arms overhead, their taut, lined muscles reflecting motion and tension, the guitar at his waist askew as if in mid-swing around his body. This snapshot aims to remind us of the singer in the midst of a live performance. The photograph only mimics, however, the performer's live and embodied act, since Marley is merely posing (and posed) for the camera as if he is onstage. It is actually a further step removed from live performance than the snapshot of an actual live performance used, for example, for the cover of the Bob Marley and the Wailers' album *Live!* from 1975.

While the photograph on the cover from 1976 represents Marley's star image while he was alive, in their subsequent appearances the photographs from the Annie Leibovitz series are framed to emphasize aspects of Marley's posthumous incorporation into American culture. All together, the three covers demonstrate the evolution of the meaning of Marley's sound from live act to recorded word to iconic image. They reveal the covering over or epidermalizing function of the gaze in pinning the black male performer, in the flesh and in his voice, to certain images of his sound. They demonstrate the phallicizing of the performer-celebrity as his hardened outer image, his look, his faciality. Here the image itself becomes a prosthetic phallus, not an "organic part," as Žižek describes, but an "excessive" attachment.

The *Rolling Stone* cover from 1994 features a close-up of the performer's face. Leibovitz captures Marley's almost ecstatic enjoyment in his own music, his facial expression—open-mouthed, eyes closed, hair flying—portraying graphically his pleasure in his own voice. Almost thirty years earlier, in 1948, Sartre noted the significance of the black male voice in the cultural changes beginning to sweep over the colonial world. Speaking of the emergence of the Negritude poets in Francophone Africa and the Caribbean, he warned his white European readers, "When you removed the gag that was keeping these black mouths shut, what were you hoping for? That they would sing your praises?"[1] He continued: "These black men are addressing themselves to black men about black men; their poetry is neither satiric nor imprecatory: it is an awakening to consciousness."[2] Sartre focused on the Orphic, self-referential dimension of the Negritude poet's lyrical voice. Another thirty years later, the Caribbean poet Édouard Glissant identified the Rastafarian as inheriting the legacy of the Negritude poet, sounding out the depths of a black male subjectivity that had heretofore existed on the margins but was coming into its own in the 1970s. For Glissant, this was a barbarian voice moving from sound and noise into speech.

The evolution of Marley's voice from the black noise of the Third World into a form of North American speech, however, was only made possible by a genre translation that shifted the meaning and message of Marley's music from reggae into rock and roll. On *Rolling Stone*'s cover from 1994, as the camera zooms in on Marley's face—faciality as the sign that sits at the intersection of black subjectification and signification—Marley's voice is imaged as Word, that is, coded into the symbolic order as a certain kind of facialized, symbolic sound—"Sex, Drugs and Rock and Roll." This cover incorporates Marley's voice and sound as a North American musical form. Reggae is rock and roll when framed and given meaning as such by an American music industry.

It is the more recent retrospective cover, however, from 2005, that demonstrates most acutely the mortification of Marley's rock-and-roll image, and the incorporation of his music as it is effected through his image (see figure 4.1). On the cover from 2005, we move from the animated performer captured as if live and active onstage to a shot which, while taken in 1976, is apt in 2005 since it freezes the performer's body and demeanor as if he is lying in a crypt. Marley's flying dreadlocks now lie stiffly and horizontally to the side rather than swinging out and away from his head; his closed eyes and partially open mouth now look more like a sleeping face; his arms akimbo are held close in to his body and parallel the wide V of his legs, as opposed to the more active opening out of his body into the two V's of spread arms and legs on the cover from 1976; and finally, his guitar now lies horizontally still and at rest, the limp phallus now as much a posed element of the photograph as any of its other highly composed and symmetrical features.

Together these three *Rolling Stone* covers, and many of the album and CD covers, posters, and T-shirt images of Marley produced since his death, work in ways that are similar to Bert Williams's song sheets from the early twentieth century. They *mortify* the performer, freezing and framing him onto the symbolic grid. They tie his voice, speech, and blackness to the image on the surface of the epidermalizing gaze. They *photo-graph* the subject, placing him in the social picture and on the cultural screen in a fixed way. With Bob Marley, the image's power to mortify also takes on an additional dimension in light of the performer's still vibrant, posthumous musical presence. Bob Marley's cover image also *immortalizes* him; it preserves an ideal image of the performer, as a transcendent, Imaginary form removed from the late twentieth-century context of the black freedom struggle that Marley's music became a sound track for in the 1970s.

Leibovitz's beautiful photographs freeze Marley in time, images from one shoot reanimating the artist every ten to twenty years in a timeless moment that stretches symbolically between 1976 and 1994, and then again between 1994 and 2005. They are the closest the symbolic grid can get to capturing Marley's incorporeality as it extends beyond his death. The *Rolling Stone* images extend the life of the body of the performer, holding his death in abeyance, in deferral, turning his presence in death into a new kind of symbolic life. Placed together and deconstructed, they also reveal the ways meaning sediments onto the flesh and voice of the black male performer.

The Marley we find in American popular culture today wears a skin layered over by the explicitly phallic meanings of blackness that attached to him and other male performers of the 1970s across the black and decolonized world. Sartre's and Glissant's perceptive linkings of voice, Negritude, and Rastafarianism set the stage here for thinking about Marley's posthumous skin act in terms of the converging phallic meanings attached to blackness during the era of decolonization. Boyeur's "my skin is my country," Lamming's "in the castle of my skin," both reflect the attempt to idealize blackness and the skin in the context of the freedom struggle, an idealization that also figures the black (male) body as individuated, whole, hardened, and closed. Among the many ways of reading Marley's fear of amputation, as quoted in the epigraph above, is as a fear of castration placed, certainly, in specific historical, religious, and political contexts, but also aligning itself with an epistemic belief in the necessary seamlessness and closure of the impregnable, autonomous body.

The 1950s through the 1970s marked a pivotal moment in which blackness emerged as a phallic signifier, that is, in which a form of political speech about blackness re-signified black identity in distinctly phallic and heteronormative terms, privileging freedom as a kind of individuated autonomy rather than as embodied in the relational capacities of the black subject. Sartre's use of the myth of Orpheus to describe the Negritude poets was prescient for, unlike Oedipus and Hamlet, whose sins were based on their desire for the mother, both Caliban's and Orpheus's sins include separation from primary female figures—the mother, the wife—separation, that is, from an echo of the fleshy, relational male self left behind and figured both as female and as somehow not-whole. In performances of black masculinity for a postcolonial era, such as Marley's, this self is abandoned in favor of a closed, hardened, self-sufficient ideal that would also be perfect for incorporation into North American culture in the form of a black, hyper-heterosexual masculinity. Simultaneously, in the Jamaican context, this image of black masculinity constructs the black sexual relation as a heterosexual unity of two subjects united into one ideal, closed form.

Marley had already achieved global recognition at the time of his death on May 11, 1981. His funeral in the hills of the rural village of Nine Miles, Jamaica, where he was born, drew a crowd of thousands, a response similar in reverence if not quite in size to Michael Jackson's memorial in the United States in 2009. News of Marley's death echoed around the world and his posthumous success continues to far outweigh his sales records while he was alive. Following his induction into the United States' Rock and Roll Hall of Fame, in 1999 *Time* magazine named *Exodus* "Album of the Century." In 2001 Marley was awarded the Grammy Lifetime Achievement Award; in 2004 he ranked No. 11

on *Rolling Stone*'s 100 Greatest Artists of all Time.[3] *Legend: The Best of Bob Marley and the Wailers*, the LP collection that Tuff Gong/Island Records issued three years after Marley's death, is still reggae's best-selling album both in the United States and in the world.[4] After his death the singer's widow proclaimed that Bob Marley's spirit would never fade, that "before he finally closed his eyes," her husband promised "that he'd [still] be here."[5] His prophecy appears to have come true. Today Marley's active legacy resurrects the man and the performer perpetually for his family and fans worldwide.

The messianic overtones of Rita Marley's comment, however, also mark the ways in which Bob Marley has remained caught "between two deaths," that is, in that particular state in which an individual's human being and meaning seem to persist in the symbolic realm beyond the physical life of his body.[6] Marley's bodiliness recedes in the face of his image; his physiognomy assumes a meaningfulness in the symbolic order that far outweighs his mortal death and life. *Rolling Stone*'s continual use of Leibovitz's photographs offers one example of the ways the "liveness" of a performer can be socially constructed, the life of the performer reproduced to fit a certain narrative, Marley's actual life overshadowed by his immortal life.

As recently as 2011, another retrospective in *Goldmine: The Music Collector's Magazine* argued that Marley's induction into the Hall of Fame "proved . . . rock 'n' roll had finally grown up."[7] This linking of the genre's maturation with the evolution of Marley's music was also evoked in the cover image of the four-disc CD box set, *Songs of Freedom* (1992), released by Tuff Gong/Island Records. Produced with the intention of introducing Marley to a new generation of listeners, the box set's packaging gave new life to Marley's voice by placing him in an acoustic setting. The acoustic represents "a sign of authenticity for the blues rock and folk of the 1960s and 1970s," part of a chain of signifiers linking the rock performer to his guitar.[8] This is partly because, in rock culture, the guitar is the musical instrument that helps to define the musical genre's sound, the lead guitar solo functioning as a kind of phallic metonym for the lone performer sitting or standing under the spotlight and singing directly to his audience.

In the years leading up to his death, Marley and his producers worked to ensure his success with American and European audiences by changing his music to accommodate the electric guitar and by adding other "rock/pop stylizations."[9] As Michael Veal describes, his "music was often recorded at better-equipped studios outside of Jamaica and was marked by high-end production values, more sophisticated chord progressions than were the local norm, and [the use of] electronic synthesizers and lead guitar solos."[10] Taking his music to the world stage, Marley adopted some of the bodily style and central tropes of rock and roll to present himself, self-signify, as an American-styled rock performer. *Songs of Freedom* uses these signs of rock-and-roll authenticity such as the acoustic guitar to move Marley from the public vibrancy of the concert stage to a more intimate setting.

Bob Marley's associations with a rock-and-roll mode of performance matter in an even more profound sense, however, having to do with the privileging of liveness itself. In American rock culture, liveness is the very marker of an authentic musical performance. It legitimates the act as the soulful expression of the individual artist-singer. As Philip Auslander describes: "The concept of rock authenticity is linked with the romantic bent of rock culture, in which rock music is imagined to be truly expressive of the artists' souls and psyches, and as necessarily politically and culturally oppositional."[11] Auslander argues that the tendency in performance studies to privilege live over mediated and recorded performance, even to assert fundamental ontological differences between the two, "is not especially productive."[12] The very category of the live only makes sense in relation to its other, the (technologically) reproducible performance: "Historically, the live is actually an effect of mediatization, not the other way around. It was the development of recording technologies that made it possible to perceive existing representations as 'live.' Prior to the advent of those technologies (e.g., sound recording and motion pictures), there was no such thing as 'live' performance, for that category has meaning only in relation to an opposing possibility."[13]

The rock star's live performance is itself the constructed, authentic act that authorizes the recording as an imitation of the performance itself, as a record of the liveness that gives the rock performance its meaning. Liveness, then, understood in symbolic terms, signifies that evanescent quality of the body that is never fully representable in the cultural and symbolic order, that kernel of the incorporeal body that escapes the image and is therefore privileged, in its absence, through its surrogates and surrogation in performance.

In a similar manner, a certain narrative about Bob Marley's life, what was significant about his performance while he was alive, continues to stand in for, shape, and authenticate our posthumous reception of his work. Much in the same way one's likeness can be socially constructed rather than being a mere mirror of the self, Bob Marley's liveness and "aliveness" were subject to ideological mediation from the minute he stepped onto the stage. Liveness (subjectification) is subject to likeness (symbolic signification and mediation) and in Marley's case both evolve in the second, symbolical life attached to his musical career and image after his death. The life of the American Marley was summed up in four parts in *Songs of Freedom*, each CD accompanied by a representative likeness of Marley's face. The facialization of the performer frames his voice, the box set literally providing a cover story of the performer, reproduced in the accompanying images of his face.[14]

In pointing to this imaged or photo-graphed Marley, the aim is to emphasize and demystify the ways we have come to understand the voice of the "live Marley" through the filter of a number of reproduced and prerecorded images. The discourse of a cultural gaze already constructed him as a rock performer while alive and now reconstructs him as a live icon while dead. In rock culture, authenticity is linked to the image of the performer: "Our ability to visualize the performance of rock music as we listen to it is dependent on the availability of visual artifacts that show us what the musicians look like in performance."[15] These artifacts include record covers, magazine and press photographs, the type of artifact chosen to introduce Bob Marley here rather than his reggae music or lyrics. They provide evidence for the ways in which Marley was defined in the American context through his image as much as his sound. Photographed, mortified, incorporated, and immortalized in the image of the live rock performer, this aspect of his performance is kept scopically alive and forever symbolically preserved in an American-led, global music market.

What would it mean to get back to a different sense of Marley's incorporeal voice, to listen for his corporeal sound without an image? Elsewhere I have argued that his incorporation points to "the increased corporate control over, and commercialization of" his work, and to "the specific way in which this has been accomplished symbolically."[16] To be "incorporate" means to be without body or material substance and Marley's cultural and symbolic importance has increased in a North American Imaginary the more incorporate he has become, an "ethereal icon, one removed from the very specific social and political context of reggae production in the 1970s."[17] This chapter explores how one might resurrect an incorporeal Marley, the man as a body-without-an-image, and an intercorporeal Marley, the performer whose relations occur on the threshold of the skin.

What does it mean to see, understand, experience Bob Marley today as a legendary voice? Where is Bob Marley, and where is he not? Is there another way to tell his story, one that includes his iconic status as a performer but also situates his life and voice in relation to the other forces shaping it rather than as the expressive vehicle for a narrative of the lone, self-sufficient man and his guitar? The myths of black Orpheus and Caliban structure our contemporary relation to black male performers as autonomous voices somehow shorn from their communities and from the more private aspects of their lives. This version of Marley's story as a performer limits us to seeing blackness, and the black voice, as circumscribed within certain notions of freedom and autonomy that rest on phallic appreciations of our bodies, our subjectivities, our relations, and our skins.

In her autobiography, *No Woman No Cry*, Rita Marley resituates Bob Marley's phallic cover story within the context of his life as a man, as a lover, and as a father, that is, as a sexual and relational subject. In doing so, she retells Bob Marley's story as part of the couple's duet, her narrative also revealing some of the broader features of a black, Jamaican, Rastafarian discourse about heterosexuality in the postindependence period. Rita Marley's female voice accompanies Marley's in recounting their shared life as a black musical couple, while at the same time, a different form of reggae music, dub reggae, also accompanied Marley's lyrical voice and live performance style. Like Rita Marley's autobiography, dub provides a different way of telling the story of Jamaican music during the 1970s.

Alongside his rock image, Bob Marley's politics of live performance were also tied to a very vibrant, black, Jamaican, and Third World politics. And yet, as his reggae became increasingly global in the First World contexts of Britain and the United States, his conscious lyrics and politics were incorporated within a rock aesthetic celebrating live embodied performance. What ultimately facilitated this convergence is an aspect of the lyrical voice of the reggae musician that also made it conducive to certain phallic representations of the liberated black male self. Marley's version of reggae music, dominated by the voice and lyrics of the lone performer, creates a political space in which the phallic signifier of racial difference takes on a new, powerful, subaltern affect and meaning. The Rastafarian performer is both a new Third World idealization of the masculine body of Negritude and black power politics—turning the black penis into the phallus—and the authorization of difference as a form of political speech emitting from the black male body.

The discourse of a black male subject became incredibly layered and sophisticated in the militant, black power, gendered politics of the Rastafarian. This context very much shapes Bob Marley's voice. However, there are other Marleys. The performer can also be understood through his silences, especially as these silences are reproduced in his social relations. In privileging certain musical and political understandings of Marley's liveness, we miss other aspects of his story, the repeated, missed encounters of the body-with-skin—the black male body lost to its phallic, epidermal signifiers and idealized surrogates—with the body-in-the-flesh, stripped of its phallic coverings. This body-in-the-flesh reappears in Marley's intimate relations, in the musical soundscape that surrounded him, and in the legacy both have left behind in the music of Marley's living sons.

The Phono-Graphed Black Voice: Reggae as a Phallic Difference

Reggae in the realm of the "audio-visual" corresponds to "poetry."
—ÉDOUARD GLISSANT, *Caribbean Discourse*

Does the voice of the persecutor differ sharply from the persecuted voice?
The secret may be that they are both the same; that there are not two voices.
—MLADEN DOLAR, *A Voice and Nothing More*

Recently, both Fred Moten and Alexander Weheliye have demonstrated that in relation to black performance, the difference technological mediation brings to live performance is not that between the live and authentic voice versus the mediated black body.[18] Rather, it is between the subject photo-graphed and the subject *phono-graphed*, that is, the black subject as a mortified image versus as a written, recorded, but also revivified and revivifying sound. Lacan privileged voice, sound, and the ear as important aspects of, as he termed it, an invocatory drive. This was precisely because of the ways in which, unlike the image and the gaze, the circuit of desire between the voice and ear, which runs between our desire to hear the self, to hear the other, and to be heard as the other hears us, can never be completely closed. In the context of Bob Marley's performance of black voice, Lacan's psychoanalytic notion of the open circuit between the voice and the ear raises the question, what desires did the black voice of the 1970s arouse in different subjects during that era? Is it possible that both the persecutor and the persecuted, the neo-imperial First World and the neocolonial Third World, were hearing, as Dolar's epigraphic statement slyly asks, one and the same voice?

Founded in the 1930s, the Rastafarian movement burst onto the world scene in the 1970s primarily due to the reggae of Bob Marley and the Wailers. Leonard Barrett describes:

> From North America to mother Africa, a new sound can be heard from the Caribbean haunting the places where Black people get together for music and dancing. From the prestigious Hotel Ivoire in Abidjan on the Ivory Coast to the secluded Meridian Hotel built by Kwame Nkrumah in the seaside city of Tema in Ghana . . . the driving Trench Town music captures and transports the listener. The effect of reggae is pure magic; it is Africa, Jamaica, [] liminal music that sings of oppression in exile, a longing for home, or for a place to feel at home.[19]

Barrett focuses first on reggae's sound, but his reference to the singer also highlights the ways Marley's lyrics disciplined reggae's sound with the Word.

Marley's strengths included not just his talents as a performer but also as a songwriter, his lyrics translating the liberatory elements of ideologies of blackness such as Negritude into terms relevant for a later era of decolonization, and simultaneously, into a language of freedom that could be heard by a white audience. The "liminal music that sings of oppression in exile, a longing for home, or for a place to feel at home" was also, as Michael Veal describes, a "logogenic" discourse in which "comprehensible words are the basis of the song."[20] The artist is the primary center of attention, the song functions as a speech act, and the singer's voice becomes "the bearer of an utterance, the support of a word, a sentence, a discourse."[21] The performer's focus is on directing a message, addressing his audience as intimately and as compellingly as he can with the lyrical power of his first-person, poetic, and prophetic voice. In this aspect of the voice it is the carrier of meaning, the support, the voice box, of the signifier, with an almost messianic capacity to turn animalistic, fleshy sound into transcendent meaning.[22]

Marley's apotheosis as the Third World prophet and "Natural Mystic" speaks as much to the jeremiadic content of his lyrics as to his Orphic power to link the most fleshly aspects of the black voice to the Word: "In the beginning was the Word, but in order for the Word to manifest itself, there has to be a mediator, a precursor in the shape of John the Baptist, who identifies himself precisely as . . . the voice crying in the desert, while Christ, in this paradigmatic opposition, is identified with the Word. . . . Thus the progression from voice to meaning is the progression from a mere — albeit necessary — mediator to the true Word: there is only a small step from linguistics to theology."[23] In Negritude Sartre heard "the far-away tam-tam in the streets of Dakar at night; voo-doo shouts from some Haitian cellar window . . . this slobbery, bloody poem full of phlegm, twisting in the dust like a cut-up worm . . . this double spasm of absorption and excretion."[24] Marley's Rastafarian music facilitates the transmutation of the flesh and sound of the black (male) voice, like the body and blood of Christ, into the logic and structure of discourse: "This illusion of transcendence accompanied the long history of the voice as the agent of the sacred, and the highly acclaimed role of music was based on its ambiguous link with both nature and divinity. When Orpheus, the emblematic and archetypal singer, sings, it is in order to tame wild beasts and bend gods; his true audience consists not of men, but of creatures beneath and above culture."[25] Music facilitates the transformation of the fleshiness of the voice into a form of symbolic, transcendent meaning that then appears to heal the split, or compensate for the fleshy voice of the body left behind by the symbolic order. The singing voice turns vocal utterance into meaning, more than it(s) sounds: "Of course this promise of a state of some primordial fusion to which the voice should bear witness is always a retroactive construction. . . . The voice as the bearer of a deeper sense, of some profound message, is a structural illusion, the core of a fantasy that the singing voice might cure the wound inflicted by culture, restore the loss that we suffered by the assumption of the symbolic order."[26] More so even than the poem, the musical lyric turns the materiality of the black voice as noise and bodily presence, into meaning, message, the discourse of phallic signification. If, as Glissant argues, reggae was an audiovisual poetry, did it exceed the values and frames of a phallic discourse?

Marley's music was, in both form and content, a way of linking, Orphically, sound to transcendent Word, the unheard and non-signifying cry of the slave articulated as meaningful utterance. The language that he used to turn black noise into meaning privileged difference as a central unit in the translation of black experience. Toward the end of *The Four Fundamental Concepts of Psychoanalysis*, Lacan notes that mass media have a globalizing capacity to enhance the alienating effects of the voice and the gaze, "stratospheriz[ing]" one and overstimulating the other.[27] Marley's is certainly a planetarized and stratospherized voice, but the spread of his universalist message is not just due to technology. His messianic performance converted black sound, both literally and figuratively, into a signifying difference, difference being the ur-Word, the master signifier, of a modern, symbolic order.

If the singing voice cures the wound inflicted by culture, providing the illusion of return to some transcendent form of being, Marley's music complicated this by also affirming difference as a higher, transcendent, historical value. His musical performance followed the essential logic of a phallic discourse — to make what was not-whole whole, to unite the fleshy parts of the body into one skin-image. Sounding out the cut of racial difference that organizes a modern symbolic order founded in colonial discourses, he simultaneously claimed to heal that cut, leaving a certain wounded aspect of the black male voice behind as it cuts away to become a closed carrier of meaning and aesthetic pleasure.

The voice in its connection with meaning is "a sound which appears to be endowed in itself with the will to 'say something,' with an inner intentionality," implying "a subjectivity which 'expresses itself.'"[28] Hence Sartre's description of the Negritude poem as the carrier for a new expression of black male subjectivity: "Because it is subjectivity written in the objective, Negritude must take form in a poem, that is to say in a subjectivity-object."[29] He also described this "subjectivity-object," the poem itself as a signifying form, as the "*negritude*-object . . . snatched" from the poet "like a cry of pain, of love and of hate."[30] With the negritude-object the poet reverses the gaze, that is, identifies the social gaze as an epidermalizing, interpellating force: "For three thousand years, the white man has enjoyed the privilege of seeing without being seen; he was only a look—the light from his eyes drew each thing out of the shadow of its birth; the whiteness of his skin was another look, condensed light. The white man—white because he was man, white like daylight, white like truth, white like virtue—lighted up the creation like a torch and unveiled the secret white essence of beings. Today, these black men are looking at us, and our gaze comes back to our own eyes."[31] Facialization, epidermalization, both dress black and white bodies in racial meanings and skins: "Our whiteness seems to us to be a strange livid varnish that keeps our skin from breathing—white tights, worn out at the elbows and knees, under which we would find real human flesh the color of black wine if we could remove them."[32] The Negritude poet used language to shine a different kind of light on these symbolic processes and epidermal codes.

Glissant recognized the Rastafarian voice of the 1970s as the reincarnation of the cry of the Negritude poet, a different kind of organic black intellectual of the Caribbean, and reggae as an "audiovisual" form of poetry. Glissant also noted, however, that the Rastafarian voice and lyric would not be recognized immediately as a new form of the "negritude-object" because it deviated from the official form and rhetoric of a black liberatory politics. Glissant felt that the Rastafarians were "the inevitable 'invasion of barbarians' to the intellectual dream of the learned."[33] The latter were the nationalist and postcolonial intellectuals "ill at ease" with Rastas who, as "extremist adherents," had taken academic theories of black history to heart: "Can the traditional intellectual who has produced his theory of negritude accept the Rasta who applies it in a concrete way?" What differentiates Marley from the Negritude poet, as the voice of the Rasta who applies Negritude in a concrete way, is that while the Rastafarian singer also turns the gaze back on itself, in addition, he reinvokes and voices the rhetoric of a political desire for difference that undergirds the gaze as an interpellating, social, and historical form. The Rastafarian's voice recalls, in a way the written word alone cannot, the affective power of difference as a form of political desire and as a way of understanding and organizing modern societies.

It is probably no coincidence that in the 1970s, in the midst of the very same forces that were shaping Bob Marley and his music, Michel Foucault gave a series of lectures that captured almost perfectly a Rastafarian sensibility organized around the historical, racial awareness of political persecution. In these lectures Foucault updated for a decolonizing age the discussion of difference that attached earlier to the epidermalized black and colonial body.[34] Foucault's historicizing of "race" as an aspect of a discourse of "race war" rested on Carl Schmidt's notion that politics depended on the identification of one's friends and enemies. Specifying such identifications as subject to historical forces rather than natural laws, in his lectures Foucault essentially provides a genealogy for modern politics as inherently built on an episteme of difference.

This genealogy consisted, in quick summary, of three components. First, the "binary mode [of] race war" rests on the determination of multiple, minute differences between peoples: "the basic elements that make the war possible, and then ensure its continuation, pursuit, and development: ethnic differences, differences between languages, different degrees of force, vigor, energy, and violence; the differences between savagery and barbarism; the conquest and subjugation of one race by another." In seventeenth-century Europe, alongside the dominant episteme of resemblance, an emergent discourse begins to politicize difference as a justification for splitting the social body into two parts: "The social body is basically articulated into two races"; the language of a "clash between two races" becomes a stand-in for marking political differences that run through society "from top to bottom." This theory of difference then takes on an "openly biological transcription" in a "materialist anatamophysiology." The shift from anatomical to physiognomic understandings of difference and the body then gets articulated to nationalist discourses in Europe and to "European policies of colonization."[35]

A second transcription in the nineteenth century translates the biological into the social: "[After] the first—biological—transcription of the theory of permanent struggle and race struggle. . . . you find a second transcription based upon the great theme and theory of social war, which emerges in the very first years of the nineteenth century, and which tends to erase every trace of racial conflict in order to define itself as class struggle."[36] Ending his genealogy, Foucault argues that it is this social theory that branches off in two directions, into the grand narratives of dialectical materialism and into the racial evolutionism and biological determinism of the nineteenth century.

Like Seth, Wynter, and other scholars pursuing a genealogy of race as a discourse of difference, Foucault draws the link between events in Europe and the discovery and colonization of the New World. What is useful for thinking about Marley's voice in terms of Foucault's theory of race war is the identification of certain strands of political discourse during decolonization as resting on a discourse of difference that was not particular to the black and colonial world. If anything, the black voice was speaking a new dialect of a discourse of political difference that had a long history in colonial modernity. With the theory of race war, Foucault essentially historicizes and theorizes this modern discourse, providing a genealogy that ranges from the physiognomic discourses of the body to the social discourses of history to the biopolitical discourses of the present. Marley's moment represents the point at which the politics of class war and race struggle were once more articulated together, offering a reminder of sorts of the links between discourses of racial difference and the historical realities of class struggle.

Bob Marley's elaboration of this discourse of race war as a Rastafarian, Third World form of political speech about the global class struggle can be seen in the song "War." In 1976 Marley set to music the words from a speech that Haile Selassie I delivered in California in February 1968. In "War," Marley moved the speech beyond one African nation's political circumstances, bringing together music and older discourses of Ethiopianism and contemporary decolonial geopolitics to describe a new and worldly black discourse on race. As Marley wails, "Everywhere is war—Me say war. . . . Dis a war," the importance of the song's lyrics diminishes.[37] They are sounded out by the accent, the intonation, the timbre of a Third World voice that signifies and marks the racial difference. Foucault's theory offers a powerful lens for interpreting Marley's music, and the politicized Rastafarian voice it epitomizes, because the vindicationist affect of race war that he describes also shapes the tone and accent of Marley's Third World voice. The power and affective style of race war discourse becomes, in Marley's hands, a discourse of racial vindicationism that is doubly determined. It offers a vindication of the black race's history in colonial modernity, and it reveals that racial discourse is the core element of a vindicationist sense of history that drives modern politics.

The Ethiopianist and jeremiadic bent of Rastafarian millenarianism translated the discourse of race war into a powerfully affective discourse, voice, and music enhancing those emotional elements of black political speech that cannot be put into words—the hortatory voice, the voice of lament, the syncopated silences and groans that resonate with the drumming heartbeat of the oppressed. In "Exodus," the singer's call for black movement admonishes black and colonial peoples not just to look back at but also to turn away from the light of the gaze, from the sight of sovereign power: "Open your eyes and look within: / Are you satisfied (with the life you're living)?"[38] The voice that recounts "the history of the race struggle" speaks not in the light of the gaze but from its shadows, as Foucault describes: "The story of the race struggle will of course speak from the side that is in darkness, from within the shadows. It will be the discourse of those who have no glory."[39] It exceeds the signifier by expressing itself in "a disruptive speech, an appeal," a lamentation or wail.[40]

Rastafarianism, as a religio-political discourse, recounts a historical memory of racial struggle that exceeds the normal chain of signifiers. Foucault described it as disqualified, never fully acknowledged in official accounts of history. Instead, the consciousness of racial struggle is "a sort of prophetic rupture" similar to "epic, religious, or mythical forms [recounting] the misfortune of ancestors, exiles, and servitude."[41] It functions as a kind of jeremiadic, biblically informed common sense—one of those "singular, local knowledges, the noncommonsensical knowledges that people have, and which have in a way been left to lie fallow, or even kept in the margins."[42] These knowledges of struggle, felt in the black body as "suffering," people carry with them as a deep structure to their political understanding of world history.

In Marley's lyrics, the rhetoric of vindication is a discursive force that simultaneously enhances and disciplines the emotional accents, intonations, and timbres, the noise of the black voice. As Marley's invocatory voice travels between subjects of different races and political creeds, articulating in his particular accented style, his locally inflected tone, a desire for difference with profound political and historical meanings, it pushes rhetorical and sonic effects into the signifying elements of the Word. Marley's vindicationist themes of exile, spiritual conviction, and a Rastafarian religious vision communicated the rhetoric of historical racial struggle as a shared meaning uniting the performer and the listener in a shared understanding of difference, bringing difference as a shared meaning into black sound.

In the 1970s, Marley's conscious lyrics, the lyrics of the sufferers, represented a black political form of signifying that drew on a discourse of race struggle deeply embedded in Atlantic culture and re-voiced in contemporary reggae sounds, in the drum percussion beats moving alongside the tenor rasp of Marley's voice. Foucault described the speaker of this disqualified discourse as the barbarian rather than the savage—not the innocent man outside of history but the barbarian who takes a position against history from within a civilization. The Rastafarian, using both the signifier and the voice to reclaim a black subject occupying the split within civilization, would require the signifier to stretch its skin, those "white tights, worn out at the elbows and knees," to accommodate the expansion of the discourse of difference to accommodate the meanings of race and difference attached to and voiced by black bodies.[43] Rather than being merely a discourse about black identity, however, when the political discourse of difference reappears in a black voice it also returns it to the hearer and listener as a reversible, self-reflexive echo of himself. With music as its vehicle for travel, in the open circuit between two like subjects of different races, the black voice's assertion of difference is integrated in the listener as a new kind of discourse about freedom.

Before rap and hip-hop, reggae was one of the first postcolonial, oppositional musical forms to take the alienated and dispossessed consciousnesses of black urban youth as its raw material for a new, pan-African image of the black male subject. Referencing the Rastafarian practice of referring to oneself as the "I and I," Marlene Nourbese Philip describes the "I-mage" as the psychic figure that results from the colonial subject's internal struggle to redefine images of the self.[44] As political performers, Marley and the Wailers represented the voice of the buffalo soldier, the urban outcast inhabiting the ghettos and trench towns of Kingston, Jamaica, in the 1960s and 1970s, who in emancipating himself from mental slavery sings of the decolonizing spirit of his times, delivering a postcolonial critique of the West in its neocolonial relationship to the Caribbean. By translating the condition of black subjects specifically into a story of oppression and redemption legible in the symbolic order, the Rastafarian black prophet enacted what Fanon could not imagine in *Black Skin, White Masks*, but went on to analyze in *The Wretched of the Earth*—the turning of the phobogenic black penis into the phallus, an act not unlike the New Negro's efforts in an earlier era to turn the body of the slave into an Imaginary face. Marley universalized the black condition into a human condition by translating blackness into a political discourse of difference rather than a biological one.

In his posthumous American incarnations, the Third World accent of Marley's music has been hidden at worst, pushed to the past at best, by the framing of his music within a rock-and-roll code. The signifier always works to discipline the voice, as Mladen Dolar describes: "We stumble on the voice [in that] which is seemingly recalcitrant to the signifier: the accent, the intonation, and the timbre. [Accent] brings the voice into the vicinity of singing, and a heavy accent suddenly makes us aware of the material support of the voice which we tend immediately to discard. It appears as a distraction, or even an obstacle, to the smooth flow of signifiers and to the hermeneutics of understanding. Still, the regional accent can easily be dealt with, it can be described and codified."[45] Over time, the codification of Marley's reggae as rock and roll removes, as Dolar describes further, the "linguistic class struggle" from the voice. Since the ruling norm is nothing but "an accent which has been declared a non-accent in a gesture which always carries heavy social and political connotations," one covers over or epidermalizes the Third World accent and the historical sensibility that comes with it by merely rewriting it as another kind of American pop sound.[46]

If we think of gender, however, also as a symbolic code, the dress or face of the signifier can also hide a bodily mark or accent. In the late 1940s, Sartre celebrated Negritude's closing up and resolution of a new sense of blackness in the image of an androgynous black male self: "For our black poets . . . being comes out of Nothingness like a penis becoming erect. . . . He is 'flesh of the flesh of this world'; . . . he is both Nature's female and its male. . . . This spermatic religion is like the tension of a soul balancing between two complementary tendencies: the dynamic feeling of being an erect phallus, and that more deaf, more patient, more feminine, of being a growing plant. Thus negritude is basically a sort of androgyny."[47] The androgynous male self of Negritude offers the fiction of a black masculinity invulnerable to the cut of sexual difference, somehow using the scar of racial difference to resist full symbolic assimilation and reconstitute himself as whole. In reality, as much as the accent, timbre, and intonation of the voice can recall different sounds, they can also be subjugated to the word in the signifying order, and sound can be overdetermined by image.

This was certainly the case with the constant harnessing of the sound of the buffalo soldier to certain images of black masculinity, one performed live onstage in the persona of the rock musician, but the other performing a black phallic difference in the social world and private life of the Rastafarian rude boy in the Caribbean. The historical sensibility of the buffalo soldier produced in Jamaican popular culture the closed and idealized image of the urban male hero, the "Rude Boy Tuff Gong" as Bob Marley was named in his early days as a young singer in Trench Town. This was also the image popularized by Marley's contemporary, Jimmy Cliff, in his portrayal of the urban legend gangster man Rhyging in the film *The Harder They Come* (1972).[48] Cliff's Rhyging is a twentieth-century buffalo soldier who makes himself whole again through acts of violence, creating in his aggressively phallic acts the cutting away of the body for a new mirror I-mage of the black male self.

Both rock and roll and reggae carry forward fantasies of an androgynous masculinity, an idealized, self-sufficient masculinity that can somehow cover over its inscription by sexual and racial difference, dressing the flesh of the black signifier in a new phallic covering that drowns out other dimensions of the black male self. There were other acoustic dimensions, however, to the performance of a postcolonial, Caribbean, Third World black masculinity in Marley's moment. Hearing them now requires a re-attunement to dub reggae's refocusing of the sonic elements cut away by a phallic discourse of liberation, and a reappraisal of the black female voice also as an acoustic echoing of phallic difference that portrays more relational dimensions of the Rastafarian performer's life.

The Dub Voice: Trimming the Barber to Find the Silences Within

Music, and in particular the voice, should not stray away from words which endow it with sense. —MLADEN DOLAR, *A Voice and Nothing More*

Does the I-mage of a militant Afro-Jamaican masculinity of the 1970s leave anything out? When Glissant observed that both the Rasta and his reggae poetry articulated a disqualified form of Caribbean knowledge, a Negritude from the gut, he also heard an undertone that "finds its expression as much in the explosion of the original cry . . . as in the imposition of lived rhythms."[49] Could this cry that stands out against the backdrop of "lived rhythms" also be what Lacan described as "the cry [that] does not stand out against a background of silence, but on the contrary makes the silence emerge as silence?"[50] In other words, is there a different way of hearing the black male sufferer not just along the chain of signification but also in the silences and rhythms between his words?

At the end of the *Legend* version of "Exodus" we get a brief acoustic sense of dub, a synthesizer-heavy form of reggae music that developed in the 1970s concurrent with Bob Marley's success. As Marley and his musicians chant the chorus, "movement of Jah people" six times, a minute and a half before the end of the song one begins to hear a flutter forming in the background of their words. The voices cut the chant up into the shouted word, "Move!" repeated thirteen times, while echoes and reverberations of the men's voices, of the guitar, of the horns, open up the structure of the song. As "Exodus" closes, three more repetitions of "movement of Jah people" turn Marley's speech, the speech of the subject, into pure sound. His voice conveys first a chant of reverberating meaning and then breaks down into a nonsensical, chopped-up, echoing noise.

In "Exodus" as elsewhere, dub techniques recorded both the noise and the linguistic meaning conveyed in the black voice, the silence as much as the sound, the break and cut as much as the utterance within the word. The word "incorporate" holds within it the phonetic ghost of a reference to the incorporeal body; similarly Marley's immortality in death holds the traces of a black male "sufferer" whose bodily echo we hear in dub reggae music, on the raspy edge of the male singer's voice, between the chirps of the reggae rock guitar. Dub reggae's sound effects both mirror (produce a copy of) and echo (sound out) the syncopated pulsations of a fading subject that flicker in and out at the very moment the subject asserts him or herself in language. If the subject gains from the mirror-likeness a sense of closure necessary for creating a sovereign ego, dub sounds recall not the voice or gaze of the subject but rather the ear. The ear is a rim space on the fleshy, permeable body, reminding one of one's openness to others and to the world. It provides an acoustic mirror or window to the self, and an intercorporeal channel to the other: "In the field of the unconscious the ears are the only orifice that cannot be closed. Whereas *making oneself seen* is indicated by an arrow that really comes back toward the subject, *making oneself heard* goes towards the other."[51] Like the acoustic mirrors used prior to World War II on the Maltese and British coasts, reflecting and concentrating sound waves as early warning systems, the ear is that fleshy protrusion that can tune in not just to speech but to the various types of sounds and silences before, between, and beneath one's words.

In a discussion of dub as a musical technology, Michael Veal traces the two different paths reggae music took during the seventies, one that focused on the live black artist, the other that focused on innovations in the black soundscape. Dub reggae creates an audiovisual soundscape of haptic or synesthetic sound, sounds that leave an opening for images and affects in the listener that are not determined by a song's lyrics. For example, in "Ali Baba," a dub song recorded by John Holt in 1970, the lyrics describe a nonsensical dream landscape in which meaning is generated from a set of fantasy images rather than any conscious messages.[52] "Ali Baba"'s lyrics are literally about dreams, the nonsense language of a dub unconscious, with allusions and free associations to the story of Ali Baba from "The Arabian Nights" and other canonical children's stories such as *Alice in Wonderland* and *The Three Blind Mice*. "Ali Baba"'s lyrics evoke precisely the kind of dream or fantasy landscape dub technicians would then reproduce and repeat in sound.

As Marley was extending his Rastafarian racial message to audiences around the world, the dub reggae artist developed a very different performance style, one that competed in many respects with the more rock-based ideology of live musical performance.[53] Whereas Marley's "roots and culture" reggae spotlighted the performer, dub reggae emphasized the sound engineers, the "technicians" and "scientists" manipulating sound to create a more textured, sonic landscape. As a musical culture, dub works through the instrumental remixing of previously recorded songs. Usually a dub recording will remove vocals, emphasizing instead the drum and bass, thereby stripping down a track to create a "riddim." In dub, a riddim then travels through its initial recording into subsequent remixes and repetitions. In this "reverberating soundscape," of lyrics reduced to fragments of texts interspersed with gaps or interludes of sound, dub creates what Veal describes as a "pathogenic" discourse, "pure sound arising from emotion" rather than meaning attached to words.[54] Dub is precisely the kind of music Dolar describes in the epigraph, which confounds the voice's efforts to make meaning and sense from the song's lyrics and words.

After the first cut of "Ali Baba," produced between 1969 and 1970 by Duke Reid and released by Treasure Isle, was a hit, in 1975 Bunny Lee then recut the song for another singer, Jackie Edwards, and it was at this point that the dub engineer's work with the song began to define it more than the singer's. In King Tubby's version, "I Trim the Barber," reggae lyrics interrupt the lines from the canonical children's stories.[55] Silences, echoes, whistles, thuds, also interrupt and distort the sound of the word "reggae" itself into "are, are, are," a pure phonetic sound. King Tubby partially removes the vocals in Holt's original song and adds in as an additional layer extensive reverb, panoramic delay, and the occasional dubbing in of vocal or instrumental snippets such as the intermezzo from the original version. As large segments of lyrics are replaced by ambient sound, Tubby creates a kind of atmospheric effect in which the soundscape asks you to think about previousness, about what is now missing, what is no longer there, now that King Tubby has trimmed Ali Baba's song.

Communications equipment often pick up acoustic echoes from each other that color sound, disrupting and altering an original sound by others in the ambient space. Every noise, every static disruption, which contemporary echo cancelers seek to filter out of communication technology was consciously brought back into the dub song and arranged by the dub engineer. "Harmonic resolutions were subverted by sound processing," Veal describes, as dub engineers intentionally disrupted sonic flow with non-signifying sounds.[56] "Equalization and filtering devices" were used to create "reverb and delay" and other "timbral and textural effects"; "microphone 'bleed-through' and secondary signals" were used to create acoustic echoes and the "inclusion of extraneous material and non-musical sound."[57] The pops and clicks, tracking errors and distortions, pitch variations and higher sensitivity that make the LP a less ideal recording device than the CD were precisely the kinds of sounds the dub artist and deejay integrated into the dub record as a scratch, mark, noise on the record itself.

As much as accent, tone, and timbre can recall the voice in the word, similarly, tonal accents and timbral effects functioned in dub as open-ended sonic signifiers. By cutting lyrics, emphasizing both song fragments and the gaps echoing between them, dub songs "often surpass the one-dimensionality of the original lyrics in their cryptically evocative power, allowing more open-ended opportunities of lyrical interpretation."[58] As a number of producers continued to rework the original rhythms and lyrics of "Ali Baba," they combined nonsense lyrics and new sound effects to create an even more intense space of fantasy for the listener. "I Trim the Barber" was only one of a series of at least fifty songs that used the original drum and bass rhythm and some of the vocals from "Ali Baba," but all now given the loose narrative premise of a war between barbers and dreadlocks.

Over a series of songs Baba becomes the Barber and his opponent is Natty Dread, for example in the Aggrovators' cut, "Natty Dread Conquer the Barber." In two other well-known cuts, Dr. Alimantado's "I Killed the Barber" and Dirty Harry's "Poor Barber," one hears the sounds of gunshots, and Dr. Alimantado plays further with the children's story references by proclaiming: "I know who shot the Barber / . . . It was Tom, Tom, the Piper's Son . . . [gun shots]."[59] In "Bury the Barber," Jah Stitch posits that a woman is ultimately behind the barbers' and the dreadlocks' war. Many of "Ali Baba"'s remixed riddims explicitly develop the phallic fantasy of the reggae artist and deejay as a transcendent dubber, and the dreadlock as refusing to be trim or cut.

Whereas the emphasis in Marley's music was on conveying emotion and speech, dub songs emphasized rhythm, interrupting lyrics with the sounds of an ambient soundscape, de-emphasizing and distorting the vocal role and presence of a sole, central, unifying performer. However, the sound producer or engineer in the recording studio was as masculine a figure as the artist-performer onstage. The male deejay reconstitutes himself as a producer-performer who can make musical meaning out of dub's nonsense sounds, putting himself and the song back together against the break.[60] Once again, the reggae artist as a transcendent dubber continues to refuse to be trimmed or cut, wants to be the one doing the cutting.

While dub may be a more abstract or conceptual musical space, it also bears the marks of gendered differences. The body of the dub performer splits into the listening male producer making sense of the music in the recording studio, and the female listener experiencing the music bodily in her movements in the dance hall. Kaja Silverman argues in *The Acoustic Mirror* that women's voices on film often become vehicles for fantasmatic male projections of the female self. This is certainly one way of thinking about the place of the female dub listener in reggae culture. As Veal reminds us, dub took its name not only from musical and performance lingo but also from its reference to a style of erotically charged dancing and the act of sex itself—dubbing was sex, and the deejay as dubber metaphorically and literally set the rhythm groove.[61] Rhythm is the most prominent aspect of dub music because, in its local Jamaican context, dub reggae was as much a sensual as a specular activity. Dub rhythms were created to be danced to in the libidinal space of the dance hall, not just watched as performed onstage.

A more diminished understanding of the dance hall and its dub rhythms would see it as a feminized space subordinate to that of the engineer. However, dub rhythms also facilitate a different kind of listening experience, one involving the aural and acoustic, as opposed to the speech and form-producing, body. Dub creates a sense of the body as a cavernous space with its own reverberations and echoes, not unlike a movie's ability to evoke a kinesthetic and visceral sense of the filmic body. The dance hall also privileges the body and the ear as a reverberating space of gender discourses. The listener of dub is not just the feminized body; she is also the bodily subject turned inside out—a pure ear focused and interpellated by the sound waves of a gendered signifying order. In the dance hall, dub and other forms of reggae music expressed not just the liberatory urges and potential of a people but also the sexual codes and gendered social relations shaping that people's sense of community.

In theorizing the sonic as an aspect of a historicized, diasporic black subjectivity, Fred Moten describes blackness as speaking in the musical "break," that is, not in black speech but in the "the breaking of such speech, the elevating disruptions of the verbal that take the rich content of the object's/commodity's aurality outside the confines of meaning."[62] What needs to be emphasized here is the ways the black musical break disrupts a phallic discourse and opens up a space for reimagining the role of a female, consensual, acoustic voice. This female sound is more than the mere mirror or fantasmatic projection of the black male performer. The non-phallic voice in the break also echoes the depths of the black male performer's subjectivity, his bodily and affective depths that exceed his signifier and image, which bleed over or leak out of his musical performance like the uncontrollable sonic elements of a dub sound.

Throughout *In the Break*, Fred Moten refers "quasi-obsessively" to the "sexual cut," thereby introducing a more subtle reading of the difference sex makes to the sonic in articulating a more marginalized and silenced aspect of black identity.[63] Moten links the black musical break, the mark of racial difference that marks the signifier, explicitly to the sexual cut, the mark of sexual difference that founds the symbolic order. In the breaks between black sounds, we hear the effects of symbolicization as they inscribe themselves upon the sexuality of the black subject. Moten traces the epidermal marks of symbolic capture on Spillers's scarred black body as they are heard in the sensory register, in the scratch of the record, the chirrup of a plucked guitar string, the sound stuck in the gullet of the black male signifier, the rasp at the back of Marley's throaty cry. The sexual cut disrupts the seamless flow of the signifier. It is essentially that mark that prevents our collapsing of the phallus and the penis into an androgynous masculinity somehow exempt from the vulnerabilities, the wounds, the relational dependencies, produced and felt in the sexual relation.

Certain sounds essentially make visible again the mark of the body on the mirror image, the sound of the throaty gullet at the back of the signifier intent on hiding the voice. In explicating what he means by the sexual cut, Moten quotes a long and difficult passage by Nate Mackey, who describes hearing the sexual cut, tellingly enough, in the "characteristic, almost clucking beat one hears in reggae."[64] Here Mackey emphasizes the *hearing* of the cut; and what he hears in it, in "the syncopation [that] comes down like a blade," is "a 'broken' claim to connection." The sexual cut makes visible, sounds out, a prior brokenness before the claim to symbolic meaning and Imaginary identity in phallic wholeness. Mackey's notion of the "cut" refers directly to the dynamic Lacan described, whereby the subject loses a sense of him or herself at the very moment of taking on the phallic signifier, leaving the unconscious in a "profound, initial, inaugural, relation" to the cut of language itself.[65] A gendered androgyny, that is, gendered and sexual identities imaged and imagined as hardened and whole unto themselves, as impermeable, are precisely the opposite of Spillers's fleshy body, ungendered because it shows its Imaginary markings rather than covering them up in epidermal skin.

The signifying cut leaves a kind of mark, a leftover scar, as the sign of a bodily past irrecoverable and forever lost to the subject cut away from a more primordial sense of living, sensational being. For Mackey, reggae marks this cut with a particularly forceful and aggressive sound. However, this is partly because reggae's sonic portrayal of the break from the signifier doubles and echoes its lyrical expression of the vindicationist force of race war.

As reggae sounds evoke the break, reggae lyrics construct a new claim to connection as the basis for the performer's unifying black political speech. Mackey continues: "Here I put the word 'broken' in quotes to get across the point that the pathos one can't help hearing in that claim mingles with a retreating sense of peril, as though danger itself were beaten back by the boldness, however 'broken,' of its call to connection. The image I get is one of a rickety bridge (sometimes a rickety boat) arching finer than a hair to touch down on the sands."[66] As if spinning aural images from a dub track himself, Mackey describes the Rastafarian's call for unity as an effort to boldly "beat[] back" the dangers of the colonial past. The voice of the sufferer calls the community to action—"Move!"—but it is still haunted by the sense of "peril," of lack, of unending deprivation, produced from displacement and exile. It is a "rickety bridge" whose creaking tenuousness is captured in the plucking sounds of the reggae song's guitar strings.

Mackey's notion of the cut hinges on this sense of brokenness, where severance from the past and movement into a triumphalist, politically independent and sovereign future still carries along with it the traces, the scratches, of something the black male subject has to leave behind in order to authorize himself and his speech. Like the mysterious lamella, Lacan's membranous layer of tissue pit with orifices, the entity he leaves behind is the impossible body without an image, unmarked by either sexual difference or racial difference.[67] To capture this flickering sense of being, Mackey describes his own ambient dreamscape with reggae as its haunting backdrop:

> Listening to Burning Spear the other night, for example, I drifted off to where it seemed I was being towed into an abandoned harbor. I wasn't exactly a boat but I felt my anchorlessness as a lack, as an inured, eventually visible pit up from which I floated, looking down on what debris looking into it left. By that time, though, I turned out to be a snake hissing, "You did it, you did it," rattling and weeping waterless tears. Some such flight (an insistent *previousness* evading each and every natal occasion) comes close to what I mean by "cut."[68]

For Mackey the sexual cut produces a phallic black subject aware that he has had to divest himself of something — "looking down on what debris [is] left" — in order to lay claim to the signifier — "You did it, you did it."

Throughout his discussion, Moten evokes Mackey's very complex passage as a way of characterizing how black sound carries, along with speech, "an insistent *previousness* evading each and every natal occasion," that aspect of living being, the lamella, that "flies off" when the subject enters the symbolic order, just as "the membranes of the egg in which the foetus emerges on its way to becoming a new-born are broken."[69] More straightforwardly, this complex notion of the sexual cut captures the ways in which the black male subject, now understood as always split by his speech, leaves something else of his self behind, some vulnerability, some insecurity, some brokenness, that Moten and Mackey believe resounds within the spaces and intervals of certain black musical forms.

In *On Feminine Sexuality*, Lacan describes how the male subject denies his own broken claim to connection, his own not-wholeness, with phallic speech.[70] He also describes the phallic subject's mystification by a form of feminine discourse that escapes phallic categorization and closure. In dominant discourses of subjectivity, the (male) subject who understands himself according to a logic of the phallus $\$$, that is, he is subject(ed) to the phallic function, believes that in "having" woman whom he constructs as his object of desire (a), he also now "has" the phallus in his possession. This is the structure of patriarchy—in possessing ~~Woman~~ a man shores up his sense of his authority and legitimacy. Woman is barred because she is nothing but a phantasm, a fantasy, an acoustic mirror, a fantasmatic projection and object of man's construction.

In this vision of subjectivity organized by phallic desires, **Woman** does not exist. The discourse itself precludes a real relationship to a living, breathing woman who is more than the object of the male subject's fantasies. Instead, from within phallic discourse woman recognizes that she is the subject of lack $\cancel{A}$. Lacking the phallus, barred from the phallus, not-whole, she can never *have* the phallus but can only *be* the phallus in male fantasy. Whereas in dominant, phallocentric, logocentric discourse Woman is deeply circumscribed by and subordinate to men's desires and needs, Lacan uses logical formulas to demonstrate how **Woman** can also stand for what escapes phallic discourse. She is the impossible point of contradiction that puts the lie to a phallic discourse's effort to retain a sense of coherency and logical consistency.

The logical contradiction **Woman** represents is analogous to and can be explained further by a logical conundrum known as the Barber's Paradox.[71]

"Barber's Paradox"

Suppose there is a town with just one barber, who is male. In this town, every man keeps himself clean-shaven, and he does so by doing exactly one of two things:

1. Shaving himself, or
2. Going to the barber.

Another way to state this is: The barber shaves only those men in town who do not shave themselves. All this seems perfectly logical, until we pose the paradoxical question:

Who shaves the barber?

This question results in a paradox because, according to the statement above, he can either be shaven by:

1. himself, or
2. the barber (which happens to be himself).

However, **none** of these possibilities are valid. This is because:

* If the barber **does** shave himself, then the barber (himself) *must not* shave himself.

* If the barber **does not** shave himself, then he (the barber) *must* shave himself.

The Barber's Paradox and Lacan's formulas of sexuation both point to a paradox of set theory, namely, that the thing that defines a set (the Human, the set of men and women as Man, the Barber who cannot shave himself) also falls outside of the set (Man, Woman, as a discursive construct, does not encompass everything that it means to be human men and women).[72]

The point of the Barber's Paradox is precisely that, following the rules of logical discourse, it describes an impossible scenario, one that does not work out. At the very point at which the rules of language fail, this failure reveals another kind of truth about language. Illogical statements, logical paradoxes, demonstrate language's incoherence. Joan Copjec describes Lacan's formula for sexual difference similarly.[73] Just as there is always a barber who escapes the terms of the set he is supposed to help define—all men in the town who need shaving—similarly, in Lacan's formula, while no woman can escape the discursive, it is also true that there is something about women that is indeterminate, not determined by phallic discourse (and something about men as well). As Copjec describes **Woman**: "She is the failure of the limit, not the cause of the failure."[74] Copjec captures succinctly here woman's potentially indeterminate status as the form of Man that is not (phallically) male, that escapes the (phallic) terms of the discourse, just as somehow the barber escapes from the set of shaved men. Both Lacan's formulas of sexuation and the Barber's Paradox demonstrate forms of lalangue, a nonsensical language and word game that stymies the signifying Other.[75]

King Tubby's "I Trim the Barber" speaks, both directly and obliquely, to the Barber's Paradox. The paradox puts to the test the dubber's confidence that he can be both trimmed and uncut at one and the same time, whole and not-whole, part of the sum and the sum of the parts. The dub song tries to escape that paradox of language, that something always escapes meaning, by moving in two opposing directions. On the one hand, the Rastafarian dubber tries to do an end run around the paradox, imagining himself as the ultimate phallic signifier who transcends and cuts all others. On the other hand, the soundscape surrounding the dub voice suggests the possibility of other discourses and sonic forms, sounds that echo through the signifier and go beyond it.

If woman's discourse represents the very possibility that something escapes phallic discourse at its limit, not surprisingly, one finds throughout the history of Western aesthetics a concern that music is a woman's discourse because it produces sound that can detach itself from the Word. "Music, and in particular the voice, should not stray away from words which endow it with sense; as soon as it departs from its textual anchorage, the voice becomes senseless and threatening—all the more so because of its seductive and intoxicating powers.

Furthermore, the voice beyond sense is self-evidently equated with femininity, whereas the text, the instance of signification, is in this simple paradigmatic opposition on the side of masculinity. . . . Music is a woman."[76] In her autobiography Rita Marley offers another music, another discourse, on Bob Marley that goes further than phallic categorization and symbolicization. Rather, her discourse operates as a kind of focusing tuner, reflecting (on) the echoes of the black male performer both hidden and revealed in the heterosexual love relation, existing in the spaces between his lyrics and words. The autobiography certainly offers a feminist account of a black marriage subject to the rules of patriarchy and a heteronormative discourse of monogamy. However, it also provides a text of the ways in which the female voice can strip the black male performer of his phallic skin. As much a story about her husband as herself, *No Woman No Cry* presents Bob Marley as a sexual subject stripped of his androgyny and firmly placed in the sexual and gender politics of his moment. Rita Marley performs her own version of stripping the riddim as she discloses the impasse the Rastafarian couple finds themselves in when neither partner can fully compensate for what is not whole in the other.

Stripping the Black Male Performer: The Love Letter and Relations of the Flesh

The duet (*duo*) . . . the love letter, they're not the sexual relationship. They revolve around the fact that there's no such thing as a sexual relationship.
—JACQUES LACAN, *On Feminine Sexuality*

My sense is that waterless tears don't have a thing to do with romance, that in fact if anything actually breaks it's the blade. "Sexual" comes into it only because the word "he" and the word "she" rummage about in the crypt each defines for the other, reconvening as whispers at the chromosome level as though the crypt had been a crib, a lulling mask, all along. In short, it's apocalypse I'm talking, not courtship.
—FRED MOTEN QUOTING NATHANIEL MACKEY, *In the Break*

For Mackey, as for Lacan, both men and women have constructed their life stories, their romances, as a way of thwarting that deeper sense of a brokenness or irrecoverable previousness to the self before language. Sexual difference, like the scratch on the record, like the scar of racial difference on the body, records the inescapably split nature of modern subjectivity, leaving only a trace, on the rim of the body, of the bodily self prior to signification. Love fills the space of "waterless tears"—of the raw flesh without its epidermal cover—with "the search by the subject, not of the sexual complement, but of the part of himself, lost forever, that is constituted by the fact that he is only a sexed,

FIG 4.2. Cover art for Damian Marley album *Mr. Marley* (Ghetto Youths, 1996).

living being, and that he is no longer immortal."[77] And when gendered scripts and romantic fantasies of love fail, the sexual or love relation becomes a kind of crypt in which the subject "rummages about" pretending that it had been "a crib, a lulling mask, all along." In the same way, Bob Marley's immortality continues to muffle the cry of the black male body's vulnerability as mortal flesh rather than immortal image.

In one of Marley's most famous love songs, "No Woman No Cry," the male, first-person voice tells his lady not to cry while the sufferer's repeated chant, "I remember," evokes the social context in which the young couple's love affair is forged, the local and historically specific setting of Trench Town in the postcolonial, urban landscape of Kingston, Jamaica.[78] To sing a song with a message, as Bob Marley has done for populations across the globe, assumes the presence of a stable subject as the fixed source or origin of the song's statement. This stable subject could then be described as retaining some kind of "signature" or ownership over his or her utterance. The performer's signature becomes more complicated, however, when, as Derrida describes: "the debt includes [another] . . . with whom I myself have worked, discussed, exchanged ideas, so that if it is indeed through him that [others] have 'read' me, 'understood' me, and 'replied' to me, then I, too, can claim a stake in the 'action' or 'obligation,' the stocks and bonds, of this holding company, the Copyright Trust."[79]

Also titling her autobiography *No Woman No Cry*, Rita Marley describes Bob Marley's musical legacy as the result of a collaboration between husband and wife. His words were forged in the context of their shared relation, their conversations as a couple making music together in the Trench Town setting: "So many of Bob's lyrics reflect our personal life. . . . When Bob wrote he didn't always write alone. . . . So that most of the lyrics you come across, especially in the early times, pertained to the life we shared."[80] Despite her own role as the primary defender of the family's legal rights to Bob Marley's musical image and material, in her autobiography Rita Marley refutes the copyright's claim to the truth of the performer. As if the original Marley was always already someone who was "divided, multiplied, conjugated, shared," in her autobiography Rita Marley borrows lyrics from some of Bob Marley's most popular songs and claims at least a partial share in the performer, as a product of the duet that was their musical marriage.[81]

An analysis of Rita Marley's autobiography that focused simply on the construction of her gendered identity in the context of broader structures of patriarchy would find ample evidence for the way her narrative repeats and reinscribes all the discourses that position women "naturally" in heterosexual symbolic orders as child bearers, social reproducers—woman as phallic object. As a *duet* of black identification, however, her account of the Marleys' relationship also reveals what escapes phallic discourse and the race narrative, exposing those aspects of blackness and black masculinity that the race narrative cannot encompass. Rita Marley's autobiographical voice is that of a woman asserting her knowledge and rights as a cohabitating lover, partner, and wife of the singer. *No Woman No Cry* is less a solo act than a performance of the gendered and sexual black female self that makes visible how the heterosexual dynamics of her and Bob Marley's love relationship, "what remains veiled in law, namely, what we do in that bed—squeeze each other tight," shapes their musical and intimate collaboration over the years of his life and career.[82]

Rita Marley offers her own cover of Bob Marley and it is the song, the image, the story that has never been told. As Anna Marie Smith describes what Rastafarianism excludes as a political identity: "The productivity of contiguous and overlapping discourses which contribute to differentiation of blackness, discourses organized around gender or sexuality, for example, tended to be muted."[83] This muting, when reflected in a black female voice, reveals how destabilizing black desire can be to the race narrative. Smith's perspective on Rastafarianism agrees with V. Spike Peterson's argument more broadly that, while "heterosexism is *not* the most visible or apparently salient aspect of political identities and their potential conflicts . . . heterosexism may be the historically constructed 'difference' we most need to see—and to deconstruct."[84] In the Marleys' political context, Rastafarianism articulates a heterosexualizing logic that is part of the genealogy of the black race-war politics that emerged from Jamaica in the 1970s.

No one knew better than Rita Marley how reggae recording studios functioned as gendered spaces during this period, shaped by dominant patriarchal and heteronormative discourses. Studio One as she describes it was "less like a business and more like a family affair," and women were allowed entrance only in very narrowly defined roles.[85] Rita met Bob Marley and his partners, Bunny Wailer and Peter Tosh, while she was a member of the Soulettes, a female singing group who provided backup for many of the new and emerging acts that included the Wailers. And yet, she noted that "it was important to all three of the Wailers to see that Dream [her cousin and singing partner] and I were being raised strictly, that we had discipline from our house, that we had been brought to Coxsone by older men who knew music. Robbie in particular seemed to take that as something very positive."[86] Despite her own professional identity she was aware that, in the men's eyes, she needed to maintain her standing as a respectable Jamaican woman.

There were aggressive efforts within Rastafarianism to police heterosexuality and female sexuality. These policing strategies were not in opposition to the realm of pleasure and sexual desire. Rather, they were intimately tied up in the radical decolonizing of black sensuality in Rastafarian discourse, "where the black body [which] had been the site of disciplining and neutralization of difference . . . was now redefined as a highly visible signifier of black pride." However, as Smith describes further, while "the revaluation of the black body as goodness was coupled with a revaluation of sensual pleasures," heterosexuality was also highly privileged, as was "the assertion of the virility of the black male and the representation of the black woman's fundamental role as a childbearer. Sexual practices, as long as they do not contradict these principles, are revalued as good in themselves. Homosexuality, contraception and abortion, however, are usually represented as taboo."[87] What Smith essentially describes is a containment of the consensual black body—multisensorial and polysexual—within a Rastafarian phallic discourse. Trying to erase from the black body the effects of the colonizer's discourse of racial difference, Rastafarianism reinscribed that body within certain constructions of sexual difference emphasizing black male virility and female fertility only. This heterosexualizing logic then reaffirms certain aspects of the vindicationist race war narrative.

As it emerged in the 1930s and developed into the 1970s, Rastafarianism was a politics of essences. Since the essentialist arguments of race-war discourses claim that the "'essence' or true character of an identity has been concealed through the work of forces which are external to that 'essence': that is, the forces of oppression and domination," Rastafari discourse "draws a single frontier between the white racist system and the suffering black people."[88] Rastafari discourse singularizes; that is, it defines the group based on an unassailable cohesiveness and unity that cannot be breached: "The Babylonian system is represented as ultimately failing to penetrate and subvert blackness."[89] It becomes a condition of battle that each side in the race war be different from the other and indivisible unto itself: "For Rastafari, the constitution of identity was not a matter of a complex play of heterogeneous subject positions, of which Rastafari-blackness was one among many, but of an increasingly totalizing identity which did not admit contradictory identities (such as homosexual blackness or anti-Rastafari blackness). The return to essence entailed a total clarification of multiplicity and contradiction in experiences and identities such that the social became represented as a simple two-camp system."[90]

Rastafarianism's antihomosexual discourse is a function of its polarized, racialized stance, since it is precisely in the realm of sexuality and desire that heterogeneous desires and identifications rear their heads, potentially destabilizing Rastafarian sexual politics from within. As a discourse of race war that cannot tolerate the fissures, the splits, the cracks that are always already a part of the sexual relation, Rastafarianism engaged in its own "homogenizing project" of defining blackness in the singular terms of Oneness.[91]

Recounting their first real date, Rita firmly positions herself and Bob Marley in a romantic space separate from the cultural screen and describes their interaction as a sensuous communication involving gazes and touches: "He took me to the Ambassador, our local Trench Town [movie] theater. . . . Most of the time we were looking into each other's eyes. . . . Our eyes were always our way of communicating, and instead of looking at the screen we were looking into each other's eyes and then we were kissing . . . and I realized that this could go on to something else that I really couldn't even think about, so don't let's think about it, let's just look at the screen!"[92] As the screen moves more explicitly into their relationship, however, it causes the first moments of alienation between the couple. When Rita is pregnant with their third child, JAD Records, an American group that signed Marley before his later and much greater success with Chris Blackwell and Island Records, approached the couple. As Rita describes further: "Americans can speak, they give you a picture on the wall that looks great." Soon she becomes enamored with the new kind of picture she can make of herself and for "Mr. Marley" in the North American cultural context: "So I had a new look, and even after three children I had a new interest too from Mr. Marley. Later, when we were alone, he took a long look at me and said, 'Wow, so you went and got yourself a fresh face!'"[93]

This American picture soon reveals its blind spot, however, when Marley is asked to perform a kind of androgyny, a performative and unattached heterosexuality, which removes him from his own private life and identity within his family:

> Back then, all the magazine stories I'd read as a girl had said that when you got married it was understood that you were going to be married for life, you were going to be devoted. . . . When we got to New York, though, a new element was added, because it was a record company recommendation that you shouldn't let your fans know you were married. How could you be a devoted husband and sell records? I didn't know this until I read, in a newspaper interview: "Bob, we hear you're married— is it true you're married to Rita?" And his answer was, "Oh no, she's my sister!"[94]

When she discusses this with her husband, Bob deflects and silences his wife's concerns by applying the Rastafarian discourse of Oneness to their love relation:

> "Listen, man," he said. "Just cool." . . . "Because look at this," he went on. "Let me show you something. . . ." He was drawing something in the palm of his hand, showing me a circle. "Listen, Rita," he said. "You see this circle, this is like life, where we have to go around different places and meet different people. But inside this circle, this is where we are, you and me. And you see this line that go around it? Nobody can break that line to come into the circle with you and me, it's protected. This is me, this is you, this is the children, all the important people are inside this ring. Anything happens outside it doesn't have a proper meaning, and nothing can get inside."[95]

With the image of the unbroken line, Bob reconstructs seamlessly the relationship between the race narrative and the heterosexual contract, asserting their "them-twoness" as a Oneness.[96] In the community of One, the people on your side remain safely enclosed within a ring of identity that no one can breach, and the promise of being "them-two," developing a real relationship with the other as a like subject, collapses into the space "inside this circle, this is where we are, you and me."

The fundamental dilemma in the heterosexual model of love is that we get in our own way. The desire to truly commune with someone else—to become them-two—is disrupted by the fact that our desire is tied up in the narcissistic need to feel "as one," undivided and whole within oneself and in the presence of the other. Lacan describes love as "impotent, though mutual, because it is not aware that it is but the desire to be One, which leads us to the impossibility of establishing the relationship between 'them-two.'"[97] The (hetero)sexual relationship essentially cloaks the self's narcissistic need to find him or herself, that lost or missing part, in the beloved.[98] Rastafarianism fit very much within this model of a phallic, heterosexualizing discourse that "provides a sense of a bounded identity which functions as an 'armor' in terms of the rigidity and fixity that it offers . . . a 'fortress' in which the subject searches in vain for a 'lofty, remote inner castle.'"[99] This fortress of the race narrative does not protect Rita Marley from the intra-racial violence that erupts when the circle of the heterosexual relation does not hold.

In later years, when Rita decides during one phase of their marriage that she can no longer tolerate Bob Marley's many infidelities, she draws a line: "I told him plain, straight out, if you're going to be doing this, we will not have a sexual relationship. We will have a relationship because we're already family, but as far as sexual involvement is concerned, no."[100] Rita's attempt to end their sexual relationship produces a violent response: "The next time Bob came back to Jamaica, I was almost raped. Because this is where I had drawn the line—'I'm not having sex with you.' But he insisted: 'You're my wife and I want you!' And so we had sex."[101] The scene literally enacts the traumatic realization that "there's no such thing as a sexual relationship," no real mutuality and them-twoness in the romantic myth of complete Oneness.[102]

That first American scene with JAD Records is also one of the last moments in the text where Rita Marley gives space to Marley's justifications for his behavior throughout their marriage. Instead, Rita Marley increasingly turns her husband's renowned lyricism against him, framing his justifications as more "blah blah blah," a form of nonsense lalangue. Lacan calls the romantic stories, idealizations, and fantasies that the subject produces, as a defensive tactic to "take[] the place of the missing partner," a "jouissance of the blah blah."[103] When Rita decides to engage in her own sexual relationship outside of the marriage, she describes her husband's jealous confrontation with her lover in these terms, black male speech as sound without meaning, a bric-a-brac of language erected to hide the truths and traumas of the self: "When Bob showed up there (as usual with a girl in the car), he left the girl and came down to the riverbank, yelling, 'Hey, Tacky, you're seeing my woman! And blah blah blah . . .' And carried on like a wild man! . . . I got very upset."[104] In a second scene close to his death, as Bob Marley's contract with Island Records approached its end he made new promises to Rita: "He'd be a better father, spend more time with his children, he'd be a better husband, he'd be a better friend . . . blah blah blah. We laughed and talked all night. Promises, and oh. . . ."[105] Rita Marley turns him down because, at this point, the Rastafarian fantasy of a Oneness proclaimed from the shadows has lost its luster—"I'm not gonna live in the darkness, I told myself, I have to be where the light shines." Confronting what Bob Marley's words and sexual acts have represented for both of their lives, she sees the truths behind the blah blah blah and reveals the role she has played in his heterosexist fantasies: "I was his eye, I was his pain; when things were not right, I would be the shoulder. I created home for him anywhere I was. And he loved that."[106] Rita Marley subverts the race narrative articulated in Bob Marley's songs with another transcription of blackness coded into the "blah blah blah" of their lives together as a couple.

Rita and Bob Marley's relationship would go through multiple iterations of the conversation they first began in that hotel room in the United States. As *No Woman No Cry* continues, the radical resignation in Rita Marley's autobiographical voice registers her demystification of the courtship romance and her apocalyptic acceptance that there is no liberatory model inherent in black heterosexuality beyond a confrontation with the limits of what we can know about our sexual selves and desires. This is the harsh reality she sees her husband denying in his relationships with women other than herself. Bob Marley's infidelities force Rita Marley to wrestle with the secret of heterosexuality, the "not-wholeness" enacted through the sexual relationship that serves as a cover for what is missing in the self: "After he became public property . . . even the whole woman thing was becoming a problem for him. They might enjoy sex, but he wasn't enjoying his life. Sex is one thing. But what happens afterward? What can you give? What is your contribution? And that's what's lacking in most of Bob's relationships; the one-night stands were becoming physically and spiritually boring—that took a lot out of him."[107]

Rita sees Bob Marley in ways he is unable to see her, and her writing of this different story allows her to traverse fantasies of heterosexuality in exchange for self-knowledge but also for an appreciation of the black male performer in all his vulnerability and inadequacy. As Lacan also explains: "There's no such thing as a sexual relationship because one's jouissance of the Other taken as a body is always inadequate—perverse. . . . [However], isn't it on the basis of the confrontation with this impasse, with this impossibility by which a real is defined, that love is put to the test?"[108] As Rita struggles with the fact that her relationship is not working out, the players and the relationship keep moving forward. The Marleys's love emerges and takes shape in the gap between them as two desiring subjects.[109]

Like the Barber's Paradox, it is another paradox of the sexual relationship that it never really works out—there is no perfect love relation or idealized sexual relationship, as the epigraph from Lacan famously describes.[110] It is precisely the working out of this truth over the course of a lifetime, and over the course of relationships, that constitutes the encounter Lacan feels comfortable approximating or calling love: "It is in their courage in bearing the intolerable relationship," the lack of harmony or unity between self and other, "that friends, recognize and choose each other. This ethics is manifestly 'beyond-sex.'"[111] This discourse of "friendship" is also Rita Marley's final song as she looks back at her marital duet with Bob Marley:

> At that time, the husband-wife thing seemed to me an unbreakable bond—you're bound to this relationship. . . . The vow alone was proof enough. . . . I never anticipated most of the things that happened because when I married, like most nineteen-year-old girls, I thought we were just going to be this way, love and happiness always. But marriage was a definite, real commitment to me, and added to it was that I always felt in sympathy with Bob and felt that I would always be his friend, come what may. It seemed more than a husband and wife thing with us; we were friends or, to look at it another way, despite whatever happened between us, we *decided* to be friends.[112]

Here, deciding to be friends means not denying how both the man and the myth failed her. Rather, friendship is the form of relation left behind after a real confrontation with the inadequacies and gaps in the other and in the self, the absences the sexual relationship romanticizes, fills up, and covers over.

In his final moments, Bob Marley partly set in play the conditions for his immortalization when he delayed his own cancer treatments because of his deeper psychic and spiritual fear of being cut. As he asserted, "Rasta no abide amputation . . . I and I . . . don't allow a mon ta be dismantled . . . no scalpel shall crease me flesh! . . . Rastamon live out."[113] In his declaration, Marley held on to the ideal of an uncut, phallic immortality even as he approached death.

In contrast, the photograph with his father that Damian Marley uses as the cover image of his first album, *Mr. Marley*, is very much an image of the mortal man (see figure 4.2). As Žižek describes, it is an image of "the flesh one never sees, the foundation of things, the other side of the head, of the face, the secretory glands par excellence, the flesh from which everything exudes, at the very heart of the mystery, the flesh in as much as it is suffering, is formless, as its form in itself is something which provokes anxiety."[114] This image of a haggard Marley, his face drawn and his body already beginning to be ravaged by his affliction, photo-graphs the uncanny possibility of the black male performer falling out of the symbolic and back into his fleshy body.

In what is clearly a family photograph, Damian Marley sits on Bob Marley's lap as an infant, the father off-center and partly covered by his son. The son protrudes from the rim of the father's unseen mouth, both a speaking and a silencing. This is the very image of a "previousness that escapes each natal occasion," the previousness of the father at the moment of the son's emergence, and also the previousness of the father's own status as flesh mirrored in the infantile skin on the belly and arms of his newborn son.[115] The photo is pasted onto a brown, papery or leathery skin-like flap, a hide, upon which both of their names are inscribed, Mr. Marley and Jr. Gong. The lamella-like brown flap beneath them is the very image of the skin marked up and left behind, as both the father and the son enter into the field of the visual and the symbolic order. This brown under-skin is also the membrane separating the photographic image from the voices of the father and the son recorded on the vinyl album inside.

In this cover image, the son offers a tribute to the father as a man of living flesh but also the son's voice leaves behind a father whose death is written on his face. Marley's drooping locks, drawn face, and erased mouth become the uncanny skin-image, the fleshy under-skin, of black male facialization, that needs to be shed and left behind for his son(s) to emerge into their own symbolic maturity. A number of Bob Marley's sons went on to pursue solo careers as performing and recording artists like their father, namely, Ziggy Marley, Julian Marley, Ky-Mani Marley, Stephen Marley, and Damian Marley. In our contemporary moment, Bob Marley's sons reproduce "likenesses" of the father, that is, symbolically repeating *themselves* as visual performances of his face. In this way, they become not so much his copies as signs in their own right. Their public images represent a visual language that can be easily recognized, a set of codes established from the 1970s when Bob Marley stood before the mirror of global culture, his face and body becoming the central signifiers for the kind of embodied, Third World, black male subjectivity his liveness came to represent for the decolonizing era.

Defacing Race, Rethinking the Skin

Every perception is doubled with a counter-perception . . . is an act with two faces, one
no longer knows who speaks and who listens. Speaking-listening, seeing-being seen,
perceiving-being perceived, circularity (it is because of it that it seems to us that perception
forms itself *in the things themselves*).
—MAURICE MERLEAU-PONTY, *The Visible and the Invisible*

On the cover of the issue of the *Economist* dated January 19–25, 2013, underneath the headline "How will history see me?" there is a photograph of President Barack Obama straightening his collar and bow tie as he faces a mirror
(see figure C.1). The cover image captures perfectly what Merleau-Ponty describes as the circularity of performance as a signifying act, its ability to blur
the line between the one "who speaks" and the one "who listens." If the skin of
the face acts as a kind of second, a surrogate or double for the human head, its
success lies in its ability to collapse the gap between the head and the face, the
man and his image-mask. "Covers," public images, serve as a kind of epidermal
covering for black celebrity, luring the gazer, the audience, into believing that
the sign for a subject, the body-image or the face, represents the subject-(in)-
his or herself. This collapsing creates a counter-perception and hides the fact
that to stand before the interpersonal or sociocultural mirror is always already
"an act with two faces." The skin act encompasses both the objectified self-
performance and the subjectifying position of the performing self.

Cover images also become part of a visual lexicon of popular culture.
Perhaps that is why the *Economist* photograph resembles so strikingly two
twentieth-century images discussed previously in *Skin Acts*. The first, one of

FIG C.1. Cover
of the *Economist*
magazine, Janu-
ary 19–25, 2013,
featuring Barack
Obama.

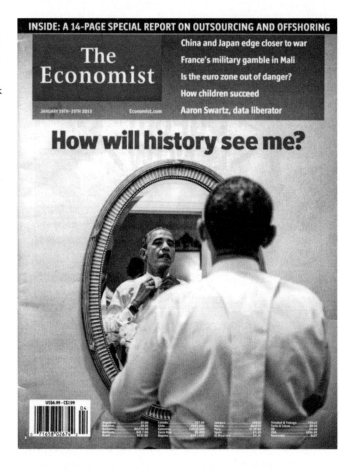

the photographs that appeared in the *Vanity Fair* spread from the first decades of the century, pictures Bert Williams in his dressing room (see figure 1.6). Promoting Williams and Walker's blackface minstrel show, the caption described the actors as performing a "most novel and valuable set of faces." The second comes from the very different medium of film, a scene from Harry Belafonte's *The World, the Flesh and the Devil*. Forty years later than the *Vanity Fair* photo spread but sixty years before the *Economist*'s cover image of President Obama, this scene includes for a few frames a shot of Ralph staring into and then smashing a mirror. This act occurs after he comments on the painting he holds in his hand, Winslow Homer's *The Gulf Stream* (1899), depicting a lone black male lost at sea. In all three instances, Williams, Belafonte, and Obama, black men known for their public presence, are caught, or posed as caught, in the act of being *photo-graphed*, in the Lacanian sense I have been using throughout. They are captured, symbolically, in the very act of standing (or sitting) before the mirror and preparing a face for the public gaze.

It is important to note that these men are caught in the act of *preparing to be* photo-graphed rather than simply as the objects produced by the photographing itself. As such, all three sights capture the different dimensions of the black male performer's chiasmic self-reflexivity—seeing, being seen, but also, seeing oneself—as he prepares himself for facing the gaze. They demonstrate each male figure's awareness of his own *faciality*, to use Deleuze and Guattari's term, or what Erving Goffman also describes as the "front of an individual," a person's "socialized self," captured best by the sign of the face emblematized in portraiture.[1] These images of the man in the mirror also capture epidermalization—that is, blackness reflected back from the cultural screen as an afterimage, a covering, a skin-image, of a subject who might locate and experience himself in other ways. The face in the mirror accompanies the body before the mirror, and the latter, in motion on the edge of the cultural screen, signifies something more about the performing self as a body-in-the-act. Finally, then, these images also capture what we cannot see, the back as a figure for everything about the performer the photo-graphing cultural grid cannot capture, or can capture only as the absence of a cover or covering, an uncanny image of nothingness, the hidden face of the flesh.

This doubling of the performer and his image—his surrogate, his shadow—a tripling, according to Fanon, of body, gaze, and self, or flesh, skin, and face, is precisely the lens through which *Skin Acts* has been thinking about specific black male performances. It should now be clear, however, that blackness functions here as the canary in the coal mine for an epistemic phallicizing of modern subjectivity that affects multiple racial subjects and revolves around the skin. Black masculine performances throw into relief the power of the gaze to reify the surface as a mere image, that is, as an encapsulating symbolic container that has meaning only as a reflection of difference in the symbolic and imaginary orders. Black masculine performances highlight the ways in which the gaze seeks to find and locate racial or sexual differences as essentialized features of the body-with-skin; to position that skinned body within the frame, on the cultural screen, as primarily a scopic or specular sight; and to use that covering image or double skin to mask other corporeal, sensational, kinesthetic, visceral, affective, desiring, attaching, intercorporeal, consensual, shadowy, virtual, unincorporated dimensions of the embodied subject. It has been my intention here to use the site of performance, and the black male body particularly, as a simultaneously phallicized and epidermalized (hardened) symbolic site. In addition, much as Belafonte does in the mirror, I aim to smash the edges of the frame that the scopic, epidermalizing sight of race provides, demonstrating instead the manifold ways in which the skin acts against and in excess of, as much as in alignment with, the power of the gaze.

Skin Acts offers a narrative and an argument concerning what a repertoire of images of four particular black male performers has to say about race, performance, visuality, and the particular tropes of the face and the skin, in dominant discourses of race and difference that have come to characterize modernity. The 1890s moment of Winslow Homer's painting begins a cultural trajectory, with both synchronic and diachronic features, that attempts to answer the very question the *Economist's* headline poses of President Obama, "How will history see me?" However, whereas the *Economist's* question suggests concerns about idealization or defamation, reputation and recognition or denial, my discussion in *Skin Acts* aims to take us well beyond the question's framing terms. Not only are there a number of things history can see, retrospectively, in black male performances, but also these features will change in historically specific ways over time. Also, there will always be something about embodied performance and black subjectivity that cultural history cannot capture by sight alone. Rather, our cultural histories of blackness will have to mobilize other senses, other haptic and synesthetic optics, to represent a hint of the complexity of what gets performed when a racialized subject — accompanied by his double, his afterimage, his surrogate — steps onto a sociocultural stage.

It was in the New Negro moment at the very turn of the twentieth century that black male performers in the United States first claimed the power to frame their own faces, deploying portraiture to capture their vision of a social self. George Walker's and Bert Williams's *Vanity Fair* photographs were taken in the heyday of two converging cultural developments, the rise of the New Negro movement and the flourishing of photography. The portrait photograph, however, far from being a more authentic representation of the black ex-slave at the dawn of the new century, is the very medium through which the modern black subject was turned further into a sign. Racialized physiognomy became the ur-trope of a blackness that could be recognized, given meaning, when seen. In Williams and Walker's cultural moment, where "the white audience wanted to look," to borrow the telling phrase from the *Vanity Fair* photo series, was on a likeness of blackness as a racial difference evident, glaringly, in physiognomy. Once "the head and its elements are facialized, the entire body also can be facialized, comes to be facialized as part of an inevitable process."[2] The body of the black subject was not just racialized, but facialized, in the portrait photography of the New Negro, to produce respectable New Negro men and women as powerful visual signifiers of the race's civic potential.

If the cartoon image of the black face as a "real coon," itself a defacing of black physiognomy as the ur-sign of racial difference, also extended itself over the body, then in an epidermalized visual logic the face serves as both a metaphor and a metonym for the skin. The skin is inscribed with its own history of serving as a modern sign for what it means to be human. This was precisely the insight Fanon marked in his titling of *Black Skin, White Masks*, namely, that "the skin is so to speak, the body's face, the face of its bodiliness."[3] By the turn of the twentieth century, white American audiences were already trained to see black corporeality reductively, as meaningful only in terms of the epidermal surface. A logic beginning in early modernity and solidifying during the Enlightenment defined epidermalized human difference as a feature of a hardened, bodily impermeability.

The body-with-skin becomes an important resource in the conversion of an acting body into an image on the film screen. As demonstrated in close readings of the physical dimensions of Paul Robeson's acting and cinematic performances, however, there is always a man, a perceptible embodiment, beneath or accompanying the image. Film in particular, as a set of "moving pictures," can capture the traces of the body-without-an-image and activate the intercorporeal space between the active performer and the seemingly passive and invisible spectator.

In Winslow Homer's painting of the bare-chested male in *The Gulf Stream*, this poor, stripped slob, all alone and afloat on the Black Atlantic, is more than a mere pornotrope of blackness. The image, not unlike the one of George Walker baring his back to the camera in the *Vanity Fair* photo spread, certainly demonstrates how the skin can display itself to the camera as a visible sign of the black subject's bodiliness (see figure 1.7). However, the stripped black male body as *imago*, as a phobogenic object that produces anxiety in Fanon's words, can also represent a brush up against the Real, the uncanny reality of our fleshy corporeality. It was Fanon, in his capacity as both a colonial thinker and a psychiatrist, who provided us with ways of thinking about the encounters between the gaze, the face, and the skin, as more than merely the reified units of a discursive lexicon of race that shapes modernity.

In a way consonant with an interpretation of the blackface mask less as a (derogatory) likeness of the black face and more as an extraction of that face from the body, taking its meanings one step farther away from the corporeality of the black subject, Fanon described the ways in which the modern subject in general has learned to replace our sense of our fragmented, porous, sensational, grotesque bodies with an image of the whole body, polished, perfected, and sealed up in the symbolic order, for the other's gaze. The famous "mirror stage" in Lacanian psychoanalysis is precisely the moment when the subject/psyche gains an understanding of itself as a surface projection reflected in a mirror. This reflected mirror image becomes the self's body-image, that is, literally a visual representation—one might say, a facialization or epidermalization—of the self's experience of him or herself out in the world as based on his or her physiognomic likeness. We all know Fanon's more famous elaboration on this to argue that the white gaze literally gives the black colonial subject back a body-image of himself as nothing more than his skin. However, we also need to remember that Fanon described a different, experiential, sensational, kinesthetic, and visceral sense of the body that is lost when the epidermal schema falls on the black subject like a mantle or mask.

Fanon's "corporeal schema," the subject-as-body, what Deleuze, Guattari, and Brian Massumi also describe as the body-without-an-image, crumbles once the subject discovers his black body as it is constructed from Symbolic material, from language, from the discourse of the Other.[4] However, just prior to that moment, in its residual sensations, this third person or triple consciousness tied to a bodily or sensational ego experiences a "body that isn't cast out" by the mirror stage, by the symbolic order, but rather, is "completely at the limit, at an extreme, outward edge that nothing closes up," a body at the very edge of our self-perception.[5] In a fascinating and lengthy footnote directly engaging Lacan's mirror-stage thesis, Fanon argues ingenuously that, for the white subject who looks in the mirror for a decorporealized, idealized body-image of the self, black skin functions as a kind of uncanny imago, a spectral, haunting image of the discarded body left behind as an unwanted remainder by the mirror image.[6] The paradigmatic trope of that body left behind is none other than the flesh, the skin stripped of its imaginary reflections and symbolic meanings.

The poor slob on the raft is a figure for bared flesh, that is, for everything abject, vulnerable, fleshy, de-idealized about the modern subject writ large. To make this metaphor even more literal, his blackness is not simply a sign for his racial difference; it is now also, in Fanon's hands, the uncanny specter of the white subject's splitting of psyche and soma, the splitting off of his own fleshy corporeality to create a more abstract, conceptual, symbolic mirror image of the self. Here Fanon gives us another fascinating word for this process, not a form of scopic vision—seeing oneself from the outside as the other sees us—but a *heautoscopic* vision—projecting our own insides outward, as if separate

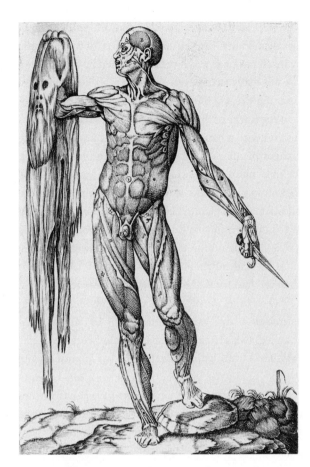

FIG C.2. *Anatomia del corpo humano.* Juan Valverde de Amusco, Rome 1559. Copperplate engraving. Courtesy of the National Library of Medicine.

from the self.[7] The skin, thickened into visibility with its racialized meaning as a sign of human difference, requires just such an act, the extraction of a part of the human body from the corporeal to give it a meaning in the mirror of the gaze that is separate from oneself.

The image that I have found most useful for conceptualizing this fleshy, cut-away, heautoscopic experience of the embodied self—as a whole body stripped of its separated skin—is that of the ecorche, an image popular in Western art history. The ecorche is a figure drawn, painted, or sculpted to show the muscles of the body without skin (see figure c.2). If the body-image in the mirror is of the self's muscular, idealized self-image, not surprisingly, "one of the definitions of the Lacanian real is that it is the flayed, skinned body, the palpitation of raw, skinless flesh."[8] As Žižek describes further: "Let us recall the uncanniness, and even disgust, we experience when we endeavor to imagine what goes on just under the surface of a beautiful naked body—muscles, glands, veins, etc. In short, our relating to the body implies the suspension of what lies beneath the surface, and this suspension is an effect of the symbolic order—it can occur only insofar as bodily reality is structured by language. In the symbolic order, we are not really naked even when we are without clothes, since skin itself functions as the 'dress of the flesh.'"[9] Throughout the history of Western art, the ecorche or the image of the body stripped from its skin has developed the same associations with a hard and defined body that would come to dominate idealized images of the skin as a container of difference. Even Vesalius spoke of surface muscularity as an anatomical norm, whereby, "the transparent, elastic quality of skin is a desirable characteristic in the muscular male body, for what it allows to shine through bears the positive connotation of vitality and virility."[10] As Benthien further describes this symbolic dressing of the flesh in a gendered skin: "The notion of the skinless body as a positive image in Western culture is still radically masculine. The male subject can, as the ultimate liberation fantasy, free itself of its skin, while the female subject remains bound within it."[11] Over time, the male body that "symbolically, gradually closed into an 'impermeable body'" was figured visually in images of the naked body where the finely drawn articulation of the male figure's muscles evokes and mirrors the attention traditionally given to the bared muscles and tendons of the ecorche.[12]

In contrast, the process of "phallicizing" the male body "gave rise to the opposing concept of the female body as 'a vessel, a container,' as a 'hollow space with an enveloping, smooth external skin.'"[13] Benthien notes that in this gendered visual regime, the male "must not forget that she is at the same time 'a bag of rot inside the skin' . . . not a potent muscle structure under the skin but rather a bloody mass of flesh," a "formless femaleness."[14] Consequently there are very few representations of the female ecorche, a woman "seen without a skin in her fleshly nakedness."[15] And if there are few female ecorches in the history of Western art, it is virtually impossible to draw a black ecorche that would somehow remain racially marked. The black ecorche is the epitome of the body without an image, that is, it is an impossible image in a symbolic order in which blackness signifies as the epidermal outer layer of the skin. How does one mark the ecorche's blackness if such an outer, epidermal layer is stripped away? The black ecorche poses an obvious conundrum for a racial theory that depends on external skin to secure an immutable sense of racial "difference."

In her work Invisible Men (2009), Dutch Caribbean artist Patricia Kaersenhout strives to create just such an impossible image of a heautoscopic black masculinity stripped of its symbolic skin. Colorfully painting over "the pages of an old biology book, with its illustrations of intestines, skin structure, hair, the

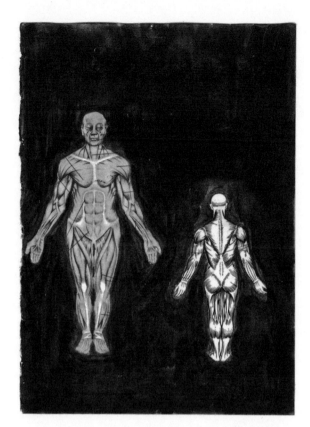

FIG C.3. *Invisible Men.*
Patricia Kaersenhout,
2009. Published by
Eindeloos uitgevers
with graphic design by
Vivienne van Leeuwen.

digestive system, and so on," she reimagines what is culturally invisible about black masculinity as a wounded, exposed, skinned body, stripped back to its visceral, internal flesh (see figure C.3).[16] In its most horrific form, the flesh as a marker of the stripped, skinned body is a phantasm marking symbolic death, the frightening failure of language (to symbolize, epidermalize, facialize, racialize).[17] This unsymbolizable kernel of the Real—in this case, precisely what is unrepresentable about blackness—appears as a "black hole" or "crack in the texture of reality."[18] What we encounter in this black hole of the signifier "is simply the body stripped of its skin," a "spectral apparition that fills up the hole of the real."[19] Understood in this way, race is not merely a social construction but also a symbolic language, an imaginary visual code, and epidermalization is both black skin and white mask, a modern skin condition, not simply a black condition.

Heautoscopy, then, represents the look that strips away imaginary and symbolic skins to expose the raw, holey fleshiness of the subject within. In *Skin Acts* I model such a heautoscopic look by contrasting Bob Marley's continued sym-

FIG C.4. *If I Were A. . . .* Courtesy of the artist. © Elia Alba, 2003. Photocopy transfers on fabric, acrylic, acrylic medium, zippers. 65 inches in length. Distorted and digitally manipulated images of the artist's body transferred onto fabric.

bolic liveness, his increased symbolic meaningfulness after his death in cover images and covers of his music, with his aliveness as evident in his social and affective relations. The image of his body in the years just before his death, as a body slowly being stripped or flayed of its symbolic skin, also stands as a membrane or bridge between the living, historical Marley and the Marley alive in death. The specter of this rarely seen, fleshy image of Marley haunts Damian Marley's album cover, the performer's visage profoundly disturbing in its cadaverous haggardness, presenting the defaced image of the performer as vulnerable and weakened but also as an affectively and haptically attached father (see figure 4.2).

The body-image or mirror image is always preceded by Fanon's corporeal third-person consciousness, the body left standing *before* or in front of the mirror, a body one experiences through other haptic and tactile senses that include, but are not exclusive to, the visual. This is the body experienced both in and as its fleshy skin, as in Jamaican American artist Sandra Stephens's life-size video installation *Skin*, with its lumps, folds, creases, and orifices (see figure 1.1). This is an idea of the (black) bodily self not as a costume but as a hide, one that feels both tactile and grotesque, as in Dominican American artist Elia

Alba's piece *If I Were A . . .* (2003), where skin suits mimic the ways the skin can exist as an internal object-representation, the subject's experience of him or herself as a front turned inward, or inside out (see figure c.4). This is not identity as performativity but rather, in its most frightening guise, a self shorn to almost a caricature of the material, embedded within the desexualized real.

What does the face of the black male performer look like in this mode, exposed without an idealized, symbolic, phallic covering? One might imagine Merleau-Ponty's two-faced act in the picture of the black male head buried beneath a facial mask, which peers out at us from the cover of the Evergreen edition of *Black Skin, White Masks* (1968) (see figure c.5). The image of a black male head that serves as Kaersenhout's cover for *Invisible Men* defaces epidermal blackness in a different way than Fanon's masked man. Here, as the face of the black male is covered over by his innards, his visceral self is also exposed (see figure c.6). Inspired by Ralph Ellison's canonical text of African American masculinity, *Invisible Man*, Patricia Kaersenhout aims less to make the black male subject socially and culturally visible in the way of New Negro portrait photography than to render what cannot be idealized and scopically fetishized about the black male subject, his embodied fleshiness. Throughout *Invisible Men* this is figured literally as his blood, guts, and viscera, in uncanny images of a re-corporealized black masculinity that necessarily appears phobogenic within the terms of the symbolic order.

Powerful as Kaersenhout's image is, in the realm of performance we find even more immediate modes for experiencing, not just seeing, the corporeality of the performer and imagining alternative ways of thinking about black masculinity once stripped from its skin. In *Skin Acts*, my goal has been to situate black male performances at this chiasmic confluence of intersections — between the gaze and the skin, the face and the body, the flesh and the act. While noting, certainly, blackness's symbolic meanings as racialized discourse, I have also offered alternative sights and methods of analysis to complement our tried and true discussions of black objectification, fetishization, or reification as pure image. The preceding readings try to imagine and expose an embodied black male subject who stands before his image in the mirror of the gaze, experiencing his body simultaneously in ways that cannot be captured by that image or mirror. In the experience of living in, being in, one's skin, the flesh is an aspect of the self one discovers on the edge, on the hide just as it is being shed, just as one enters the symbolic order to stand before the Other's gaze.

Performance provides a space for rediscovering, in our experiencing and readings of actors' particular gestures, their specific embodiments of their

FIG C.5. Cover of Frantz Fanon's *Black Skin, White Masks* (Evergreen edition, 1968).

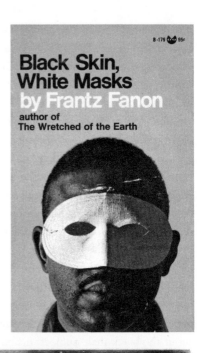

FIG C.6. *Invisible Men.* Cover image. Patricia Kaersenhout, 2009. Published by Eindeloos uitgevers with graphic design by Vivienne van Leeuwen.

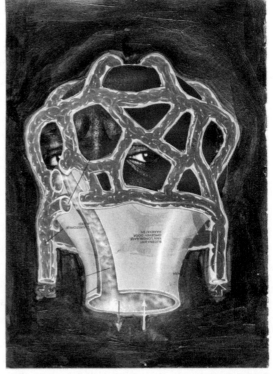

parts in their personal, corporeal styles, those performance strategies or skin acts that serve as another site for the (in)corporeal exceeding of the frames and boundaries of the symbolic image and phallic signifier. As much as the *Vanity Fair* photographs of Williams and Walker at the turn of the century created fetishized images of each face in its own individual box on the grid, taken together they also suggest the motility of Bert Williams's body in the act of performing his "facial stunts." The two photos of Williams in his dressing room looking into the mirror capture quite literally that space between the body-image and the body-without-an-image, as the performer's (black) face floats in the mirror alongside, in front of, the image of his actual body, which sits on our side of the frame (see figure 1.6). The body looking exists beside the body being looked at. Here the back of the performer is not posed but rather in action, preparing for the act as an "interaction-in-the-making," and given a place as such within the frame. Contrasting, even, with the refusal of display that characterizes contemporary photographer Lorna Simpson's famous images of the backs of black women, the imaged backs of Obama, Williams, and Belafonte are *neither* guarded nor displayed (also see figure c.1). They are merely in the process of engaging in an action, in the act of preparing a mirror image of the self.

Ultimately, *Skin Acts* strives to recover the way in which these kinds of unexpected gestures and undramatic images can be reread as precisely those uncanny moments when a shot, a photograph, an image captures a different kind of sight of the black male body in the act. This sight is a tripling of the self of the performing black male consciousness, first as the seen (the face, the skin); second, as the uncanny unseen (the hide, the insides); and third, as the self-reflexive self seeing itself in the act (the polyvocal, sensory corporeality of the skin). When Ralph Burton smashes the image of his own face in the mirror, as the shadow of his head hovers over Homer's painting, and as his body turned with his back toward the camera, looks on, we get precisely the kind of layered, palimpsest-like image that I have tried to unpack here using concepts such as faciality, epidermalization, heautoscopy, and intercorporeity as tools.

In regards to the *Economist*'s image of Obama and the question, "How will history see me?" I hope I have demonstrated that answering this question fully in Obama's case would require much more than the study of one image and act, but rather, a close reading of many of his performances, public, imagined, private, posed, using some of the methodologies and analytic tropes I have demonstrated. What I can say now about this particular cover image is that it offers a very different picture of Obama than the famous one Shepard Fairey produced for his first presidential campaign. In the slick, twenty-first-century style of portraiture exemplified in Fairey's now-iconic poster, the black male human head is smoothened, virtualized, colorized, and deracinated. Fairey's rendering of Obama is very much an image of The Face, inviting us to write ourselves into a new vision of America as a colorful, multiracial, postracial utopia.[20] This is not just the post-racial body but also a new form of facialization that tries once again to color over the flesh with new codes and signifiers of a mediated blackness, the irreal images of a colorblind gaze.[21] In contrast, in the cover image of the *Economist*, the face that looks back at us in the mirror belongs to a body slightly to the left or right of the symbolic frame, what Bert Williams described as standing beside himself, and the face is not simply refused—after all, one can see it clearly in the mirror. Rather, it is the gap between the face and a body whose movement can never be fully pictured that the photograph ultimately captures. Obama's back is as much a metaphor for his absence—in the Derridean sense, whereby the man is not actually here in his image but rather the image is a stand-in—as it is a marker of his emergent presence in a more phenomenological sense and experiential bodily mode. The back represents the man, the performing self, caught on the edge of motion. His cover image and backward-facing double stand in for all the other dimensions of corporeal experience that go into his act, as he faces off against his afterimage reflected in the Other's gaze.

preface

1. Frantz Fanon, *Black Skin, White Masks*, trans. Charles Lam Markmann (New York: Grove Weidenfeld Press, 1967), 109.

2. Quoted in Cary D. Wintz's *Encyclopedia of the Harlem Renaissance* (New York: Routledge, 2004), 1210.

3. Gerald Bordman, *Musical Theatre: A Chronicle* (New York: Oxford University Press, 1978), 190.

4. Hortense Spillers, "Mama's Baby, Papa's Maybe: An American Grammar Book," *Diacritics* 17, no. 2 (Summer 1987): 67.

5. Cornel West, *Restoring Hope: Conversations on the Future of Black America*, ed. Kelvin Shawn Sealey (Boston, MA: Beacon Press, 1997), 4.

6. Henry Louis Gates Jr., "Belafonte's Balancing Act," *The New Yorker*, August 26, 1996, 133.

7. Many of these forms fall into the genre of the "public photograph" Maurice Wallace describes in *Constructing the Black Masculine: Identity and Ideality in African American Men's Literature and Culture, 1775–1995* (Durham, NC: Duke University Press, 2002). This genre can include "the magazine cover, the book jacket, the news photo, the billboard, the exhibit portrait, even the criminal mug shot" (25). In *Skin Acts* I argue that the public photograph functions as a metonym for some of the "covering" functions of the skin itself, which include hiding, protecting, and mimicking the self through physiognomy. See also Kenji Yoshino's inventive uses of the term "covering" in *Covering: The Hidden Assault on Our Civil Rights* (New York: Random House, 2007) to represent the various forms of the "cover-up" society encourages when blacks and Asians are required to act white and gays and lesbians to act straight.

introduction. FLESHING OUT THE ACT

1. Toni Morrison, *Beloved* (New York: Random House, 2004), 104.

2. William Faulkner, *Absalom, Absalom* (New York: Random House, 1986), 111–112.

3. Hortense J. Spillers, "Mama's Baby, Papa's Maybe: An American Grammar Book," *Diacritics*, Vol. 17, No. 2 (Summer, 1987): 64–81, 65, 66, 66, 67. Spillers also describes

this body as ungendered so that blackness can be assigned new gendered meanings in a colonial discursive order — the captive black body as hypersexual, a thing, other, and "pornotroped" as powerless (67).

4. Spillers, "Mama's Baby," 67.

5. Spillers, "Mama's Baby," 67.

6. See Nicole Fleetwood for a discussion of how and why epidermalized black femininity retains its associations with the flesh, even signifying as "excess flesh" (*Troubling Vision: Performance, Visuality and Blackness* [Chicago: University of Chicago Press, 2011], 9).

7. Spillers, "Mama's Baby," 68.

8. Spillers, "Mama's Baby," 70.

9. Spillers, "Mama's Baby," 70.

10. Michael Taussig, *What Color Is the Sacred?* (Chicago: University of Chicago Press, 2009), 137. In "Off-Colour," the sixth chapter of *The Book of Skin*, Steven Connor also draws the link between European perceptions of the skin and of color more broadly (Ithaca, NY: Cornell University Press, 2004), 147–177.

11. Taussig, *What Color Is the Sacred?*, 159. In *Europe's Indians: Producing Racial Difference, 1500–1900* (Durham, NC: Duke University, 2010), 3, Vanita Seth re-creates the links between epistemic shifts in Western thought and forms of colonial discourse, arguing that we must pay closer and deeper attention to "the epistemic conditions that enabled the thinking of difference at different historical junctures," conditions that included "Europe's interaction with the colonial non-West" (3–5). In her history of "difference," she points to the period from the Enlightenment to the nineteenth century as the historical moment when skin color becomes increasingly associated in scientific treatises as the "physiological basis for the difference" between the African and the European. Her work corresponds with Claudia Benthien's history of the skin in which she describes the contrast drawn between the African as the "skin person" and the European as the "eye person," that is, the one defined epidermally in relation to the other, defined scopically or through the power of the gaze. Claudia Benthien, *Skin: On the Cultural Border between Self and World* (New York: Columbia University Press, 2004), 159, 152.

12. Kaja Silverman, *Flesh of My Flesh* (Stanford, CA: Stanford University Press, 2009), 1.

13. Seth's discussion of the epistemic privileging of similitude in the medieval period parallels Connor's discussion of "the mythical logic of homology (as *a* is to *b*, so *x* is to *y*)" that shapes the relationship between humoral theory and notions of the skin in the Middle Ages (*The Book of Skin*, 19). Both accounts allow us to reattach medieval and early modern notions of alikeness to a more contemporary discourse of relationality one can find, for example, in the work of Caribbean thinker Édouard Glissant, for whom the history of colonial modernity created a layered "poetics of relation" that extends across New World and Old World space and time: Édouard Glissant, *Poetics of Relation* (Ann Arbor: University of Michigan Press, 1997). As relationality emerges as a new paradigm for intersubjective relations both in psychoanalytic theory and in sensation and affect studies, it behooves those of us working in black diaspora studies to recover the discourses of relationality that have also shaped the articulations of the black experience throughout the Americas.

14. In another aspect of this intervention, scholars counter the association of same-ness and resemblance with what is bad about sight or naïve about representation. We see this critique of sameness throughout Peggy Phelan's discussion of identification in *Unmarked: The Politics of Performance* (London: Routledge, 1993), see especially chap-ters 3 and 4, and also in Silverman's discussion of the *selfsame body* in *The Threshold of the Visible World* (New York: Routledge, 1996), see chapter 1. Others such as Hardt and Negri have argued that difference is an a priori assumption of empire, postmodernism's modus operandi rather than subversive opposite number (see their complex discussion of difference in the section entitled "Alternatives within Empire," in Michael Hardt and Antonio Negri, *Empire* [Cambridge, MA: Harvard University Press, 2001]). Gilroy ex-tends this critique of difference in more explicitly racial terms in *Against Race*, where much like Silverman in *Flesh of My Flesh*, he puts faith in the utopian dimensions of perceiving sameness in the face of overdetermined, dominant discourses of difference. Gilroy's hope is that such perceptions could lead to alternative modes of congenial inter-action between humans across racial, subjective lines (see the conclusion to *Against Race: Imagining Political Culture Beyond the Color Line* (Cambridge, MA: Harvard Univer-sity Press, 2000) but also Gilroy's discussions of "conviviality" throughout his later work *Postcolonial Melancholia* (New York: Columbia University Press, 2006).

15. See Martin Jay's *Downcast Eyes: The Denigration of Vision in Twentieth-Century French Thought* (Berkeley: University of California Press, 1994) for an account of the position of vision in the works of leading figures and in Western thought and culture. In a number of discourses across continental philosophy, art history, postcolonial theory, and feminist film studies, the spectating subject has been seen as synonymous with the master in the Hegelian dialectic of the master and the slave, and with the existential Self (or subject) in relationship to the Other (object). Such a perspective also shapes bell hooks's *Black Looks: Race and Representation* (Boston, MA: South End Press, 1992), where she describes the "imperial gaze" as "the look that seeks to dominate, subjugate, and colonize. This is especially so for white people looking at and talking about blackness" (7). Hooks's de-scription of this gaze evokes Jean-Paul Sartre's characterization of the look as unequivo-cally shaped by structures of domination (*Being and Nothingness* [New York: Washington Square Press, 1992]), and John Berger's description in *Ways of Seeing* (New York: Viking Press, 1973) of the white male subject of the gaze as the "spectator-owner," inhabiting this viewing position in relationship to the European art form of the female nude (56, 63). In contemporary theory, the spectator is the subject who faces the painting, looks at the colonized, and watches the film screen. In film studies, for the canonical work on the spectator, see Laura Mulvey's *Visual and Other Pleasures* (New York: Palgrave Macmil-lan, 1989). In African American cultural studies, Maurice Wallace provides an in-depth theorization of the gaze in relation to race and black masculinity in *Constructing the Black Masculine: Identity and Ideality in African American Men's Literature and Culture, 1775–1995* (Durham, NC: Duke University Press, 2002) where he describes the gaze as "an accu-mulation of social, psychic, and symbolic affects through which social subjects are 'screened'" (182). For Wallace, the central problem of black masculinity is a problem of the visual—"the monocularistic gaze of Western racialism" serves as "the signal menace

to the coherence of the black masculine corporeal ego"—and the black male subjected to the dual dilemma of invisibility and hypervisibility is the victim of a "frame (-up)" (6, 34, 10). Wallace also refers to Kaja Silverman's discussions of the gaze, the look, and the screen throughout *The Threshold of the Visible World*. Focused primarily on the hegemony of the visual in constructions of black masculinity, Wallace nevertheless points to certain forms of performance that may hold the key to preventing this fixing of the black male body by the gaze, whereby "the performative properties of the black masculine [could] reappropriate the objectified body" (12, 14). *Skin Acts* picks up where Wallace leaves off, also theorizing what is less visible to the gaze, the dynamic interaction between the resisting, fleshy black look and the object of *its* sight, the embodied white gazer.

16. Naomi Segal, *Consensuality: Didier Anzieu, Gender and the Sense of Touch* (Amsterdam: Rodopi B. V., 2009).

17. Laura U. Marks, *The Skin of the Film: Intercultural Cinema, Embodiment, and the Senses* (Durham, NC: Duke University Press, 2000); Jennifer Barker, *The Tactile Eye: Touch and the Cinematic Experience* (Berkeley: University of California Press, 2009).

18. The turn to focusing on human affinities across difference also comes with new approaches to representation. For example, Kaja Silverman describes and uses a logic of *analogy* in *Flesh of My Flesh* and Marks argues that Third World films rely more on *mimetic* modes that emphasize the imitation of touch, rather than *representative* modes that center on the image as visual metaphor.

19. Nina G. Jablonski, *Skin: A Natural History* (Berkeley: University of California Press, 2006). As evident in the dialogue between Jablonski's study, Connor's *Book of Skin*, and Benthien's *Skin*, a more material discussion of the skin can also provide the humanities disciplines with a more cross-disciplinary vocabulary, bridging the humanities, the social sciences, and the psychosocial sciences, in thinking about intersubjective and intercultural relations.

20. Brian Massumi, *Parables for the Virtual: Movement, Affect, Sensation* (Durham, NC: Duke University Press, 2002), 9; he also terms this "relation."

21. Massumi, *Parables*, 9.

22. Massumi, *Parables*, 259. Massumi's mantra, "passage precedes construction," is meant to remind us of a body in motion and in social interaction prior to social construction (8).

23. See Jessica Benjamin, *Like Subjects, Love Objects: Essays on Recognition and Sexual Difference* (New Haven, CT: Yale University Press, 1995). This turn to relationality, the interpersonal, and the intersubjective, as posing very different understandings of identity and difference, distinguishes more recent schools of American psychoanalysis from their more traditional Freudian counterparts, and also from Lacanian models. For a helpful discussion of the differences between contemporary psychoanalytic schools, see Stephen A. Mitchell and Margaret J. Black, *Freud and Beyond: A History of Modern Psychoanalytic Thought* (New York: Basic Books, 1995).

24. See Silverman for more on this notion of the "incorporative" (*Threshold*, 22).

25. Didier Anzieu, *The Skin Ego: A Psychoanalytical Approach to the Self* (New Haven, CT: Yale University Press, 1989). Anzieu adds the "skin ego" as another locus of the

unconscious to both the Freudian oedipal narrative and the Lacanian focus on language as the structuring medium of the unconscious. Skin theorists and scholars working in affect and sensation studies have picked up on Anzieu's highly complex model that focuses, for example, on eight psychic functions of the skin and the conditions that result when these functions are disrupted.

26. As Merleau-Ponty describes in *The Visible and the Invisible* (Evanston, IL: Northwestern University Press, 1968) in a working note entitled "Flesh of the World—Flesh of the Body—Being": "My body is made of the same flesh of the world (it is a perceived), and moreover that this flesh of my body is shared by the world, the world reflects it, encroaches upon it and it encroaches upon the world . . . they are in a relation of transgression or overlapping. . . . This means a sort of "reflectedness" [of the body] . . . it touches *itself*, sees *itself*. . . . It is not an act, it is a being at" (248–249).

27. Anzieu, *The Skin Ego*, 62.

28. In "'All the Things You Could Be by Now, If Sigmund Freud's Wife Was Your Mother': Psychoanalysis and Race," in *Female Subjects in Black and White: Race, Psychoanalysis, Feminism*, ed. Elizabeth Abel, Barbara Christian, and Helene Moglen (Los Angeles: University of California Press, 1997), Hortense Spillers also describes this mode of self-reflectivity and self-reflexivity as an "interior intersubjectivity," as the "locus at which self-interrogation takes place" in the black subject, a locus that she argues might emerge more clearly as a site of study when one engages in a "psychoanalytic cultural criticism, or psychoanalytics" of black subjectivity (138).

29. Throughout "Mama's Baby, Papa's Maybe," Spillers argues for keeping distinct the African slave who has been assigned a racial, epidermal meaning on the skin, and the captive African subject who is still "flesh" just prior to his or her racialization in New World history.

30. See Kimberlé Crenshaw's canonical essays, "Demarginalizing the Intersection of Race and Sex: A Black Feminist Critique of Antidiscrimination Doctrine, Feminist Theory and Antiracist Politics," in *The Black Feminist Reader*, ed. Joy James and T. Denean Sharpley-Whiting (Malden, MA: Blackwell Publishing, 2001), 208–238, and "Mapping the Margins: Intersectionality, Identity Politics, and Violence against Women of Color," in *The Public Nature of Private Violence: The Discovery of Domestic Abuse*, ed. Martha Albertson Fineman and Roxanne Mykitiuk (New York: Routledge, 1994), 93–120. For Spillers's description of a "psychoanalytics" of blackness, see "All the Things You Could Be," 138. For an example of the convergence of intersectional and psychoanalytic approaches, see Jared Sexton's reconciling of Jacques Lacan's account of the sexual relationship with issues of sexuality and miscegenation in black and racialized contexts in *Amalgamation Schemes: Antiblackness and the Critique of Multiracialism* (Minneapolis: University of Minnesota Press, 2008).

31. Sylvia Wynter, "Beyond Miranda's Meanings: Un/silencing the 'Demonic Ground' of Caliban's 'Woman,'" in *Out of the Kumbla: Caribbean Women and Literature*, ed. Carole Boyce Davies and Elaine Savory Fido (Trenton, NJ: Africa World Press, 1990), 355–371. Spillers's and Wynter's canonical essays are founding black feminist theoretical texts for this study.

32. Connor, for example, describes "the early Christian tradition [as having] a decidedly ambivalent attitude towards the skin," much of that ambivalence stemming from their focus on the body as anatomy. The skin was perceived "only as that which is to be breached in order to gain access to the hidden innards of the human body" (*Book of Skin*, 13). This attitude, continuing into the eleventh century and beyond, was reflected in the work of Andreas Vesalius, the author of the foundational text of modern anatomy. In *De humani corporis fabrica (On the Fabric of the Human Body)*, the removal of the skin is "the emblematic act of this production of knowledge" that allows the human body to come into view as the "anatomical idea" (Benthien, *Skin*, 43, 45). "The actuality of the skin may have been invisible to the anatomist," Connor continues, but this begins to change by the middle of the sixteenth century. Connor arrives at a conclusion very similar to Wynter's, namely, that "the figural and the physiognomic" start to blend as modes of perceiving the human from the early to mid-1600s and, as Benthien also begins her eighth chapter, "As early as the seventeenth century, visually differentiated skin color becomes the primary characteristic by which ethnic difference is defined" (*Skin*, 145). Benthien's and Connor's accounts corroborate not only Wynter's theoretical premise but also Kim Hall's careful literary-historical argument that in the writings of the Renaissance poets and playwrights there is a relationship between the epidermal meanings of such words as "fair," "dark," or "complexion" and their separate but related function as poetic metaphors: Kim Hall, *Things of Darkness: Economies of Race and Gender in Early Modern England* (Ithaca, NY: Cornell University Press, 1996). Shakespeare's language figures prominently in Wynter's, Benthien's, and Connor's accounts as linguistically marking the moment of the shift away from anatomy to a more physiognomic apprehension of the human body.

33. Seth, *Europe's Indians*, 176.

34. Seth, *Europe's Indians*, 178.

35. Seth, *Europe's Indians*, 176.

36. In *Skin*, Benthien describes the body of the Middle Ages as a "grotesque body" completely at odds with a more modern, post-Baroque conception of "an entirely finished, completed, strictly limited body" from which nothing "protrudes, bulges, sprouts, or branches off" (38). For Seth, the medieval body is like Merleau-Ponty's overlapping flesh in that it also has "transgressive characteristics" such as "physiological confusion (anatomical disarrangement of human body parts or the intermingling of human and animal physiques)" (*Europe's Indians*, 177). Seth is interested in emphasizing this grotesque body's specifically nonracial character (175).

37. Seth, *Europe's Indians*, 183.

38. Seth, *Europe's Indians*, 183.

39. Seth, *Europe's Indians*, 183.

40. Seth, *Europe's Indians*, 183. Seth continues, "Whereas the two-sex model of the body that was to emerge in the late eighteenth century (and continues into our own time) presumes a radical incommensurability and distinctiveness between male and female anatomy, the one-sex model that saw little corporeal variation between men and women attributed the body with a greater degree of fluidity and transformative power" (183–184).

41. Connor, *The Book of Skin*, 18; Connor also describes this as a "nesting involution of the body" that duplicates medieval cosmology, "the universe being articulated by an endless series of such enclosures of the same within the same."

42. In *The Book of Skin*, Connor describes the slow emergence of the word "complexion" as a synonym for the skin in the medieval and early modern periods (10, 19).

43. Connor, *The Book of Skin*, 15.

44. Benthien, *Skin*, 38–39.

45. Benthien continues: "The main events in the existence of this grotesque body thus happen through other bodies and substances . . . eating, drinking, defecation, copulation, pregnancy, sickness, death, and decomposition as the kinds of 'acts of the bodily drama' that occur at the 'confines of the body and the outer world'" (*Skin*, 38).

46. Massumi, *Parables*, 57; also see Silverman's discussion of proprioception and the bodily ego in the first chapter of *Threshold*.

47. Massumi, *Parables*, 58–59.

48. Merleau-Ponty, *The Visible*, 134. Drawing very much from Merleau-Ponty's notion of "the flesh of the world" in *The Visible and The Invisible* (248), Silverman, Barker, and Segal all utilize the trope of the flesh as a way of talking about bodily subjectivity. Whereas Merleau-Ponty focuses on the phenomenological relationship between the self and the world, Barker examines the relationship between flesh and the film screen, and for Segal the flesh is the ultimate figure for consensuality. For Brian Massumi, who seeks to move us outside of the frame of the mind-body dichotomy, flesh becomes the entryway into theorizing the incorporeal body—the body in motion that can never be captured by sight without being immobilized in a frame.

49. Merleau-Ponty, *The Visible*, 134.

50. Merleau-Ponty, *The Visible*, 138.

51. Merleau-Ponty, *The Visible*, 138.

52. Merleau-Ponty, *The Visible*, 215.

53. Connor, *Book of Skin*, 40. As he describes further, "We habitually envisage that in-betweenness in terms of membranes, borders, boundaries. But these are themselves abstracted forms of the skin, the skin emblazoned, stretched out, explicated," the skin as a metaphoric rather than material model of relation.

54. Anzieu, *The Skin Ego*, 10.

55. Merleau-Ponty, *The Visible*, 138, 140–141.

56. Jacques Lacan, *The Four Fundamental Concepts of Psychoanalysis*, ed. Jacques-Alain Miller, trans. Alan Sheridan (New York: W. W. Norton, 1998), 81–82, 181. The drives, an element of the Lacanian psyche that scholars have taken up much less comprehensively and systematically than his models of the Imaginary and the Symbolic, is a crucial arena for fleshing out an intersectional theory of racial and sexual difference in *Skin Acts*.

57. Lacan, *Four Fundamental Concepts*, 196. The diagram of the partial circuit of the drive is on page 178 and is described on 179 in *Four Fundamental Concepts*.

58. Lacan, *Four Fundamental Concepts*, 151.

59. For Lacan, in the body the sexual cut represents not a fixed genital difference, but rather, sexuation as a signifying difference that grounds the modern symbolic order.

Lacan tells us, "In the psyche, there is nothing by which the subject may situate himself as a male or female being" (*Four Fundamental Concepts*, 204). Sexual difference emerges in the face of the signifier's inability to deal with the libido as undifferentiated living being, and with the Real as something we are irrevocably denied access to except through the lens of language and signification.

60. Jacques Lacan, *On Feminine Sexuality, the Limits of Love and Knowledge*, ed. Jacques-Alain Miller and Bruce Fink (New York: W. W. Norton, 1999), 57.

61. Anzieu, *The Skin Ego*, 10. By reminding us that the sex act can be both "the deepest psychical contact and the most complete form of skin contact with one and the same person," "the act of love" as "two lips touching," and the phallus itself as "an equally sensitive surface" and fold of the skin, Anzieu points us toward a reimagining of the phallus as enfolded, invaginated skin, this time with the vagina turned inside out, another return to the medieval one-sexed body.

62. Lacan, *Four Fundamental Concepts*, 178; a diagram of the libido-organ or libido-body is on page 187 in *Four Fundamental Concepts*.

63. Lacan, *Four Fundamental Concepts*, 178. Lacan also describes the reflexivity of the drive, "making oneself seen, heard, sucked, shitted" (187).

64. The triangular diagram of the Imaginary, the Symbolic, and the Real appears in *On Feminine Sexuality*, 90. As Lacan also describes, in the "domain of the drive" we meet "something that has an irrepressible character even through repressions—indeed, if repression there must be, it is because there is something beyond that is pressing in" (*Four Fundamental Concepts*, 162). The drive is the outcome of the subject's encounter with a Real that only manifests as an obstacle: "The real is the impact with the obstacle; it is the fact that things do not turn out all right straight away." The drive is the "irrepressible" force of an "irrepresentable" reality that can only appear as a remainder or kernel of the Real. Sexual desire functions as the most intense form of pressure from an irrepressible Real that presses in upon a sensational body. Segal describes something similar, quoting Anzieu: "The orifices [. . .] become erogenous zones . . . by being figures or points of intense, rapid pleasure on a ground of the global sensuality of the skin" (*Consensuality*, 192). So the sexual body, the body cut by sexual difference, can be both an erogenous pathway back to the sensational body and a libidinously charged experience of what presses in upon it from the Real.

65. Lacan, *Four Fundamental Concepts*, 197. "Whenever the membranes of the egg in which the foetus emerges on its way to becoming a new-born are broken, imagine for a moment that something flies off, and that one can do it with an egg as easily as with a man, namely the *hommelette*, or the lamella."

66. Slavoj Žižek, "The Lamella of David Lynch," in *Reading Seminar XI: Lacan's Four Fundamental Concepts of Psychoanalysis*, ed. Richard Feldstein, Bruce Fink, and Maire Jaanus (Albany: State University of New York Press, 1995), 205. Lacan also describes the lamella as a mythic organ representing "an infinitely more primal form of life" ("Position of the Unconscious," in *Reading Seminar XI*, 273). Including both anatomical sexes, the lamella represents the "sphericity of primordial Man as much as his division," that aspect of living being that exists prior to signification and capture by the specular image.

Another of Lacan's descriptions of the lamella, as "[Aristophanes's] primitive double-backed creatures in which two halves are fused together [and] separated later by a surgical operation," suggests a being who looks much like Vanita Seth's monsters of medieval fables ("Position of the Unconscious," 273).

67. Lacan, "Position of the Unconscious," 273.

68. Lacan, "Position of the Unconscious," 273; Lacan, *Four Fundamental Concepts*, 197.

69. Lacan, "Position of the Unconscious," 273; Lacan, *Four Fundamental Concepts*, 197.

70. In Lacanian theory, these are the three movements or loops of the drive, the active, the passive and the reflexive, which ultimately produce the subject of desire.

71. For Massumi, there is an experience of the body that slips away from and cannot be captured by discourse, and yet still remains as a part of the subject's experience of his or her self. "The skin is faster than the word," Massumi states, and there is a "disconnection of signifying order from intensity," intensity here describing "incipient action and expression" (*Parables*, 25, 30). Massumi also theorizes "a different order of connection [between body and self] operating in parallel" to the body described by the signifier, translated in language (24).

72. For Lacan there is also an important distinction between libidinous and genital desire, both of which connect to the sexual relation. The genital is what we turn to when our libidinous desire for wholeness cannot be satisfied. The genital is a screen, the psyche invested with sexual fantasies, whereas the libidinous is the absent cause of the sexual desire that propels us toward those fantasies and desired, partial replacement objects. The genital seeks objects of desire, an intrapsychic or incorporative relationship with beloved, desired objects; the libidinous is the very cause of desire, the lost object or like subject that is always missing, for whom the subject of desire finds its partial replacement, remnant, remainder in the physical organs of the body. In the skin ego, the body itself is the remainder of this lost object-cause of desire, as much a set of orifices as it is a sealed-up mass, and therefore the skin can provide an entryway back to a phantom experience of the body of species-being.

73. Fanon, *Black Skin*, 109; Silverman, *Threshold*, 133. For Silverman, the gaze reappears and functions in the symbolic order as the cultural screen.

74. Feminist scholars have also studied this cry, including bell hooks in "Feminism as a Persistent Critique of History: What's Love Got to Do with It?" and Lola Young in "Missing Persons: Fantasizing Black Women in *Black Skin, White Masks*," both included in *The Fact of Blackness: Frantz Fanon and Visual Representation*, ed. Alan Read (Bay Press: Seattle, WA, 1996), 76–85 and 86–101, respectively); also see Michelle Wright, *Becoming Black: Creating Identity in the African Diaspora* (Durham, NC: Duke University Press, 2004).

75. Fanon, *Black Skin*, 114–116.

76. Massumi, *Parables*, 3. Massumi's follow-up question is, "How does a body perform its way out of a definitional framework that is not only responsible for its very 'construction,' but seems to prescript every possible signifying and countersignifying move as a selection from a repertoire of possible permutations on a limited set of predetermined terms? How can the grid itself change?" Recognizing that "the very notion of movement

as qualitative transformation is lacking" from these accounts of a body constructed by the social order and overdetermined by the symbolic grid, Massumi answers his question theoretically by beginning in and with the body in motion, and seeing that body as a virtual body.

77. Fanon, *Black Skin*, 109.

78. Fanon, *Black Skin*, 109.

79. Fanon, *Black Skin*, 110–111.

80. Benthien, *Skin*, 29.

81. Gilroy, *Against Race*, 103–104.

82. Gilroy, *Against Race*, 37.

83. See Lacan, *Four Fundamental Concepts*, 106, with an accompanying diagram of the relation between the gaze and the screen.

84. Silverman suggests that we are essentially moving between the Imaginary and the Symbolic, between the look and the gaze, when we move between the eye, the camera lens, and the cultural screen (*Threshold*, 132). While the look is purely imaginary, the basis of our mirror images of both the ideal self and the beloved Other, the Imaginary is codependent on the Symbolic as the space where the Other defines us. If symbolic identification means being placed on a grid, the visual is the vehicle, the medium, for that emplacement; and vice versa, if the symbolic grid maps onto the visual field as a screen, then the Imaginary screen is precisely where and when difference chiasmically enters the field of vision. As she states further: "I would like to propose that the screen is the site at which social and historical difference enters the field of vision. . . . It intervenes not just between the gaze and the subject-as-spectacle, but also between the gaze and the subject-as-look, and between the object and the subject-as-look. . . . It does not merely 'open,' like a door or a window, onto what it obstructs, but rather substitutes itself for the latter. It must consequently determine how the gaze and the object, as well as the subject, are 'seen'" (134). Silverman also defines the screen as "the conduit through which social and historical variability is introduced not only into the relation of the gaze to the subject-as-spectacle, but also into that of the gaze to the subject-as-look. The screen represents the site at which the gaze is defined for a particular society, and is consequently responsible both for the way in which the inhabitants of that society experience the gaze's effects, and for much of the seeming particularity of that society's visual regime" (135).

85. Benthien, *Skin*, 11.

86. Benthien, *Skin*, 9.

87. Benthien, *Skin*, 12.

88. See Fanon, *Black Skin*, 111, where he also describes "the corporeal schema" that "crumbled" in the face of the gaze as an experience of "being aware of my body in the third person."

89. Fanon, *Black Skin*, 111. Silverman also describes this as the sensational or bodily ego made up of "all tactile, cutaneous, and kinaesthetic sensations," which exists in the subject in the gap between the specular mirror image and one's corporeal "container whose shape determines in advance the imaginary 'contents' which can be put into it"

(*Threshold*, 13, 12). Whereas Silverman draws her definitions of the bodily ego from the work of the Viennese neurologist and psychoanalyst Paul Schilder, *The Image and Appearance of the Human Body* (1935), she not only talks about a dermal layer of subjectivity similar to Didier Anzieu's skin ego but also parallels Fanon's efforts to define a third corporeal consciousness, which he draws, ironically, from the work of a contemporary of Schilder, Jean L'hermitte's *L'Image de Notre Corps* (Nouvelle Revue Critique: Paris, 1939).

90. Fanon, *Black Skin*, 111.

91. Silverman, *Threshold*, 9.

92. Sigmund Freud, "Three Contributions to the Theory of Sex," in *The Basic Writings of Sigmund Freud*, ed. and trans. A. A. Brill (New York: Modern Library, 1995), 567.

93. Freud, "Three Contributions," 536.

94. Freud, "Three Contributions," 572.

95. Freud, "Three Contributions," 536. For Freud this also explains why, even as "'beauty' is rooted in the soil of sexual stimulation . . . the sight of [the genitals] which provokes the greatest sexual excitement, can really never be considered 'beautiful.'"

96. Fanon, *Black Skin*, 161.

97. Lacan, *Feminine Sexuality*, 4.

98. In psychoanalytic terms, it is only when the "sensational" or "proprioceptive" ego of "muscular and cutaneous sensation" is closed up that the "visual imago" of the ideal self can emerge (Silverman, *Threshold*, 31). The feeling of "ownness" is supported by the symbolic, and "the proprioceptive ego is always initially disjunctive with the visual image . . . a unified bodily ego comes into existence only as the result of a laborious stitching together of disparate parts" (17). For Silverman also, Fanon's discussion reveals "what it is about the black male body" that "disrupts the unity of the white male corporeal ego" (*Threshold*, 31). Fanon notes, "Every time the subject sees his image and recognizes it, it is always in some way 'the mental oneness which is inherent in him' that he acclaims" (*Black Skin*, 161). Here he describes the fundamental function of the mirror stage to provide the subject with a certain sense of closure necessary to the emergence of an individuated, autonomous self. This sense of oneness and self-closure is lost when the hysterical subject becomes aware of his or her own split nature in language, that is, upon entering the symbolic order—a subject never fully "at one" with or coterminous with the self. Remembering the split-off skin ego or libido-body generates a sense of trauma, the fearful reminder that one has left behind the life force, the libido, the forces of desire, that drive the self. Both Silverman and Fanon argue that the image of the black self as Other precipitates this kind of traumatic splitting.

99. As Fanon states: "European culture has an *imago* of the Negro which is responsible for all the conflicts that may arise [and] on the [film] screen the Negro faithfully reproduces that *imago*. . . . [On the film screen]—one is no longer aware of the Negro but only of a penis; the Negro is eclipsed. He is turned into a penis. He *is* a penis" (*Black Skin*, 170).

100. Fanon, *Black Skin*, 165, 167, 177; Lacan, *Four Fundamental Concepts*, 170.

101. Fanon, *Black Skin*, 154–159.

102. Freud, "Theory of Sex," 580.

103. It was always Freud's sense that "there is no pure masculinity or femininity either in the biological or psychological sense" ("Theory of Sex," 581). Rather, gendered sexuation is the result of a fundamentally social process of finding appropriate objects for one's desire, the rules of which are governed by the oedipal complex. Feminists and queer studies theorists have criticized psychoanalysis for this oedipal supremacy of the phallus in thinking about human sexuality. Silverman even argues that the very problem of linking the phallus with the male genital organ is the way it naturalizes the oedipal narrative as a primary social fiction for all male and female gender identification. Significant schools of American psychoanalytic theory and clinical practice have dispensed with Freudian drive theory and de-prioritized the applicability of the oedipal complex for contemporary psychic phobias and psychological conditions. However, Lacan's rewriting of the phallus as a "function of the written" in *On Feminine Sexuality*, a work produced much later in his career than either his discussions of the mirror stage or of the signifying order, opens up the possibility of thinking about the phallus as the sign for a hegemonic discursive order—a heteronormative, patriarchal discursive order—that organizes other signifiers, like women or blacks, according to their "phallic function" (Lacan, *On Feminine Sexuality*, 90). When we give up the erogenous body, what we are told to replace it with is the phallic signifier, that is, a form of our sexuality sublimated in certain heteronormative forms.

104. The trope of the phallus takes two forms in psychoanalytic theory. On the one hand, it is associated with the penis when, in imaginary fantasies of the self and their subsequent translation on the cultural screen, it represents dominant fictions of masculinity. Above and beyond its associations with masculinity, however, in the symbolic order the phallus represents the power of the signifier to define us. It is both what names or speaks the subject and what alienates him from himself. Thus, when Gilroy says black epidermal skin has become a sign, another way of saying this is that it functions as a phallic signifier for blackness. As such, it is not unrelated to a whole class of phallic signifiers that both name and alienate the subject, of which the most fundamental one is the phallus itself. Why? The phallus represents precisely the fact that the subject is tied up inextricably in both the social realm of linguistic subjectification and sexual differentiation, and the bodily realm of consensuality and erogeneity.

105. Silverman, *Threshold*, 30.

106. Fanon, *Black Skin*, 151, 159. The phobogenic Negro object presents the other side of the beloved as love object, the black subject as the image of alterity in relation to the self. Much of black studies and critical race theory has focused on this racial other in constructions of blackness. The Uncle Bucks, Toms, mammies, jezebels, and other "pornotropes" studied by scholars are precisely the "negrophobic" images of blackness like this phobogenic or phobic object we find translated into popular culture. Fanon himself moves back and forth between the psychic and popular cultural realms as he draws from American popular culture and from his clinical case studies to describe "the Negro" as the black imago of the other. See a range of works in black cultural studies engaged in this type of analysis, including: Thomas Cripps's *Making Movies Black: The Hollywood Message Movie from World War II to the Civil Rights Era* (New York: Oxford Uni-

versity Press, 1993) and Donald Bogle's *Toms, Coons, Mulattoes, Mammies and Bucks: An Interpretive History of Blacks in American Film* (New York: Continuum, 2001); also more recently, Wallace's *Constructing the Black Masculine*; Harvey Young's *Embodying Black Experience: Stillness, Critical Memory and the Black Body* (Ann Arbor: University of Michigan Press, 2010); Kara Keeling's *The Witch's Flight: The Cinematic, the Black Femme, and the Image of Common Sense* (Durham, NC: Duke University Press, 2007); and Nicole Fleetwood's *Troubling Vision: Performance, Visuality and Blackness* (Chicago: University of Chicago Press, 2011).

107. In *On Feminine Sexuality*, Lacan contrasts the desexualized Real with the sexual relation when he states, "We speak therein of fucking, and we say that it's not working out. . . . This sexual relationship, insofar as it's not working out, works out anyway — thanks to a number of conventions, prohibitions, and inhibitions that are the effect of language" (32–33).

108. Lacan, *Four Fundamental Concepts*, 172. As he explains further: "On the one side, Freud puts the partial drives and on the other love. . . . The drives necessitate us in the sexual order — they come from the heart. To our great surprise, he tells us that love, on the other hand, comes from the belly, from the world of yum-yum," that is, fantasy as driven by bodily instincts and needs (189).

109. Robert Mapplethorpe's iconic *Man in Polyester Suit* is one of those images that function both as a racial pornotrope and as a phobogenic object producing anxiety. For more extended discussions of Mapplethorpe's images of the black male body, see Kobena Mercer, "Reading Racial Fetishism: The Photographs of Robert Mapplethorpe" in *Welcome to the Jungle: New Positions in Black Cultural Studies* (New York: Routledge, 1994).

110. Silverman, *Threshold*, 151; Lacan, *On Feminine Sexuality*, 92.

chapter one. SEEING FACES, HEARING SIGNS

1. George Walker, "The Real 'Coon' on the American Stage," CD booklet in *Bert Williams: The Early Years, 1901–1909*, Archeophone, 2004. All cites taken from pages 16–17.

2. See Rena Fraden's "Acting Properly," in *Blueprints for a Black Federal Theatre, 1935–1939* (New York: Cambridge University Press, 1994) for her description of the presumption in the 1930s that black American actors were "naturally" theatrical, that is, to be black was automatically to act (black). For more on early twentieth-century black actors, also see Susan Curtis, *The First Black Actors on the Great White Way* (Columbia: University of Missouri Press, 1998).

3. Gilles Deleuze and Felix Guattari, "Year Zero: Faciality," in *A Thousand Plateaus: Capitalism and Schizophrenia*, trans. Brian Massumi (Minneapolis: University of Minnesota Press, 1987), 167.

4. Deleuze and Guattari, "Year Zero," 176.

5. Deleuze and Guattari, "Year Zero," 181.

6. See Henry Louis Gates Jr., "The Trope of a New Negro and the Reconstruction of the Image of the Black," *Representations* 24 (fall 1988): 129–155, and his "Preface" to *Black Male: Representations of Masculinity in Contemporary American Art*, ed. Thelma

Golden (Whitney Museum of American Art, New York: Harry N. Abrams, 1994), 11–14. Maurice Wallace also discusses the early New Negro's investment in the visual politics of the portrait, its (false) promise to "counter the spectragraphic frame (-up) through rituals and pictorial self-representations of disciplined, domesticated individualism and abstract disembodiment" (*Constructing the Black Masculine: Identity and Ideality in African American Men's Literature and Culture, 1775–1995* [Durham, NC: Duke University Press, 2002], 10). Studying widely circulated images of two leading figures from the late nineteenth century, Prince Hall and Martin Robison Delaney, he argues that while they may seem to be "approximating a cultural ideal of black masculinity for the eighteenth and nineteenth centuries, their republican posings inversely highlight the pitfalls of pictorialization each man's picture seeks to resolve. For at precisely the moment the one or the other poses, he apprehends himself *as an image* and submits willy-nilly to the hegemony of camerican social vision that has previously abjected him and required his portraited self-display in the first place" (10).

7. Gates describes Washington's collection in more detail in "Trope of a New Negro"; for an account of the exposition and 150 of the photographs Du Bois chose, see *A Small Nation of People: W. E. B. Du Bois and African American Portraits of Progress*, ed. David Levering Lewis and Deborah Willis (New York: HarperCollins Publishers, 2003). For more on the visual culture of the Harlem Renaissance more broadly, see Shawn Michelle Smith, *Photography on the Color Line: W. E. B. Du Bois, Race, and Visual Culture* (Durham, NC: Duke University Press, 2004); Cherene Sherrard-Johnson, *Portraits of the New Negro: Visual and Literary Culture in the Harlem Renaissance* (New Brunswick, NJ: Rutgers University Press, 2007); Martha Jane Nadell, *Enter the New Negroes: Images of Race in American Culture* (Cambridge, MA: Harvard University Press, 2004); Caroline Goeser, *Picturing the New Negro: Harlem Renaissance Print Culture and Modern Black Identity* (Manhattan: University Press of Kansas, 2006); Mary Ann Calo, *Distinction and Denial: Race, Nation, and the Critical Construction of the African American Artist, 1929–40* (Ann Arbor: University of Michigan Press, 2007); and Anne Elizabeth Carroll, *Word, Image, and the New Negro: Representation and Identity in the Harlem Renaissance* (Bloomington: Indiana University Press, 2007).

8. Deleuze and Guattari, "Year Zero," 170.

9. Deleuze and Guattari, "Year Zero," 181.

10. Caryl Phillips, *Dancing in the Dark* (New York: Knopf, 2005), 4.

11. Phillips, *Dancing in the Dark*, 6.

12. Phillips, *Dancing in the Dark*, 4.

13. A number of works have explored this trope of the Victorian gentlemen as a model for early New Negroes from both the United States and the Caribbean. See Belinda Edmondson, *Making Men: Gender, Literary Authority and Women's Writing in Caribbean Narrative* (Durham, NC: Duke University Press, 1999); Judith Stein, *The World of Marcus Garvey: Race and Class in Modern Society* (Baton Rouge: Louisiana State University Press, 1986); Martin Summers, *Manliness and Its Discontents: The Black Middle Class and the Transformation of Masculinity, 1900–1930* (Chapel Hill: University of North Carolina

Press, 2004); and Marlon B. Ross, *Manning the Race: Reforming Black Men in the Jim Crow Area* (New York: NYU Press, 2004).

14. Phillips, *Dancing in the Dark*, 14.

15. For her rich discussion of the black dandy, see Monica L. Miller, *Slaves to Fashion: Black Dandyism and the Styling of Black Diasporic Identity* (Durham, NC: Duke University Press, 2009).

16. Gates, "Trope of a New Negro" and "Preface"; also see Michelle Mitchell, *Righteous Propagation: African Americans and the Politics of Racial Destiny after Reconstruction* (Durham: University of North Carolina Press, 2004). Analyses of these images within black visual and performance studies focus on the symbolic visual languages in which blackness was spoken at the turn of the twentieth century and African Americans' efforts to speak back using different visual codes (e.g., Wallace's *Constructing the Black Masculine* and Young's *Embodying Black Experience: Stillness, Critical Memory and the Black Body*, [Ann Arbor: University of Michigan Press, 2010]). Here I focus on the symbolic affinities between different kinds of images of the blackface minstrel, be they forms of portraiture or caricature, which then necessitates a turn away from the visual in analyzing the full intercultural impact of Bert Williams's performances.

17. Racist caricatures of blackness in the United States at the turn of the century therefore reinforced a process, a visual regime of epidermalization, from the nineteenth-century, which had transatlantic, Euro-American origins and a deeper genealogy in colonial modernity.

18. Gates includes an image of this song sheet among others in "Trope of a New Negro," 149, 150.

19. Deleuze and Guattari, "Year Zero," 167.

20. Deleuze and Guattari, "Year Zero," 181.

21. Steven Connor, *The Book of Skin* (Ithaca, NY: Cornell University Press, 2004), 19. As he describes further: "Racial theory always imagines black skin to be thickened or doubled, a bodily mask which impedes rather than assists the passage of light" (162). The blackface mask literalizes this belief as an epidermal and physiognomic fact.

22. Kaja Silverman, *The Threshold of the Visible World* (New York: Routledge, 1996), 22–25. See also Peggy Phelan's discussion, "Developing the Negative: Mapplethorpe, Schor and Sherman," in *Unmarked: The Politics of Performance* (London, UK: Routledge, 1993), 34–70. A number of scholars have explored the importance of photography's emergence in the late nineteenth and early twentieth centuries for the study of cultural modes of representation and performance. Silverman demonstrates, for example, that the "necessary condition" for the photograph's cultural prominence was its capacity for "sustaining the belief in the equivalence of photograph and referent" (*Threshold*, 130). Historicizing Lacan's metaphor of the gaze as a camera that "photo-graphs" the subject, Silverman elaborates, "In the wake of the camera, the eye can clearly be seen to be the site for the induction of a specific kind of vision" whereby "the gaze confers identity only through an irreducibly exterior image which intervenes between it and the object. And like the camera, the gaze provides the subject with a specular body at the same time that

it abolishes his or her existential body" (131, 150). The camera then imitates the symbolic power of the gaze to project for the subject an ideal image of the self, while simultaneously repressing the bodily ego, that sense of one's "existential body." Peggy Phelan argues that portrait photography specifically "tries to make an inner form, a (negative) shadow, expressive: a developed image which renders the corporeal, a body-real, as a real body" (*Unmarked*, 36). And Wallace uses the notion of a "camerical metonymy" to describe the photograph's mimicry of the ways in which "the racialist gaze congeals black male bodies into [] statued rigidities" of themselves (*Constructing the Black Masculine*, 7). Here I am arguing that early twentieth-century photographic technologies helped formalize a process of epidermalization that was already a constitutive part of the audience's gaze upon and reception of the blackface minstrel. Both Williams and Walker had much less agency in shifting the visual terms and logic operative in the reception of black performances at the turn of the century, but the problem was less in photography than in its source — the gazing consciousness of the period itself, where scopic dynamics central to the performance of blackness were codified in the minstrel act and only further reified in the photographic image of blackface.

23. Fanon, *Black Skin*, 109. Also, in *Bodies of Dissent: Spectacular Performances of Race and Freedom, 1850–1910* (Durham, NC: Duke University Press, 2006), Daphne Brooks describes this series as an artifact of the struggle to define black performance in natural rather than cultural terms: "Although Williams and Walker engage in the 'natural,' the [*Vanity Fair*] article celebrates the 'novel' quality of their 'posed' 'stunts,' their staged acts" (235). She also describes the series as "spectacularizing the corporeality of these performers" and presenting the black body "as the fundamental plot for the white spectator" (238).

24. The twinkle in Walker's eye signals to the viewer that he is the one creating his performance — demeaning or not, its very campiness suggests craft rather than a natural image.

25. In the photograph, his smiling face turned sideways for our viewing links the skin of his back to his recognizable black face. One might think this is a sexualizing image of Walker, emphasizing his masculinity in his (suggested) bare chest and backward-turned muscleman pose. However, the engine of eroticization in this distinctive image is less his gender per se than his gender encased in black skin. What this particular photograph does is to emphasize the epidermal surface of his back as a metonym for the face portrayed in the other images. The associations of the thickened blackness of the blackface mask as a second skin of difference are drawn downward here to Walker's back. Marked in an almost painterly way, the bare skin or flesh of the performer becomes another canvas of blackness available for the viewers' pleasure.

26. John Berger, *Ways of Seeing* (New York: Viking Press, 1973), 10, 9. Here his image is itself representative of a "sight," the gaze as a lost act of seeing that passes between the viewer and the viewed, in the space that lies between Williams and Walker and the original photographer behind the camera. In Lacan's psychoanalytic account of the gaze and the look, the subject becomes a sight in the gaze of the Other, an image to be looked

upon, but also, one's sight or way of looking back becomes a site for the subject formation of both (black, performing) self and (white, viewing) other.

27. Brian Massumi, *Parables for the Virtual: Movement, Affect, Sensation* (Durham, NC: Duke University Press, 2002), 9.

28. While in every close-up in the bottom row Williams looks directly at the camera and the viewer, in most of Walker's shots he looks askance, out of the corner of his eye or up above the viewer. In the two shots in which Walker directly faces the viewer, his facial grimaces are so extreme that his lips draw our attention away from his eyes. The latter remain unfocused while most of the energy and activity in Walker's face is oriented toward the arrangement of his mouth. Williams's gaze, in contrast, forces us to rest, even if for a moment, on the idea that there is an audience outside the frame to whom he is looking, to whom his look is appealing and communicating, and who are looking back at the sight he represents.

29. Deleuze and Guattari, "Year Zero," 181.

30. In *Constructing the Black Masculine*, Wallace is skeptical that any pose can be subversive enough to resist "the hegemony of photographic vision in modern racialism" (48). He continues, "Not even in speech acts . . . is one entirely safe from the spectragraphic threat" because of the posing subject's "fundamental reliance on the very hegemony of vision" (12). In his study of Bert Williams, Louis Chude-Sokei tries to reclaim some agency for a black performing consciousness by positioning the performer's look back as inhabiting the role of spectator in relationship to the black body: "To claim the role of the spectator is to project oneself on the other side of one's oppression and gaze back at the caged black self as a fiction. . . . The 'Negro' exists merely as an object to be scrutinized and constructed from without. . . . By claiming that spectator function . . . one could elude and evade that gaze by silently supplanting its meanings with one's own" (*The Last 'Darky': Bert Williams, Black-on-Black Minstrelsy, and the African Diaspora* [Durham, NC: Duke University Press, 2005], 168–169). In *Skin Acts* the presumption is that while the ability to evade the spectragraphic gaze is near to impossible, the performer can situate and position that gaze from his perspective by re-embodying the invisible spectator as a sight (that is, the historical subject for whom such an image constitutes an identifiable audience behind the gaze).

31. In the shot of Williams caught in the act of "dressing down" for the viewer, without his mask and in the process of changing his clothes, he is very much in a liminal space between his onstage and offstage performances. He is the pictorial representation of the split subject, the subject split off from his capture by the specular image and his framing by language. And in the double of his face floating in the mirror and darkened in shadow, he reminds us that the disappeared subject may also exist somewhere else other than in his mirror image. Williams's repeated image also makes us think of the viewer of the image in a recursive mirror, projected inward ad infinitum.

32. Phillips, *Dancing in the Dark*, 10.

33. Bert Williams, "The Comic Side of Trouble," CD booklet in *Bert Williams: The Middle Years, 1910–1918*, Archeophone, 2002–2005, 11–19. Phillips builds his fictional

portrayal of Williams and Walker in *Dancing in the Dark* from similar essays and interviews by the two performers. For a more extended discussion of this essay and Williams's self-consciousness as a comedian, see Michelle Stephens, "The Comic Side of Gender Trouble and Bert Williams' Signature Act," in "Diaspora" special issue, *Feminist Review* 90 (2008): 128–146.

34. In *The Signifying Monkey: A Theory of African-American Literary Criticism* (New York: Oxford University Press, 1988), Gates used the word "signifyin(g)," with its unusual orthography, to represent "repetition with a signal difference" as it appears in black literature and rhetorical traditions. The "signifyin(g) difference" in black writing, speech, and other oral forms includes the use of repeated tropes that represent the speaking black voice in writing and elements of parody, pastiche, and figuration, that is, rhetorical strategies that focus our attention on "the manner in which language is used" (xxiv–xxviii). I change the spelling of the word slightly here, to "signifyin'," to incorporate the combined issues of syncopation and punctuation that are also aspects of the black letter as I describe them below.

35. Jacques Lacan, "The Instance of the Letter in the Unconscious, or Reason Since Freud," in *Écrits: A Selection*, trans. Bruce Fink (New York: W. W. Norton, 2002), 138–168.

36. Phillips, *Dancing in the Dark*, 3. The Caribbean Harlem Renaissance poet Eric Walrond linked West Indian immigrants and African Americans in Harlem across their national and intra-ethnic differences by asserting "no amount of urbanization . . . can deprive the Negro of his enormous capacity as a creator of music and folk song. [In] Georgia, Alabama, Africa, or the West Indies . . . Philadelphia, Chicago or New York this spirit-thing which differentiates the Negro from the Eskimo, for example, again struggles to the surface." (See Eric Walrond, "Negro Folk-Song," in *"Winds Can Wake Up the Dead": An Eric Walrond Reader*, ed. Louis J. Parascandola [Detroit, MI: Wayne State University Press, 1998], 132). For Walrond, the dialect speech and folk mannerisms of the black peasant articulated an everyday life-world that was shaped by socioeconomic and cultural circumstances that were diasporic in scope.

37. The blackface act highlights the black face as the be-all and end-all signifier of blackness, and this effect only increases as audiences become more sensitive to its racial connotations over time. In contrast, by focusing on the more vocal aspects of Bert Williams's performance, his voice in relationship to the gaze of his audience, we interrupt the process by which he becomes nothing more than a stereotype, the minstrel detached from the material conditions of his aesthetic production and performance. By focusing on the sound of the black letter, we also attend to a mode of black cultural address that, rather than being a counter or contrast to the signifier, wages a battle with the signifier on the scopic terms in which blackness is constructed. It puts the uncanny object-voice that exceeds the signifier back into the image of sound, that is, inscribed into the letter itself as recorded on the page of a libretto or dramatic text. As the drawing spans writing and image, so too does syncopation span sound, the image of the sound, and speech.

38. Paul Laurence Dunbar, "A Banjo Song," in *Lyrics of Lowly Life* (New York: Dodd, Mead and Company, 1896), 42–44 (digital reproduction by BiblioLife, LLC); Wayne F.

Cooper, ed., *The Dialectic Poetry of Claude McKay* (contains *Songs of Jamaica* and *Constab Ballads*) (Freeport, NY: Books for Libraries Press, 1972).

39. For more on blacks in the early years of the recording industry, see Tim Brooks, *Lost Sounds: Blacks and the Birth of the Recording Industry, 1890–1919* (Champaign: University of Illinois Press, 2004); Marva Griffin Carter, *Swing Along: The Musical Life of Will Marion Cook* (New York: Oxford University Press, 2008).

40. The oral and rhetorical features of black dialect speech and folk music, the accented, colloquial, "broken" grammatical forms and informal rhythms heard in the diction of black Caribbean peasants and African American sharecroppers and ex-slaves, represented a very different mode of cultural address to whites and an alternative medium for representing modern blackness. For more on the folk and a black vernacular sound and aesthetic, see: J. Martin Favor, *Authentic Blackness: The Folk in the New Negro Renaissance* (Durham, NC: Duke University Press, 1999) and Paul Allen Anderson, *Deep River: Music and Memory in Harlem Renaissance Thought* (Durham, NC: Duke University Press, 2001).

41. Edward Kamau Brathwaite, "History of the Voice," in *Roots* (Ann Arbor: University of Michigan Press, 1993), 271; Gates, *Signifying Monkey*, xxiv.

42. Signifyin(g) is also what Jacques Lacan calls "lalangue," which his translator Bruce Fink describes as "the acoustical level of language, the level at which polysemy is possible due to the existence of homonyms . . . the level at which language may 'stutter'" (*On Feminine Sexuality, the Limits of Love and Knowledge*, ed. Jacques-Alain Miller and Bruce Fink (New York: W. W. Norton & Company, Inc., 1999), 44). For Žižek it is "the space [in language] of illicit pleasures that defy any normativity: the chaotic multitude of homonymies, word-plays, 'irregular' metaphoric links and resonances." Slavoj Žižek, *How to Read Lacan* (New York: W. W. Norton, 2007), 71. The "stutter" was a crucial aspect of Bert Williams's vocal performances, demonstrating precisely the ways in which sound and rhetorical play in black speech also function as unconscious instances of the black letter. The vocal signifier holds the trace of an invocatory drive, the pleasure in hearing oneself speak, being heard, hearing the Other, that circles between the word and the ear, both sealing up and opening up the ear to the echoes of sound and speech in the body.

43. Jacques Lacan, *The Four Fundamental Concepts of Psychoanalysis*, ed. Jacques-Alain Miller, trans. Alan Sheridan (New York: W. W. Norton & Company, Inc., 1998), 143, 270.

44. Slavoj Žižek, "'I Hear You with My Eyes'; or, The Invisible Master," in *Gaze and Voice as Love Objects*, ed. Renata Salecl and Slavoj Žižek (Durham, NC: Duke University Press, 1996), 93.

45. Jennifer DeVere Brody, *Punctuation: Art, Politics, and Play* (Durham, NC: Duke University Press, 2008), 2, 5. Brody also describes her interest in artists struggling with "the predominately visual rather than strictly grammatical understandings of punctuation," that is, "punctuation marks as visual (re)marks," and attends to the punctuation-image as a surface mark, the skin rather than the signifying meaning of "logos (the word)." Punctuation thereby offers another way of thinking about, playing with, the black letter.

46. Thomas L. Riis, ed., "*In Dahomey* in Text and Performance," in *The Music and Scripts of* In Dahomey (Madison, WI: A-R Editions, 1996), xxxi.

47. Riis, "*In Dahomey*," xxxi.

48. Brathwaite, "History of the Voice," 273.

49. Brathwaite, "History of the Voice," 289, 271. Brathwaite accompanied his discussion with a tape recording of poets reading and speaking Anglophone Caribbean poetry, highlighting, for example, the "trouble" the poet Claude McKay had "with his syllables": "His Clarendon syllables are very 'evident,' and he didn't always say 'the,' but sometimes said 'de' . . . and these elisions, the sound of them, subtly erode, somewhat, the classical pentametric of the sonnet" (277). Now a classic of Caribbean literature, in "History of the Voice" Brathwaite argued that Caribbean rhetorical traditions, accents, and sounds constituted a "nation language" that defined the developing postcolonial cultures and nation-states of the region. His observations extend beyond the Caribbean as he used examples from other black musical traditions to emphasize the links between the national and a broader, regional, and transnational, aural and oral discourse of blackness. Henry Louis Gates Jr. (in *Signifying Monkey*) and Houston Baker have traced similar histories of African American speech and sound in oral and rhetorical practices of signifyin(g) and sounding. Baker also describes African American orality and rhetoric as a form of nation language when he states, "Turn-of-the-century black spokespersons provide tactics, strategies, and sounds that mark a field of possibilities for an emergent Afro-American *national* enterprise [that] can be fittingly characterized as the establishment of a mode of *sounding* reality that is identifiably and self-consciously black and empowering." Houston Baker, *Modernism and the Harlem Renaissance* (Chicago: University of Chicago Press, 1987), 71. For Baker, however, the "absurd noises" of minstrelsy represented a deformation black intellectuals and artists worked to filter. My focus instead is on how minstrelsy represented in each sound and letter its own kind of black speech act, that is, a project of defining a black aesthetic through sound and voice, especially evident in a close reading of the language of a production such as Williams and Walker's *In Dahomey*.

50. Ralph Ellison definitively separated the two in *Shadow and Act* (New York: Quality Paperback Book Club, 1994) when he stated: "Although the figure in black face looks suspiciously home-grown, Western and Calvinist to me, [others identify] it as being related to an archetypal trickster figure, originating in Africa. Without arguing the point I shall say only that if it *is* a trickster, its adjustment to the contours of 'white' symbolic needs is far more intriguing than its alleged origins, for it tells us something of the operation of American values as modulated by folklore and literature" (51–52).

51. Édouard Glissant, *Caribbean Discourse: Selected Essays* (Charlottesville: University of Virginia Press, 1989), 146.

52. Glissant, *Caribbean Discourse*, 122–123. The jouissance of psychoanalysis is complicated by the very real condition of enslavement, for it is the black subject's journey (back) to erotic pleasure that then becomes cautious and silent, attentive to gender codes of respectability that govern Victorian, and by extension black, bodies in postemancipation periods throughout the Americas. The slave, representing a stage of subjectivity between the specular and the social I, enters into language understanding his or her sexual difference as always already defined by slavery and racial discourses.

53. "African American Performers on Early Sound Recordings, 1892–1916," in *The*

Library of Congress Presents: Music, Theater and Dance, April 12, 2007, Library of Congress, accessed May 8, 2007, http://memory.loc.gov/cocoon/ihas/loc.natlib.ihas.200038862 /default.html.

54. Žižek, "'I Hear You with My Eyes,'" 92. "Voice vivifies whereas gaze mortifies," he also states, the voice bringing to life or into social view something that has heretofore been unrecognized; whereas the image captures, arrests, freezes something that remains dead or mute in the gaze. Together the gaze and the voice form a chiasmus in the way they structure our experience as a contemporary audience looking at and listening to a Bert Williams recording.

55. William Shakespeare, *The Tempest*, Act 3, Scene 3 (New York: W. W. Norton, 2003).

56. Riis, "*In Dahomey*," xxv. Riis also adds that "black audiences were probably most aware of any subtle subversions of the style" (vxxv).

57. Brathwaite, "History of the Voice," 271. The voice was also an important vehicle for Bert Williams in marking his own West Indian identity as distinct from African Americans. Like Claude McKay, Williams intentionally kept his West Indian accent offstage and Louis Chude-Sokei argues that this was for political reasons. Representing cultural and ethnic forms of blackness that were literally unrecognizable, and therefore unmarketable, to American audiences, during the 1920s, West Indian immigrants in Harlem such as McKay, Williams, and Eric Walrond were forced to perform African American racial identities, appropriating the minstrel mask and other sanctioned performances of black identity "in order to construct a face," that is, to be recognized as black in and by audiences in the United States (Louis Chude-Sokei, *The Last "Darky*," 104, 14). A broader politics of black orature beyond ethnic identity can be read in Williams's continued use of his accent. His accented speech marked, like an "oral signature," his disappearing corporeal schema beneath an American racial epidermal schema. In other words, as a Caribbean immigrant subject Williams sought to mark in his vocal expression a form of blackness that is not just identity, not just ethnicity, and not just history but also the black hole or gap in the self from which the performer as lost body, as no/body, speaks. See also Antonio Brown, "Performing 'Truth': Black Speech Acts," *African American Review* 36, no. 2 (2002), accessed September 16, 2007, http://findarticles.com/p/articles /mi_m2838/is_2_36. Elaborating on Jacques Derrida's notion of the speech act in *Limited Inc.* (Evanston, IL: Northwestern University Press, 1988), in his own notion that "Black Speak" acts, Brown argues that black vernacular accents perform "an 'oral signature' that marks the presence of the 'author' as the 'person who does the uttering, as the origin, the source, in the production of the statement.'"

58. As Peggy Phelan asks in the context of film, "If presence is registered not through a visible body but through a voice, an invisible but audible consciousness, how are the models of identification between spectators and their screen surrogates [i.e., the performers] challenged?" (*Unmarked*, 71).

59. Riis, "*In Dahomey*," xliii.

60. Riis, "*In Dahomey*," xliii. Hence Williams's continued reputation as one of the first great black comedians. For more on his comedic career and African American humor

more broadly, see Mel Watkins, *Stepin Fetchit: The Life and Times of Lincoln Perry* (New York: Random House, 2006) and his edited anthology, *African American Humor: The Best Black Comedy from Slavery to Today* (Chicago: Lawrence Hill Books, 2002); and the DVD *Comedians* in the box set *That's Black Entertainment* (S'more Entertainment, 2007).

61. Riis, "*In Dahomey*," xliii.

62. Bert Williams, "Nobody," *The Early Years, 1901–1909*, Archeophone, August 21, 2004, CD.

63. The ironic structure of the chorus projects two "nobodies" to the audience, the "coon" enunciated in the first person in the song's lines, and the actor, the performer, recognized unconsciously by the audience as the performing consciousness creating, with a wink, the first-person "I" as an identity-effect of the subject in the song. Since irony is precisely that "form of utterance that postulates a double audience, consisting of one party that hearing shall hear and shall not understand, and another party that, when more is meant than meets the ear, is aware both of that more and of the outsiders' incomprehension" (from H. W. Fowler, in *Modern English Usage* referenced in Wikipedia entry on irony, http://en.wikipedia.org/wiki/Irony, May 14, 2007, accessed November 27, 2013), in order to "get" the joke the audience must remain aware of the performing consciousness who is the "I" of his discourse performed in the song. Otherwise, the humor of the song, which exists in the gap of meaning between the subject and his discourse, falls flat.

64. "Nobody" performs multiple layers of irony as it gestures to the performer's own lack of social presence as a reality and condition determining the song's production. While Williams's (white) interlocutors could unconsciously recognize the speaker and appreciate the humor of his song, those same interlocutors would consciously disavow the black performer's like subjectivity in their shared everyday culture. In "Nobody" the singer colludes with the hearer by consciously and ironically performing the disappearance of the black subject and allowing the hearer to pretend to not see him doing it. In "Nobody," Bert Williams, in the very act of asserting that he is doing nothing, is nevertheless still performing a comment on the act of passivity that frames where his audience wishes to look.

65. Riis, "*In Dahomey*," xliii. Ellen Donkin describes this as taking "a subject position outside the performance" as opposed to the "subject voice within the performance narrative," in "Mrs. Siddons Looks Back in Anger," *Critical Theory and Performance*, ed. Janelle G. Reinelt and Joseph R. Roach (Ann Arbor: University of Michigan Press, 2007), 327.

66. Riis, "*In Dahomey*," xxxii.

67. Brathwaite, "History of the Voice," 272, 264.

68. Riis, "*In Dahomey*," xxx.

69. Keeping in mind Brathwaite's analysis of how both syncopation and accented speech can create thick racial and political meaning from mere sounds, the syllabic structure of the words used in *In Dahomey*'s scripts and song lyrics make them worthy of close reading and semiotic analysis. It has been difficult for critics to do a systematic analysis of the structure of *In Dahomey*'s libretto given its amorphous shape. Both the

choice and order of interpolated songs and the language and sequence of events in the script were apt to change without notice from one performance to another. However, at least six identifiable pieces were signature songs of the show, appearing as part of almost every performance and serving as advertisements for the show when released as single recordings. Their placement clearly enhanced specific points in the show's narrative. Often they functioned as a sort of chorus amplifying on but also diverging from the themes and events driving the scenes they were placed between.

70. Bert Williams, "Broadway in the Jungle" or "On Broadway in Dahomey Bye and Bye," in *The Music and Scripts of* In Dahomey, ed. Thomas L. Riis (Madison, WI: A-R Editions, 1996), 111–114.

71. Chude-Sokei, *The Last "Darky,"* 183.

72. In a song with a similar theme, "My Castle on the Nile," the American dream of social mobility in limitless space is implicit but the humor of the song turns on the naive African American's belief that a royal genealogy is the key asset for upward movement. As Bert William's sing-songy voice mimics ironically the action of the first line—"Dere ain't no use in try'n to rise up in de so-cial scale"—the lines that follow state—"You got to have an-ces-tral halls an' den you mus'-n't fail / To prove dere's in-di-go mixed in yo' blood." Here the song makes a clear ironic reference to the "one drop rule" as itself the most significant feature of black blood in a racist American context. (James W. Johnson, Bob Cole, and Rosamond Johnson, "My Castle on the Nile," lyrics in Riis, *Music and Scripts*, 94, 95).

73. Ellison, *Shadow and Act*, 48–49.

74. For more on the conventions of Renaissance comic drama, see Susan Snyder, "The Genres of Shakespeare's Plays," in *The Cambridge Companion to Shakespeare*, ed. Margreta de Grazia and Stanley Wells (Cambridge, MA: Cambridge University Press, 2001), 83–98. There are two extant versions of the *In Dahomey* script, which Thomas Riis includes in *The Music and Scripts of* In Dahomey, each produced and copyrighted respectively for the show's American and English productions.

75. I use the terms "delineator" and "interlocutor" as puns referencing the minstrel tradition. Early white minstrels wearing blackface were called "Ethiopian delineators," referring to their roles as actors portraying or delineating an African American character. A specific troupe of white minstrels, the Christy Minstrels, who originated many of the features of the early minstrel shows in the 1840s, included an opening act with a semicircle of blackfaced performers on stage, a tambourine player at one end (Mr. Tambo) and a bones player at the other (Mr. Bones). These two men traded jokes and repartee with the man in the middle of the semicircle known as the interlocutor (Mr. Interlocutor).

76. Riis, "The Script" in *Music and Scripts*, xlix.

77. Deleuze and Guattari, "Year Zero," 181.

78. Riis, "The Script," xlix–1.

79. The full ironic meaning of Dr. Straight's statement depends on our understanding these two deferrals, how what he says about his actions and intentions in the now relates to his actions as we can anticipate them later. In other words, Dr. Straight's lies are actu-

ally performative truths, for in the moment of his speech his desire to advertise his product does take the place of his desire to sell it, and his intent to give something away does replace, for that moment, his desire to make money in some other moment.

80. John Willett, ed., *Brecht on Theatre: The Development of an Aesthetic* (New York: Hill and Wang, 1964), 137.

81. Willett, *Brecht on Theatre*, 191.

82. Willett, *Brecht on Theatre*, 191.

83. Depending on the audience, the white audience in the theatre or the black viewers seated in the higher, segregated balconies, Dr. Straight is either the buffoon with his overly ostentatious language or the crafty hustler playing off of the gullibility of the crowd.

84. Riis, "The Script," xlix–1.

85. Riis, "The Script," lii.

86. Riis, "The Script," liv (emphasis mine).

87. Lacan, *Écrits*, 413; *Écrits: A Selection*, 139.

88. Lacan, "Seminar on 'The Purloined Letter,'" in *Écrits*, 6–51.

89. For most critics, the language of *In Dahomey* is flawed in the ways Fanon objected to when he saw himself mirrored in the Other's eyes as "above all else, above all: 'Sho' good eatin'" (*Black Skin*, 112). The inability to appreciate the satiric dimensions of *In Dahomey*'s script, the ways the show addressed the audience in multiple registers, is partly due to its burlesque mixing of high style and low subject matter. A full comprehension of *In Dahomey*'s burlesque effect requires a knowledge of the performance features of black signifyin' and linguistic syncopation.

90. Riis, "The Script," liii.

91. Riis, "The Script," liii.

92. Riis, "The Script," liii.

93. Lacan: "Included in object *a* is *agalma*, the inestimable treasure that Alcibiades declares is contained in the rustic box the figure of Socrates is to him" (*Écrits*, 699; *Écrits: A Selection*, 310).

94. Riis, "The Script," lii.

95. Marvin Katilius-Boydstun, "The Semiotics of A. J. Greimas: An Introduction," *Lituanus: Lithuanian Quarterly Journal of Arts and Sciences* 36, no. 3 (fall 1990), accessed November 27, 2013, http://www.lituanus.org/1990_3/90_3_02.htm.

96. Riis, "The Script," liv.

97. As a malapropism it plays on the signifying properties of the letter itself, the pleasure one can get from the slippage of sounds, vowels, and consonants between *epi-* and *cata*-leptic.

98. See the classic Quintilian definition of metalepsis as "an intermediate step . . . to that which is metaphorically expressed, signifying nothing in itself, but affording a passage to something," in *Quintilian's Institutes of Oratory*, book 8, chapter 6, April 17, 2006, http://rhetoric.eserver.org/quintilian/8/chapter6.html, accessed July 3, 2012.

99. Harold Bloom, *A Map of Misreading* (New York: Oxford University Press, 1975), 183, 74.

100. Riis, "The Script," liii.

101. Riis, "The Script," li.

102. Audre Lorde, *Sister Outsider* (Freedom, CA: Crossing Press, 1984).

103. Merleau-Ponty, *The Visible and the Invisible*, ed. Claude Lefort, trans. Alphonso Lingis (Evanston, IL: Northwestern University Press, 1968), 154.

104. Audre Lorde, "Coal" from *The Collected Poems of Audre Lorde* (New York: W. W. Norton, 2000), 6.

105. Lacan, *Écrits*, 417. The diagram "Gentlemen and Ladies" is on page 416; *Écrits: A Selection*, 143. The diagram is also on page 143.

106. In "'Ladies,' 'Gentlemen,' and 'Colored': The Agency of (Lacan's Black) Letter in the Outhouse," *Cultural Critique* 41 (winter 1999): 108–138, Maia Boswell adds to Lacan's image of the gendered bathrooms the segregated bathroom reserved for people of color. The door of the colored bathroom "closes up" the black subject in the room, or body, of race; the black subject cannot cross from race into gender in an American grammar of difference. Boswell explains that, in contrast, she wants "to open up . . . the way in which the racial other can appear set outside of the signifying chain." To do so, Boswell focuses on the materiality of the signifier, the signifyin' capacities of the black letter, to sound out the lost, incorporeal, black body.

107. Lacan, *Écrits: A Selection*, 144.

108. Lacan, *Écrits: A Selection*, 145.

109. Lacan, *Écrits: A Selection*, 145.

110. For meaning to emerge there must be closure—each sentence must have an ending, and the period or full stop is the opposite of a silently speaking apostrophe. Jennifer DeVere Brody's tongue-in-cheek comment applies here also, that the type of ending the period performs is "perhaps the ending of girlhood and entrance into [con]scripted signifiers of sexuality" (*Punctuation*, 137).

111. This biblical line was also favored by Renaissance sonneteers wishing to demonstrate their poetic prowess by using elaborate figures of speech to do the seemingly impossible, to make blackness beautiful (or, in the language and imagery of the times, to wash white the blackamoor's or the Ethiop's skin). This could be seen as another tradition the wordsmiths and songwriters of *In Dahomey* are signifyin' on; see the discussion below of the songs "Society" and "Brown-Skin Baby Mine" from *In Dahomey*. For more on the trope of washing the blackamoor white, see Hall, *Things of Darkness: Economies of Race and Gender in Early Modern England* (Ithaca, NY: Cornell University Press, 1996), 107–108; and Srinivas Aravamudan's *Tropicopolitans: Colonialism and Agency, 1688–1804* (Durham, NC: Duke University Press, 1999), 1–3.

112. Discussing "the dimension by which the subject is to be inserted into the picture," the photo-graphing function of the social and symbolic gaze, Lacan draws on the concept of mimicry to emphasize the gap between what a thing mimics (what it camouflages itself as) and what it is: "what might be called an *itself* that is behind" (*Four Fundamental Concepts*, 99).

113. For an illuminating study of the politics of gender and heterosexuality during this period, see Anastasia Curwood's *Stormy Weather: Middle-Class African American Marriages*

between the Two World Wars (Chapel Hill: University of North Carolina Press, 2010). For more on black heterosexual intimacy, also see Candace Jenkins's *Private Lives, Proper Relations: Regulating Black Intimacy* (Minneapolis: University of Minnesota Press, 2007). Gender troubles manifest in completely opposite ways for the men in the Williamses' and Walkers' marriages. Bert Williams descends into alcoholism and impotence while George Walker pursues the objects of his desire with a relentless hypersexuality and willingness to cross racial lines. In a parallel contrast, for their black female partners the denial of their status as desiring, sexual women drives Ada Walker to further success as an entertainer after both male performers' deaths while Lottie Williams slips into depression and cultural obscurity.

114. Lacan, *Four Fundamental Concepts*, 117.

115. Phillips, *Dancing in the Dark*, 112, 113.

116. Phillips, *Dancing in the Dark*, 112, 113.

117. Phillips, *Dancing in the Dark*, 112, 113.

118. Phillips, *Dancing in the Dark*, 128.

119. Phillips, *Dancing in the Dark*, 14–16.

120. Phillips, *Dancing in the Dark*, 14.

121. Phillips, *Dancing in the Dark*, 128.

122. Paul Laurence Dunbar, Will Marion Cook, and Will Accoe, "Society," lyrics in Riis, *Music and Scripts*, 149.

123. Will Marion Cook and Cecil Mack, "Brown-Skin Baby Mine," lyrics in Riis, *Music and Scripts*, 19.

124. Merleau-Ponty, *The Visible*, 263. Lacan was also struck by this image of "the turning inside-out of the finger of a glove," which he uses to describe how "consciousness, in its illusion of *seeing itself seeing itself,* finds its basis in the inside-out structure of the gaze" (*Four Fundamental Concepts*, 82).

125. Finding the circular relationship between the performer and his audience in the act is not the same as the study of reception even though the latter can support this hermeneutic endeavor. Rather, a type of reading is necessary that can re-embody the image, placing it back in its performative context, not just in a historical or biographical recounting of that context but in an analysis of the traces of that context left behind on the surface of the text itself.

126. Lacan reminds us that even if the signifier "brings forth a subject from a being that cannot yet speak . . . at the cost of freezing him," the subject remains a potentiality, a "ready-to-speak" ("Position of the Unconscious," in *Reading Seminar XI: Lacan's Four Fundamental Concepts of Psychoanalysis*, ed. *Richard Feldstein, Bruce Fink, and Maire Jaanus* [Albany, NY: State University of New York Press]), 269. For Massumi, the incorporeal body "is as concrete doesn't," that is, it does not do, act, as it is captured in vision and thought (*Parables*, 1). And Judith Butler reminds us in *Excitable Speech: A Politics of the Performative* (New York: Routledge, 1997) that even when the voice is silent the body speaks, and embodied performances that use the power of gesture to make meaning can communicate in ways that both run parallel to and are at odds with the speech act.

chapter two. BODYLINES, BORDERLINES, COLOR LINES

Epigraph 1: Paul Robeson, in *Paul Robeson Speaks: Writings, Speeches, Interviews, 1918–1974*, ed. Philip S. Foner (New York: Citadel Press Books, 1978), 67.

Epigraph 2: Paul Schilder, quoted by Kaja Silverman in *The Threshold of the Visible World* (New York: Routledge, 1996), 131.

1. Gertrude Stein, *The Autobiography of Alice B. Toklas* (New York: Vintage Books, 1990), 237–238.

2. Stein, *The Autobiography of Alice B. Toklas*, 238.

3. See chapter 3 of Vanita Seth's *Europe's Indians: Producing Racial Difference, 1500–1900* (Durham, NC: Duke University Press, 2010) and, in relation to the portrayal of black men at the turn of the century, see chapter 2 of Hazel Carby's *Race Men* (Cambridge, MA: Harvard University Press, 1998) for her discussion of images of the African at the turn of the century and their relationship to African American masculinity and the ideal of citizenship. The stripping of the black male performer from "tradition," for example, the African past of the slave, also facilitated his entrance into the "history" of the modern American nation.

4. Steven Connor, *The Book of Skin* (Ithaca, NY: Cornell University Press, 2004), 19. In *Second Skin: Josephine Baker and the Modern Surface* (New York: Oxford University Press, 2011), Anne Cheng demonstrates that modernists held a fascination with surfaces. Relying on skin theorists such as Didier Anzieu, she discusses how this fascination shaped perceptions of Josephine Baker's performance of blackness. While Cheng restricts her discussion to Baker, in *Skin Acts* I argue that this phenomenon has a broader applicability across both modernism and the history of interracial and intercultural skin encounters in the New World. The skin therefore shapes a number of different kinds of performances of blackness across gendered and geographic lines. *Skin Acts* also focuses more explicitly on the function of the sexual relation, intimacy, and relationality in interpersonal relations, as these circulated around the skin as the interface between the performer as a surface-object or image, and the depths of a black "interior intersubjectivity" (Hortense Spillers, "'All the Things You Could Be by Now, If Sigmund Freud's Wife Was Your Mother': Psychoanalysis and Race," in *Female Subjects in Black and White: Race, Psychoanalysis, Feminism*, ed. Elizabeth Abel, Barbara Christian, and Helene Moglen [Berkeley, CA: University of California Press, 1997], 138).

5. Paul Robeson Jr., *The Undiscovered Paul Robeson: An Artist's Journey, 1898–1939* (New York: John Wiley and Sons, 2001), 345–346. Salemme's life-size sculpture disappeared soon after it was made, so in the mid-1980s the sculptor re-created a half-size version of the original statue in clay, which is the model one often sees in contemporary photographic reproductions. Carl Van Vechten's photograph of the statue in Salemme's studio in 1937 is a wonderful exception.

6. Robeson Jr. describes his father as "unabashed in posing nude" because "he felt he was participating in a worthy artistic venture" (Robeson Jr., *The Undiscovered Paul Robeson*, 90).

7. Robeson Jr., *The Undiscovered Paul Robeson*, 90–91. Robeson Jr. also describes: "What Tony [Salemme] recalled most was the magnetism of Paul's personality. Everyone

was drawn to him, especially women. 'Paul was very talented, and women really went at him from all directions—all kinds of women'" (91). Robeson was "remarkably at home in this eclectic, urbane group," according to his son (90).

8. Robeson Jr., *The Undiscovered Paul Robeson*, 348.

9. Naomi Segal, *Consensuality: Didier Anzieu, Gender and the Sense of Touch* (Amsterdam, New York: Rodopi B. V., 2009), 138.

10. Quoted by Kaja Silverman, *The Threshold of the Visible World* (New York: Routledge, 1996), 13.

11. The photographer Christian Walker coined the phrase "miscegenated gaze" in his discussion of the work of Jeffrey Scales, Leah Karp, and Lyle Ashton Harris, contrasting the subjective black gaze and the white colonialist gaze in photographs and texts by Robert Mapplethorpe and F. Holland Day, in the text for the exhibition catalog of *No More Heroes: Unveiling Masculinity* (San Francisco, CA: SF Camerawork), published as *Camerawork Quarterly* 18, nos. 3 and 4 (summer/fall 1991).

12. See Harvey Young's discussion in *Embodying Black Experience: Stillness, Critical Memory and the Black Body* (Ann Arbor, MI: University of Michigan Press, 2010) of the portrayal and enactment of black "stillness" in artistic mediums, useful for thinking about Robeson's composed "sitting" for the sculptor, the camera, and the curious modernist's gaze.

13. Segal, *Consensuality*, 136.

14. John Berger, *Ways of Seeing* (New York: Viking Press, 1973), 52–63.

15. For more on the gendered representations of the ecorche in Western art, see Claudia Benthien, *Skin: On the Cultural Border Between Self and World* (New York: Columbia University Press, 2004), 94. As she describes: "The notion of the skinless body as a positive image in Western culture is still radically masculine. The male subject can, as the ultimate liberation fantasy, free itself of its skin, while the female subject remains bound within it." She continues, "Undressing a woman of her skin would destroy the myth of her being other," that is, would strip her of her symbolic skin.

16. Segal quotes this description from Rainer Maria Rilke's notion of the sculptural (*Consensuality*, 127).

17. Segal traces the shifting "aspects of modern engagements with the sculptural that have to do with the physical, sensual and affective dimensions of the encounter between viewer and work" (*Consensuality*, 135). In minimalist sculpture, for example, unlike the neoclassical, "physical effects are less representational than visceral" and "their sensuality has to do with their shape, how they stand in space" (136). These conflicting tendencies were part of the aesthetic regime within which modernists such as Salemme and Muray worked, shaping the different sensory traces we find in their representations of a body such as Robeson's in their respective artistic mediums.

18. As Segal describes further, "All sculptural things dramatize the confrontation between the body of the viewer located in a specific place and the 'body' of the object s/he finds there" (*Consensuality*, 137).

19. See Silverman, *Threshold*, 30; however, *Negro Spiritual* clearly created quite a bit of phobic anxiety for the Philadelphia group who chose not to exhibit it.

20. H. D., "Red Roses for Bronze," in *Collected Poems, 1912–1944* (New York: New Directions, 1986), 211–215. H. D. denies Robeson's influence on "Red Roses for Bronze" in a letter Susan Stanford Friedman includes in *Analyzing Freud: The Letters of H. D., Bryher and Their Circle* (New York: New Directions, 2002). In her footnote, Friedman clarifies that it may not have been whether the poem was inspired by Robeson that was at issue but the nature of the inspiration, especially given H. D.'s sketch about her relationship with Robeson that she wrote during the same period. As Friedman describes: "Although H. D. was certainly attracted to Paul Robeson, she did not have an affair with him, unlike a number of white women admirers of the time. In the poem "Red Roses for Bronze" and the story "Two Americans," H. D. explores her resistance to joining the horde of adoring white women and her connection with Robeson on different grounds—their common identities as 'borderline' artists and 'exiles' from America" (440). See also Susan McCabe's discussion in chapter 4, "H. D.'s Borderline Bodies," in *Cinematic Modernism: Modernist Poetry and Film* (New York: Cambridge University Press, 2009). In addition to McCabe's and Cheng's work (*Second Skin*), modernists' fascination with New Negro celebrities such as Robeson and Josephine Baker has been explored by Petrine Archer-Straw in *Negrophilia: Avant-Garde Paris and Black Culture in the 1920s* (London: Thames and Hudson; New York: W. W. Norton, 2000). Archer-Straw uses the term "negrophilia" for what McCabe describes as "the avant-garde's co-opting of blackness as a form of transgression and as 'a sign of their modernity'" (*Cinematic Modernism*, 172). Finally, see James Smethurst's *The African American Roots of Modernism: From Reconstruction to the Harlem Renaissance* (Chapel Hill: University of North Carolina Press, 2011) for an original take on how the New Negroes of Bert Williams's generation influenced the modernists and the New Negroes of the Harlem Renaissance era.

21. H. D., "Red Roses for Bronze," 211.

22. H. D., "Red Roses for Bronze," 211.

23. Quoted in Silverman, *Threshold*, 13.

24. H. D., "Red Roses for Bronze," 212.

25. Brian Massumi, *Parables for the Virtual: Movement, Affect, Sensation* (Durham, NC: Duke University Press, 2002), 15, 24.

26. Jacques Lacan, *The Four Fundamental Concepts of Psychoanalysis*, ed. Jacques-Alain Miller, trans. Alan Sheridan (New York: W. W. Norton & Company, Inc., 1998), 103.

27. As Jean-Luc Nancy argues in *Corpus* (New York: Fordham University Press, 2008): "Let there be writing, not *about* the body, but the body itself. Not bodihood, but the actual body. Not signs, images, or ciphers of the body, but still the body. This was once a program for modernity" (9).

28. Nancy, *Corpus*, 11. Recognizing the sensory limit of the body is for Nancy a not-so-simple matter of recognizing that writing contains within it both the desire to represent and to connect (9). As he also states, "But, finally, it has to be said that touching upon the body, touching the body, *touching*—happens in writing all the time" (11).

29. Nancy, *Corpus*, 11.

30. Silverman, *Threshold*, 198.

31. Massumi, *Parable*, 50.

32. Jennifer Barker, *The Tactile Eye: Touch and the Cinematic Experience* (Berkeley, CA: University of California Press, 2009), 15. Barker's concept of the film having a body is incredibly useful and works well with Massumi's notion of the body without an image.

33. Carby, *Race Men*, 113–132. In her discussion of C. L. R. James's notion of the bodyline in *Beyond A Boundary* (Durham, NC: Duke University Press, 1993) Carby contrasts James's and the modernist's aesthetic theories, describing James as using "a cultural aesthetic of body lines in direct opposition to the modernist strategies of cultural producers like Muray or Macpherson." Macpherson was the director of the modernist avant-garde film *Borderline*, starring Robeson and his wife Essie Robeson, which I discuss in more detail below.

34. The term "bodyline," meaning literally "in the line of the body," specifically derives from the actions of the British team in the 1932–1933 cricket season. In *Beyond A Boundary*, the bodyline becomes James's metaphor for the sublimation of postcolonial tensions between Britain and her colonies onto the cricket field.

35. See Massumi, *Parables*, 59, for his discussion of gesture as a "muscular memory of relationality" on a cultural grid imagined as a sports field.

36. See also Carby's discussion in *Race Men*, with more examples of Muray's photographs.

37. James, *Beyond a Boundary*, 202. In "'What Is Art?'" James's goal is to demonstrate that "in addition to being a dramatic, cricket is also a visual art." He names as his interlocutors "the aestheticians of painting, especially the modern ones, [who] are the great advocates of 'significant form,' the movement of the line, the relations of colour and tone" (James, *Beyond a Boundary*, 199). For James the most significant, aesthetic effect of the line was that it captured movement and action, not simply form and shape.

38. James, *Beyond a Boundary*, 200. For his discussion James draws from such works as Bernard Berenson's studies of the Venetian and Florentine painters of the Renaissance (published in 1894 and 1896 respectively), and *Esthétique et Histoire Des Arts Visuels* (Éditions Albin Michel: Paris, 1953). He contrasts Berenson's observations with John Berger's comments on the abstract painting's exclusive focus on "the line and relations of line" (*Ways of Seeing*).

39. James, *Beyond a Boundary*, 200; emphasis in the original.

40. Massumi, *Parables*, 50. In the 1960s C. L. R. James was describing exactly the kind of bodily memory Massumi theorizes, whereby proprioception "register[s] movement without also registering its arrest" in the form of the visual image, which is, "movement as captured in a still, snapshot, or tableau" (*Parables*, 59).

41. Massumi, *Parables*, 49.

42. James, *Beyond a Boundary*, 207.

43. Massumi, *Parables*, 49.

44. James, *Beyond a Boundary*, 205: "Whereas in the fine arts the image of tactile values and movement, however magnificent, is permanent, fixed, in cricket the spectator sees the image constantly re-created, and . . . has standards which he carries with him always."

45. James, *Beyond a Boundary*, 203.

46. James, *Beyond a Boundary*, 206.

47. James, *Beyond a Boundary*, 200, 205.

48. Massumi, *Parables*, 77.

49. James, *Beyond a Boundary*, 199.

50. C. L. R. James, "Paul Robeson: Black Star," *Black World* 1 (November 1970): 106–115.

51. C. L. R. James, "Paul Robeson: Black Star," in *At the Rendezvous of Victory: Selected Writings* (London: Allison and Busby, 1984), 257, 256.

52. In her introductory paragraph in the Table of Contents of *Black Masks* 13, no. 2 (October/November 1998), editor Beth Turner argues that "Robeson studied Stanislavski acting from the early moments of his career, yet others—and he—proclaimed his lack of acting." She substantiates this statement in her essay in the same issue, entitled "Paul Robeson: The Consummate Actor/Activist" (*Black Masks* 13, no. 2 [October/November 1998]: 5–6, 18–19).

53. For more of a discussion of critics' responses to Robeson's physicality, see Martin Duberman, *Paul Robeson: A Biography* (New York: New Press, 1989) and Michelle Stephens, "'I'm the Everybody Who's Nobody': Genealogies of the New World Slave in Paul Robeson's Performances of the 1930s," in *Hemispheric American Studies*, ed. Caroline F. Levander and Robert S. Levine (New Brunswick, NJ: Rutgers University Press, 2007), 166–186.

54. As Richard Dyer describes, the kinesics of performance include those attributes such as "facial expression, voice, gestures (of hands, arms, mainly; but also limbs), body posture, body movement" as "signs we give vs. give off" alongside speech in any given performance. *Stars* (London: British Film Institute, 2008), 134, 139.

55. Lacan, *Four Fundamental Concepts*, 100.

56. Lacan, *Four Fundamental Concepts*, 101.

57. Lacan, *Four Fundamental Concepts*, 101. As Lacan also states: "He gives something for the eye to feed on, but he invites the person to whom this picture is presented to lay down his gaze there as one lays down one's weapons."

58. Lacan, *Four Fundamental Concepts*, 92.

59. Lacan, *Four Fundamental Concepts*, 112: "If one wishes to deceive a man, what one presents to him is the painting of a veil, that is to say, something that incites him to ask what is behind it." Lacan's fortuitous use of the metaphor of the veil reminds us that the Du Boisian trope of the veil was also one of the inaugurating gestures of the Harlem Renaissance. In response to another rhetorical question—"*What is the desire which is caught, fixed in the picture but which also urges the artist to put something into operation?*"— Lacan argues that a subject escapes the eye's attention by casting instead a projection of the self onto the other's field of vision, onto both the eyes of an audience (others) and the cultural screen (the Other) (92).

60. Lacan, *Four Fundamental Concepts*, 107.

61. Silverman, *Threshold*, 157; Lacan, *Four Fundamental Concepts*, 110. If the painter-actor offers the gaze a lure, the painter-actor's gesture comes along with it, lying on the surface of the offering as an unassimilable remainder: "The gesture is always present there [and] there can be no doubt that the picture is first felt by us, as the terms *impres-*

sion or *impressionism* imply, as having more affinity with the gesture than with any other type of movement" (Lacan, *Four Fundamental Concepts*, 115).

62. Massumi, *Parables*, 9.

63. In Lacan's words again: "All action represented in a picture appears to us as a battle scene, that is to say, as something theatrical, necessarily created for the gesture" (*Four Fundamental Concepts*, 115).

64. Maurice Merleau-Ponty, *The Visible and the Invisible*, ed. Claude Lefort, trans. Alphonso Lingis (Evanston, IL: Northwestern University Press, 1968), 264.

65. Robert E. Welsh, "David W. Griffith Speaks," *New York Dramatic Mirror*, January 14, 1914, 49, 54.

66. Philip Auslander, *Liveness: Performance in a Mediatized Culture* (New York: Routledge, 1999). If anything, Auslander describes the video camera's and the film or television director's efforts "to recreate the perceptual continuity of the theatre" and copy "the effect of the theatre spectator's wandering eye" (19). Theatre directors always have to factor in the spectator's gaze, creating, for example, "focal points in the staging that are equivalent to camera views." In *Liveness* he also argues that the live event can be as regulated by ideological forces as the reproducible one and, as James argued, spectatorial memory can exist as much in the watching of the image of an action as in watching the action itself.

67. Auslander, *Liveness*, 11.

68. Actors and actresses provide another link across the dramatic media of the stage and the screen. Richard Dyer argues throughout *Stars* that a film star's charisma is constituted by much more than the screen image. Rather, his or her "itness," to use Joseph Roach's term, encompasses an audience's previous knowledge and experience of the actor's voice, biography, and particular kinesthetic language. Joseph Roach, *It* (Ann Arbor, MI: University of Michigan Press, 2007). This was especially true by the time Robeson came to his role in *Borderline* in 1930. The actor had already established a reputation and recognizable presence as an athlete, singer, and stage star.

69. Carby, *Race Men*, 67.

70. Duberman, *Paul Robeson*, 131.

71. Carby, *Race Men*, 67–68.

72. Duberman, *Paul Robeson*, 130.

73. Barker, *Tactile Eye*, 81.

74. Quoted in Carby, *Race Men*, 67.

75. For more on the "dystopic fantasy of the body in bits and pieces" on the screen, see Silverman, *Threshold*, 20, 29, 30, The collage also mimics the director's modernist editing technique of clatter montage first theorized by Sergei Eisenstein. The guiding premise of clatter montage was that a film should actively engage the spectator visually such that he or she would have to move beyond any cursory sense of plot to the meanings conveyed more formally from the striking juxtaposition of images. Hence why *Borderline*'s director felt the camera was the real actor, for the film's shots were a crucial aspect of the filmmaker's technique. For many film scholars, montage places the power to determine a film's meaning primarily in the hands of the director and out of the hands of the actors.

Contemporary acting scholar Patrick Tucker argues that in film more broadly one cannot privilege the actor because "not denying the power of [the actor's] wonderful performance . . . to give all credit to the actor denies both the presence of the director, and the editor who . . . chooses those takes designed to create a desired effect." Patrick Tucker, *Secrets of Screen Acting*, 2nd ed. (New York: Routledge, 2003), 104. I would argue, however, that similar to the work that clatter montage requires of an audience to attend to the movements of the camera and the technical sequences of shots, there is also a process of racial, intercultural meaning-making occurring as we watch *Borderline*, and this layer of meaning is best captured in the black and white actors' movements and gestures. In *Borderline*, Eisenstein's cinematic theories regarding clatter montage must be juxtaposed against Stanislavski's method of physical acting, "based on broad strokes, on a lot of 'out front' acting and melodramatic presentational techniques [to which] the famous and revered director added his techniques," both serving to enhance some of the film's unconscious meanings (Tucker, *Secrets of Screen Acting*, 102).

76. In his classic essay on semiotic theory, "The Interaction of Semiotic Constraints" (trans. François Rastier, *Yale French Studies* 41, Game, Play, Literature [1968]: 86–105), A. J. Greimas followed the Freudian model and mapped French culture as a social system of sexual relations. He formulated a combinatory that included four types of sexual relations: legitimate (conjugal love) and illegitimate (incest and homosexuality), prescribed (male adultery) and forbidden (female adultery) (93–97). For a critical feminist response to these categories, see Christine Brook-Rose's "Woman as a Semiotic Object," in *Poetics Today* 6, no. 1/2, The Female Body in Western Culture: Semiotic Perspectives (1985): 9–20. Miscegenation is such a feared and prohibited taboo, however, that it remains a silent term in Greimas's totalizing schema. This is despite the realities of such relations described by black artists and performers living in Paris and traveling throughout France at various points during the twentieth century (for more on blackness and sexuality in French society and culture, see Michel Fabre, *From Harlem to Paris: Black American Writers in France, 1840–1980* (Champaign: University of Illinois Press, 1993); T. Denean Sharpley-Whiting, *Black Venus: Sexualized Savages, Primal Fears, and Primitive Narratives* (Durham, NC: Duke University Press, 1999); Bennetta Jules-Rosette, *Black Paris: The African Writers' Landscape* (Champaign: University of Illinois Press, 2000); Tyler Stovall, *Paris Noir: African Americans in the City of Light* (New York: Mariner Books, 1998 and *French Civilization and Its Discontents: Nationalism, Colonialism, Race (after the Empire)* (New York: Lexington Books, 2003); Brent Edwards, *The Practice of Diaspora: Literature, Translation, and the Rise of Black Internationalism* (Cambridge, MA: Harvard University Press, 2003); Shay Youngblood, *Black Girl in Paris* (New York: Riverhead Books, 2001); Theresa Runstedtler, *Jack Johnson, Rebel Sojourner: Boxing in the Shadow of the Global Color Line* (Berkeley: University of California Press, 2102); and Archer-Straw, *Negrophilia*.

77. Jean Walton, *Fair Sex, Savage Dreams: Race, Psychoanalysis, Sexual Difference* (Durham, NC: Duke University Press, 2001), 46.

78. See Duberman, *Paul Robeson*, for a comprehensive discussion of the Robeson's marriage and the actor's affairs. In the year of *Borderline*'s filming, Essie Robeson pub-

lished a biography of her husband in which she described the tensions in their marriage caused by her concerns with his infidelities. Eslanda Robeson, *Paul Robeson, Negro* (New York: Harper and Brothers, 1930). Essie would later discover her husband's affair with the white actress Peggy Ashcroft, who played his leading lady Desdemona in his first stage performance of *Othello*, also in 1930. The *Othello* stage production was fraught with controversy concerning the possibilities of an onstage kiss between Robeson and Ashcroft. According to Ashcroft, the controversy only heightened the sexual tension of their romance, as she exclaimed, "How could one not fall in love in such a situation with such a man!" (as quoted by Lindsey Swindall in *The Politics of Paul Robeson's* Othello [Jackson: University Press of Mississippi, 2011], 31). Also see Robeson Jr.'s interpretation of the role the actor's infidelities played in Essie Robeson's decision to write the biography (*The Undiscovered Paul Robeson*, 173).

79. In the transatlantic intercultural environment of the 1930s, Robeson's film performances worked to authorize and regulate safe forms of white viewing of black male bodies, both in Europe and in the United States. A film such as *Borderline* negotiated the miscegenated gaze by moving the action of black heterosexuality to the safe space of Europe, farther away from a white American gaze.

80. In *Fair Sex*, Jean Walton argues that precisely what is missing from the film, billed explicitly as a psychological study of race and race relations, is a sense of the psychology of the two main black characters, Pete and Adah, played by Robeson and his wife Essie. As she states: "The Robesons are not 'borderline' in the sense that the white characters are, insofar as Thorne's perverse sexual appetites (indexed by his excessive drinking and cross-racial desire) and Astrid's sexual jealousy are posited as the root of their borderline status. . . . [The Robesons' characters] are understood as representing the healthy, heterosexual couple untainted by the neuroses that result from (white) civilization" (61). Drawing also on H. D.'s portrayal of Robeson in "Two Americans," Walton describes Pete as representative of a "white fantasy of the premoral, natural, indeed sexualized quality of the black mind," and Adah as the film's tragic mulatta, a "cipher, functioning as the external stimulant that triggers the internal reactions in the minds of the other characters . . . but never rendered as a subject herself" (60, 49). My reading of the film demonstrates the dimensions of the black actors' performances that we miss when we assume their status as mere ciphers overrides their bodily presence and interaction with the camera, revealing other dimensions of the film as a performance text.

81. Massumi, *Parables*, 64, 76.

82. Massumi, *Parables*, 47.

83. See in particular the introduction and chapter two of Barker's *Tactile Eye*.

84. Black love is far from simple and natural in *Borderline*. Rather, it serves as a racial catalyst for the social upheaval in the town, drawing Thorne's and the other white characters' increasingly irrational responses. It also mimics New Negro couples' real-life negotiations of gendered romantic ideals and the challenges of the black sexual relation in an interracial cultural setting (see Anastasia Curwood, *Stormy Weather: Middle-Class African American Marriages between the Two World Wars* (Chapel Hill, NC: University of

North Carolina Press, 2010); Candace Jenkins, *Private Lives, Proper Relations: Regulating Black Intimacy* (Minneapolis, MN: University of Minnesota Press, 2007). Read with the New Negro's sociocultural context in mind, *Borderline* has the capacity to engender much more complex readings of the sexual borderlines shaping both white and black couples across the modern color lines of race.

85. See discussions of both the New Woman and the New Negro in Adele Heller and Lois Rudnick, eds., *1915, the Cultural Moment: The New Politics, the New Woman, the New Psychology, the New Art and the New Theatre in America* (New Brunswick, NJ: Rutgers University Press, 1991).

86. In terms of the "tut-cut," my thanks to Robert Hill for first revealing to me this connection between the classic flapper's haircut and black female "Egyptian cut" hairstyles of the 1920s and 1930s. Few have commented on Adah's evocation of such classic New Negro female characters as the heroines in Nella Larsen's novels of the 1930s, *Quicksand* and *Passing*, in *The Complete Fiction of Nella Larsen: Passing, Quicksand, and the Stories* (New York: Anchor Books, 2001). See Judith Butler's "Passing, Queering: Nella Larsen's Psychoanalytic Challenge," in *Female Subjects in Black and White: Race, Psychoanalysis, Feminism*, ed. Elizabeth Abel, Barbara Christian, and Helene Moglen (Berkeley, CA: University of California Press, 1997), 266–284, for her linking of Larsen's novel with the complexities of miscegenation as a sexual taboo central to modern identity formation.

87. Unlike the blues women of the Harlem Renaissance Carby describes in *Cultures in Babylon: Black Britain and African America* (London: Verso, 1999), left behind as their men migrated north, in *Borderline* Adah is the one on the move, leaving Astrid and Thorne behind in their domestic tension, and ultimately, leaving Pete behind at the end of the film. Adah shares the blues woman's attitude of sexual independence, albeit in a more "refined," middle-class form. In the story line she makes her own sexual choices, including fulfilling the forbidden fantasy of crossing the sexual color line. In contrast, H. D. portrays Astrid as a fragile, delicate, female hysteric whose jealousy and "neuroses" position her as the ultimate figure of lack—lacking her husband, lacking the erotic charge of interracial desire, lacking an erotically stylized body. Draped in diaphanous clothing throughout the film, her silken shawl is itself a metaphor for the thinness of the veil of skin protecting her from her emotions.

88. The film opens with an argument between Adah and Thorne in the privacy of his bedroom, with a shot of Adah on the floor as if pushed there by Thorne in the heat of the argument. Despite the suggestion of violence, Adah is represented as if she is the legitimate female partner in this scene. She is the one in the bedroom with Thorne as the two engage in a passionate domestic quarrel, while Astrid stands pathetically outside, until she desperately calls on Pete to get Adah away from Thorne.

89. Later on in the film, Astrid confronts Thorne in the downstairs tavern of a public rooming house. In gestures further dramatized by captions, Astrid yells the epithet "Nigger lover!" thereby naming miscegenation as Thorne's real crime, not adultery. Her accusation underscores the problem of the film, which is not the white characters' extra-

marital desires for the black couple per se, but rather the fact that "they are niggers, my dear!" The white couple struggles with the permeability of racial desire, which is also the source of their neuroses and psychopathologies of the skin.

90. For a discussion of the ways in which films serve as "acoustic mirrors" of American gendered and sexual relations, silencing women both literally and figuratively by confining them to the diegetic action of a film rather than its more self-conscious meta-narrative, see Kaja Silverman's *The Acoustic Mirror: The Female Voice in Psychoanalysis and Cinema* (Bloomington: Indiana University Press, 1988). For her discussion of masculinity on film more broadly, see Kaja Silverman, *Male Subjectivity at the Margins* (New York: Routledge, 1992).

91. Adah is like the blotch-shaped death's head in Hans Holbein's painting *The Ambassadors* that so fascinated Lacan: "The secret of this picture [that] is given at the moment when, moving slightly away, little by little, to the left, then turning around, we see what the magical floating object signifies" (*Four Fundamental Concepts*, 92). In this instance, the magical object she reveals is the space of the film itself, its racial and cinematic conditions of production. She punctures the narrative drama of the confrontation between the two male characters, drawing our attention instead to the movement on the screen itself. Shifting our attention away from the diegetic action in the film, she is that player in the field who, in catching our spectating eye, makes us self-conscious and throws us off our game (Massumi, *Parables*, 77). In her sway around Robeson's body she also reshapes the contours of his bodyline, reminding us of the incorporeal male actor who animates the character in the narrative.

92. Barker, *Tactile Eye*, 81.

93. Both men try on new identities in *Borderline*—Pete is freed from the stereotype of the marauding black rapist, and Thorne from the role of the proper, calm, superior white gentleman. Also, just before Thorne storms into the tavern to confront Pete, another white male protagonist, the tavern's male pianist, gazes longingly at a photograph of Robeson he has taped to his piano. In its own act of mimicry, the camera pays homage to the invisible framing activity of photography and, as it shifts to a close-up of the photograph, it demonstrates the kind of recursive motion it is capable of that a photograph cannot mimic in turn.

94. Robeson's gestures convey an ironic awareness that in acting as the savior of Adah's virtue, he is reenacting a posture of masculinity she does not require. Even though Pete is confused and indignant when Thorne first enters the room, when his confusion clears and he perceives Thorne as a threat, his decisive, masculine actions are undermined by small fumbles. There is a subtle comedy in one shot as the camera pauses at Pete's feet, parodying his efforts to "arm" himself psychologically as he reaches under the bed for his shoes in preparation for his confrontation with Thorne. The look of menace mixed with amusement (almost a quiet sneer felt more in our contact with his eyes than with his smile) that Pete assumes at the door is a pose meant to be both sardonic and intimidating, a true performance, in both the literal and the figurative sense of the word, of the act of masculine confrontation the scenario seems to require.

95. Duberman, *Paul Robeson*, 131.

96. Massumi, *Parables*, 76.

97. Richard Dyer, *Heavenly Bodies: Film Stars and Society* (New York: Routledge, 2003), 126.

98. Dyer, *Heavenly Bodies*, 136.

99. Dyer, *Heavenly Bodies*, 113. Dyer's critique is informed by Berger's description of a regime of looking instituted in the early modern period in which "*men act* and *women appear*. Men look at women. Women watch themselves being looked at. *This determines not only most relations between men and women* but also the relation of women to themselves" (Berger, *Ways of Seeing*, 47, emphasis in original). In her canonical essay, "Visual Pleasure and Narrative Cinema" (in *Visual and Other Pleasures* (New York: Palgrave Macmillan, 1989), Laura Mulvey elaborated on Berger's observations as they relate to women and female spectators, while in "Ways of Not Seeing: (En)gendered Optics in Benjamin, Baudelaire, and Freud," in *Loss: The Politics of Mourning*, ed. David Eng and David Kazanjian (Berkeley: University of California Press, 2003), 396–425, Alys Eve Weinbaum describes how this dominant sight line evolves in the nineteenth century to reveal the very instability of the modern European male subject in an urban setting.

100. See Lindsey Swindwall's excellent account of the politics of these three performances (*The Politics of Paul Robeson's Othello*).

101. H. D., "Red Roses for Bronze," 212.

102. Massumi, *Parables*, 60.

103. Slavoj Žižek, "The Lamella of David Lynch," *in Reading Seminar XI: Lacan's Four Fundamental Concepts of Psychoanalysis*, ed. Richard Feldstein, Bruce Fink, and Maire Jaanus (Albany, NY: State University of New York Press, 1995), 208; Massumi, *Parables*, 59.

104. As Duberman describes the plot further: "Based on Claude Williams and Dorothy Holloway's *The Kingdom of the Zinga*, the film . . . tells the story of John Zinga (played by Robeson), a London dockworker whose glorious bass voice is accidentally discovered, launching him into international success as a concert singer. . . . . Zinga learns that [he is also] the King of Casanga. Abandoning his concert career to return to his people, he is met with scorn . . . until he bursts into sacred song, thus persuading them of his royal heritage" (*Paul Robeson*, 204). Many of these plot elements replicate events in Robeson's own artistic career. Zinga's rise to national and international fame as a concert opera singer mirrors Robeson's own early fame as a performer of the spirituals; the character's "discovery" of an African past resembles Robeson's own ideological journey tracing the roots of African American identities in African culture and folklore; and the film's locating of the roots of a black singer's voice in a continental past parallels Robeson's own tracing of the spirituals back to Old World cultures and political forms. Consciously or not, *Song of Freedom* allowed Robeson to communicate his own individual story as a broader metaphor for the race's quest for self-knowledge and cultural liberation. Proof that this story line addressed a communal need among black audiences was evidenced by the fact that, of all his films, *Song of Freedom* was one of the few to find favor in Harlem. As Duberman also recounts, "the Pittsburgh *Courier* welcomed *Song of Freedom* as the 'finest story of colored folks yet brought to the screen' . . . [and] Langston Hughes wrote Essie, 'Harlem liked *Song of Freedom*.'"

105. In another intertextual moment, the character's innovations to the sacred song

are reminiscent of Robeson's real-life changes to the song "Old Man River" to suit his political purposes (for more on this, see the documentary *Paul Robeson: Tribute to an Artist* directed by Saul J. Turell and narrated by Sidney Poitier, distributed by Janus Films in 1979 and part of the Criterion DVD Collection released in 2007).

106. Massumi, *Parables*, 59.

chapter three. THE PROBLEM OF COLOR

1. James Baldwin, "Unnameable Objects, Unspeakable Crimes," BlackState.com, http://www.blackstate.com/baldwin1.html, accessed September 13, 2009, originally published in *Ebony*, ed., *The White Problem in America* (Chicago: Johnson, 1966), 173–181. This version of the essay is slightly different from the version reprinted as "The White Man's Guilt," in *James Baldwin: Collected Essays* (New York: Literary Classics of the United States, 1998), 722–727. Specifically, the latter excludes the Belafonte anecdote.

2. Baldwin, "Unnameable Objects."

3. Baldwin continued reflecting on the young white women's reactions, stating ruefully, "God knows what was happening in the minds and hearts of those girls. Perhaps they would like to be free." In this essay and throughout his writings, Baldwin often linked race relations to deeper psychological and unconscious concerns in American culture of the 1950s. As he also stated regarding Belafonte: "One does not need to be a student of Freud to understand what buried forces create a matinee idol, or what he represents to that public which batters down doors to watch him" ("Unnameable Objects").

4. For a discussion of the ways in which the discourse of "sexual equality" and the fear of the "brown girl" always shadowed discourses of "social equality" in the 1950s, see St. Clair Drake and Horace R. Cayton, *Black Metropolis: A Study of Negro Life in a Northern City* (Chicago: University of Chicago Press, 1993), 41–45, 497.

5. Baldwin, *Collected Essays*, 552.

6. Baldwin, *Collected Essays*, 504.

7. Film's ability to deny the presence and determinative role of its audience created in its stead a disembodied figure, a kind of cipher for the audience, which presents an ethereal but omniscient viewpoint with no eye attached to it. The film camera becomes the perfect figure for the disembodied big Other, the subject who knows what the audience does not have to know, who sees what the audience does not want to or is not yet ready to see.

8. Baldwin, *Collected Essays*, 500.

9. Baldwin, *Collected Essays*, 500.

10. Baldwin, *Collected Essays*, 501.

11. Baldwin's critical perspective on film and on the Hollywood film industry grew even sharper following his attempt to write the screenplay of a film about Malcolm X. He described: "Having fallen into the trap of accepting 'technical' assistance, I would not, at the cutting point, be able to reject it; and the script would then be cut according to the 'action' line, and in the interest of 'entertainment' values" (*Collected Essays*, 552). Baldwin realized that "all meaning was being siphoned out" of the scenes he wrote for

the screenplay: "The adventure remained very painfully in my mind, and, indeed, was to shed a certain light for me on the adventure occurring through the American looking-glass" (553). In his experience, the author was not the one in control of the semiotic or imaginary meanings of the film-text.

12. John Patterson, "If Only It Was 1960 Again," *Guardian*, May 10, 2008.

13. See Charles Eidsvik, "Machines of the Invisible: Changes in Film Technology in the Age of Video" and Jean-Pierre Geuens, "Through the Looking Glasses: From the Camera Obscura to Video Assist," for more on color and "glance esthetics" versus "gaze esthetics" in film production of the 1950s, in Brian Henderson and Ann Martin, eds., *Film Quarterly: Forty Years—A Selection* (Berkeley: University of California Press, 1999), 346, 382.

14. Jean-Paul Sartre, "Black Orpheus," *Massachusetts Review* 6, no. 1 (autumn 1964–winter 1965): 15.

15. James Baldwin, *Tell Me How Long the Train's Been Gone* (New York: Vintage Books, 1998), 482.

16. Baldwin, *Collected Essays*, 36–37.

17. All of Van Vechten's photographs included in *Skin Acts* share this distinctive feature of capturing a signature aspect of the performer or artwork, as is also the case in Van Vechten's photograph of Salemme's statue (see figure 2.2). The photograph of the statue *Negro Spiritual*, taken slightly from the side, presents an impression of the sculpture almost in the round. This effect is enhanced by its placement in space, in the studio alongside other objects that emphasize by their proximity the statue's solidity and size. Here, Van Vechten's studio photographs of Belafonte capture the lushness of color film technologies, the sensuality but also arrested movement of Belafonte's posed body, and the exoticism of tropicalized and orientalized settings and props.

18. Baldwin, *Collected Essays*, 136.

19. Arnold Shaw, *Belafonte: An Unauthorized Biography* (New York: Chilton, 1960), 255.

20. Shaw, *Belafonte*, 252.

21. Shaw, *Belafonte*, 255.

22. Baldwin, *Collected Essays*, 40.

23. Joseph Roach, *It* (Ann Arbor, MI: University of Michigan Press, 2007), 1.

24. Eidsvik, "Machines of the Invisible," 346.

25. Baldwin, *Collected Essays*, 39–40.

26. For more on miscegenation and interracial couples on-screen, see Thomas Wartenberg, *Unlikely Couples: Movie Romance as Social Criticism* (Boulder, CO: Westview Press, 1999). Also see Susan Courtney's *Hollywood Fantasies of Miscegenation: Specular Narratives of Gender and Race* (Princeton, NJ: Princeton University Press, 2004) for a more specific discussion of miscegenation in film in response to television's popularity.

27. The magazine cover is from the issue of *Tan* published in January 1955.

28. Baldwin, *Collected Essays*, 40. Baldwin also observed about *Carmen Jones*: "It is one of the most important all-Negro movies Hollywood has yet produced [because] the questions it leaves in the mind relate less to Negroes than to the interior life of Americans" (39–40).

29. Baldwin, *Collected Essays*, 37.

30. Baldwin, *Collected Essays*, 35.

31. Baldwin, *Collected Essays*, 619.

32. Baldwin, *Collected Essays*, 617.

33. Baldwin, *Collected Essays*, 35.

34. For more on U.S.-Caribbean relations in the period, see Harvey Neptune, *Caliban and the Yankees: Trinidad and the United States Occupation* (Chapel Hill: University of North Carolina Press, 2007), and Michelle Stephens, "The First Negro Matinee Idol: Harry Belafonte and American Culture in the 1950s," in *Left of the Color Line: Race, Radicalism, and Twentieth-Century Literature of the United States*, ed. Bill V. Mullen and James Smethurst (Chapel Hill: University of North Carolina Press, 2006), 223–238.

35. Belafonte's musical crowning as North America's calypso king was in dialogue with the calypso kings also rising to prominence in the Caribbean islands during this period, the group of artists working in the region from which Belafonte's calypso tunes originated. The meaning of the term "calypso king" had markedly different resonances in the Caribbean at this time, however, as male performers such as the Mighty Sparrow became mass popular heroes and organic intellectuals for the people, expressing an emerging national consciousness in Caribbean islands such as Trinidad and Jamaica. Belafonte's calypso, on the other hand, was a popular but still marginal fad in the United States, his form of calypso having little musical impact in the islands. Nevertheless, Belafonte's celebrity in the United States led to transnational stardom and took on a magical aura in the islands above and beyond his popularity as a performer. It was this charismatic appeal that would allow him to transition from being America's calypso king to becoming the nation's first black matinee idol. See Henry Louis Gates Jr., "Belafonte's Balancing Act" (*The New Yorker*, August 26, 1996, 167), for Belafonte's discussion of his own transformations of his calypso voice, how he "modified the dialect [and] put it into a rhythm that was more closely identified with the American scene" (167). For more on the politics and cultural history of calypso, see Gordon Rohlehr's "Sparrow as Poet," in *David Frost Introduces Trinidad and Tobago*, ed. Michael Anthony and Andrew Carr (London: Andre Deutsch, 1975). For more on the construction of Belafonte's calypso career and West Indian identity in the United States, see Lisa McGill, *Constructing Black Selves: Caribbean American Narratives and the Second Generation* (New York: NYU Press, 2005).

36. Thomas Cripps, *Making Movies Black: The Hollywood Message Movie from World War II to the Civil Rights Era* (New York: Oxford University Press, 1993), 263. The cast included James Mason and Michael Rennie (English), Joan Fontaine and Joan Collins (American transplants of British descent), Patricia Owens (Canadian), Stephen Boyd (Irish), Hartley Power (American), Dorothy Dandridge (African American), and Harry Belafonte (African American of Jamaican descent).

37. See Richard Wright's analysis of Bandung in *The Color Curtain: A Report on the Bandung Conference* (Jackson: University Press of Mississippi, 1994).

38. As Baldwin described in "Princes and Powers": "Hanging in the air . . . were the great specters of America and Russia, of the battle going on between them for the domination of the world. The resolution of this battle may very well depend on the earth's

non-European population" (*Collected Essays*, 145). Also see Jean Lacouture, "The First Conference of the Third World," *Le Monde Diplomatique*, May 2005, for more on the "Third World" designation and reception of the conference in the world media. The years that followed the conference would see the fracturing of this already fragile alliance and notion of a unified black and colonial world in the wake of movements for national independence in the Caribbean and Africa, and civil rights and black power struggles in the United States and other First World venues throughout Europe.

39. Sartre, "Black Orpheus," 13.

40. Baldwin, *Collected Essays*, 156, 157.

41. The debates at the conference played out some of the differences within the black world and the differing relationships of various national groups to a developed First World. In "On National Culture," Fanon's presentation at the Second Conference of Negro-African Writers and Artists that took place in Rome in 1959, he addressed some of the tensions of national differences within black consciousness, and his essay would go on to become one of the key pieces in *The Wretched of the Earth* (New York: Grove Weidenfeld, 1963).

42. Baldwin, *Collected Essays*, 157.

43. Baldwin, *Collected Essays*, 160–161.

44. The reflections of Fanon, both a psychoanalyst and a phenomenologist, in *Black Skin, White Masks* are comparable to Baldwin's in reflecting a similar investment in the space of the black interior, especially within the black male, and in the psychosexual space of the white Imaginary in both European and American popular culture.

45. *Bright Road* is a story about two black schoolteachers set in the American south and based on the story "See How They Run," by Mary Elizabeth Vroman, a fourth-generation schoolteacher from the British West Indies. The story ran in the issue of the *Ladies' Home Journal* dated June 1951. *Carmen Jones* is an adaptation of Bizet's Italian opera *Carmen* and retells a tale of murderous passion, with Belafonte playing the lead role of the angry black male lover.

46. As Shaw described further, Belafonte's prominence in magazine articles that year included "a long story" in the *Saturday Evening Post*, "a week-long serial" in the *New York Post*, a "picture spread" in *Life*, a "long feature story" in *Look*, and the entire music section of *Time* devoted to an article entitled "Wild about Harry" (*Belafonte*, 253–254). All of these pieces appeared within four months of each other between April and July 1957, and it was in the pages of *Life* magazine that Belafonte would receive his title as "the first Negro matinee idol in our entertainment history." As is often the case in show business, notoriety and controversy bring the star more fame than talent affords the actor. Shaw recounts multiple instances of white female fans' adoration, including their thefts of posters advertising his shows and the verbal scuffles resulting from husbands' shouts, "Do I have to pay to watch you steal my wife?" (*Belafonte*, 253–254).

47. Similar controversies surrounded Robeson's kiss with his white female costar, Uta Hagen, onstage in *Othello*, demonstrating the carryover in North American culture of issues related to the performance of race and sexual relations, particularly involving black male actors, from the theatrical stage to the cinematic screen.

48. In "'To Kiss Or Not to Kiss?,'" in "Island in the Sun," *Ebony*, July 1957, 33–37. Both lead actors commented on the offensive nature of the prohibition, Belafonte observing, "I definitely think that the movie industry has a policy which prohibits love-making and kissing between interracial couples."

49. The magazine covers are from the issue of *Jet* dated October 1956 and the issue of *Ebony* dated July 1957.

50. Harry Belafonte, "Why I Married Julie," *Ebony*, July 1957.

51. His charisma, as C. L. R. James described about celebrity in general, was the product of both his talent as a performer and his appeal or allure as a "personality," to use Shaw's language of the period (*Belafonte*, 253).

52. In *Colonial Desire: Hybridity in Theory, Culture and Race*, Robert Young reminds us of the degree to which theories of race were also "covert theories of desire" at key moments of colonial encounter (New York: Routledge, 1995), 9. He reattaches sexuality to the typically racialized figure of the creole and argues that through colonial discourses of hybridity we can identify "the emergence of desire in history, its genealogy and its disavowal in the history of racialized thought" (26, xi).

53. Sean X. Goudie, *Creole America: The West Indies and the Formation of Literature and Culture in the New Republic* (Philadelphia: University of Pennsylvania Press, 2006).

54. Toward the end of the film, a white female character, Sylvia Fleury, sums up her assessment of whites' future relationship to the island's changing political realities. She suggests to her husband, Maxwell Fleury, that they move to New England where appliances can take the place of servants. The film reminds American audiences that they inhabit a utopian, white racial space outside of the tensions of a hellish paradise, the politically independent black Caribbean. Despite the romanticism of the film's title, the real utopia in the film is an America of the 1950s where concerns about racial hierarchies and structures of colonization are washed away by the benefits of consumer culture.

55. Langston Hughes, "Jamaica," *Ebony*, November 1948, 45–50, 45.

56. The Fleurys are one of the more powerful families among the island's creole elite. Questions of generational inheritance, what is the status of the relationship between the sons of the master and the sons of the slave, all coalesce in the film's representation of Fleury's insecure manhood. His fears regarding whether he is man enough for his wife are underscored by the phallic prop of a foreign cigarette he finds in an ashtray in his home, lying beside another with the imprint of his wife's lipstick. All of these provide the not so subtle, but ultimately misleading, clues that his wife is involved in something that is sexually illicit.

57. See Drake and Cayton, *Black Metropolis*, 41–45, 497.

58. He terms this "lactification," the imperative that "the race must be whitened," which reflects the woman of color's incorporative identification with whiteness, swallowing whiteness, so to speak, like mother's milk (Frantz Fanon, *Black Skin, White Masks*, trans. Charles Lam Markmann [New York: Grove Weidenfeld Press, 1967], 47, 59–60). He also states that she is the very figure for "the sexual myth—the quest for white flesh—perpetuated by alienated psyches" (81). Fanon's discussion of the heterosexual woman and man of color's desires for their white counterparts in *Black Skin, White Masks*

can be looked at more broadly as an attempt to theorize black heterosexuality and desire, and the gendered structures of the black unconscious, as governed by the interdiction of the miscegenation taboo. In his discussion of the woman of color's desire as a perverted form of interracial love, Fanon reveals that he is as much a prisoner to the misogyny and phallocentrism of psychoanalytic discourse and colonial discourse in his time. His inability to imagine a black female interior and a legitimate form of black female inter-racial desire mirrors some of Freud's less sophisticated depictions of female sexuality as a phallic lack—in the woman of color's sexual quest whiteness becomes the phallic lack. The woman of color carries the psychic burden of a racial inferiority complex that in actuality both the black male and female subject share, the effects of the colonial rela-tion on their sexuality in relation to whiteness.

59. Baldwin, *Collected Essays*, 554.

60. As one viewer insightfully observes about the scene in an online discussion of the DVD of the film by viewers on amazon.com (accessed May 1999): "Dandridge and her white lover were even not allowed to kiss in their romantic scenes. In fact, [he] could say 'in love' (not 'I love you') only after persistent pressure from Dandridge, who looks totally lost in the summer cottage after he professes his love. In an awkward moment of indecision Dorothy quickly puts on a record then abruptly brushes her cheek against his face when they should be kissing hard." The actress's gesture, what she can say about interracial desire with her face and body, complicates Fanon's negative characterization of the woman of color as lacking agency in her own desires.

61. Fanon, *Black Skin*, 75.

62. When Belafonte sings along with them, his emerging career as a folk performer and Caribbean calypso king is brought into the diegetic action of the film.

63. "Island in the Sun," *Ebony*, July 1957, 33–37.

64. Fanon, *Black Skin*, 46.

65. Excerpt from *Island in the Sun* © 1957. Courtesy of Twentieth Century Fox. Written by Alfred Hayes. All rights reserved.

66. See Jared Sexton's *Amalgamation Schemes: Antiblackness and the Critique of Multi-racialism* (Minneapolis, MN: University of Minnesota Press, 2008) for a discussion of the fallacies of the interracial romance in the context of a (hetero-)sexual relation that never works out.

67. As Slavoj Žižek argues, what characterizes modernity is not repressed desires, but rather, repressed prohibitions, where "beneath the appearance of free choice is an even more oppressive demand." *For They Know Not What They Do* (London: Verso, 2008), 93.

68. Fanon, *Black Skin*, 78. Žižek uses similar terms to describe what it means to tra-verse and give up one's fantasy narratives: "'Protect me from what I want' means: 'Pre-cisely when I seem to protect my authentic innermost longing, "what I want" has already been imposed on me by the patriarchal order that tells me what to desire, so the first con-dition of my liberation is that I break the vicious cycle of my alienated desire and learn to formulate my desire in an autonomous way'" (*For They Know Not What They Do*, 39).

69. As an early "end of the world," or "doomsday scenario," film, *The World, the Flesh and the Devil* is part of a subgenre that includes other classics such as *The Last Man*

on Earth (1964), *The Omega Man* (1971), and the more recent blockbuster *I Am Legend* (2007). While explicitly a remake of *The Omega Man, I Am Legend* also makes key references to *The World, the Flesh and the Devil*. Above and beyond both films' black male lead protagonist, the New York city scenes, the interaction with idealized mannequins, the main protagonist's truck filled with supplies, and his frequent radio announcements out to the rest of the world, all evoke central tropes from Belafonte's film, the lead actor Will Smith admitting that he had Belafonte's film in mind while portraying his role.

70. As one contemporary reviewer from the *New York Times* described, "the fancy begins to crumble and the weird spell begins to break when the screenplay calls for the arrival of another man." Bosley Crowther, "Movie Review—The World, the Flesh and the Devil," *New York Times Review*, May 21, 1959.

71. See chapter 2, "The Interpassive Subject: Lacan Turns a Prayer Wheel," in Žižek's *How To Read Lacan* (New York: W. W. Norton, 2007).

72. As Baldwin states, "For, I have seen the devil, by day and by night, and have seen him in you and in me. . . . It is at that moment when no other human being is real for you, nor are you real for yourself" (*Collected Essays*, 571).

73. Baldwin, *Collected Essays*, 567.

74. In his description for *Weathering the Storm: Inside Winslow Homer's Gulf Stream* (Mercer University Lamar Memorial Lectures [Athens: University of Georgia Press, 2004]), Peter H. Wood describes the historical context of the painting in the 1890s: "Viewed in light of such events as the Spanish American War, the emergence of Jim Crow practices in the South, and the publication of Rudyard Kipling's epochal poem 'The White Man's Burden,' *The Gulf Stream* takes on deeper layers of meaning" (accessed November 28, 2013, http://www.amazon.com/Weathering-Storm-University-Memorial -Lectures/dp/0820326259). The storm on the horizon, the sharks and flying fish in the water, the sugarcane stalks protruding from the boat's hold—these are just some of the elements in what Wood reveals to be a richly symbolic tableau of the Black Atlantic world, linking the histories of Africa, the Caribbean, and the United States. It is a perfect image of what Hortense Spillers also historicizes as "those African persons in 'Middle Passage' . . . literally suspended in the 'oceanic,' in a state of unmitigated loneliness" ("Mama's Baby, Papa's Maybe: An American Grammar Book," *Diacritics* 17, no. 2 (Summer, 1987): 72). The "oceanic feeling" Spillers evokes, analogous to undifferentiated being, made Freud nervous because it seemed to promise some other space, like Merleau-Ponty's flesh of the world, for example, that the subject could fall back on as a refuge from civilization, the divisive symbolic order one can never really escape. However, Kaja Silverman finds in Freud a more hopeful understanding of the oceanic as a feeling of limitlessness that can lead the subject to a more relational self: "He is not talking about the manic pleasure of an imperial ego; the oceanic feeling is 'imposed' upon us as a 'fact,' and it is a 'sensation' instead of a thought—the sensation of the 'contact' between ourselves and other beings" (Kaja Silverman, *Flesh of My Flesh* [Stanford, CA: Stanford University Press, 2009], 29).

75. As Crowther complains in his *New York Times* review from 1959: "A passionately

sincere, pictorially brilliant, monumentally silly example of how people who are obsessed with the race question tend to see everything in Black and White . . . the audience is asked to believe that when most of humanity has been wiped out by a cloud of radioactive sodium, the three people who have managed to save their skins will spend most of their time worrying about the color of them."

76. M. P. Shiel, *The Purple Cloud* (London: Chatto and Windus, 1901).

77. Shiel, *The Purple Cloud* ebook, http://www.gutenberg.org/files/11229/11229-h/11229-h.htm.

78. See such writers as Junot Diaz, *The Brief Wondrous Life of Oscar Wao* (New York: Riverhead Books, 2008), and theorists such as Paul Gilroy, *Postcolonial Melancholia* (New York: Columbia University Press, 2006); Édouard Glissant, *Caribbean Discourse: Selected Essays* (Charlottesville, VA: University of Virginia Press, 1989); and Lois Parkinson Zamora, *Writing the Apocalypse* (New York: Cambridge University Press, 1993), for more on various forms of colonial apocalypticism and postimperial nostalgia that shape both the founding of the New World and the decolonization of the Caribbean and Africa.

79. Silverman, *Flesh*, 30.

80. In Amiri Baraka's play *The Sidney Poet Heroical in 29 Scenes* (New York: I. Reed Books, 1979), this narcissistic figure is the object of satire. Baraka's Belafonte-like character, Larry Alifonte, describes himself as "the real star . . . I'm God pure and simple, a trinity of three layers Great White Hope. The baldbrained Cadillac Othello. The Calypso Jesus. The grinning loyal soldier. The mix-match ancestor. Theblownupgoodguy" (scene 19). For Baraka the specular image of the black male performer in a white cultural setting can only be one of a caricature dancing manically underneath dazzling, Technicolor lights, as he illustrates on the cover of *The Sidney Poet Heroical* with a cartoon image of the black male performer.

chapter four. IN THE FLESH, LIVING SOUND

1. Jean Paul Sartre, "Black Orpheus," *The Massachusetts Review* 6, no. 1 (autumn 1964–winter, 1965): 13.

2. Sartre, "Black Orpheus," 16.

3. Behind the Beatles, Bob Dylan, Elvis Presley, Jimi Hendrix, and Aretha Franklin, but ahead of Stevie Wonder, Marvin Gaye, U2, Bruce Springsteen, and Michael Jackson.

4. All of this despite the fact that it entered the Billboard charts at No. 168 and peaked at No. 54 when it was released, and from a performer who never had a Top 40 single nor won a Grammy Award during his lifetime.

5. Rita Marley and Hettie Jones, *No Woman No Cry: My Life with Bob Marley* (New York: Hyperion, 2004), 1.

6. See Lacan's discussion of the state of being "between two deaths" in *The Seminar of Jacques Lacan: The Ethics of Psychoanalysis*, ed. Jacques-Alain Miller, trans. Dennis Porter (New York: W. W. Norton, 1997), 248, 270. Also see Slavoj Žižek, *How To Read Lacan* (New York: W. W. Norton, 2007), 89.

7. Dave Thompson, "Bob Marley: Rock Hall's Reggae Legend," in *Goldmine: The Music Collector's Magazine*, Bob Marley Hall of Fame, Special Issue, April 2011, 66–71, 66.

8. Philip Auslander, *Liveness: Performance in a Mediatized Culture* (New York: Routledge, 1999), 82.

9. Michael Veal, *Dub: Soundscapes and Shattered Songs in Jamaican Reggae Music* (Middletown, CT: Wesleyan University Press, 2007), 4.

10. Veal, *Dub*, 4.

11. Auslander, *Liveness*, 81.

12. Auslander, *Liveness*, 55.

13. Auslander, *Liveness*, 50. Auslander's debate with Peggy Phelan (*Unmarked: The Politics of Performance* [London: Routledge, 1993]) concerning the authenticity of the live versus the recorded repeats in a slightly different form the debate between Diane Taylor in *The Archive and the Repertoire: Performing Cultural Memory in the Americas* (Durham, NC: Duke University Press, 2003) and Joseph Roach in *Cities of the Dead: Circum-Atlantic Performance* (New York: Columbia University Press, 1996) on the status of memory versus forgetting as the ground of authenticity in circum-atlantic performance. My interest in these debates revolves around the differences between repetition (or surrogation, that is, the reproduction of what is always already forgotten or missing, left behind) and re-production (the production of a copy) in the psychic transaction between the black male performer who is always already constructed, and the (white) audience/listener whose liveness is often forgotten.

14. The box set recounts, in his songs, in the accompanying booklet, and in these images, his early musical beginnings in rocksteady (paired with a Motown-derived, short-hair look); followed by his radicalization as "rude boy Tuff Gong" in Trenchtown (accompanied by an image of the singer in the beginnings of his bushy, short-hair, dreadlocked Afro); the subsequent politicization of both the man and his lyrics in a broader Third World moment of decolonization, revolution, and struggles for independence (marked by his Che Guevara-esque image against a background of flames); and finally his apotheosis as the icon of struggle, freedom, and liberation, a transcendent, universal ideal (accompanied by the messianic image of Marley as the saintly, long-haired Rasta, the "Natural Prophet," placed before a sea of water).

15. Auslander, *Liveness*, 86. He elaborates: "Rock listeners do visualize the musicians while listening to recordings [and] listening to rock on records engages the visual imagination in a highly developed way."

16. Michelle Stephens, "Babylon's 'Natural Mystic': The North American Music Industry, the Legend of Bob Marley, and the Incorporation of Transnationalism," *Cultural Studies* 12, no. 2 (April 1998): 139–167, 141.

17. Stephens, "Babylon's 'Natural Mystic,'" 142–143.

18. See Fred Moten, *In the Break: The Aesthetics of the Black Radical Tradition* (Minneapolis: University of Minnesota Press, 2003) and Alexander G. Weheliye, *Phonographies: Grooves in Sonic Afro-Modernity* (Durham, NC: Duke University Press, 2005).

19. Leonard E. Barrett Sr., *The Rastafarians* (Boston, MA: Beacon Press, 1997), 18.

20. Veal, *Dub*, 66.

21. Dolar, *A Voice*, 12.

22. As Dolar also states: "What singles out the voice against the vast ocean of sounds and noises, what defines the voice as special among the infinite array of acoustic phenomenon, is its inner relationship with meaning. . . . The voice is an opening toward meaning" (*A Voice*, 13).

23. Dolar, *A Voice*, 16.

24. Sartre, "Black Orpheus," 35.

25. Dolar, *A Voice*, 31.

26. Dolar, *A Voice*, 31.

27. As Lacan states: "The voice—partly planetarized, even stratospherized, by our machinery—and the gaze, whose ever-encroaching character is no less suggestive, for, by so many spectacles, so many phantasies, it is not so much our vision that is solicited, as our gaze that is aroused" (*The Four Fundamental Concepts of Psychoanalysis*, ed. Jacques-Alain Miller, trans. Alan Sheridan [New York: W. W. Norton & Company, Inc., 1998], 274).

28. Dolar, *A Voice*, 14–15.

29. Sartre, "Black Orpheus," 51–52.

30. Sartre, "Black Orpheus," 35.

31. Sartre, "Black Orpheus," 13.

32. Sartre, "Black Orpheus," 14.

33. Édouard Glissant, *Caribbean Discourse: Selected Essays* (Charlottesville: University of Virginia Press, 1989), 108.

34. Michel Foucault, *"Society Must Be Defended": Lectures at the College de France, 1975–1976*, trans. David Macey (New York: Picador, 2003).

35. Foucault, *"Society Must Be Defended,"* 60.

36. Foucault, *"Society Must Be Defended,"* 60.

37. Bob Marley, "War" lyrics, Alan Cole and Carlton "Carly" Barrett, in *Rastaman Vibration* (Perfs. Bob Marley and the Wailers. Tuff Gong/Island Records, 1976).

38. Bob Marley, "Exodus" lyrics, originally released by Island Records in 1977 (*Legend: The Best of Bob Marley and the Wailers*. Perfs. Bob Marley and the Wailers. Tuff Gong/Island Records, 1984).

39. Foucault, *"Society Must Be Defended"*: "We came out of the shadows, we had no glory and we had no rights, and that is why we are beginning to speak and to tell of our history" (70).

40. Foucault, *"Society Must Be Defended,"* 70.

41. Foucault, *"Society Must Be Defended,"* 71. Within black diasporic traditions this narrative form of the racial jeremiad has had a "fairly recognizable structure" as David Scott describes, usually beginning with "a dark age of oppression and domination . . . followed by the emergence of the great struggle against that oppression and domination, and the gradual building of that struggle as it goes through ups and downs . . . but moving steadily and assuredly toward the final overcoming." David Scott, "Interview with Stuart Hall," BOMB *Magazine* 90 (winter 2004–5). Classic anticolonial texts such as C. L. R. James's *The Black Jacobins* and Frantz Fanon's *The Wretched of the Earth* rely on this narrative structure to tell a history of the race that legitimates the act of revolution.

42. Foucault, *"Society Must Be Defended,"* 8.

43. Sartre, "Black Orpheus," 14.

44. Marlene Nourbese Philip, *A Genealogy of Resistance: Essays* (Toronto, Ontario: Mercury Press, 1999), 44–45.

45. Dolar, *A Voice*, 20.

46. Dolar, *A Voice*, 20.

47. Sartre, "Black Orpheus," 40.

48. *The Harder They Come*, directed by Perry Henzell and starring Jimmy Cliff, New World Pictures, 1972. The film tied the emergence of reggae as a new form of black urban music to the lives of the rude boys in the streets of Kingston, the latter performing what Deborah Thomas has described as a "modern blackness" that replaced the creole complexes of the immediate, post-national independence period. Deborah Thomas, *Modern Blackness: Nationalism, Globalization, and the Politics of Culture in Jamaica* (Durham, NC: Duke University Press, 2004). It also linked that identity transnationally to what was emerging in the urban streets of London and New York among black populations of West Indian and North American descent. For more on the film, see the critical essays in *Ex-iles: Essays on Caribbean Cinema*, ed. Mbye B. Cham (Trenton, NJ: Africa World Press, 1992).

49. Glissant, *Caribbean Discourse*, 108–109.

50. Lacan, *Four Fundamental Concepts*, 26.

51. Lacan, *Four Fundamental Concepts*, 195. As Lacan also describes, the very reason why the voice and the ear, the object and the source of the invocatory drive, are linked so closely to the "opening/closing of the gap of the unconscious" is because both have "the privilege of not being able to close" (200).

52. John Holt, "Ali Baba," Treasure Isle, 1970.

53. More and more, scholars are describing dub techniques as a prescient form of electronic music-making and musical production that set the stage for much of the ways in which popular music has developed in the eighties and continues today (see Veal in particular). In this sense, the reproduction and reproducibility of Bob Marley's voice in the present works according to a dub logic rather than a rock logic of liveness.

54. Veal, *Dub*, 66.

55. King Tubby remix, "I Trim the Barber," in *King Tubby's Special, 1973–1976*, CD, Trojan Records, UK, 1995.

56. Veal, *Dub*, 73.

57. Veal, *Dub*, 71–74.

58. Veal, *Dub*, 65.

59. Dr. Alimantado and Bunny Lee, "I Killed the Barber" ("Natty Dread Kill the Barber"), Greensleeves, 1976.

60. In a Sprite commercial from 2011, cracks in Drake's skin open up to reveal musical equipment and technology—the turntable, woofer, speakers—integrated into the very body of the deejay performer. However, the sequence ends with these sound elements sealed back up into the seamless, hardened skin of the performer Drake.

61. This socio-sexual reality carries over from the dub era to lovers' rock and to the slackness of dance-hall reggae. Dub reggae and dance-hall music are libidinal sites for

the evocation and enactment of private drives and fantasies, and the public deployment of black (hetero-)sexual and gendered norms.

62. Moten, *In the Break*, 6: In the clicks, tics, horns, nonsensical sounds and pulsating rhythms of certain forms of black music, Moten hears, "the transference of a radically exterior aurality that disrupts and resists certain formations of identity and interpretation by challenging the reducibility of phonic matter to verbal meaning or conventional musical form." This is the materiality of the black letter transferred now to the black musical signifier, the black note, which retains in its "material trace" a missed encounter with the fleshy body erased from, but also left-over and hovering just on the edge of, written meaning.

63. Moten, *In the Break*, 258, 6.

64. Moten, *In the Break*, 258–259. The passage is taken from Nathaniel Mackey's *Bedouin Handbook* (College Park, MD: Sun and Moon Press, 2000). The line "an insistent previousness evading each and every natal occasion" from Mackey's work serves as one of Moten's epigraphs and a touchstone throughout *In the Break* (for some of its appearances, see 55, 73, 83, 98).

65. Lacan, *Four Fundamental Concepts*, 43.

66. Moten quoting Mackey, *In the Break*, 259.

67. Lacan describes the lamella as that which represents "not sexed polarity, the relation between masculine and feminine, but the relation between the living subject and that which he loses by having to pass, for his reproduction, through the sexual cycle" (*Four Fundamental Concepts*, 199).

68. Moten quoting Mackey, *In the Break*, 259.

69. Moten quoting Mackey, *In the Break*, 259; Lacan, *Four Fundamental Concepts*, 197.

70. Lacan, *On Feminine Sexuality, the Limits of Love and Knowledge*, ed. Jacques-Alain Miller and Bruce Fink (New York: W. W. Norton & Company, Inc., 1999), 78. See his discussion and chart of the formulas of sexuation.

71. For this description and more on the "Barber's Paradox," see *Wikipedia*, http://en.wikipedia.org/wiki/Barber_paradox, accessed July 2, 2012.

72. As Moten also describes this, quoting Derrida: "I would speak of a sort of participation without belonging—a taking part in without being a part of, without having membership in a set. . . . The set comes to form by invagination an internal pocket larger than the whole" (*In the Break*, 258). We arrive once again at the notion of invagination, which is the very quality Moten ascribes to blackness and black music (6). Invagination, in symbolic terms, represents the fact that something always escapes the phallic signifier, that difference is itself part of a larger, invaginated set.

73. See Joan Copjec's very helpful discussion in chapter 8, "Sex and the Euthanasia of Reason," in *Read My Desire: Lacan against the Historicists* (Cambridge, MA: MIT Press, 1996), 201–236.

74. Copjec, "Sex and the Euthanasia of Reason," 236.

75. For more on lalangue, see Dolar, *A Voice*, 143.

76. Dolar, *A Voice*, 20.

77. Moten, *In the Break*, 259; Lacan, *Four Fundamental Concepts*, 205.

78. Bob Marley, "No Woman No Cry" lyrics, originally released by Island Records in 1977 (*Legend: The Best of Bob Marley and the Wailers*. Perfs. Bob Marley and the Wailers. Tuff Gong/Island Records, 1984).

79. Jacques Derrida, *Limited Inc.* (Evanston, IL: Northwestern University Press, 1988), 31.

80. As Rita Marley describes at more length: "So many of Bob's lyrics reflect our personal life. . . . Sometimes, on tour . . . while we were performing ['No Woman No Cry'] he'd use the opportunity to come over to me onstage and put his arm around my shoulder, with sometimes a kiss or a whisper 'I love you' in my ear. . . . I could go on and on about what song meant what, because basically when Bob wrote he didn't always write alone. . . . He might call to say, 'Did you read what I did last night. . . .' Or 'How does this sound?' Or 'Did I spell this right?' Or 'Was that the right way to say it?' So that most of the lyrics you come across, especially in the early times, pertained to the life we shared. I don't want to make it seem as if I'm claiming them, but we did a lot of writing together" (*No Woman No Cry*, 140).

81. Derrida, *Limited Inc.*, 31.

82. Lacan, *On Feminine Sexuality*, 2–3.

83. Anna Marie Smith, "Rastafari as Resistance and the Ambiguities of Essentialism in the 'New Social Movements,'" in *The Making of Political Identities*, ed. Ernesto Laclau (London: Verso, 1994), 180.

84. V. Spike Peterson, "Sexing Political Identities/Nationalism as Heterosexism," *International Feminist Journal of Politics* 1, no. 1 (June 1999): 56.

85. Marley, *No Woman No Cry*, 17.

86. Marley, *No Woman No Cry*, 16.

87. Smith, "Rastafari," 179–180.

88. Smith, "Rastafari," 175, 176–177.

89. Smith, "Rastafari," 177.

90. Smith, "Rastafari," 181.

91. Smith, "Rastafari," 177.

92. Marley, *No Woman No Cry*, 24–25.

93. Marley, *No Woman No Cry*, 66, 72.

94. Marley, *No Woman No Cry*, 72–73.

95. Marley, *No Woman No Cry*, 73–74.

96. The "them two" is a term Lacan uses in *On Feminine Sexuality* to describe the real appreciation of another's otherness, the other's like subjectivity (in being as inaccessible to the self as the self is to the other) (6).

97. Lacan, *On Feminine Sexuality*, 6.

98. In Lacan's words, "Phallic jouissance is the obstacle owing to which man does not come," both literally and figuratively, in the sense of finding himself, but also "does not come . . . to enjoy woman's body, precisely what he enjoys is the jouissance of the organ," namely, a phallic organ that "is not related to the Other as such" but really to the self (*On Feminine Sexuality*, 7).

99. Smith, "Rastafari," 197, quoting Lacan, *Écrits*, 4–5.

100. Marley, *No Woman No Cry*, 112–113.

101. Marley, *No Woman No Cry*, 114.

102. This is Lacan's controversial statement in *On Feminine Sexuality*, that, at least in relationship to heterosexuality, "there's no such thing as a sexual relationship" because of how the subject and Woman are positioned within phallic discourse (12, 34). Any love relation in which the love-object cannot be seen in their like subjectivity would also qualify, however, as a relation struggling against the reality of them-twoness.

103. Lacan, *On Feminine Sexuality*, 63.

104. Marley, *No Woman No Cry*, 112.

105. Marley, *No Woman No Cry*, 156.

106. Marley, *No Woman No Cry*, 156.

107. Marley, *No Woman No Cry*, 156.

108. Lacan, *On Feminine Sexuality*, 145.

109. As Lacan also states movingly, out of "love's approach" "something emerges," each subject's sense of self that evolves out of the understanding of what one has missed in the other (*On Feminine Sexuality*, 145–146).

110. Lacan reminds us early in *On Feminine Sexuality*: "For everything having to do with the relations between men and women, what is called collectivity, it's not working out. It's not working out, and the whole world talks about it, and a large part of our activity is taken up with saying so" (32).

111. Lacan, *On Feminine Sexuality*, 85.

112. Marley, *No Woman No Cry*, 62.

113. Marley, *Songs of Freedom* CD booklet and Timothy White, *Catch a Fire: The Life of Bob Marley* (NY: Henry Holt, 1983), 3–4. White's cover provides the rare image of a more haggard Marley toward the end of his career.

114. Slavoj Žižek, *Enjoy Your Symptom! Jacques Lacan in Hollywood and Out* (New York: Routledge, 1992), 21.

115. The son's voice is also built on the evocation of his own mortality in the infantile portrait of a young Damian Marley at the very start of his life.

conclusion. DEFACING RACE, RETHINKING THE SKIN

1. As quoted in Jennifer Law's "Knowledge Is Made for Printing: Joscelyn Gardner's Creole Portraits Series," in *Joscelyn Gardner: Bleeding and Breeding*, exhibit catalogue (Ontario, Canada: Station Gallery, 2012), 12.

2. Gilles Deleuze and Felix Guattari, "Year Zero: Faciality," in *A Thousand Plateaus: Capitalism and Schizophrenia*, trans. Brian Massumi (Minneapolis, MN: University of Minnesota Press, 1987), 170.

3. Steven Connor, *The Book of Skin* (Ithaca, NY: Cornell University Press, 2004), 29.

4. Frantz Fanon, *Black Skin, White Masks*, trans. Charles Lam Markmann (New York: Grove Weidenfeld Press, 1967), 111.

5. Jean-Luc Nancy, *Corpus* (New York: Fordham University Press, 2008), 11.

6. Placed in the chapter as an aside, this parenthetical discussion offers the most

provocative clues to Fanon's synthesis of (explicitly) the Freudian unconscious, the Lacanian Imaginary, and (implicitly) Didier Anzieu's theories of a sensational or bodily skin ego. All four theories converge around the status of a mysterious "apprehension" or apparition Lacan describes as appearing upon the subject's emergence into self-consciousness, and then disappearing as the subject fully enters the symbolic order. There is a subtle and crucial difference, however, between Anzieu's and Lacan's notions of the mirror stage. For Anzieu the skin ego is actually a pre-Imaginary, pre-Symbolic stage of subjective development. The body-image in the mirror is preceded by an image of the body *before* the mirror, that is, the body *as its flesh or skin*.

7. Fanon's translator describes heautoscopy as "the vivid psychological awareness and examination of one's own internal organs as if they were outside oneself—an extreme hypochondria" (*Black Skin*, 164). This description corresponds remarkably to Lacan's notion of the partial object or *objet a*: "The *objet a* is something from which the subject, in order to constitute itself, has separated itself off as organ" (Jacques Lacan, *The Four Fundamental Concepts of Psychoanalysis*, ed. Jacques-Alain Miller, trans. Alan Sheridan [New York: W. W. Norton & Company, Inc., 1998], 103). I am suggesting here that the similarity is not accidental—both psychiatrists are attempting to define a similar psychic condition.

8. Slavoj Žižek, "The Lamella of David Lynch," in *Reading Seminar XI: Lacan's Four Fundamental Concepts of Psychoanalysis*, ed. Richard Feldstein, Bruce Fink, and Maire Jaanus (Albany: State University of New York Press, 1995), 208.

9. Žižek, "The Lamella of David Lynch," 208.

10. Claudia Benthien, *Skin: On the Cultural Border Between Self and World* (New York: Columbia University Press, 2004), 86–87.

11. Benthien, *Skin*, 94. As she also states, femaleness is either "the dark and muddy breeding ground in the depths of the body" or "the smooth and beautiful sheath-façade that surrounds this body but not in the powerful and vigorous, though profane, intervening layers of muscle and tissue" (89).

12. Benthien, *Skin*, 89.

13. Benthien, *Skin*, 89.

14. Benthien, *Skin*, 94.

15. Benthien, *Skin*, 90.

16. Patricia Kaersenhout, *Invisible Men* (Den Haag, the Netherlands: Eindeloos Publishers, 2009), foreword.

17. This is the horrific aspect of the flesh William Faulkner evokes, in terms of race explicitly, when a character in *Absalom, Absalom* describes her sense "that my entire being seemed to run at blind full tilt into something monstrous and immobile, with a shocking impact too soon and too quick to be mere amazement and outrage at that black arresting and untimorous hand on my white woman's flesh. Because there is something in the touch of flesh with flesh which abrogates, cuts sharp and straight across the devious intricate channels of decorous ordering . . . let flesh touch with flesh, and watch the fall of all the eggshell shibboleth of caste and color too" (*Absalom, Absalom* [New York: Random House Inc., 1986], 111–112).

18. Žižek, "The Lamella of David Lynch," 208.

19. Žižek, "The Lamella of David Lynch," 208; also see "'I Hear You with My Eyes'; or, The Invisible Master," in *Gaze and Voice as Love Objects*, ed. Renata Salecl and Slavoj Žižek (Durham, NC: Duke University Press, 1996), 113.

20. The Obamacizing craze that followed Shepard Fairey's poster, with websites such as Obamiconme.com offering to allow anyone to manipulate their image to look like the poster's head shot, gives us all the opportunity to facialize ourselves according to the new terms of the symbolic order inaugurated by Barack Obama's election. As Peter Schjeldahl describes, the poster's effect and "abstract associations" depend on a graphic technique "refined by Andy Warhol—of polarizing photographs into solid darks and blank lights, thus rendering volumetric subjects dead flat." The flattened image then becomes the site for an imaginative rebuilding of the face in symbolic and idealizing terms. In this instance, Barack Obama's visage becomes a study "of concerted purpose, guarded against fatuity by coolly candid deliberation. The effect is that of epic poetry in an everyday tongue," the perfect combination of the exalted and the vernacular necessary for a political candidate ("Hope and Glory: A Shepard Fairey Moment," *The New Yorker*, February 23, 2009, http://www.newyorker.com/arts/critics/artworld/2009/02/23/090223craw _artworld_schjeldahl, accessed July 7, 2012).

21. When Paul Gilroy in *Against Race: Imagining Political Culture Beyond the Color Line* (Cambridge, MA: Harvard University Press, 2000) and Emmanuel Eze in *Achieving Our Humanity: The Idea of the Postracial Future* (New York: Routledge, 2001) first introduced the term "post-racial," they used it to indicate the epistemological project and deconstructive process of stripping languages of race and difference from the signifier, historicizing them, showing their genealogy, and thereby stripping the racialized body to show its historical meanings. Gilroy also hoped for a new type of vision that could see the raced body as "absolutely penetrable . . . refigured as the transient, epiphenomenon of coded visible information." For Gilroy, this would be the sign that epidermalization, "that aesthetic, that gaze, and that regime of power are irrecoverably over" (*Against Race*, 47).

Abel, Elizabeth, Barbara Christian, and Helene Moglen, eds. *Female Subjects in Black and White: Race, Psychoanalysis, Feminism*. Los Angeles: University of California Press, 1997.

"African American Performers on Early Sound Recordings, 1892–1916." *The Library of Congress Presents: Music, Theater and Dance*. April 12, 2007. http://memory.loc.gov /cocoon/ihas/loc.natlib.ihas.200038862/default.html. Accessed May 8, 2007.

Anderson, Paul Allen. *Deep River: Music and Memory in Harlem Renaissance Thought*. Durham, NC: Duke University Press, 2001.

Anzieu, Didier. *The Skin Ego: A Psychoanalytical Approach to the Self*. New Haven, CT: Yale University Press, 1989.

Aravamudan, Srinivas. *Tropicopolitans: Colonialism and Agency, 1688–1804*. Durham, NC: Duke University Press, 1999.

Archer-Straw, Petrine. *Negrophilia: Avant-Garde Paris and Black Culture in the 1920s*. London: Thames and Hudson, 2000.

Auslander, Philip. *Liveness: Performance in a Mediatized Culture*. New York: Routledge, 1999.

Baker, Houston. *Modernism and the Harlem Renaissance*. Chicago: University of Chicago Press, 1987.

Baldwin, James. "Unnameable Objects, Unspeakable Crimes." http://www.blackstate .com/baldwin1.html. Accessed September 13, 2009.

Baldwin, James. *James Baldwin: Collected Essays*. New York: Literary Classics of the United States, 1998.

Baldwin, James. *Tell Me How Long the Train's Been Gone*. New York: Vintage Books, 1998.

Baldwin, James. *Go Tell It on the Mountain*. New York: Doubleday, 1952.

Baraka, Amiri. *The Sidney Poet Heroical in 29 Scenes*. New York: I. Reed Books, 1979.

"Barber's Paradox." *Wikipedia*. http://en.wikipedia.org/wiki/Barber_paradox. Accessed July 2, 2012.

Barker, Jennifer. *The Tactile Eye: Touch and the Cinematic Experience*. Berkeley: University of California Press, 2009.

Barrett Sr., Leonard E. *The Rastafarians*. Boston, MA: Beacon Press, 1997.

Belafonte, Harry. "Why I Married Julie." *Ebony*, July 1957.

Benjamin, Jessica. *Like Subjects, Love Objects: Essays on Recognition and Sexual Difference.* New Haven, CT: Yale University Press, 1995.

Benthien, Claudia. *Skin: On the Cultural Border between Self and World.* New York: Columbia University Press, 2004.

Berenson, Bernard. *Esthétique et Histoire Des Arts Visuels.* Paris: Éditions Albin Michel, 1953.

Berger, John. *Ways of Seeing.* New York: Viking Press, 1973.

Bloom, Harold. *A Map of Misreading.* New York: Oxford University Press, 1975.

Bogle, Donald. *Toms, Coons, Mulattoes, Mammies and Bucks: An Interpretive History of Blacks in American Film.* New York: Continuum, 2001.

Bordman, Gerald. *Musical Theatre: A Chronicle.* New York: Oxford University Press, 1978.

Boswell, Maia. "'Ladies,' 'Gentlemen,' and 'Colored': The Agency of (Lacan's Black) Letter in the Outhouse." *Cultural Critique* 41 (winter 1999): 108–138.

Brathwaite, Edward Kamau. "History of the Voice." In *Roots: Essays in Caribbean Literature,* 259–304. Ann Arbor: University of Michigan Press, 1993.

Brooks, Daphne. *Bodies of Dissent: Spectacular Performances of Race and Freedom, 1850–1910.* Durham, NC: Duke University Press, 2006.

Brooks, Tim. *Lost Sounds: Blacks and the Birth of the Recording Industry, 1890–1919.* Champaign: University of Illinois Press, 2004.

Brook-Rose, Christine. "Woman as a Semiotic Object." *Poetics Today* 6, no. 1/2. The Female Body in Western Culture: Semiotic Perspectives (1985): 9–20.

Brown, Antonio. "Performing 'Truth': Black Speech Acts." *African American Review* 36, no. 2 (2002).

Butler, Judith. *Excitable Speech: A Politics of the Performative.* New York: Routledge, 1997.

Butler, Judith. "Passing, Queering: Nella Larsen's Psychoanalytic Challenge." In *Female Subjects in Black and White: Race, Psychoanalysis, Feminism,* edited by Elizabeth Abel, Barbara Christian, and Helene Moglen, 266–284. Berkeley, CA: University of California Press, 1997.

Calo, Mary Ann. *Distinction and Denial: Race, Nation, and the Critical Construction of the African American Artist, 1929–40.* Ann Arbor: University of Michigan Press, 2007.

Carby, Hazel V. *Cultures in Babylon: Black Britain and African America.* London: Verso, 1999.

Carby, Hazel V. *Race Men.* Cambridge, MA: Harvard University Press, 1998.

Carroll, Anne Elizabeth. *Word, Image, and the New Negro: Representation and Identity in the Harlem Renaissance.* Bloomington: Indiana University Press, 2007.

Carter, Marva Griffin. *Swing Along: The Musical Life of Will Marion Cook.* New York: Oxford University Press, 2008.

Cham, Mbye B., ed. *Ex-iles: Essays on Caribbean Cinema.* Trenton, NJ: Africa World Press, 1992.

Cheng, Anne Anlin. *Second Skin: Josephine Baker and the Modern Surface.* New York: Oxford University Press, 2011.

Chude-Sokei, Louis. *The Last "Darky": Bert Williams, Black-on-Black Minstrelsy, and the African Diaspora.* Durham, NC: Duke University Press, 2005.

Connor, Steven. *The Book of Skin*. Ithaca, NY: Cornell University Press, 2004.

Cooper, Wayne F., ed. *The Dialectic Poetry of Claude McKay*. Freeport, NY: Books for Libraries Press, 1972.

Copjec, Joan. *Read My Desire: Lacan against the Historicists*. Cambridge, MA: MIT Press, 1996.

Courtney, Susan. *Hollywood Fantasies of Miscegenation: Specular Narratives of Gender and Race*. Princeton, NJ: Princeton University Press, 2004.

Crenshaw, Kimberlé. "Demarginalizing the Intersection of Race and Sex: A Black Feminist Critique of Antidiscrimination Doctrine, Feminist Theory and Antiracist Politics." In *The Black Feminist Reader*, edited by Joy James and T. Denean Sharpley-Whiting, 208–238. Malden, MA: Blackwell Publishing, 2001.

Crenshaw, Kimberlé. "Mapping the Margins: Intersectionality, Identity Politics, and Violence Against Women of Color." In *The Public Nature of Private Violence: The Discovery of Domestic Abuse*, edited by Martha Albertson Fineman and Roxanne Mykitiuk, 93–120. New York: Routledge, 1994.

Cripps, Thomas. *Making Movies Black: The Hollywood Message Movie from World War II to the Civil Rights Era*. New York: Oxford University Press, 1993.

Crowther, Bosley. "Movie Review—The World, the Flesh and the Devil." *New York Times Review*, May 21, 1959.

Curtis, Susan. *The First Black Actors on the Great White Way*. Columbia: University of Missouri Press, 1998.

Curwood, Anastasia. *Stormy Weather: Middle-Class African American Marriages between the Two World Wars*. Chapel Hill: University of North Carolina Press, 2010.

Deleuze, Gilles, and Felix Guattari. "Year Zero: Faciality." In *A Thousand Plateaus: Capitalism and Schizophrenia*. Translated by Brian Massumi, 167–191. Minneapolis: University of Minnesota Press, 1987.

Derrida, Jacques. *Limited Inc*. Evanston, IL: Northwestern University Press, 1988.

DeVere Brody, Jennifer. *Punctuation: Art, Politics, and Play*. Durham, NC: Duke University Press, 2008.

Diaz, Junot. *The Brief Wondrous Life of Oscar Wao*. New York: Riverhead Books, 2008.

Dolar, Mladen. *A Voice and Nothing More*. Cambridge, MA: MIT Press, 2006.

Donkin, Ellen. "Mrs. Siddons Looks Back in Anger." In *Critical Theory and Performance*, edited by Janelle G. Reinelt and Joseph R. Roach, 317–333. Rev. Ed. Ann Arbor: University of Michigan Press, 2007.

Doolittle, Hilda. "Red Roses for Bronze." In *Collected Poems, 1912–1944*. New York: New Directions, 1986.

Drake, St. Clair, and Horace R. Cayton. *Black Metropolis: A Study of Negro Life in a Northern City*. Chicago: University of Chicago Press, 1993.

Duberman, Martin. *Paul Robeson: A Biography*. New York: New Press, 1989.

Dunbar, Paul Laurence. *Lyrics of Lowly Life*. New York: Dodd, Mead, 1896.

Dyer, Richard. *Stars*. London: British Film Institute, 2008.

Dyer, Richard. *Heavenly Bodies: Film Stars and Society*. New York: Routledge, 2003.

Ebony, ed. *The White Problem in America*. Chicago: Johnson, 1966.

Edmondson, Belinda. *Making Men: Gender, Literary Authority and Women's Writing in Caribbean Narrative*. Durham, NC: Duke University Press, 1999.

Edwards, Brent. *The Practice of Diaspora: Literature, Translation, and the Rise of Black Internationalism*. Cambridge, MA: Harvard University Press, 2003.

Eidsvik, Charles. "Machines of the Invisible: Changes in Film Technology in the Age of Video." In *Film Quarterly: Forty Years — A Selection*, edited by Brian Henderson and Ann Martin, 340–349. Berkeley: University of California Press, 1999.

Ellison, Ralph. *Shadow and Act*. New York: Quality Paperback Book Club, 1994.

Eze, Emmanuel. *Achieving Our Humanity: The Idea of the Postracial Future*. New York: Routledge, 2001.

Fabre, Michel. *From Harlem to Paris: Black American Writers in France, 1840–1980*. Champaign: University of Illinois Press, 1993.

Fanon, Frantz. *Black Skin, White Masks*. Trans. Charles Lam Markmann. New York: Grove Weidenfeld Press, 1967.

Fanon, Frantz. *The Wretched of the Earth*. New York: Grove Weidenfeld, 1963.

Faulkner, William. *Absalom, Absalom*. New York: Random House, 1986.

Favor, Martin. *Authentic Blackness: The Folk in the New Negro Renaissance*. Durham, NC: Duke University Press, 1999.

Feldstein, Richard, Bruce Fink, and Maire Jaanus, eds. *Reading Seminar XI: Lacan's Four Fundamental Concepts of Psychoanalysis*. Albany: State University of New York Press, 1995.

Fleetwood, Nicole. *Troubling Vision: Performance, Visuality and Blackness*. Chicago: University of Chicago Press, 2011.

Foner, Philip S., ed. *Paul Robeson Speaks: Writings, Speeches, Interviews, 1918–1974*. New York: Citadel Press Books, 1978.

Foucault, Michel. *"Society Must Be Defended": Lectures at the College de France, 1975–1976*. Trans. David Macey. New York: Picador, 2003.

Fraden, Rena. *Blueprints for a Black Federal Theatre, 1935–1939*. New York: Cambridge University Press, 1994.

Friedman, Susan Stanford. *Analyzing Freud: The Letters of H. D., Bryher and Their Circle*. New York: New Directions, 2002.

Freud, Sigmund. "Three Contributions to the Theory of Sex." In *The Basic Writings of Sigmund Freud*, edited and translated by A. A. Brill, 519–597. New York: Modern Library, 1995.

Gates Jr., Henry Louis. *Thirteen Ways of Looking at a Black Man*. New York: Random House, 1997.

Gates Jr., Henry Louis. "Preface." In *Black Male: Representations of Masculinity in Contemporary American Art*, edited by Thelma Golden, 11–14. New York: Whitney Museum of American Art, Harry N. Abrams, 1994.

Gates Jr., Henry Louis. *The Signifying Monkey: A Theory of African-American Literary Criticism*. New York: Oxford University Press, 1988.

Gates Jr., Henry Louis. "The Trope of a New Negro and the Reconstruction of the Image of the Black." *Representations* 24 (fall 1988): 129–155.

Geuens, Jean-Pierre. "Through the Looking Glasses: From the Camera Obscura to Video Assist." In *Film Quarterly: Forty Years—A Selection*, edited by Brian Henderson and Ann Martin, 372–391. Berkeley: University of California Press, 1999.

Gilroy, Paul. *Postcolonial Melancholia*. New York: Columbia University Press, 2006.

Gilroy, Paul. *Against Race: Imagining Political Culture Beyond the Color Line*. Cambridge, MA: Harvard University Press, 2000.

Glissant, Édouard. *Poetics of Relation*. Ann Arbor: University of Michigan Press, 1997.

Glissant, Édouard. *Caribbean Discourse: Selected Essays*. Charlottesville: University of Virginia Press, 1989.

Goeser, Caroline. *Picturing the New Negro: Harlem Renaissance Print Culture and Modern Black Identity*. Manhattan: University Press of Kansas, 2006.

Golden, Thelma, ed. *Black Male: Representations of Masculinity in Contemporary American Art*. New York: Whitney Museum of American Art, Harry N. Abrams, 1994.

Goudie, Sean X. *Creole America: The West Indies and the Formation of Literature and Culture in the New Republic*. Philadelphia: University of Pennsylvania Press, 2006.

Greimas, A. J. "The Interaction of Semiotic Constraints." Trans. François Rastier. *Yale French Studies* 41, Game, Play, Literature (1968): 86–105.

Hall, Kim. *Things of Darkness: Economies of Race and Gender in Early Modern England*. Ithaca, NY: Cornell University Press, 1996.

Hardt, Michael, and Antono Negri. *Empire*. Cambridge, MA: Harvard University Press, 2001.

Heller, Adele, and Lois Rudnick, eds. *1915, the Cultural Moment: The New Politics, the New Woman, the New Psychology, the New Art and the New Theatre in America*. New Brunswick, NJ: Rutgers University Press, 1991.

hooks, bell. "Feminism as a Persistent Critique of History: What's Love Got to Do with It?" In *The Fact of Blackness: Frantz Fanon and Visual Representation*, edited by Alan Read, 76–85. Seattle, WA: Bay Press, 1996.

hooks, bell. *Black Looks: Race and Representation*. Boston, MA: South End Press, 1992.

"Irony." Wikipedia, http://en.wikipedia.org/wiki/Irony. Accessed May 14, 2007.

Jablonski, Nina G. *Skin: A Natural History*. Berkeley: University of California Press, 2006.

James, C. L. R. *Beyond A Boundary*. Durham, NC: Duke University Press, 1993.

James, C. L. R. *The Black Jacobins: Toussaint L'Ouverture and the San Domingo Revolution*. New York: Vintage Books, 1989.

James, C. L. R. *At the Rendezvous of Victory: Selected Writings*. London: Allison and Busby, 1984.

James, C. L. R. "Paul Robeson: Black Star." *Black World* 1 (November 1970): 106–115.

Jay, Martin. *Downcast Eyes: The Denigration of Vision in Twentieth-Century French Thought*. Berkeley: University of California Press, 1994.

Jenkins, Candace. *Private Lives, Proper Relations: Regulating Black Intimacy*. Minneapolis: University of Minnesota Press, 2007.

Jules-Rosette, Bennetta. *Black Paris: The African Writers' Landscape*. Champaign: University of Illinois Press, 2000.

Kaersenhout, Patricia. *Invisible Men*. Den Haag, The Netherlands: Eindeloos Publishers, 2009.

Katilius-Boydstun, Marvin. "The Semiotics of A. J. Greimas: An Introduction." *Lituanus: Lithuanian Quarterly Journal of Arts and Science* 36, no. 3 (fall 1990). http://www .lituanus.org/1990_3/90_3_02.htm. Accessed November 27, 2013.

Keeling, Kara. *The Witch's Flight: The Cinematic, the Black Femme, and the Image of Common Sense*. Durham, NC: Duke University Press, 2007.

Lacan, Jacques. *Écrits: The First Complete Edition*. Trans. Bruce Fink. New York: W. W. Norton, 2007.

Lacan, Jacques. *Écrits: A Selection*. Trans. Bruce Fink. New York: W. W. Norton, 2002.

Lacan, Jacques. *On Feminine Sexuality, the Limits of Love and Knowledge*. Eds. Jacques-Alain Miller and Bruce Fink. New York: W. W. Norton, 1999.

Lacan, Jacques. *The Four Fundamental Concepts of Psychoanalysis*. Edited by Jacques-Alain Miller. Translated by Alan Sheridan. New York: W. W. Norton, 1998.

Lacan, Jacques. *The Seminar of Jacques Lacan: The Ethics of Psychoanalysis*. Edited by Jacques-Alain Miller. Translated by Dennis Porter. New York: W. W. Norton, 1997.

Lacan, Jacques. "Position of the Unconscious." In *Reading Seminar XI: Lacan's Four Fundamental Concepts of Psychoanalysis*, edited by Richard Feldstein, Bruce Fink, and Maire Jaanus, 259–282. Albany: State University of New York Press, 1995.

Lamming, George. *In the Castle of My Skin*. New York: McGraw-Hill, 1953.

Larsen, Nella. *The Complete Fiction of Nella Larsen: Passing, Quicksand, and the Stories*. New York: Anchor Books, 2001.

Law, Jennifer. "Knowledge Is Made for Printing: Joscelyn Gardner's Creole Portraits Series." In *Joscelyn Gardner: Bleeding and Breeding*, 9–17. Exhibition catalogue. Ontario, Canada: Station Gallery, 2012.

Levering Lewis, David, and Deborah Willis, eds. *A Small Nation of People: W. E. B. Du Bois and African American Portraits of Progress*. New York: HarperCollins, 2003.

L'hermitte, Jean. *L'Image de Notre Corps*. Paris, 1939: Nouvelle Revue Critique.

Lorde, Audre. "Coal." In *The Collected Poems of Audre Lorde*. New York: W. W. Norton, 2000.

Lorde, Audre. *Sister Outsider*. Freedom, CA: Crossing Press, 1984.

Mackey, Nathaniel. *Bedouin Handbook*. College Park, MD: Sun and Moon Press, 2000.

Marks, Laura U. *The Skin of the Film: Intercultural Cinema, Embodiment, and the Senses*. Durham, NC: Duke University Press, 2000.

Marley, Bob. CD booklet in *Songs of Freedom*. Tuff Gong, 1992.

Marley, Rita, and Hettie Jones. *No Woman No Cry: My Life with Bob Marley*. New York: Hyperion, 2004.

Massumi, Brian. *Parables for the Virtual: Movement, Affect, Sensation*. Durham, NC: Duke University Press, 2002.

McCabe, Susan. *Cinematic Modernism: Modernist Poetry and Film*. New York: Cambridge University Press, 2009.

McGill, Lisa. *Constructing Black Selves: Caribbean American Narratives and the Second Generation*. New York: NYU Press, 2005.

Mercer, Kobena. *Welcome to the Jungle: New Positions in Black Cultural Studies*. New York: Routledge, 1994.

Merleau-Ponty, Maurice. *The Visible and the Invisible*. Ed. Claude Lefort. Trans. Alphonso Lingis. Evanston, IL: Northwestern University Press, 1968.

Miller, Monica L. *Slaves to Fashion: Black Dandyism and the Styling of Black Diasporic Identity*. Durham, NC: Duke University Press, 2009.

Mitchell, Michelle. *Righteous Propagation: African Americans and the Politics of Racial Destiny after Reconstruction*. Chapel Hill: University of North Carolina Press, 2004.

Mitchell, Stephen A., and Margaret J. Black. *Freud and Beyond: A History of Modern Psychoanalytic Thought*. New York: Basic Books, 1995.

Morrison, Toni. *Beloved*. New York: Random House, 2004.

Moten, Fred. *In the Break: The Aesthetics of the Black Radical Tradition*. Minneapolis: University of Minnesota Press, 2003.

Mullen, Bill V., and James Smethurst, eds. *Left of the Color Line: Race, Radicalism, and Twentieth-Century Literature of the United States*. Chapel Hill: University of North Carolina Press, 2006.

Mulvey, Laura. *Visual and Other Pleasures*. New York: Palgrave Macmillan, 1989.

Nadell, Martha Jane. *Enter the New Negroes: Images of Race in American Culture*. Cambridge, MA: Harvard University Press, 2004.

Nancy, Jean Luc. *Corpus*. New York: Fordham University Press, 2008.

Neptune, Harvey. *Caliban and the Yankees: Trinidad and the United States Occupation*. Chapel Hill: University of North Carolina Press, 2007.

Parascandola, Louis J., ed. *"Winds Can Wake Up the Dead": An Eric Walrond Reader*. Detroit, MI: Wayne State University Press, 1998.

Peterson, V. Spike. "Sexing Political Identities/Nationalism as Heterosexism." *International Feminist Journal of Politics* 1, no. 1 (June 1999): 34–65.

Phelan, Peggy. *Unmarked: The Politics of Performance*. London: Routledge, 1993.

Philip, Marlene Nourbese. *A Genealogy of Resistance: Essays*. Toronto, Ontario: Mercury Press, 1999.

Phillips, Caryl. *Dancing in the Dark*. New York: Knopf, 2005.

Quintilian's Institutes of Oratory, book 8, chapter 6. http://rhetoric.eserver.org/quintilian /8/chapter6.html. Accessed July 3, 2012.

Read, Alan, ed. *The Fact of Blackness: Frantz Fanon and Visual Representation*. Seattle, WA: Bay Press, 1996.

Reinelt, Janelle G., and Joseph R. Roach, eds. *Critical Theory and Performance*. Ann Arbor: University of Michigan Press, 2007.

Riis, Thomas L., ed. "*In Dahomey* in Text and Performance." In *The Music and Scripts of In Dahomey*, xiii–xlvi. Madison, WI: A-R Editions, 1996.

Riis, Thomas L. *The Music and Scripts of In Dahomey*. Madison, WI: A-R Editions, 1996.

Riis, Thomas L. "The Script." In *The Music and Scripts of In Dahomey*, xlvii–lxxii. Madison, WI: A-R Editions, 1996.

Roach, Joseph. *It*. Ann Arbor: University of Michigan Press, 2007.

Roach, Joseph. *Cities of the Dead: Circum-Atlantic Performance*. New York: Columbia University Press, 1996.

Robeson, Eslanda. *Paul Robeson, Negro*. New York: Harper and Brothers, 1930.

Robeson Jr., Paul. *The Undiscovered Paul Robeson: An Artist's Journey, 1898–1939*. New York: John Wiley and Sons, 2001.

Rohlehr, Gordon. "Sparrow as Poet." In *David Frost Introduces Trinidad and Tobago*, edited by Michael Anthony and Andrew Carr, 73–83. London: Andre Deutsch, 1975.

Ross, Marlon B. *Manning the Race: Reforming Black Men in the Jim Crow Area*. New York: NYU Press, 2004.

Runstedtler, Theresa. *Jack Johnson, Rebel Sojourner: Boxing in the Shadow of the Global Color Line*. Berkeley: University of California Press, 2012.

Salecl, Renata, and Slavoj Žižek, eds. *Gaze and Voice as Love Objects*. Durham, NC: Duke University Press, 1996.

Sartre, Jean-Paul. *Being and Nothingness*. New York: Washington Square Press, 1992.

Sartre, Jean-Paul. "Black Orpheus." *Massachusetts Review* 6, no. 1 (autumn 1964–winter 1965): 13–52.

Scott, David. "Interview with Stuart Hall." BOMB *Magazine* 90 (winter 2004–5). 2–13.

Segal, Naomi. *Consensuality: Didier Anzieu, Gender and the Sense of Touch*. Amsterdam: Rodopi B. V., 2009.

Seth, Vanita. *Europe's Indians: Producing Racial Difference, 1500–1900*. Durham, NC: Duke University Press, 2010.

Sexton, Jared. *Amalgamation Schemes: Antiblackness and the Critique of Multiracialism*. Minneapolis: University of Minnesota Press, 2008.

Shakespeare, William. *The Tempest*. New York: W. W. Norton, 2003.

Sharpley-Whiting, T. Denean. *Black Venus: Sexualized Savages, Primal Fears, and Primitive Narratives*. Durham, NC: Duke University Press, 1999.

Shaw, Arnold. *Belafonte: An Unauthorized Biography*. New York: Chilton, 1960.

Sherrard-Johnson, Cherene. *Portraits of the New Negro: Visual and Literary Culture in the Harlem Renaissance*. New Brunswick, NJ: Rutgers University Press, 2007.

Shiel, M. P. *The Purple Cloud*. London: Chatto and Windus, 1901. Ebook. http://www.gutenberg.org/files/11229/11229-h/11229-h.htm.

Silverman, Kaja. *Flesh of My Flesh*. Stanford, CA: Stanford University Press, 2009.

Silverman, Kaja. *The Threshold of the Visible World*. New York: Routledge, 1996.

Silverman, Kaja. *Male Subjectivity at the Margins*. New York: Routledge, 1992.

Silverman, Kaja. *The Acoustic Mirror: The Female Voice in Psychoanalysis and Cinema*. Bloomington: Indiana University Press, 1988.

Smethurst, James. *The African American Roots of Modernism: From Reconstruction to the Harlem Renaissance*. Chapel Hill: University of North Carolina Press, 2011.

Smith, Anna Marie. "Rastafari as Resistance and the Ambiguities of Essentialism in the 'New Social Movements.'" In *The Making of Political Identities*, edited by Ernesto Laclau, 171–204. London: Verso, 1994.

Smith, Shawn Michelle. *Photography on the Color Line: W. E. B. Du Bois, Race, and Visual Culture*. Durham, NC: Duke University Press, 2004.

Snyder, Susan. "The Genres of Shakespeare's Plays." In *The Cambridge Companion to Shakespeare*, edited by Margreta de Grazia and Stanley Wells, 83–98. Cambridge, UK: Cambridge University Press, 2001.

Spillers, Hortense J. "'All the Things You Could Be by Now, If Sigmund Freud's Wife Was Your Mother': Psychoanalysis and Race." In *Female Subjects in Black and White: Race, Psychoanalysis, Feminism*, edited by Elizabeth Abel, Barbara Christian, and Helene Moglen, 135–158. Berkeley: University of California Press, 1997.

Spillers, Hortense J. "Mama's Baby, Papa's Maybe: An American Grammar Book." *Diacritics* 17, no. 2 (summer 1987): 64–81.

Stein, Gertrude. *The Autobiography of Alice B. Toklas*. New York: Vintage Books, 1990.

Stein, Judith. *The World of Marcus Garvey: Race and Class in Modern Society*. Baton Rouge: Louisiana State University Press, 1986.

Stephens, Michelle A. "The Comic Side of Gender Trouble and Bert Williams' Signature Act." "Diaspora" special issue. *Feminist Review* 90 (2008): 128–146.

Stephens, Michelle A. "'I'm the Everybody Who's Nobody': Genealogies of the New World Slave in Paul Robeson's Performances of the 1930s." In *Hemispheric American Studies*, edited by Caroline F. Levander and Robert S. Levine, 166–186. New Brunswick, NJ: Rutgers University Press, 2007.

Stephens, Michelle A. "The First Negro Matinee Idol: Harry Belafonte and American Culture in the 1950s." In *Left of the Color Line: Race, Radicalism, and Twentieth-Century Literature of the United States*, edited by. Bill V. Mullen and James Smethurst, 223–238. Chapel Hill: University of North Carolina Press, 2006.

Stephens, Michelle A. "Babylon's 'Natural Mystic': The North American Music Industry, the Legend of Bob Marley, and the Incorporation of Transnationalism." *Cultural Studies* 12, no. 2 (April 1998): 139–167.

Stovall, Tyler. *French Civilization and Its Discontents: Nationalism, Colonialism, Race (after the Empire)*. New York: Lexington Books, 2003.

Stovall, Tyler. *Paris Noir: African Americans in the City of Light*. New York: Mariner Books, 1998.

Summers, Martin. *Manliness and Its Discontents: The Black Middle Class and the Transformation of Masculinity, 1900–1930*. Chapel Hill: University of North Carolina Press, 2004.

Swindall, Lindsey. *The Politics of Paul Robeson's Othello*. Jackson: University Press of Mississippi, 2011.

Taussig, Michael. *What Color Is the Sacred?* Chicago: University of Chicago Press, 2009.

Taylor, Diana. *The Archive and the Repertoire: Performing Cultural Memory in the Americas*. Durham, NC: Duke University Press, 2003.

Thomas, Deborah. *Modern Blackness: Nationalism, Globalization, and the Politics of Culture in Jamaica*. Durham, NC: Duke University Press, 2004.

Tucker, Patrick. *Secrets of Screen Acting*. 2nd ed. New York: Routledge, 2003.

Turner, Beth. "Paul Robeson: The Consummate Actor/Activist." *Black Masks* 13, no. 2 (October/November 1998): 5–6, 18–19.

Veal, Michael. *Dub: Soundscapes and Shattered Songs in Jamaican Reggae Music*. Middletown, CT: Wesleyan University Press, 2007.

Vroman, Mary Elizabeth. "See How They Run." *Ladies' Home Journal*, June 1951.

Walker, Christian. "The Miscegenated Gaze." *No More Heroes: Unveiling Masculinity* (San Francisco, CA, SF Camerawork). Exhibition catalogue. *Camerawork Quarterly* 18, nos. 3 and 4 (summer/fall 1991).

Walker, George. "The Real 'Coon' on the American Stage." CD booklet in *Bert Williams: The Early Years, 1901–1909*. Archeophone, 2004.

Wallace, Maurice. *Constructing the Black Masculine: Identity and Ideality in African American Men's Literature and Culture, 1775–1995*. Durham, NC: Duke University Press, 2002.

Walton, Jean. *Fair Sex, Savage Dreams: Race, Psychoanalysis, Sexual Difference*. Durham, NC: Duke University Press, 2001.

Wartenberg, Thomas E. *Unlikely Couples: Movie Romance as Social Criticism*. Boulder, CO: Westview Press, 1999.

Watkins, Mel. *Stepin Fetchit: The Life and Times of Lincoln Perry*. New York: Random House, 2006.

Watkins, Mel. *African American Humor: The Best Black Comedy from Slavery to Today*. Chicago: Lawrence Hill Books, 2002.

Weheliye, Alexander G. *Phonographies: Grooves in Sonic Afro-Modernity*. Durham, NC: Duke University Press, 2005.

Weinbaum, Alys Eve. "Ways of Not Seeing: (En)gendered Optics in Benjamin, Baudelaire, and Freud." In *Loss: The Politics of Mourning*, edited by David Eng and David Kazanjian, 396–425. Berkeley: University of California Press, 2003.

West, Cornel. *Restoring Hope: Conversations on the Future of Black America*, edited by Kelvin Shawn Sealey, 3–34. Boston: Beacon Press, 1997.

White, Timothy. *Catch a Fire: The Life of Bob Marley*. New York: Henry Holt, 1983.

Willett, John, ed. *Brecht on Theatre: The Development of an Aesthetic*. New York: Hill and Wang, 1964.

Williams, Bert. "The Comic Side of Trouble." CD booklet in *Bert Williams: The Middle Years, 1910–1918*. Archeophone, 2002–2005.

Wintz, Cary D. *Encyclopedia of the Harlem Renaissance*. New York: Routledge, 2004.

Wood, Peter H. *Weathering the Storm: Inside Winslow Homer's Gulf Stream*. Mercer University Lamar Memorial Lectures. Athens: University of Georgia Press, 2004.

Wright, Michelle. *Becoming Black: Creating Identity in the African Diaspora*. Durham, NC: Duke University Press, 2004.

Wright, Richard. *The Outsider*. New York: Perennial, 2003.

Wright, Richard. *The Color Curtain: A Report on the Bandung Conference*. Jackson: University Press of Mississippi, 1994.

Wynter, Sylvia. "Beyond Miranda's Meanings: Un/silencing the 'Demonic Ground' of Caliban's 'Woman.'" In *Out of the Kumbla: Caribbean Women and Literature*, edited by Carole Boyce Davies and Elaine Savory Fido, 355–371. Trenton, NJ: Africa World Press, 1990.

Yoshino, Kenji. *Covering: The Hidden Assault on Our Civil Rights*. New York: Random House, 2007.

Young, Harvey. *Embodying Black Experience: Stillness, Critical Memory and the Black Body.* Ann Arbor: University of Michigan Press, 2010.

Young, Lola. "Missing Persons: Fantasizing Black Women in *Black Skin, White Masks.*" In *The Fact of Blackness: Frantz Fanon and Visual Representation*, edited by Alan Read, 86–101. Seattle, WA: Bay Press, 1996.

Young, Robert J. C. *Colonial Desire: Hybridity in Theory, Culture and Race.* New York: Routledge, 1995.

Youngblood, Shay. *Black Girl in Paris.* New York: Riverhead Books, 2001.

Zamora, Lois Parkinson. *Writing the Apocalypse.* New York: Cambridge University Press, 1993.

Žižek, Slavoj. *For They Know Not What They Do: Enjoyment as a Political Factor.* London: Verso, 2008.

Žižek, Slavoj. *How to Read Lacan.* New York: W. W. Norton, 2007.

Žižek, Slavoj. "'I Hear You with My Eyes'; or, The Invisible Master." In *Gaze and Voice as Love Objects*, edited by Renata Salecl and Slavoj Žižek, 90–126. Durham, NC: Duke University Press, 1996.

Žižek, Slavoj. "The Lamella of David Lynch." In *Reading Seminar XI: Lacan's Four Fundamental Concepts of Psychoanalysis*, edited by Richard Feldstein, Bruce Fink, and Maire Jaanus, 205–220. Albany: State University of New York Press, 1995.

Žižek, Slavoj. *Enjoy Your Symptom! Jacques Lacan in Hollywood and Out.* New York: Routledge, 1992.

discography

Dr. Alimantado and the Aggrovators. "Natty Dread Conquer the Barber." In *If Deejay Was Your Trade: The Dreads at King Tubby's, 1974–1977.* Perf. Dr. Alimantado. Bunny Lee, 1975. CD. Blood and Fire, 1995.

Dr. Alimantado and Bunny Lee. "I Killed the Barber ("Natty Dread Kill the Barber")." Perf. Dr. Alimantado. Greensleeves, 1976.

Cole, Alan, and Carlton "Carly" Barrett. "War." Lyrics. *Rastaman Vibration.* Perfs. Bob Marley and the Wailers. Tuff Gong/Island Records, 1976.

Cook, Will Marion, and Cecil Mack. "Brown-Skin Baby Mine." Lyrics. In *The Music and Scripts of* In Dahomey, edited by Thomas L. Riis, 19–21. Madison, WI: A-R Editions, 1996.

Dunbar, Paul Lawrence, Will Marion Cook, and Will Accoe. "Society." Lyrics. In *The Music and Scripts of* In Dahomey, edited by Thomas L. Riis, 142–154. Madison, WI: A-R Editions, 1996.

Holt, John. "Ali Baba." Lyrics. Perf. John Holt. Treasure Isle, 1970.

Johnson, James W., Bob Cole, and Rosamond Johnson. "My Castle on the Nile." Lyrics. Perf. Bert Williams. In *The Music and Scripts of* In Dahomey, edited by Thomas L. Riis, 94–95. Madison, WI: A-R Editions, 1996.

King Tubby and John Holt. "I Trim the Barber." In *King Tubby's Special, 1973–1976.* Perfs. Jackie Edwards and King Tubby and The Aggrovators. Attack, 1973. CD. Trojan 1995.

King Tubby. "Bury the Barber." In *If Deejay Was Your Trade: The Dreads at King Tubby's, 1974–1977*. Perf. Jah Stitch. Jackpot, 1977. CD. Blood and Fire, 1995.

King Tubby, King Jammy, Dirty Harry, and the Aggrovators. "The Poor Barber." In *At The Controls*. Perf. King Tubby. Bunny Lee, 1975/1976. CD. Ackee Dist., 2012.

Marley, Bob. *Songs of Freedom*. CD box set. Tuff Gong, 1992.

Marley, Bob. "Exodus." Lyrics. *Legend: The Best of Bob Marley and the Wailers*. Perfs. Bob Marley and the Wailers. Tuff Gong/Island Records, 1984.

Marley, Bob. "No Woman No Cry." Lyrics. *Legend: The Best of Bob Marley and the Wailers*. Perfs. Bob Marley and the Wailers. Tuff Gong/Island Records, 1984.

Rogers, Alex, and Al Johns. "Broadway in the Jungle" or "On Broadway in Dahomey Bye and Bye." Lyrics. Perf. Bert Williams. In *The Music and Scripts of* In Dahomey, edited by Thomas L. Riis, 111–114. Madison, WI: A-R Editions, 1996.

Williams, Bert. "Nobody." *The Early Years, 1901–1909*. Perf. Bert Williams. CD. Archeophone, 2014.

filmography

Borderline. Dir. Kenneth Macpherson. Pool Films. Perfs. Paul Robeson, Eslanda Goode Robeson, Hilda Doolittie, Gavin Arthur. Originally released in 1930. DVD. New York: Criterion Collection, 2007.

Bright Road. Screenplay by Emmet Lavery. Dir. Gerald Mayer. Perfs. Paul Robeson, Dorothy Dandridge. Originally released in 1953. DVD. Beverly Hills, CA: Metro-Goldwyn-Mayer, 2012.

Carmen Jones. Screenplay by Harry Kleiner. Dir. Otto Preminger. Perfs. Dorothy Dandridge, Harry Belafonte, Pearl Bailey. Originally released in 1954. DVD. Century City, CA: Twentieth Century Fox, 2002.

Comedians. In *That's Black Entertainment*. Dirs. William Greaves and G. William Jones. Originally released in 1990. DVD. Sherman Oaks, CA: S'more Entertainment, 2007.

Harder They Come, The. Dir. Perry Henzell. Perf. Jimmy Cliff. Originally released in 1972. Atlanta, GA: New World Pictures, 2010.

I Am Legend. Dir. Francis Lawrence. Perfs. Will Smith, Alice Braga. Originally released in 2007. DVD. Burbank, CA: Warner Bros., 2008.

Island in the Sun. Screenplay by Alfred Hayes. Dir. Robert Rossen. Perfs. Harry Belafonte, Dorothy Dandridge, James Mason, Joan Fontaine, Joan Collins. Originally released in 1957. VHS. Century City, CA: Twentieth Century Fox, 1998.

Last Man on Earth, The. Dirs. Ubalda Ragona and Sidney Salkow. Perf. Vincent Price. Originally released in 1964. DVD. Beverly Hills, CA: Metro-Goldwyn-Mayer (MGM), 2005.

Omega Man, The. Dir. Boris Sagal. Perf. Charlton Heston. Originally released in 1971. DVD. Burbank, CA: Warner Bros., 2007.

Paul Robeson: Tribute to an Artist. Dir. Saul J. Turell. Janus Films. Perf. Sidney Poitier. Originally released in 1979. DVD. New York: Criterion Collection, 2007.

Song of Freedom. Screenplay by Paul Schrader. Dir. J. Edgar Wills. Perfs. Paul Robeson, Elisabeth Welch. Originally released in 1936. DVD. New York: Kino Video, 2000.

World, the Flesh, and the Devil, The. Dir. Ranald MacDougall. Perfs. Harry Belafonte, Inger Stevens, Mel Ferrer. Originally released in 1959. DVD. Beverly Hills, CA: Metro-Goldwyn-Mayer (MGM), 2011.

205n3, 246n52; sonic resistances or excesses to, 47–48, 51–53

color, 6–7, 10, 14, 29, 32–33, 111–21. *See also* blackness; epidermalization; film; Technicolor

"The Comic Side of Trouble" (Williams), 44

Conference of Negro-African Writers and Artists, 128, 245n41

Connor, Steven, 8, 206n13, 210n32

consensuality, xii, 8, 17–18, 25, 81, 86–93, 121, 172–83, 193. *See also* affect; relationality; skin; subjectivity

Constab Ballads and Songs of Jamaica (McKay), 45

Cook, Will Marion, 46–47, 51, 68–69

coon songs, 45–54. *See also* caricature; *In Dahomey* (Williams and Walker); *specific songs*

Copjec, Joan, 179

Crenshaw, Kimberlé, 11

creole desire, 123–40, 149

cultures: demands of, upon the self, 9; interpellation and, viii, 5, 16–17, 21–22, 38, 90, 118, 164; perceptual regimes and, 39; symbolic order and, 22–30, 32–33. *See also* discourse; subjectivity; symbolic order

dance halls, 174–75, 252n61

dance routines, 60

Dancing in the Dark (Phillips), 34, 44–54, 63, 66–68

Dandridge, Dorothy, 122–24, 126, *126*, 128–29, 131, *132*

"The Dark Is Light Enough" (Baldwin), 122–24

decolonization, x, 5, 120, 127, 140–57, 166, 183

Deleuze, Gilles, 32–34, 193, 196

Derrida, Jacques, 182, 204, 253n72

Descartes, René, 15

desexualization, 27–29, 75, 201

desire: for difference, 21, 111–21, 246n52; Lacan on, 16–19; psychoanalytical understandings of, 7, 11–20; Robeson's sculptures and, 73–74, 77–78; white neuroses and, 6, 86, 90–93, 98, 105–6, 111–21. *See also* difference; miscegenation; race and racialization; sexuality

Devil Finds Work, The (Baldwin), 146

dialect, 44–54, 69, 166–67, 222n36, 223n40. *See also* blackness; race and racialization; voice, the

difference: desire and, 21; epidermalization and, 1, 6–20, 113–14, 195, 197; faciality concept and, 32–37; the gaze and, xi; gender and, viii–x, 60–62, 198; linguistic meaning and, 58–63; phallic-, 162–80; sexuality and, 147–51, 182–83

discourse: haptic experience's resistance and, 5–6; racialization and, 21–24, 166–68; skin/flesh dichotomy and, 3–4, 180–81. *See also* symbolic order; voice, the

Dockstader, Lew, 37, *38*

"Does Belafonte Get Girl in 'End of World'?" (article), 140

Dolar, Mladen, 162, 169, 171, 250n22

double consciousness, 4, 24

Drake, 252n60

drives, 7–9, 211n56, 211n64. *See also* desire

Duberman, Martin, 88

Du Bois, W. E. B., 4, 24, 33, 37

dub reggae, 171–80, 252n61

Dunbar, Paul Laurence, 45–46, 68

Dyer, Richard, 105–6, 235n54, 236n68, 241n99

Ebony, 128, 130

echoes, 47, 69, 143, 157, 169–73, 175–80, 223n42

Economist, 191, *192*, 194, 203

Edwards, Jackie, 173

Ellison, Ralph, 53, 69, 201

embodiment: anatomy/physiognomy distinction and, 12–20, 32–33, 194; desire and, 21–30; epistemologies and, 9–10; facialization and, 33, 41; grotesque and, 13–15; haptic experience and, 2, 8; liveness aesthetic and, 153–61; relationality and, viii, 5–6, 11–20; skin's relation to, 3–4, 9, 27–29, 147–48, 189, 198–99, *199*; symbolic

whiteness: the gaze and, viii, ix, ix–x, 10, 20, 37, 44–54, 59, 111–21, 126–27, 131–32, 196; minstrel shows and, 31, 227n75; neuroses and, 6, 86, 90–93, 98, 105–6, 111–21; photography and, 64–65, 66–68, 103

White Problem in America, The (Baldwin), 111

"Why I Married Julie" (Belafonte), 129

"Will Hollywood Let Negroes Make Love?" (article), 123

Williams, Bert: blackface and, vii, 36, 39–41; career of, viii–ix; celebrity status of, 34; dance routines and, 60; fictional representations of, 44–54, 66–68; historical representations and, 5; images of, 35, 42–43, 50, 64–65, 70, 104, 156, 192, 203, 221n28, 221n30; sonic performance and, 29, 44–54, 68–69, 222n37, 225n57; W. C. Fields and, viii–ix

Williams, Lottie, 49

"Williams and Walker, Nature's Black-Face Comedians in a Series of Specifically Posed Facial Stunts" (*Vanity Fair*), 42–43

World, the Flesh and the Devil, The (film), 111, 120, 140–51, 192

Wretched of the Earth, The (Fanon), 169, 251n41

Wright, Richard, 126, 128

Wynter, Sylvia, 12–14, 166, 210n32

Young, Robert, 130, 246n52

Zanuck, Darryl F., 129

Ziegfried Follies, ix

Žižek, Slavoj, 31, 47–48, 144, 153, 155, 189, 197, 247n67

NOV 0 7 2014